MIMESIS AND THE
HUMAN ANIMAL

Rethinking Theory

GENERAL EDITOR

Gary Saul Morson

CONSULTING EDITORS

Robert Alter
Frederick Crews
John M. Ellis
Caryl Emerson

MIMESIS AND THE HUMAN ANIMAL

On the Biogenetic Foundations of Literary Representation

Robert Storey

Northwestern University Press
Evanston, Illinois

Northwestern University Press
Evanston, Illinois 60208-4210

Copyright © 1996 by Northwestern University Press. Published 1996.
All rights reserved.

Printed in the United States of America

ISBN 0-8101-1457-7 (cloth)
ISBN 0-8101-1458-5 (paper)

Library of Congress Cataloging-in-Publication Data

Storey, Robert F., 1945–
    Mimesis and the human animal : on the biogenetic foundations of literary representation / Robert
Storey.
       p.   cm. — (Rethinking theory)
    Includes bibliographical references and index.
    ISBN 0-8101-1457-7 (cloth : alk. paper). — ISBN 0-8101-1458-5 (paper : alk. paper)
    1. Mimesis in literature.   2. Literature and science.   I. Title.   II. Series.
PN56.M536S76 1996
  801—dc20   96-30678
                                                            CIP

Naturam expelles furca, tamen usque recurret.
—Horace, *Epistles,* 1.10.24

To the memory of Edward R. Hagemann,
maestro di color che sanno

Contents

Figures

Pugnacious Preface

Why should we still want to be so clever when at long last we have a chance of being a little less stupid?

—Bertolt Brecht, *Life of Galileo*

For a long time I used to go to bed early. I had pledged myself to a twilight regimen of poststructuralist literary criticism. And—what would prove to be even more soporific—of "theory." By day, when I prepared my classes, I read Sophocles and Seneca, Shakespeare and Molière, Mallarmé and Rilke and Virginia Woolf. I lingered over the lines, garlanded with annotations, in a sweet repossession of intimacy and language. I declaimed them aloud ("Le vierge, le vivace et le bel aujourd'hui!" "Wer, wenn ich schriee, hörte mich denn aus der Engel / Ordnungen?" "Against you I will fling myself, unvanquished and unyielding, O Death!") as the microwave roared over my lunch. I puzzled through their meaning in a deliberative rapture as I walked with my dog in our scruffy little neighborhood park. Afternoons were reserved for "secondary materials"; evenings for *Diacritics* and *Representations*.

It was on those evenings that a certain tedium set in. The writing (which, I was assured, rivaled the art that it explicated) struck me as often uncomfortably bad. It wasn't that it was simply clumsy—it was *that*, unapologetically, and sometimes defiantly so—but that it also seemed to revel, both smugly and pretentiously, in its own abstract obscurantism. Everyone was a philosopher, giddy, in J. L. Austin's words, with the "ivresse des grands profondeurs" and turgidly propounding the gospel according to Derrida or Kristeva or Foucault. And it was all the same gospel, since each preaches a version of what Jerome Bruner has called "the rather philosophically harebrained perspectivalism that is now living out its sunset in Paris and New Haven and in the intellectual suburbs" (*Actual Minds* 155).

As a fugitive from the college biochemistry laboratory whose first publication was a dietary study of the Yellow Fever mosquito, I felt particularly exasperated (when I was not, in Shaw's phrase, convulsed with merriment) by the caricature that this perspectivalism made of modern science. Its "framework relativism," as Paisley Livingston calls it, propagated the idea—"a notion that reappears frequently in literary debates"—"that the 'knowledges' produced by science have no truth other than that bestowed upon them by their own autonomous frameworks of concepts and prejudices" (*Literary Knowledge* 23). "Il n'y a pas de hors-texte," in Derrida's famous formulation (158); and the *texte* itself is merely a structure of relations, its "discourse" constitutive of reality (Kristeva 215). And so, although modern medicine (to borrow Livingston's own example) may adopt a different discourse from that of the practices that it's displaced, that discourse is, in Foucault's estimation, "equally metaphorical" (*Birth* xi) and so equally alienated from the real as the old.

Livingston notes in passing that framework relativism is a position generally "urged by the postmodernists" (*Literary Knowledge* 5), the latter being more or less synonymous with "the poststructuralists." But it was structuralism that gave the position currency. Peter Caws spells out its principal assumption in his *Structuralism: The Art of the Intelligible:* "Structuralists are fond of quoting von Humboldt's remark that we can never step outside the circle of our language except into some other circle of language; the general truth that this reflects is simple and obvious once one has grasped it, but it is surprising how many people still seem to think it necessary to look for transcendent grounds of certainty or of significance" (204). That this "general truth" is "simple and obvious" is a matter for the rest of this book to dispute. What I'll focus on here is Caws's contrasting such a position to "transcendent grounds of certainty or of significance."

It is, to be blunt, a false opposition, one largely bred by the ignorance of humanists about the kind of extralinguistic knowledge that the scientific disciplines pursue. "Transcendence" is, to begin with, not a goal in that pursuit: scientific knowledge is *contextualized* knowledge, emergent from a highly self-conscious sensitivity to constraints, with language only a part (and, as I shall suggest in Chapter 3, a comparatively minor part) of its matrix of constraining conditions. Its results are never "certain," though its aim is, of course, a closer and closer approximation to a *reliable* understanding of the world. For such an understanding it subjects models of that world to empirical confirmation (about which I will have more to say at the end of Chapter 1); and some of those models have withstood so successfully this process of interrogation—a process, incidentally, to which literary "theory" seems exempt—that they continue to survive (against [post]structuralist opposition) as the best equivalents of self-critical sense-making that the human imagination has yet devised.

In the life sciences, significantly for the argument of this book, the most robust of those models is evolution. To the structuralists for whom Caws speaks, evolution must appear as one "circle of language," one "language game," among a great many possible others. But for the biologist (and, increasingly, for the social scientist) it is, in the words of the critic Alexander J. Argyros, preeminently the "game of games" (107). The theory of evolution is a master "grand narrative" that grows more compelling with each roll of the evidentiary dice. "At the present time," writes Livingston, "it offers the most detailed, coherent, and well-supported hypotheses as to the origins of cognitive capacities, and thus it stands as a formidable rival to idealist ontologies in which thought is held to be free-floating and absolutely self-creating" (*Literary Knowledge* 135). The philosopher John Searle takes a stronger line: there simply is no alternative to evolutionary thinking when it comes to accounts of both the body and the mind. "Like it or not," it is "the world view we have," he observes in *The Rediscovery of the Mind;* furthermore, it "is not an option. It is not simply up for grabs along with a lot of competing world views" (90). The notion that epistemological foundationalism has been "abandoned," in Caws's words, and that "we are . . . 'freely suspended in space,' or in the nautical rather than astronautical image appropriate to the discussion of anchors 'freely floating' " (255), is a species of romance that only the most ignorant or determined of scientific illiterates can hope to cling to today. Evolution is less a "theory" (at least in the sense in which that word is used in current literary study)[1] than a fact, and, as such, it provides, not only the best perspective for an approach to human life, but also a necessary (and inevitable) replacement for the structuralist- and poststructuralist-inspired ontologies that now dominate the critico-theoretical scene. For if what Jameson calls, with rather endearing naïveté, "the heroic discovery period of poststructuralism" (*Postmodernism* 391) is over, poststructuralism and its misguided models of the human being live on. "In the 1990s," writes Frederick Crews,

> scarcely anyone finds it necessary to argue directly for poststructuralism as a distinct body of thought. Rather, poststructuralist assumptions are often (though by no means always) treated as self-evidently valid within those cutting-edge schools of practice—feminist, Marxist, gay and lesbian, ethnic, psychoanalytic, new historicist—that seek to highlight and favor previously suppressed interests within both literature and society. (Foreword vii)

The logical bankruptcy of those assumptions has been the subject of many books prior to the present one;[2] their empirical indefensibility will occupy me in the pages that follow. But only as a secondary and rather minor theme. Primarily I'll be concerned with developing a wholly alternative model, one that positions literature, in Argyros's words, within a "larger natural framework" (2–3) than most of the frameworks (with some notable exceptions) that have been erected to date. In doing so, I join a number of critics—the artisans of those exceptions in my last parenthesis—who have begun now to shorten my sleep: Argyros, whose *Blessed Rage for Order* is a remarkable application of the new chaos theory to the conceptualization of literary meaning; Livingston, who in a number of books has reintroduced sanity into discussions of such topics as scientific knowledge, human agency, and (most recently) René Girard's theory of mimesis; Ellen Dissanayake, whose *What Is Art For?* provocatively answers its question in biologically adaptive terms, and who extends those terms in compelling ways in her more recent *Homo Aestheticus;* Nancy Easterlin and Barbara Riebling, who have assembled in their collection *After Poststructuralism* one of the most stimulating guides available to the student seeking an exit from what Harold Bloom calls the "School of Resentment"; and, most important, Joseph Carroll, whose recently published *Evolution and Literary*

Theory is a brilliantly sustained argument for the complete abandonment of the poststructuralist paradigm in favor of a neo-Darwinian one. I could add the names of other scholars—Walter A. Koch (*The Biology of Literature*), Frederick Turner (*Natural Classicism*, *The Culture of Hope*), Bryan Dietrich, James Ralph Papp, Michelle Scalise Sugiyama—a list the mere numbers of which begin to suggest something very like a "movement." And an incipient movement I think it is: specifically, a turning away from the strained ingenuities, the political sophistries, the uncritical obeisances to fashionable authority that now corrupt the practices of the profession, and a turning toward a conception of literary production and appreciation as "acts"—in the words of one of the satellites of this group—"of a human brain in a human body in a human environment which that brain must make intelligible if it is to survive" (M. Turner vii–viii). What may be said to unite all these critics in their separate enterprises is the conviction that literature is "the expression of everyday capacities" (M. Turner 4), the adaptive function of which offers the single most important key for springing the literary lock.

And it must be emphasized early here that the lock is no imaginary one. "In spite of the fact," as Livingston observes,

> that current debates within literary theory have attained a vertiginous degree of verbal complexity [he is writing at the height of the "theory wars"], it is possible to characterize the key issues with a certain economy. In fact, one may venture that there is really only one fundamental issue, and that the others arise purely in relation to it. This key issue is the question of the validity of interpretation. (*Literary Knowledge* 200)

Having identified the issue with such precision, *Literary Knowledge* goes on, rather oddly, to urge that "the models, insights, and critiques *implicit* in literature" be henceforth used "to complexify, challenge, and improve the models and hypotheses guiding research within the humanities and social sciences" (266, my emphasis). Of course, the idea that literature *offers* models, insights, and critiques that are transparently visible to all sensitive readers is precisely what is denied by the concession that interpretation is the "key issue." Racine's *Phèdre* has produced almost as many models of human relations as it has attracted interpreters: one of the most recent readings describes Phèdre's "tactic" as "to propose a possible image of herself, and when she sees Hippolyte's 'blindness' before that image, to turn back on him the image that he projects of her, in order to bring him to the point of seeing himself in the same way that he would wish to see her" (Berg 429). Are we then to assume that Luce Irigaray's "specular" model of human intercourse is "implicit" in the play?

Literature is always a discourse in need of interpretation, and never so urgently in need, in fact, as when it aspires to mimetic "transparency." "Criticism has to exist," writes Northrop Frye, because "all the arts are dumb" (4). But then, having said this, Frye commits a version of Livingston's mistake, assuming that models are implicit, not in single works of literature, but in the spectacle of their totality. Such a totality can only be "grasped" by a mind bringing structure to it, of course, and the resultant world of fourfold myths, of fivefold modes, and so on, is only too obviously a Pythagorean universe of crystalline harmonies.[3] Jonathan Culler calls attention to the ghost in Frye's machine:

> His discussions of modes, symbols, myths and genres lead to the production of taxonomies which capture something of the richness of literature, but the status of his taxonomic categories is curiously indeterminate. What is their relation to literary discourse and to the activity of reading? Are the four mythic categories of Spring, Summer, Autumn and Winter devices for classifying literary works or categories on which the experience of literature is based? As soon as one asks why these categories are to be preferred to those of other possible taxonomies it becomes evident that there must be something implicit in Frye's theoretical framework which needs to be made explicit. (*Structuralist Poetics* 120)

And yet, given the current degradation of literary studies into mere tub-thumping for this or that special-interest group, one feels the force of Frye's chief complaint: "Criticism seems to be badly in need of a coordinating principle, a central hypothesis which, like the theory of evolution in biology, will see the phenomena it deals with as parts of a whole" (16).

Ironically, the comparison enunciates the principle. It's not that criticism, or literature, ever needed a conceptual universe of its own, but that each is explicable only in terms of the natural world that the human being shares with the rest of terrestrial phenomena. Neither criticism nor the animal that brings it into being, therefore, suffers under the limitations that Caws describes: "in the end it amounts to this: that we have at our disposal only the present moment and things in the world as they are, that our task is to make sense of these from a standpoint within the world, and that any pretense to an Archimidean fulcrum outside the world, or even at a remove from our own standpoint within it, is suspect" (169). What Caws's phenomenological myopia leads him to overlook (as Frye's theological enthusiasm for myth also leads him to ignore) is that the most reliable "standpoint within the world" is one that serves, simultaneously, as an Archimedean fulcrum to lift that world out of the shallows of framework relativism. The theory of evolution is the only theory of any scientific integrity that can claim to provide a starting point to answer the first two of Gauguin's fundamental questions: "D'où venons-nous? Que sommes-nous? Où allons-nous?"

But of course it provides a starting point only. And the theory itself is in its infancy. What the reader will find, then, in the pages that follow can be only a provisional answer to the question I have posed myself: What does it mean to say that art imitates life? In the question are embedded two simpler, albeit more immodest, ones—What is life? and What is art?—and, with the hubris character-istic, in Donald T. Campbell's words, of "marginal scholars who are willing to be incompetent in a number of fields at once" (qtd. in Ruse xiii), I have tried to answer both. The first is addressed in Part I of this book: Chapters 1 and 2 elaborate a general "biogrammar" of the species, arguing that human culture in its global manifestations—and, in turn, the matter of narrative—exfoliates from human biology; Chapter 3 gives the view from inside the mind, approaching the human psyche as a "Darwin machine" and analyzing, among other things, the dependency of its powers upon language. In Part II, I suggest how the findings of Part I serve as ground for literary representation, particularly for its adaptive characteristics and functions, sketching out general considerations in Chapter 4, then narrowing the focus in the next two chapters to Western tragedy and comedy. I conclude with a "reading" in Chapter 7—with an exercise in so-called practical criticism—of a book by a novelist, Iris Murdoch, who both regards herself as a mimetic artist and interestingly subverts that self-assessment by her philosophical allegiances.

This book is about the literary representation of human life as what Carroll calls a "realist" phenomenon. As he argues in *Evolution and Literary Theory*, "represen-tations of characters, settings, and plots constitute a single, continuous scale, with realism at one end and symbolism at the other."

> Figurations at the realist end of the scale represent people, objects, and actions as they appear to common observation and to the represented characters themselves. . . . Figurations at the symbolic end of the scale use the dramatic elements to represent or embody the basic forces and the fundamental structural relations within the author's own world-picture or cognitive order. (131)

Although, as Carroll points out, these forms "are not mutually exclusive," rep-resenting as they do "extreme points in a continuum within a single scale of representation" (137), they may be differentiated for the sake of analysis, and my focus here will be on what he elsewhere calls "the objective orientation": "The objective orientation tends to concentrate on depicting the personal experience of other human beings, and the subjective on constructing figurations that exemplify the relations among the elemental components of the author's cognitive order" (133). If, in other words, art is what Zola proposed it to be—"nature refracted through a temperament"—my interest is with both what is refracted and how and why the "ludic reader," in psychologist Victor Nell's phrase, profits from the refraction. What will emerge is a form of what I call "narrativic" meaning, the deciphering of which owes its authority to a competence that, as I shall argue, all human beings share. I have concerned myself only in a marginal way with the hypothetical origins of mimesis: readers interested in the latter issue should consult the fascinating article by Robert W. Mitchell, "The Evolution of Primate

Cognition," or the more speculative book by Merlin Donald, *The Origins of the Modern Mind*, or the (less rigorous) hypotheses of René Girard, particularly as they are synthesized in Livingston's *Models*.[4] And I have avoided the quagmire that beckons theorists with the promise of explaining how words themselves—on the page, in the ear—call up worlds of imaginative richness and immediacy. In fact, I make no apologies for what Culler calls "the unseemly rush from word to world" (*Structuralist Poetics* 130); like Kendall Walton, I would "break the hold that the preoccupation with language has exerted on our thinking about representation" (5).

"In contrast to current practice," Carroll writes, "a critic who aligned himself or herself with evolutionary biology would once again take the 'subject'—the living, individual, human personality—as a primary point of reference" (94–95). This I do in my first chapter, arguing that that "subject" must be newly redefined in biological instead of linguistic terms. But, although I begin with the same "primary point of reference" as Carroll, I reach rather different conclusions, and it may be useful to touch on our major disagreements for those readers to whom our common orientations may suggest that our books merely cover the same sort of ground. At one point, Carroll quotes the evolutionary theorist Donald Symons—"However universal human cognition may be, I believe that human emotion is still more basic, older, and universal, and that 'emotion has taught mankind to reason'"—and he characterizes such views as "a prejudice" (157). Symons's view is, in fact, my own, one that will be elaborated in detail in Chapter 1. Carroll is averse to such views because he apparently accepts the traditional opposition between the emotions and what he calls "the 'higher' faculties of reason and the capacity for intentional behavior" (157), an opposition that, as I hope to show, is more virtual than real. Carroll is also somewhat hostile—or better, ambivalent—toward certain strains of sociobiological theory, an ally, as I shall argue, in any effort to found literary study upon evolutionary principles. But I think that his objections (as he would agree) evaporate before recent refinements in that theory—refinements of which I have not hesitated to take advantage.

About one aspect of that theory Carroll's critique still holds: there is a fundamental "division" in the discipline. It is, as he describes it, "between those who believe that proximate causes operate in complete independence of inclusive fitness as ultimate cause and those who reduce all proximate causes to inclusive fitness" (377). Less technically, it is between theorists who regard the human being as a "hodgepodge" (to use E. O. Wilson's word) of various psychological adaptations to an ancient environment that no longer exists, and those who look upon the human being as a "fitness-maximizing" organism, each of whose capacities may be assumed to have evolved to turn social environments to its genetic advantage. For the most part, my theoretical sympathies lie on the former side of the divide, with those—like Carroll—who favor an "adaptation-executor" model of the human being, although I suspect it will turn out that the human repertoire of "proximate" mechanisms is richer than many like-minded theorists now imagine (the cost-and-benefit calculations of the resourceful neocortex figure, after all, among those mechanisms) and yet less efficient than their rivals seem to think. In other words, differences in the field will be subtly and not coarsely adjudicated, eventually, something I have tried to do in my synthesis of Chapter 2. Although it eschews the dogmatism of what Carroll tends to allude to as "strict" sociobiology, that synthesis is (*caveat lector!*) still "sociobiological," informed as it is by the orientations of two of the founders of the discipline, theorists whom Carroll himself rightly admires: the anthropologist Robin Fox and the entomologist Edward O. Wilson.

Since the S-word has appeared, it may not be amiss to grapple immediately with the chief misconception that humanists seem to harbor about it. With the various other misconceptions—that sociobiology is "biological determinism," that it posits a completely selfish human agent, that it is nothing but a congeries of "just-so stories"—I deal in both the text and the notes of the first two chapters. The point of chief mistrust, if I may judge by the curled lips of my colleagues, is that sociobiology is thought to underwrite a political program of a conservative, which is to say objectionable, kind. But sociobiology is neither a program nor a platform nor an agenda: it is a scientific theory that explains—to my mind, cogently and elegantly—a large body of fact, ethological, anthropological, sociological, psychological, endocrinological, neurological, and so on. For the purposes of this book, the fact is more important than the theory, but since the fact is most intelligible in terms of the theory, as life is most intelligible in terms of evolution in general, I have ventured to spell it out for the reader. To those who would object that there is little unequivocal proof of (that is, precisely traceable pathways for) gene-behavior connections in human beings, I would draw attention, not only to Dean Hamer's work on the so-called gay gene, which is science of impressive sophistication and rigor, but also to Darwin's remarks about the wholly indirect evidence that supported his descent-with-modification thesis:

> It has recently been objected that this is an unsafe method of arguing; but it is a method used in judging of the common events of life, and has often been used by the greatest natural philosophers. The undulatory theory of light has thus been arrived at; and the belief in the revolution of the earth on its own axis was until lately supported by hardly any direct evidence. It is no valid objection that science as yet throws no light on the far higher problem of the essence or origin of life. Who can explain what is the essence of the attraction of gravity? No one now objects to following out the results consequent on this unknown element of attraction; notwithstanding that Leibnitz formerly accused Newton of introducing "occult qualities and miracles into philosophy." (*Origin* 421)

Sensible words to keep in mind about the so-called speculations of sociobiology.

This is a book of literary theory for those who detest literary theory—and who have grown weary of the relentless politicizing of literature that has been largely engendered by that theory. I have written it, in part, as a polemicist, both because I have little expectation of being heard sympathetically by my (principally poststructuralist) opposition, no matter how moderate and conciliatory my tone, and because it seems to me time to repay that opposition for the savagery and contempt it has shown—and continues to show—toward one of the things that I most value, the scientific rationality of the so-called West. Our only point of difference is that those who have hitherto been doing the sneering seem to me, in their ignorance, incoherence, and irrationality, eminently deserving of the contempt. What follows is not intended for readers who must be cajoled into the idea of the legitimacy and general integrity of the scientific pursuit of knowledge; such readers, in the late twentieth century, strike me as intellectually unreachable. Nor is it for those for whom political rectitude forgives all squalor of logic and evidence. It is for what Virginia Woolf called the common reader, with common, if unanalyzed, intuitions, who is dispassionately curious not only about the phenomenon of literature but also about what lies on the other side of today's academic garrison wall.

My perspective (and scholarship) owes an incalculable debt to the work of Robin Fox. I encountered that work at a propitious time, having become disillusioned with the psychoanalytic paradigm on which my last book had been based. The disillusionment had begun to set in even before that book had been finished: because of the infinite flexibility of its interpretive "rules" and the improvisatory and empirically unconstrained nature of its model-building, psychoanalysis allowed me to say practically anything I wished about my literary texts; its recommendation was merely as what Frank Cioffi calls a "pseudo-science" that is virtually immune to falsification. This conclusion was confirmed when a keen-nosed reviewer (who thought he was defending the purity of the discipline) pointed out that my drawing upon different psychoanalytic "schools"—Kleinian, Sartrean, Kohutian, Laplanchean—had resulted in a "pot pourri." I had not been unaware of the perspectival diversity, but I had assumed that, as in any other science, the competing claims of its theoreticians could be resolved by a critical practice that valued both consistency and fidelity to fact (of which, alas, there didn't seem to be much, at least of a "nonfantasmatic" kind). I had thought I was producing a synthesis; I had only cooked up—the metaphor is appropriate—a lumpy and indigestible stew.

What a true synthesis was (and could be) I realized when I read Robin Fox's books. Here was resourceful scholarship founded upon the most unimpeachable of conceptual models that was expanding the frontiers of scientific knowledge in exhilaratingly provocative ways. What seemed to be happening in his work—and elsewhere outside the airless rooms of literary theory—was nothing less than a revolution in the conception of human life. As I plunged into the underbrush of his notes and bibliographies and began to explore the territories that he had already mastered—primatology, behavioral biology, neuropsychology, evolution theory— it became more and more clear that, if the study of literature were not to remain in a protracted post-sixties infancy, it had to make contact with an intellectual milieu that it hardly knew existed. I have his work to thank for ushering me into it, and even for carrying me into areas where he might regret that I've strayed. For my errors of judgment he can't be held accountable, but he must assume full responsibility for enkindling the enthusiasm that has resulted in this book. I hope he finds pleasure, if not profit, in its pages, and will accept at least the spirit of its enterprise as homage to his own.

A number of friends and colleagues have kindly indulged this long aberration and have even abetted it by reading early drafts. Shelly Brivic, Joel Conarroe, Tim Corrigan, Peter Hlavacek, Dan O'Hara, Naomi Ritter, Judith Sensibar, Bill Van Wert, Gerald Weales, and Alan Wilde all saw abbreviated versions of one or more chapters and gave helpful and encouraging replies. Geoffrey Harpham and Nancy Easterlin were, as always, indefatigably loyal in coaxing material from me and heroically self-effacing in taking the time to respond critically, shrewdly, and good-humoredly. My students listened patiently to my theories, and some helped me develop and refine them: I'm especially indebted to the contributions of Rich Alphonse, Marie Collins, Tom Devaney, Jeff Ford, Ed Flanagan, Seth Frechie, Nick Gillespie, Jack Gugliuzza, Jim Held, Lynn Kendall, Mark Pfeifer, and Neal Spector. Keith Reid-Green and Libby Ballinger chased down special references for me (although both had, undoubtedly, better things to do); my colleagues at Temple generously granted me a Study Leave so that I could make a start on the project; and Joseph Carroll offered selfless encouragement as I sought out a publisher. For permission to reprint, in somewhat revised forms, versions of Chapters 1 and 6 from *Criticism* ("'I Am I Because My Little Dog Knows Me': Prolegomenon to a Theory of *Mimesis*" and "Comedy, Its Theorists, and the Evolutionary Perspective," copyright © 1990 and 1996, respectively, Wayne State University Press, Detroit, Michigan 48202), I am grateful to the Regents of Wayne State University.

In closing, I should assure my wife, Chom, that she never (as she seemed to fear) pushed me too hard to finish: just hard enough to make it pleasant, at the end of the day, to seek her company, her talk, and her gracious spirit, and there, between her and my infrahuman muse, to imbibe the warmth for the next morning's labor. I had hoped, finally, to offer the latter muse the tangible fruit of his inspiration, and thereby give him the pleasure of shredding its pages, as he had shredded with gusto my other books. But Blackie—I record the event here in loving remembrance—died on November 16, 1994.

Part I

The World

1

"I Am I Because My Little Dog Knows Me": Of Apes and Essences

But what do we know about nature?
—Geoffrey Galt Harpham, pers. comm., April 6, 1989

The hypocrisy of past ages was usually classical and dogmatic, the hypocrisy of this age is romantic and skeptical. We pretend not to know. Instead of trying to see, we shut the curtains and revel in tragic darkness, concentrating carefully on impossible cases and taking the boring possible for granted.
—Mary Midgley, *Beast and Man: The Roots of Human Nature*

1

He was right where we thought he'd be.

He jumped up off the driveway, where we'd left him that morning, and stood staring into the headlights, his tail wagging furiously, his ears drooping in an attitude of abject humility, his whole body trembling with barely contained excitement. My wife and I were back in Philadelphia from a day in Washington, D.C., and Blackie had hardly budged from his usual station in front of the garage. His Doggie Dor had been unlocked, he had fresh water in the kitchen, but not even his thirst (which proved prodigious) had been strong enough to lure him from the spot.

I kept thinking of this scene as I reflected, the next morning, on a remark I had read recently of S. P. Mohanty's: "It is this capacity for a second-order understanding and evaluation [i.e., for a rationality "that distinguishes us from animals" (21)], which enables us to be critically and cumulatively self-aware in relation to our actions, that defines human agency and makes possible the sociality and the historicality of human existence" (22). There was little fit, of course, between the oracular academese of the passage and my physically immediate reunion with my dog, but that was a small discrepancy that I could put down to (among other things) the self-important penchant for grand pronouncements

3

that now disfigures Mohanty's profession. (Mohanty is a professor of English.) There was a more serious lack of fit, though, that tended to nag at me, and that was between the "sociality" of Blackie and Mohanty's ascribing that same sociality to "human agency" alone. It was obvious that Blackie had missed our company over that long afternoon: he was as hungry as he was thirsty, but he could hardly settle down to his doggie bowls for his joy at having us home. He kept running from one of us to the other, his tail thrashing wildly, poking at us with his muzzle for a caress, a pat, a fond look.

Of course the skeptical observer would have cautioned against our "anthropomorphizing" the scene (though that same observer wouldn't have given a second thought to anthropomorphizing any signs of internal distress if Blackie had needed a vet). Isn't Blackie's "sociality" a rather opaque kind of dependency, his "excitement" a response that his human caretakers interpret in an all-too-human way? We are obligated these days to indulge this sort of skepticism, since current advanced opinion holds that biology and "human existence" have parted company, so that whatever an observer reads into an animal's behavior is likely to be a cultural—not to say a verbal—artifact.[1] But it takes a very skeptical observer indeed to deny sociality to various undomesticated animals: ants, bees, the gregarious primates— have these been anthropomorphized, too? I am ready to grant Mohanty that "historicality" is "made possible" by human rationality, but sociality is by no means its child. The social nature of human life, a nature shared, however variously, with much of the insect and mammalian world, is the fact from which "agency" springs.

Before arguing and elaborating this point, I should give Mohanty's sentence a context. In many ways his is an interesting and important essay. He is intent on establishing a common ground for understanding human interrelations as they are distributed across cultures, races, and genders, and he is rightly impatient of the relativism that has long held sway in the "progressive" humanities and, to an influential extent, anthropology. The more radical versions (which is to say, the more fashionable versions) of the prevailing orthodoxy are quite impossible as workable propositions: "If the relativist says that everything is entirely context-specific," Mohanty observes, "claiming that we cannot adjudicate among contexts or texts on the basis of larger—that is, more general—evaluative or interpretive criteria, then why should I bother to take seriously *that very relativist claim?*" (14). Mohanty is politically savvy enough to know that he mustn't seem to be subscribing to "the ambiguous imperial-humanist myth of our shared human attributes" (13): what he calls "the Enlightenment's emphasis on a singular rationality underlying and comprehending all human activities" (2) was misplaced to begin with, he predictably declares, a relic of the Dark Ages of critical thought.

But what can we put in its place? Alluding to Talal Asad's call for a "'genuine dialogue' between anthropologist and native, the ex-colonizer and the ex-colonized,"

Mohanty writes: "A . . . dialogue of the kind Asad envisions would become possible only when we admit that crucial aspects of [a] non-Western culture may have a great degree of coherence as part of a larger web of ideas, beliefs and practices, and moreover that *some* of these aspects may be untranslatable to the language of the Western anthropologist's culture in terms of its historically sedimented and institutionally determined practices of knowing" (15). And he concludes by asserting that "the reason this would constitute the beginning of a *dialogue* is that 'we' are forced to extend our understanding by interrogating its limits in terms of [alien] categories of self-understanding" (16).

We seem to be back at the familiar poststructuralist impasse here. It's hard to imagine how an "interrogation" of anything or anyone can be carried out in "categories of self-understanding" that are alien to the inquiring mind. (Notice how quickly the phrase "in terms of" plunges the sentence into referential obscurity.) If those categories are not to some extent the interrogator's own, then communication is completely impossible. It's apparently because Mohanty recognizes this difficulty that he makes his last argumentative move, the declaration that certain "basic claims" must be formulated about *all* human "subjects": "If (as I argued against the relativist position earlier) we are to deal seriously with other cultures and not reduce them to insignificance or irrelevance, we need to begin by positing the following minimal commonality between us and them: the capacity to act purposefully, to be capable of agency and the basic rationality that the human agent must in principle possess" (21).

A disappointingly ironic conclusion. We've dismissed the Enlightenment error of history as "guided by Reason, obeying the logic of Progress and Modernization" (13), only to resurrect it in a stylishly more palatable form. Although Mohanty concedes that the conditions of the world are "not all within [human] control" (19) and that humans as "agents" are only "potentially" self-aware (20), his final emphasis is upon the purposiveness and "rationality" of the human actor, deliberately "making" his or her world. And it's obvious why the emphasis should fall there: "theoretically understanding this 'making,'" he writes, "involves redefining social structures and cultural institutions as not simply given but *constituted,* and hence containing the possibility of being changed" (19). Progress and Modernization are on the horizon, as they are in all utopian political visions.

It should be clear now why it's important for Mohanty to attribute sociality to agency and hence rationality. The human world is made by and through human relationships, and, if the making is to be purposive, those relationships must be rational. For, lacking the self-awareness consequent upon rational control, the agent is not "free" and the world cannot be "changed." The logic is simple, not to say oversimple, and Mohanty is wise not to spell it out too explicitly. But for those readers with dogs like my obstreperously social Blackie, the shakiness of the edifice is more than apparent.

In opposition to Mohanty, I argue that a sustained reflection upon human sociality leads us inevitably to a theory of human nature in which rationality (at least as Mohanty seems to conceive it) has only a secondary role. I'll use "human nature" without apology, not only because (as I'll try to show) important behavioral facts clearly warrant it, but because there can be no coherently intelligible criticism of human life and production, including art, without it. The time is long overdue for an abandonment of the cant that both structuralism and poststructuralism have foisted on the academy. That the human "subject" is "indeterminate," the artifact of history and culture and language alone, erecting structures upon their ghostly frames that must be constantly "deconstructed"—this is a piece of stupefyingly romantic fiction that can't bear much serious thought. Of course this charge has been thoughtfully (or splenetically) lodged by a number of previous critics, with most memorable vigor, for example, by Frederick Crews in "The Grand Academy of Theory." But rather than rehearse their arguments or defend the indictment myself, at least just yet, I'll let a poststructuralist take the scythe to his own premises and so clear the ground for our work.

2

Many people, it has been argued, "drift" into identity, battered by con-tingency rather than guided by will. Four characteristic stages have been identified by [Kenneth] Plummer [in *Sexual Stigma: An Interactionist Account* (1975)]: "sensitization," when the individual becomes aware of the possibility of being different; "signification," when he or she attributes a developing meaning to these differences; "subculturalization," the stage of recognizing oneself through involvement with others; and "stabilization," the stage of full acceptance of one's feelings and way of life. . . . There is no automatic progression through these stages; each transition is dependent as much on chance as on decision; and there is no necessary acceptance of the final destiny, of an open identity. Some choices are forced on individuals, whether through stigmatization and public obloquy or through political necessity. But the point that needs underlining is that *identity* is a choice. It is not *dictated* by internal imperatives.

Thus Jeffrey Weeks in a section entitled "Identity as Choice" in "Questions of Identity" (43–44), his contribution to *The Cultural Construction of Sexuality*, an anthology widely adopted in the cultural anthropology classroom. It is a passage, to mangle Wallace Stevens's phrase, that almost successfully eludes the intelligence. The first sentence immediately introduces an unresolved ambiguity: the "it has been argued" vaguely suggests that Weeks will take an opposing position on the idea that "many people . . . 'drift' into identity" or, at the very least, that he will argue that they should be "guided by will" rather than "battered by contingency." But as he summarizes Plummer's four "stages," he seems to imply that those stages are definitive, even capping the summary with refinements of his own ("There is no automatic progression through these stages"). But his final paraphrase of Plummer's position is a bizarre deformation of it: whereas Plummer seems to argue that the rather haphazard route to identity leads to recognition of what one "is"—to "full acceptance of one's feelings and way of life"—Weeks asserts that "the final destiny" is that of an "open" identity. And his last two sentences of the paragraph are in flat contradiction to Plummer's whole thesis, at least as Weeks has presented it. Identity *is* "dictated" by "internal imperatives," according to Plummer himself: his "individual" is inducted into "identity" by strong forces within and without; there is hardly any suggestion at all, in fact, that identity for him is a "choice."

Given the discontinuities in the exposition, I am not really sure what Weeks thinks he has done, but a charitable reading would conclude that Plummer's implicit fatalism need not always obtain. Identity *can* be "guided by will," according to this reading of the passage; in an "open" subject, identities are merely (as Weeks declares at the beginning of his essay) "historically and culturally specific, . . . selected from a host of possible social identities, . . . not necessary attributes of particular sexual drives or desires, . . . not, in fact, *essential*—that is naturally pre-given—aspects of our personality" (31).

But Plummer may prove as seductive for the attentive reader as he seems to have been for Weeks: What are we to do with those autonomously intractable agents of persuasion, the "feelings"? Are they, too, historically and culturally specific and so "inessential"? Not surprisingly, attempts have been made by poststructuralist anthropologists to argue that they are, that "the passions are as cultural as the devices [of political exploitation]"—an attempt dismissed by Edmund Leach as "complete rubbish." Leach's response (he is replying specifically to Clifford Geertz) is worth reproducing in full:

> I can make no sense of a line of thought which claims that "passions" are culturally defined. From my prejudiced position as a social anthropologist this passage reveals with startling clarity the ultimately radical weakness of the basic assumption of cultural anthropology, namely, that not only are cultural systems infinitely variable, but that human individuals are products of their culture rather than of their genetic predisposition. (qtd. in Levy 217)

This is, of course, the familiar spectacle of the blind men palpating the elephant: both Geertz and Leach have, as I shall argue, more or less defensible positions. But they can't be defended with the blunt verbal instruments that have been hustled into the fray. (What does it mean to say that passions "are . . . cultural"? or—with no less obscurity—that they are "culturally defined"?) And, as in most conflicts of this sort in the "human sciences," there has been little attempt by either party to repair to professional opinion: in this case, to the provocative research of the last several decades that has been amassed by psychologists of emotion.

The various theories of those psychologists are now converging upon a functional account of their subject, one that assumes, in George Mandler's words, as "a truism at this point in scientific history," that "mental structure" and therefore the operation of the emotions are "influenced by the evolutionary history of the species" (54). There is disagreement among them about many things—about the existence and identity of "primary emotions," about the relative contributions of biology and cognition to the emotion-activation process, about the role that facial-musculature feedback plays in the production and apprehension of emotion—but what most seem to agree on is that the emotions constitute a psychological system that once served (and still serves, though to a disputed extent) biologically adaptive ends.

Of central importance is the work of Robert Plutchik, currently professor of psychiatry and psychology at Bronx Municipal Hospital Center in New York. In 1980 Plutchik published *Emotion: A Psychoevolutionary Synthesis*, arguing that the emotions "serve an adaptive role in helping organisms deal with key survival issues posed by the environment" (129). Each of the so-called prototype emotions—fear, anger, joy, sadness, acceptance, disgust, expectancy, and surprise—serves one of the basic needs of the organism, fear inducing withdrawal, anger inciting attack, joy encouraging copulation, and so on. From the functional point of view, all emotions are (or at least *were*, in what developmentalist John Bowlby calls the "environment of evolutionary adaptedness" [58]) beneficial; it is to a creature's advantage to be as sensitively receptive to the "information" encoded in fear or sadness as to that in joy or acceptance (a clue, as we shall see when we turn to literature, to the pleasure of tragic catharsis). In this sense, there are no "bad" emotions (or, to use the current jargon, "dysfunctional" ones): the emotions are, in O. Hobart Mowrer's words, "of quite extraordinary importance in the total economy of living organisms and do not at all deserve being put into opposition with 'intelligence.' The emotions are, it seems, themselves a high order of intelligence" (308).

If anything, Mowrer understates the case. Not only psychologists but also neuroscientists and philosophers of emotion now emphasize what Silvan Tomkins had early contended: that the emotional affects constitute the "primary innate biological motivating mechanism" (146). Robert Ornstein, author of *The Evolution of Consciousness*, quotes E. E. Cummings' "Feeling is first." And he adds:

Feeling is first in two senses: Emotions appeared first in the mind's evolution, to operate as special-purpose organizers. Second, they are at the front line of our experiences. Since they evolved to shortcircuit deliberations, they spring quickly into action, before rational deliberation has the time to function. (92)

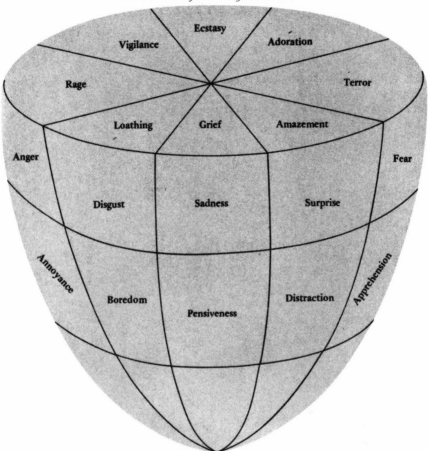

Fig. 1. Robert Plutchik's multidimensional model of the emotions. "The vertical dimension represents intensity, or level of arousal, and ranges from a maximum state of excitement to a state of deep sleep at the bottom. The shape of the model implies that the emotions become less distinguishable at lower intensities" (Plutchik 157–59). Reprinted by permission of Harper and Row, Publishers.

That emotions are "organizers" of human experience gives them very special importance. It means that they provide, in the words of Ronald de Sousa, one of the most informed and persuasive philosophers of emotion, "frameworks in terms of which we perceive, desire, act, and explain" (24). As, in effect, a behavior-disposing agent, "an emotion limits the range of information that the organism will take into account, the inferences actually drawn from a potential infinity, and the set of live options among which it will choose" (195).[2] Emotions, de Sousa therefore concludes, "can be said to be judgments, in the sense that they are what we see the world 'in terms of'" (196). Insofar as they control "salience"—"what to notice, what to attend to, what to inquire about" (191)—they control the organism itself, since "they operate by evoking whole scenarios, at a metalevel in relation to beliefs" (199). In this respect, the emotions are as powerful an operant in human behavior as "instinct" is for the "lower animals"—if, in fact, such distinctions can be maintained in the face of recent neuroanatomical research.[3]

As early as 1949, the pioneering neuroanatomist Paul D. MacLean began elaborating a model of brain functioning that, extending the research of P.-P. Broca in the last century and of J. W. Papez in this, has led to the identification of a general "limbic system," a system that has now, as Melvin Konner explains, "won almost universal acceptance as the central neural network of the emotions" (146). In a still-influential theory among non-neuroscientists, MacLean assigned that network to the "paleomammalian" brain, the second of what he calls the "triune" brain's structures, which also include the "reptilian" and "neomammalian" brains. His compartmentalizations have proved much too neat, and most neurobiologists are now skeptical of the triune-brain theory (Reiner 304), although there are those who still respect it as "a metaphor" (Isaacson 240). But their skepticism in fact rests on evidence that strengthens my own argument here. For the limbic system has since been identified, not only as a "paleomammalian" phenomenon, but as a possession of even more primitive vertebrates as well. The septum, the amygdala, and the hippocampal complex—all links in the limbic "network"—are found in reptiles, birds, amphibians, and mammals. The cingulate cortex, which seems essential, among other things, for parental behavior, can be assumed not only for avian brains but perhaps for those of the birds' remote extinct ancestors, since recent paleontological evidence suggests that some dinosaurs nurtured their young (Horner and Gorman 63; Norell et al. 782). The "emotions" (if we may thereby identify the psychological artifacts of apparently homologous brain structures) were of early evolutionary origin; their usefulness—in exciting parenting, mating, aggression, play—helps explain their robustness and their antiquity.

That both the relationships and the behaviors of complex social animals evolved roughly in the same (terrestrial) environment may also explain the apparent neural specificity of the emotions. The recent work of Paul Ekman, Robert W. Levenson, and Wallace V. Friesen suggests strongly that certain activity in the autonomic nervous system, involving heartbeat, breathing, skin temperature, and so on, is specific to at least six of Plutchik's "prototype" emotions. Their findings cast doubt on the rather widely entertained hypothesis, advanced most notably by cognitive theorists of emotion, that autonomic "arousal" is initially "undifferenti-ated" in emotion-inducing situations and that only after cognitive intercession does it acquire (out of a large potentiality of affective possibilities) the complexion of an emotional state. In short, there is now evidence, supporting Plutchik's hypotheses, that six to ten emotions (or perhaps "classes" of emotion)[4] are "primary" in human beings, if not in most of their mammalian kin—primary, no doubt, because they proved indispensable in the adaptive life of their possessors. It is these, and their "blends,"[5] that provide those metaconceptual frameworks in terms of which *Homo* negotiates its world.

None of which is to imply that the emotions are fundamentally "deterministic." De Sousa in fact argues that the emotions constitute the system that *forestalls* behavioral determinism in both human and infrahuman affairs. "A truly emotionless being," he writes, "would be either some sort of Kantian monster with a computer brain and a pure rational will, or else a Cartesian animal-machine, an ant, perhaps, in which every 'want' is preprogrammed and every 'belief' simply a releasing cue for a specific response" (190). But the "fact of biological variability," he continues, "precludes any animal-machine of the sort just described":

> Two individual ants, even two individual viruses, will not do exactly the same thing under every condition. But they come close enough: close enough in particular so that individual ants have no need of special clues to tell them how, from a repertoire of equally probable alternatives, other ants are likely to react. Ants, unlike primates, have no need for communicativeness of emotional expression. But among animals like us, to read the emotional configuration of another's body or face is to have a guide to what she is likely to believe, attend to, and therefore want and do. Such dispositions tend to be given different names depending in part on their duration: a short one is an emotion, a longer one a sentiment, and a permanent one a character trait. (191)

Not only is emotion always a highly variable affair (even as it hardens into disposition); it is also indispensable for the act of learning, an act impossible for Kantian monsters as well as for animal-machines. In such structures as the amygdala, an important part of the limbic circuit, memories are given emotional resonance (Barinaga, "How Scary Things" 887), and this "indexing" of memory apparently fulfills a necessary cognitive function. Andrew Ortony, Gerald L. Clore, and Allan Collins, all theorists of emotion, explain:

> If an organism experiences a feeling similiar to ones experienced in the past, that organism has the potential to respond on the basis of its memory of the success or failure of past responses. . . . In this way, by taking advantage of the similarities and differences between the current emotion-inducing situation and past ones that led to the same feeling, the organism can *learn* to maximize the effectiveness of its responses. So, emotional experiences can be viewed as signatures . . . for the presence of structured and distinct eliciting conditions, and for indexing memory so that, with the help of reminding

mechanisms . . . , the organism can potentially respond in the maximally appropriate manner. (177)

Of course, the "structured and distinct eliciting conditions" for emotions in human beings are by no means universally invariant, and the emotional system has had to maintain enough lability to respond to greatly diversified needs and environments, including (most notably for *Homo sapiens*) those behaviorally inflected by culture. And, indeed, the most recent research in the neurosciences is eroding the notion of a "hard-wired" brain, its information pathways generally fixed from birth—even with respect to the neural "maps" that characterize the adult nervous system. The brain is "a network," suggests Michael Merzenich, a neuroscientist at the University of California at San Francisco, "that is continually remodeling itself" (Barinaga, "Brain" 216).[6] For the theorist of emotion this helps explain how, say, the young of the Chuckchee, a people of the Russian tundra, can be taught to feel disgust merely at the sight of strange objects (Bruner, *Actual Minds* 116) or how the unmarried American teenage girl can regard with indifference the loss of virginity that so shamed her turn-of-the-century counterpart. The emotions are refined (that is to say, calibrated in intensity, extended in their specific application, and "blended" with nuance and sophistication) apparently through the operations of what de Sousa calls cultural "paradigm scenarios," which "are drawn first from our daily life as small children and later reinforced by the stories, art, and culture to which we are exposed" (182):

> Before the age of three, toddlers can understand that one person's action may lead to another's distress and that certain types of events typically cause certain emotions. They also know that by taking a sequence from an emotional scenario out of context, one can play-act or "pretend" emotions that are not actually being felt. And by the time toddlers are four or five years old, they have a very good sense of what kinds of stories lead to what simple emotions. Learning these scenarios continues indefinitely, however, as the emotional repertoire becomes more complicated. . . . Indeed, perhaps we enlarge our repertoire, much as we increase our mastery of language, well into adult life, though with increasing resistance. (183–84)

It is this process of learning that is the "cultural" contribution to the intensity, application, and sophistication of the system: in this way the emotions are "culturally defined." But it's important to stress that such a process does not imply a wholly indeterminate subject, a plastic psyche that is subsequently "constructed" as a social, gendered being. "We need to allow for the idea," de Sousa adds, "that the clash of scenarios—a certain degree of self-assertion by rebellion—is essential to ego development. And I suspect [that] the biological factors . . . bundled under the name of 'temperament' may be responsible for a great many differences between individual natures in respect of the style, strength, and direction of the rebellion" (252). "Temperament," as the developmental psychologist Jerome Kagan explains, is a largely inherited disposition to "organize the expression of emotion, especially in interpersonal contexts" (*Unstable Ideas* 129), and its power to inflect, modify, or redirect its expression, irrespective of the "lessons" of a particular scenario, is evident in the variability of human behavior even within relatively homogeneous pockets of culture.

And not only are we biologically—temperamentally—disposed to organize the emotions elicited by paradigm scenarios: we're programmed to develop (from birth, I should emphasize) what Plutchik calls their "prototypes" as well. However culturally or individually variable may be the intensity or application of the emotional system, infants in all cultures go through the same kind of changes as the basic emotions emerge from autonomic arousal. "The predictable, reliable sequence of these changes," as Ornstein (among others) observes, "indicates an innate maturational component to emotion" (*Evolution* 97). And the "innateness" of that component is further suggested by the universality—exhibited cross-culturally as well as neonatally—of the facial expression of emotions. Several important articles by Ekman and Friesen and *The Face of Emotion* by Carroll E. Izard (260) argue that at least seven basic emotions are expressed facially with quasi-pancultural intelligibility by peoples of quite disparate cultures.[7] Not surprisingly, then, we may conclude with de Sousa that "a child is genetically programmed [or "constrained," as a neuroscientist would more accurately say] to respond in [emotionally] specific ways to the situational components of some paradigm scenarios" (183), particularly of those scenarios that conform to situations in which the emotions originally evolved. What this means is that, even as the emotions are directed in their operations by the paradigm scenarios of life, those scenarios themselves are generally defined by the prototypical affects and the binary dynamics—joy/sadness, acceptance/disgust, and so forth—that give both content and structure to the emotional system.[8] Feeling is first, in other words: the emotional predispositions of the infant in large part prefigure (as, of course, natural selection would ensure) its social and cognitive interactions in the world, *and they prefigure them precisely because the constraints of the primary neural repertoire tend naturally to perpetuate such interactions.* Not only do the emotions provide a metaconceptual framework for the behavioral reality of their possessors; they dispose that reality in accordance with their own hegemonic functions and powers.

To the extent that limbic structures organize the human world perceptually, conceptually, and behaviorally, to that same extent is human culture (to pursue, for the sake of argument here, an opposition that the rest of this chapter will erode) unequivocally synonymous with nature. And that, as I have been trying to suggest, is a very great extent indeed. Far from having left biology behind, as anthropologists like Lévi-Strauss imply by conjuring up epistemic points of divide, like language or, more generally, symbolization, human beings have simply exfoliated their cultures from its genetically productive heart. And, in so doing, they have functionally (and happily) retained every bit of their much-maligned "animal nature." As most zoologists would readily admit, one has only to live with a social animal in alert and responsive intimacy to learn (as I have) how clear a continuity there is across species that are often said to be severed by the gulf of language. ("If a lion could talk," wrote Wittgenstein, "we could not understand him" [223ᵉ]. Evolutionary theory argues otherwise.) Not only do I recognize my own expectancy and surprise, my lust and fear and boredom in my dog, but I see in him my love of play and my need for physical affection and comfort from what might most accurately be called "my likes." And how much clearer is the behavioral continuity when the companion is even closer mammalian kin. Jane Goodall describes her chimpanzees:

> Chimps . . . show a capacity for intentional communication that depends, in part, on their ability to understand the motives of the individual with whom they are communicating. Chimps are capable of empathy and altruistic behavior. They show emotions that are undoubtedly similar, if not identical, to human emotions—joy, pleasure, contentment, anxiety, fear and rage. They even have a sense of humor. (qtd. in Calvin 329)

Of course, the danger in such comparisons is in naively concluding that the *quality* of the consciousness that experiences those emotions must be close to that of human perceivers: but that way lies the anthropomorphic trap. While it seems reasonable to assume that homologous brain structures give rise to similar *kinds* of behaviors in both humans and, say, chimpanzees,[9] there is no knowing what quality of consciousness (if consciousness may be assumed at all) subjectively accompanies the expression of those behaviors in the so-called infrahuman world. Despite the efforts of ethologists like Donald R. Griffin to demonstrate that consciousness is not unique to the human species, no procedures exist by which we may determine how infrahuman consciousness compares with our own and so is even deserving of the name of consciousness. To Thomas Nagel's cry in a famous essay, "I want to know what it is like for a *bat* to be a bat," we can only answer (as he does himself): "we may ascribe general *types* of experience on the basis of the animal's structure and behavior. . . . But we believe that these experiences also have in each case a specific subjective character, which is beyond our ability to conceive" (169–70).

With that caveat (an important one, as I shall suggest, when we turn to the anthropocentric character of mimesis), we may speak of a kinship and continuity across species. Darwin early recognized the continuity, and in his *Expression of the Emotions in Man and Animals* (1872) he gave the motive for the fascinating work of Konrad Lorenz and his students—most notably, for the ethological research on human cultures that has been conducted by Irenäus Eibl-Eibesfeldt. The latter's *Love and Hate* offers compelling arguments for the "ritualization" of functional nonhuman primate behaviors into expressive human signals: so the hiding movements of apes and monkeys became the human's covering of the face in shame or embarrassment that is common to all cultures; so their submissive gestures became the bows, the prostrations—the "making of oneself small"—that stamp most human encounters with rank. These (and the many others that Eibl-Eibesfeldt proposes) are conjectural derivations, of course, but they rest on an evolutionary logic that is very hard to resist. Especially when we realize that the "ritualizations" are involuntary *emotional* signals that emanate from an ancient neural circuitry still deep in the "animal" brain.

I think it's largely in that shared circuitry, beneath the destabilizations (negligible, to my mind) of language and "rationality," that human nature resides. This will probably strike most readers as both paradoxical and pointless: paradoxical because it promises to elucidate *human* attributes by confusing them with those of nonhuman species; pointless because it offers to deal with none of the *uniqueness* of human life as opposed to life in the nonhuman order. To take the last first: it's becoming increasingly clear that human uniqueness is an illusion, at least in the strict (and common) usage of the word. Self-consciousness, foresight, tool- and language-use, culture—none of these is the sole province of the human animal: "it now seems likely," write sociobiologists Richard D. Alexander and Katharine M. Noonan, "that all occur in other primate species, and chimpanzees alone may possess all five, though not in the form or to the degree that they are expressed in humans" (437). The myth of the human creature as alienated from "nature," a victim of its uniqueness, of its culture and language, rests upon a widespread ignorance of nature in general and, particularly, of our primate kin. "Nature is not an 'other,'" as the British ethologist John Hurrell Crook has declared: "We are ourselves pervaded by it. We *are* it and have always been so" ("Consciousness" 217).

As for the first objection, that comparative reference to primate kin reveals little about human realities, it ignores the profound implications of *Homo*'s indisputable evolutionary origin. To say that human beings evolved is to concede that there is much in their still-operative emotional relations that is useless, if not inimical, to modern life. "There is bound to be," de Sousa contends, "a good deal of biological atavism, and considerable variation in the levels of antiquity, in the determinants of our emotions. And this means that they will be variously well adapted to the circumstances in which they are now likely to arise" (198). This is so, as anthropologist Jerome H. Barkow reminds us, because "evolution always involves adaptation to past and not present environments" (178). Natural selection has no foresight, only an efficiency born of environmental change. And so efficacious have been our human adaptations that we have come now to master the environment itself (if we may exempt the microbial world), thereby relieving us of the selection pressures that might significantly alter our biology. As a consequence, the human being—to quote Harvard sociobiologist Edward O. Wilson—is a "hodgepodge of special genetic adaptations to an environment largely vanished, the world of the Ice-Age hunter-gatherer" (*On Human Nature* 196), dependent on its culture for those paradigm scenarios (and perhaps in the future for the genetic engineering) that may discipline its limbic inheritance.

Emotionally, in short, it is still a primate, understandable by reference to an ancient past. In the pages that follow I'll draw from that past, as best as it can be reconstructed, and offer evidence, long familiar to the behavioral biologist, for the persistence of its influence on the present. For the student of the humanities there exists no vocabulary in which to frame the terms of this discussion. "Essentialism" is the cant term that now seems to cover every instance of an extension from the particular, but essentialism of any stamp, as evolution would argue, is quite beside the point. Neither philosophical appeals to Platonic essences nor analogies drawn from subatomic physics (however seductive the latter have become for a number of postmodern "theorists") have any bearing upon how biological behavior, including the apprehension of human art, may legitimately be described. "It is not commonly understood," writes Gerald M. Edelman, the Nobel Laureate who is now director of the Neurosciences Institute,

> that there are characteristically biological modes of thought that are not present or even required in other sciences. One of the most fundamental of these is population thinking, developed largely by Darwin. Population thinking considers variation not to be an error but, as the great evolutionist Ernst Mayr put it, to be real. Individual variance in a population is the source of diversity on which natural selection acts to produce different kinds of organisms. This contrasts starkly with Platonic essentialism, which requires a typology created from the top down; instead, population thinking states that evolution produces classes of living forms from the bottom up by gradual selective processes over eons of time. . . . No such idea exists in physics— even the "evolution" of stars does not require such a notion for its explanation.

"Plato is not *even* wrong," Edelman concludes; "he is simply out of the question" (*Bright Air* 73, 153).

Also out of the question is any confusion of human nature (at least as I shall attempt to describe it) with psychological normality or moral authenticity. The natural, the normal, and the good are by no means synonymous categories: what nature contrives for the survival of the fit may—and often does—have little to do with the rights (or desired norms) of the human animal. On the other hand, we should guard against the cliché of the human "beast," harboring a savage heart of darkness in its civilized breast. Such romance shares with Freud's romance of the id the notion of unstructured instincts propelling life forward in an egomaniacally grasping bloodlust. Like all melodrama, this has its appeal, but it also has little substance. Life, as the fact of evolution argues, is an often exquisite structure born of the dynamic relations between a biological creature and its environment. That creature must solve its problems, as it were, within its special environmental constraints, and one of the most efficient means of its doing so, as R. I. M. Dunbar maintains (167), is—to return to the question that initiated our inquiry—the construction of a social world.

3

"It is a widely held opinion," writes Konrad Lorenz,

> shared by some contemporary philosophers, that all human behavior patterns which serve the welfare of the community, as opposed to that of the individual, are dictated by specifically human rational thought. Not only is this opinion erroneous, but the very opposite is true. If it were not for a rich endowment of social instincts, man could never have risen above the animal world. All specifically human faculties, the power of speech, cultural tradition, moral responsibility, could have evolved only in a being which, before the very dawn of conceptual thinking, lived in well-organized communities. Our prehuman ancestor was indubitably as true a friend to his friend as a chimpanzee or even a dog, as tender and solicitous to the young of his community and as self-sacrificing in its defense, aeons before he developed conceptual thought and became aware of the consequence of his actions. (246)

I would quibble with some of the phrasing here: "risen above" suggests a kind of transcendence that I don't think Lorenz meant to imply, and "specifically" in the fourth sentence ("specifically human") begs to be replaced by a more accurate word like "markedly." But, quibbles aside, Lorenz states the case with admirably appropriate force. The British philosopher Mary Midgley, who quotes the passage with approval, adds that, with respect to many animals—whales and wolves as well as human beings—"Social bonds structure their lives." And she italicizes the first of her concluding remarks: *"Communication, and therefore intelligence, develops only where there are these long-standing deep relationships. It may be possible for it to occur in another* context, but if so, nobody knows what it would be like" (*Beast* 275).[10]

The primate evidence in support of this position seems unequivocal to me. The Harvard anthropologist Richard W. Wrangham has surveyed the behavioral characteristics of humans, modern and "primitive," and of their closest primate kin (the gorilla, the bonobo, and the common chimpanzee) in order "to distinguish between aspects of hominoid social organization which are shared, and therefore phylogenetically conservative, and those which are variable" (53). The shared behavior, he concludes, "can be viewed as part of an 'ancestral suite' which, though admittedly hypothetical, offers a logical starting point for behavioral reconstruction at any time during human evolution" (53). In other words, such behaviors will have been exhibited not only by our distant "common ancestor" but also "in intermediate species between the [ancestor] and its living descendants" (53). One of the first and most basic of the similarities is in the "grouping patterns" of those descendants. All four of the species have "social networks" that "share a strong tendency towards closure" (58). Except for the lone traveling male (and, even more commonly, female)[11] solitariness is simply not a species-typical trait of the chimp, gorilla, or human being. Which implies strongly, of course, a semiclosed social network, not only for their common ancestor, but also for those prerational "intermediate species" that antedated *Homo sapiens sapiens*. Rousseau's myth of a "savage" humanity, "with neither a fixed dwelling nor any need for one another, . . . hardly encounter[ing] one another twice in their lives, without knowing or talking to one another" (48), is a vision of no hominid species, at least on this planet, that ever was or probably will be.

For the human primate in particular, the establishment and maintenance of strong social bonds were—and are—of the first importance.[12] The human infant is "altricial," that is, dependent on nourishment, protection, and care for a period longer than that of any other mammalian newborn, and it is because the period of weaning (and the enculturation that accompanies it) is so long that a fast emotional bond between caretaker and child is crucial. This is what Irene Elia has called "the only bedrock of primate association" (232), the necessity dictated by an internal imperative to preserve, in one's infant (or in what one is emotionally seduced into accepting as one's infant), one's own genetic code. Eibl-Eibesfeldt has argued at length that the bond is of such superordinate primacy that all sociability should be attributed to it; in short, "the roots of love," contrary to popular (and much academic) thought, "are not in sexuality [that is, adult sexual intimacy], although love makes use of it for the secondary strengthening of the bond" (*Love* 128). The bonding rites of human sexual behavior have originated in infantile or parental gestures that, even in the relations of chimpanzees, have acquired an unmistakably ritualized quality. The kiss, for example, has its probable source in the caretaker's mouth-to-mouth feeding; the "kiss with the nose" in the sniffing of kin; the "love bite" in the friendly grooming nip; the nuzzle in the infant's search for the breast. "In fact, wider sociality in its original essence," Mary Midgley properly concludes, "simply *is* the power of adults to treat one another, mutually, as honorary parents and children" (*Beast* 136).

On reflection, the implications of this are disturbing, though not because of what they may seem to corroborate to the naive disciple of Freud. Eibl-Eibesfeldt is clear on this latter point:

> Sigmund Freud, in a strikingly topsy-turvy interpretation, once observed that a mother would certainly be shocked if she realized how she was lavishing sexual behavior patterns on her child. In this case Freud had got things reversed. A mother looks after her children with the actions of parental care; these she also uses to woo her husband. (*Love* 151)

It's this last fact that tends to disturb. The First Bond (as Ibsen's Helmers discover to their despair) lays the foundations for mammalian politics. "Honorary parents and children": as adults, they are ineluctably implicated in emotional power relations— relations that are inevitably exacerbated by the natural inequalities of sex.

For if sex helps strengthen the adult pair bond, it does so in significantly skewed terms. We share with other (though not all) of our fellow primates a noticeably "dimorphic" disposition: like baboons and gorillas (but unlike gibbons and siamangs), humans are sexually differentiated by size, strength, and weight. On the average, men are taller and heavier than women; they also have slightly different anatomical structures. Their limb proportions, skeletal torsions, and muscular densities are such that they excel in competitions of running and throwing, "the archaic specialties of the ancestral hunter-gatherer males" (E. O. Wilson, *On Human Nature* 127). Darwin explained the size difference in the sexes as the result of competition for females among those ancestral males, an explanation consonant with what is now generally known of primate anatomy and behavior. Physiological dimorphism correlates with mating patterns across much of the mammalian world: usually the more pronounced the size difference within a species, the higher the average number of females consorting with reproductively active males. [13]

But dimorphism also correlates with methods of subsistence: a study of the bones of American Indian populations has suggested that there was more dimorphism in hunting-dependent tribes than in those that were dependent on agriculture (Elia 219). I raise this point to concede the justice of Stephen Jay Gould's famous criticism of evolutionary explanations of behavior. The latter— often plausible but ultimately unverifiable—are, in his words, "just-so stories" ("Sociobiology" 530), impossible to support with paleontological evidence and usually dependent for their authority upon an appeal to "alloprimate"[14] culture. There are, in fact, a number of available explanations for the dimorphism of human beings: the need for defense against predators, a need that the tool-wielding hunting male was early expected to satisfy; the result of the female's preference for larger males—for those, in other words, who promised to supply the necessities of food and protection (Wenke 100). All of these factors, interdependent as they are, probably entered into the development of dimorphism, although the narrative that they constitute remains intractably nothing but a just-so story.[15] But some of those stories are more plausible than others: the inclusiveness of vision is what matters. And those that narrate our cultural origins with inadequate reference to our prehistoric past are just-so stories of the most doubtful kind.

Such is Gerda Lerner's *The Creation of Patriarchy*, a much-admired book that justifies its title by a constructivist vision of culture. The argument takes us swiftly to the dawn of agriculture, a development that, as most anthropologists have long realized, affected crucially the organization of human life. And yet Lerner's reconstruction of the *preagricultural* past gets very short argumentative shrift. That past, she suggests (making visionary use of the present tense), is an egalitarian Eden: "matrilineal, matrilocal systems abound" (49). Then, with the appearance of sedentary communities, the foundations of patriarchy are laid: "kinship arrangements tend to shift from matriliny to patriliny, and private property develops" (49). (The Marxists can take it from there.)

But quite aside from Lerner's indifference to (or ignorance of) the voluminous primate literature, her reconstruction is weakened, initially and powerfully, by her own rather rueful concessions. However egalitarian hunter-gatherer cultures are— and the existing ones *are*, in fact, more "relaxed and egalitarian by comparison with the majority of economically more complex societies" (E. O. Wilson, *On Human Nature* 83)—in none of them do we find political equality, much less a female hegemony. "One must . . . note," Lerner reluctantly observes, "that in all hunting/gathering societies, no matter what women's economic and social status is, women are always subordinate to men in some respects." And she adds: "There is not a single society known where women-as-a-group have decision-making power *over* men or where they define the rules of sexual conduct or control marriage exchanges" (30). The hypothesized "shift from matriliny to patriliny" seems, moreover, mere fantasy. In one of the most recent, informed, and sophisticated reconstructions of early hominid society, paleoanthropologists R. A. Foley and P. C. Lee conclude that "it may be argued that polygynous male family groups *occurring within larger male kin lineages* characterized the social organization of the ancestors and earliest representatives of modern humans" (905, my emphasis). These conclusions are in accord with the independent research of Michael P. Ghiglieri as well as with Wrangham's primate model, a model that hypothesizes female exogamy for the so-called ancestral suite.

My point is that cultural—specifically economic—facts alone, at least those derived from the paleontologically recent history of our species, cannot begin to account adequately for its behavioral repertoire. (And to those who know anything about the most recent research in developmental psychology, the Freudian "facts" in which Lerner also dabbles can hardly account convincingly for them at all.) One very important fact in that repertoire—our "moderately polygynous" nature

(E. O. Wilson, *On Human Nature* 124)—is not only explicable but, according to physiologist Jared Diamond (71), predictable from the dimorphism that stamps the species. Anthropologist Melvin Konner summarizes the data:

> Of 849 human societies in the ethnographic record, George Peter Murdock
> —one of anthropology's great systematizers—found the marriage form
> called polygyny (one man to two or more women) in 708 of them (83
> percent), these about equally divided between those with usual and those
> with occasional polygyny. Most hunting-gathering societies have occasional
> polygyny. . . . Monogamy is characteristic of 137 (16 percent) of the soci-
> eties, but it must be remembered that in most of these a single individual may
> have more than one mate in succession, and because of the starkly different
> reproductive life spans in men and women, men who choose this option
> are much more likely than their female counterparts to have more than one
> family. Polyandry—a marriage of one woman to more than one man—occurs
> in 4 of the societies (less than half of one percent), and in all of these there
> are special conditions that make the pattern much less than a mirror image
> of polygyny. The human species can thus be said to be pair-bonding with a
> significant polygynous option and tendency. (273–74)

In his polygynous disposition (and other respects), the human male, as Alexander and Noonan observe, "is not particularly unusual among primate males, except that he is generally more parental than the males of other group-living species" (436).

And even in this his unusualness is an eminently relative affair. "For the most part," write primatologists David Taub and Patrick Mehlman in "Primate Paternalistic Investment: A Cross-Species View," "females and not males are the primary, and in many cases the exclusive, caretakers" of infants among human beings (75). A 1981 cross-cultural survey of eighty pre-industrial societies revealed that, in 59 percent of those societies, "fathers are rarely or never with their infants" (69). It further revealed that, even in those societies (only 4 percent) in which there is "a regular and close relationship between father and child" (73), fathers "account for only 6 percent of the direct paternal care given to infants, and they spend on average only 14 percent of their time directly interacting with infants" (69). Thus, Taub and Mehlman conclude, "if we attempt to rank human males on a scale of male-infant interaction time, . . . they fall somewhere in the middle of the continuum of this measure among all primates (i.e., they spend less time with infants than marmosets, tamarins, owl and titi monkeys, and Barbary macaques and can be ranked close to gorilla males)" (69).

As they can be ranked, metaphorically, with respect to their aggressiveness. The greater size and (in Darwin's word) "pugnacity" of the human male (*Descent* 143), relative to that of the female, are probably both consequences of sexual selection. And they are still very much with *Homo sapiens sapiens*. In a now-classic survey of gender-difference research, conducted by two "feminists (of different vintages, and one perhaps more militant than the other!)," Eleanor Emmons Maccoby and Carol Nagy Jacklin conclude that "males do appear to be the more aggressive sex, not just under a restricted set of conditions but in a wide variety of settings and using a wide variety of behavioral indexes" (*Psychology* 12, 228). The evidence, gathered from a number of different cultures and age-groups and supported by both primatological and endocrinological research, is, in Maccoby and Jacklin's words, "unequivocal" (*Psychology* 274).

Their work has not gone unchallenged, of course: Anne Fausto-Sterling's *Myths of Gender*, with which literary theorists are generally more familiar than they are with the research it addresses, is a determined attack, not only on the Maccoby and Jacklin findings, but also on all of the research that has purported to find evidence for biological predispositions in gender-typical behavior.[16] Although its integrity is seriously compromised by the unapologetic bias of its perspective,[17] *Myths of Gender* represents such an influential position in the current academic establishment that it may be useful to devote a paragraph or two to its account of human aggression.

"In arguing that sex-related differences in human aggression have a biological basis," Fausto-Sterling writes,

> Maccoby and Jacklin rely on four lines of evidence, none of which they themselves have analyzed in depth [*sic*]: (1) aggression is related to levels of sex hormones; (2) there are similar sex differences in human and nonhuman primates; (3) sex differences are found early in life before adult socialization pressures could cause them; and (4) males are more aggressive than females in all human societies for which data exist. (150)

The passage is characteristically slipshod in language—Maccoby and Jacklin are scrupulous in avoiding the word "cause" for any single line of influence—and Fausto-Sterling's subsequent discussion will not surprise that reader who, in every previous chapter, has seen all studies of a politically suspect complexion incinerated by the slash-and-burn assault. Her handling of the endocrinological data must wait for a footnote further along in this chapter; here I'd like to review her critique of both the human and the primate studies.

"The difficulty," she writes, with the human studies "revolves around the problem of observer bias" (150). Citing a 1976 paper by John and Sandra Condry in which observers of an infant of variously ascribed sex (it was a "boy" for one group, a "girl" for another) identified its behavior in gender-biased terms, Fausto-Sterling concludes that gender behavior is largely in the eye of the beholder (as the Condrys had suggested in the title of their article) and that "differences in socialization could certainly affect the development of sex-related differences in aggressive behavior" (151). The last is an unremarkable conclusion that no psychologist, I assume, would dispute, but it is typical of Fausto-Sterling's argumentative tactics that socialization becomes gradually, not an influence upon aggression, but the overridingly principal "cause." The possibility that this is so, in other words, is subtly elevated to a probability, and the discussion is closed before any attention is given to an interrogation (or formulation) of its plausibility. I quote Fausto-Sterling's conclusion: "The key biological fact is that boys and girls have different genitalia, and it is this biological difference that leads adults to interact differently with different babies whom we conveniently color-code in pink or blue to make it unnecessary to go peering into their diapers for information about gender" (152–53).

This has an air of plausibility about it, but it can't stand up to elementary questions. Why should a mere anatomical difference, to which no gender behaviors are "naturally" attached, lead adults "to interact differently with different babies"? Why wouldn't, say, a difference in eye color lead to the same differences in interaction? That *globally consistent* gender differences in behavior—behavior that bears no necessary relation (and in the case of aggression no obvious one at all) to the function of the genitalia—should result merely from the perception of those genitalia (or their signs) is an obviously illogical hypothesis.

And when we turn to Fausto-Sterling's conclusions regarding the Condry article, we find the same sort of fuzzy confusion. The experimental situation described by the article is unlike that of observers in the field, who provided much of the Maccoby-Jacklin data. Fieldworkers are asked to tabulate the frequency of specific behaviors in clearly gendered subjects; the Condrys' observers, on the other hand, were asked to disambiguate behaviors in an infant to whom a sex had been artificially assigned. Probability would argue that field-observers are prone to check their gender biases, whereas the observers of the infant in the Condry experiment were invited to exercise their own. In other words, it is plausible that, in cross-cultural studies of children's aggression, if bias becomes a factor it may very well appear in the form of "correcting for gender."

Which, apparently, is just what happens. In a more recent (1985) study by the same John Condry and David F. Ross, a film of two children, their sex disguised by snowsuits, was shown to 175 observers, who were asked to judge the degree of aggression by a so-called target child. The genders of the subjects were systematically varied, so that every combination of interaction—boy-boy, boy-girl, girl-boy, girl-girl—was presented to different groups of the observers (resulting, incidentally, in the sort of "blind" study that Fausto-Sterling advocates). The results were dramatic: "Specifically, the boy-boy condition was rated as significantly less aggressive than the other 3 conditions, which did not differ in level of perceived aggression" (225). Condry and Ross are thus led to conclude that boys' aggressiveness, in comparison to girls', is probably even greater than previously thought:

> Our results, when viewed from the perspective of a perceptual adaptation effect, suggest that the literature probably significantly underestimates the amount of aggression in boys. Thus, if we corrected the "bias" in scaling that we observed in this study, the difference between boys and girls in aggression would be even greater than the current literature (or various meta-analyses) suggests. (231)

And what of the primate evidence? Fausto-Sterling's discussion ranges rather bewilderingly over endocrinological research on rhesus monkeys (which confirms the thesis of Maccoby and Jacklin, though it is rejected as taking insufficient account of socialization by rhesus mothers), on vaguely identified "monkeys" in the wild, on baboons, both forest- and savanna-dwelling—all for the benefit of general readers who have only the fuzziest of notions, if any at all, of how each species relates to humans. She concedes at one point that, "in groups such as baboons and the great apes, males seem to be more pugnacious" (146), but she fails to add that, for many primatologists, the exclusion of *Homo sapiens* from the family of the pongids ("great apes") is as arbitrary as it is arrogant. "Even where differences exist, however," Fausto-Sterling is then quick to caution, "they are environmentally conditioned" (146). The caveat suggests that gender research is ignoring a crucial line of influence, but this observation, like the one above, on the effects of socialization, is a truism that no one denies. The Canadian anthropologist Bernard Chapais elucidates the case with respect to aggression as it emerges in humans and their primate kin:

> a host of . . . studies clearly establish that environmental factors and learning mechanisms exert a considerable hold on the expression of . . . aggression. Such strong learning influences, however, are perfectly compatible with, *and in fact require*, the existence of a neurophysiological substrate underlying aggression. Animals and humans are equipped with neural and hormonal structures underlying aggressive responses. . . . This biological foundation can be conceived as a universal set of constraints affecting the probability that an individual will act aggressively in a number of situations (e.g., being the target of an attack, seeing one's close kin receive aggression, being deprived of scarce resources, feeling exploited by a nonreciprocator, being sexually jealous, etc.). (214, my emphasis)

Aggression, in short, like most other behaviors, "is stimulus- and context-specific" (213).[18] Almost all zoologists agree today, as E. O. Wilson explains, "that none of the categories of aggressive behavior exists in the form of a general instinct over broad arrays of species" (*On Human Nature* 102). By humanists this is usually misunderstood: neither a universal "drive" demanding (Freudian) "discharge" nor a "will" to (Nietzschean) "power," "aggression" is a loose rubric for a broad class of behaviors that are elicited by different confrontational conditions and governed by different controls in the nervous system. Kenneth Evan Moyer has identified several kinds of aggression, as well as the physiological bases of a few: the former are both interspecific (predatory, fear-induced, irritable, territorial) and intraspecific (inter-male, fear-induced, irritable, territorial, maternal, instrumental or "environment-reinforced"). The focus of most studies in human behavior, before and, now, after *Myths of Gender*,[19] has been naturally on "within-species" aggression.

Among the most recent findings are that, first, aggression emerges early in preschool toddlers; second, it quickly acquires gender-typical characteristics; and, third, it changes complexion in accordance with changes in maturation. In the first years of life, there is a positive correlation among aggression, altruism, and emotionality for boys but no such correlation for girls. "Aggressiveness among girls," write psychologist E. Mark Cummings and his colleagues, "is associated with reparation for their own aggressive misconduct, but it is not associated [as it is for boys] with a generally greater sensitivity to another's distress" (184). Between the ages of about five and six, there is a shift from aggression-as-empathy to aggression-as-dominance in boys, and thereafter, at least through late adolescence, their aggressive behavior is positively correlated with their sense of self-esteem (Feshbach and Feshbach 213). That behavior often takes the form of "toughness" in general—of physical and verbal threat and abuse—the acceptance of which, at least in the West, has led L. D. Ferguson to speak of a "brutalization norm" (qtd. in Cairns 77). But for the male adolescent who seeks "leadership status" (that is, the domination and manipulation of other adolescents), "toughness," as Maccoby and Jacklin observe, may prove an ineffective tool (*Psychology* 263). Such a male may turn to what they call "Machiavellianism," in which he is generally more coercive, more free with direct lies, than his female manipulative counterpart (*Psychology* 261). But ontogeny usually recapitulates phylogeny, as it were, the maturing boy's repairing to the social graces with which the males of early hominid societies most likely were endowed—graces that reflect, in E. O. Wilson's words, "the necessities of compromise" (*On Human Nature* 86). Wilson quotes the anthropologist Robin Fox: "Controlled, cunning, cooperative, attractive to the ladies, good with the children, relaxed, tough, eloquent, skillful, knowledgeable and proficient in self-defense and hunting": such was (and, omitting the last two words, still is) the dominant "alpha" male.

But why must the latter be aggressively "tough"? The "most parsimonious" answer, writes R. B. Cairns, "is that, for humans, 'Aggression works' " (73). Or it *worked*, at least, in our "environment of evolutionary adaptedness." Aggression works, for one thing, to erect dominance hierarchies, and it is in the (now-regressive) nature of the human male, especially as he approaches reproductive age, to establish and maintain such hierarchies, particularly among his fellow males. That this tendency has its origins in a hominoid past[20] is suggested by the usual pattern of male aggression. Although, as Maccoby and Jacklin point out, "the same contingencies for aggressors' behavior" are provided by girls as well as boys, the latter "are more frequently selected as the victims of aggression despite the fact that the consequences to the aggressor are more likely to be aversive" (*Psychology* 240–41). To explain such behavior by mere "social conditioning" is to ignore this apparent anomaly—as well as the fact that adults don't seem to reinforce boys' aggression any more than discourage girls'; "in fact, the contrary may be true" (Maccoby and Jacklin, *Psychology* 360). "Aggressive expression and inhibition are highly learnable," writes Cairns, "but they are not initially established through specific learning processes" (76). And boys, as Maccoby and Jacklin conclude, are "more biologically prepared" than girls to learn them (*Psychology* 361).

They also seem more biologically prepared to learn "alliance" behavior, sharing in this, as in much else, a link with close male primate kin. Although in many Old World monkeys "escalated intergroup aggression is carried out by females as well as by males" (Wrangham 67), in neither gorillas, chimpanzees, nor human beings are females notably active in such encounters. Like their counterparts among the apes, "human females have relationships which may include strikingly friendly aspects, but they rarely involve physical aggression or systematic alliance relationships in which women form predictable alliances against other women" (Wrangham 62). This is clearly not the case with men, young or old. In cross-cultural studies of children's play, the sexes have been reported to segregate in significantly different ways. Girls tend to form intimate relationships with one or two "best friends," while boys collect in larger, often competitive play-groups, the selections for which are made on the basis of game prowess: "liking and disliking one's playmates is essentially irrelevant [for boys]. The game," write Maccoby and Jacklin, "is the thing" (*Psychology* 207). These patterns have been corroborated by human ethologist Ritch C. Savin-Williams in a carefully designed and fascinating study of adolescents at summer camp. During "free time" at the camp,

> Boys . . . engaged in sports such as basketball or tennis, usually with fellow cabinmates, or in asocial activities such as reading comic books or sleeping. On the other hand, it was uncommon for girls to spend this time with their cabin group or in organized and competitive activities; rather, they preferred to associate with sisters, cousins, hometown friends, extra-cabin friends, or a close cabin buddy in pairs and cliques, walking and talking.[21] (126)

Savin-Williams concludes that "The greater male proclivity for formulating and maintaining cohesive same-sex groups is empirically congruent with Tiger's (1969) speculations on group bonding and evolutionary theory" (128). It is Tiger's thesis, in *Men in Groups,* that "male-male bonds are of the same biological order for defensive, food-gathering, and social-order-maintenance purposes as the male-female bond is for reproductive purposes" (42).

All of which argues—to quote Maccoby and Jacklin—that "the two sexes may have chosen ["evolved" is, of course, a better word] somewhat different arenas for ego-investment" and that "each sex [has] a higher sense of self-worth in the area of more central . . . involvement" (*Psychology* 159–60). The relative structures of their social hierarchies seem to bear this out. Savin-Williams found that, although the girls of his study often showed dominance, "dominance does not appear to have been a highly desirable or discernible trait to them" (126). When his girl campers were asked to identify their most dominant member, they selected the most antagonistic girl, even though the counselors had observed that the most "maternally" assertive ("confident, loyal, kindhearted, and manipulative" [115]) had been their true group leader. Power relations were in greater daily flux among the girl campers than among the boys, and dominance was exerted by the girls in less physical and overt ways. For the boys, the dominance-submission order had been worked out very quickly, and the boys that fell into each level were generally of a fairly clear "type." The "alpha" boys were (according to their own cabinmates) the handsomest, most athletic, most physically mature, "exhibiting the confidence we have learned to expect from alpha monkeys" (qtd. in Freedman 46); their satellites included a "beta" confidant, who got on well with his superior; a "gamma" bully; a "joker" occupying a middle position; then a "quiet" and "submissive" follower, who was described by his peers as "the nerd."

If such stereotypes smack of Hollywood formula, a kind of cast-list for Bill Murray's *Meatballs,* the conclusions are not hard to draw. Maccoby and Jacklin are bold enough to draw them:

> if one sex is more biologically predisposed than the other to perform certain actions, it would be reasonable to expect that this fact would be reflected in popular beliefs about the sexes, so that innate tendencies help to produce the cultural lore that the child learns. Thus he adapts himself, through learning, to a social stereotype that has a basis in biological reality. (Of course, not all social stereotypes about the sexes have such a basis.) It is reasonable, then, to talk about the process of acquisition of sex-typed behavior—the *learning* of sex-typed behavior—as a process built upon biological foundations that are sex-differentiated to some degree. (*Psychology* 363–64)

What exactly those "foundations" are has been the object of much endocrinological research. It is probable, as many animal studies have suggested, that both androgens and ovarian hormones play a role in gender-differentiated acts of aggression, but attempts to extend such findings to human subjects have been marred by procedural flaws.[22] What seems the most suggestive endocrinological work to date on gender-related behavior has focused, not on postnatal gonadal steroid effects, but on the prenatal hormonal milieu.

Congenital adrenal hyperplasia, or the CAH syndrome, represents a dramatic intervention in fetal development of an excessive hormonal effect. CAH infants, both boys and girls, are born, because of a genetic defect, with enlarged ("hyperplasic") adrenal glands, and during gestation the secretions of those glands result in abnormally high levels of androgen. The androgen, in turn, masculinizes the bodies of CAH females: the clitoris is more or less enlarged, and the labia may resemble a scrotum. But with surgical correction (when it is needed) and treatments of cortisone or prednisone, both males and females develop normally, their sexual functioning and fertility unimpaired. Gender identity "typically agrees with the sex of rearing of the child: that is, females with CAH firmly identify as girls and women . . . , provided that sex assignment is clearly female from early childhood" (Ehrhardt and Meyer-Bahlburg 1314). And yet the gender behavior of both girls and boys seems to be significantly altered:

> Girls with CAH have been reported to show a more masculine pattern of toy preference than their unaffected sisters as well as more rough-and-tumble play, a preference for male rather than female playmates, greater tomboyism, reduced rehearsal through childhood play of adult female roles [such] as wife and mother, reduced interest in infant care, and reduced interest in physical appearance or attractiveness as compared with female controls. Boys with CAH are reported to differ from their unaffected male siblings in higher levels of intense energy expenditure in rough outdoor play and sports. (Hampson and Kimura 373–74, footnotes omitted)

That these behaviors are essentially uninfluenced by the patients' medical histories is suggested by similar studies of females whose mothers were treated with androgen-derived progestogens during pregnancy. Such progestogens, like CAH, have a masculinizing effect upon the female fetus, but the latter is born endocrinologically normal and, aside from occasional surgical correction when the clitoris is enlarged, requires no further medical treatment of any kind. "Most of these girls," write Anke A. Ehrhardt and Heino F. L. Meyer-Bahlburg, who have summarized the studies prior to 1981, "showed a behavior pattern similar to that of females with CAH" (1314).[23]

For most scientists it's now irresistibly apparent that not only is human sex-dimorphic behavior predisposed by chemical factors—Jaak Panksepp has argued recently that brain opiods play a key role in various bondings—but the human brain itself is, in the words of Sandra Witelson, "a sexualized organ" (295).[24] Witelson, one of the pioneers in work on brain lateralization over the last twenty to twenty-five years, has proposed that differences in male and female brain functioning may result in important differences in behavior. That there *is* a difference in functioning has been confirmed by James Inglis and J. S. Lawson, who, in 1981, reported that "lateralized brain lesions produce very different effects on the intelligence of men and women" (694). Males with left-hemisphere damage show impairment on the Verbal Scale, and with right-hemisphere damage on the Performance Scale, of the Wechsler Adult Intelligence Scale, but females show "selective deficits" on neither scale after comparable damage in one hemisphere or the other. Such findings have led many neuroscientists to conclude that the male's brain is functionally more asymmetric than the female's. But, as the Canadian neuropsychologist Doreen Kimura reports in a recent summary of her own research, "the most striking sex differences in brain organization may not be related to asymmetry" (124). Apparently the front-back organization is a more crucial distinguishing feature. In disorders such as aphasia or apraxia (difficulty in selecting appropriate hand movements), men and women reveal different brain deficits, those in men more localized to the back of the left hemisphere, those in women more localized to the front.

"Taken together," Kimura observes, "the evidence suggests that men's and women's brains are organized along different lines from very early in life" and that the resultant differences in cognitive patterns "arose because they proved evolutionarily advantageous" (125). It was probably, she hypothesizes, the division of labor (doubtless "quite marked" for the early hominids)—a division by which men were made responsible for hunting, defense, and tool-manufacture, women for food-gathering, garment-provisioning, and child care—that "put different selection pressures" on the brains of men and women (125). And she concludes, like Maccoby and Jacklin (as well as the host of other women who now dominate this field), that "the finding of consistent and, in some cases, quite substantial sex differences suggests that men and women may have different occupational interests and capabilities, independent of [I prefer "prior to"] societal influences" (125).

4

Kimura is speaking (as I have been writing, throughout this chapter) in a kind of statistical shorthand. "Men" and "women" are population categories, not designations for all same-sexed individuals who should be expected to share the same characteristics. As in all populations, some members (statistically, those of the bell-curve mean) are "more typical" of their sex than others. There is a good deal of overlap between categories, of course, the most aggressive woman being far more aggressive than the least aggressive man, and so on. This is variously expressed in the behavioral literature: E. O. Wilson speaks of the "probability" or "capacity" of developing "a certain array of traits" (*On Human Nature* 100, 56); Konner of an expected "range of reactions" (40); Georg Breuer of a "bandwidth" within which a sex (or species) typically operates (20). And it should go without saying that no set of characteristics or behaviors is genetically or biologically "determined." When scientists and laymen inveigh against "biological determinism," they (like Lewontin and company, in *Not in Our Genes*) are simply misrepresenting the issue. "Our species," writes Daniel G. Freedman, echoing scores of his behavioralist colleagues, "is biocultural—100% biological and 100% cultural" (108). Which is to say, as Maccoby and Jacklin imply above, that there is no separating the "innate" and the "learned."[25] Learning, to recite a formula now commonplace in learning theory, can be carried out only by an organism biologically *prepared* to learn, and the "innate" can manifest itself only if environmental conditions allow. My argument, to which I shall return at the end of this chapter, is that culture is *both* an expression and a critique of what the species as a "population" (or as a set of sexually differentiated populations) is biologically disposed to do.

That it is disposed to do anything is not even a matter of dispute in many academic quarters, especially in the enlightened humanities: the notion is simply, flatly denied. With the exception of the "maternalist" faction, most feminists (like Fausto-Sterling, for example) are resolutely set against conceding behavioral differences between the sexes, at least those induced by biology.[26] The differences that are obvious (and regnant: the "patriarchy") are merely cultural constructions: "I take *masculine* here," writes Ruth Bleier in her introduction to *Feminist Approaches to Science*, "to refer to the set of socially constructed characteristics attributed to men in the patriarchal cultures that are the context for our analyses" (15). In another essay in the same collection, Bleier attacks (how convincingly I must let the enterprising reader decide) the experimental evidence for behavioral differences biologically typical of sex, arguing against the work on aggression, for example, that "'masculinity' is a gender characteristic and, as such, culturally, not biologically, constructed" (150). A biologist herself, she notes at the end of her essay that "biological and environmental factors are inextricable, in ways that make futile any efforts to separate them" (161), but, braving the futility, she concludes with a sentence that shoves biology out the back door: "Rather than biology, it is the cultures that our brains have created that most severely limit our visions and the potentialities for the fullest possible development of each individual" (162–63).

The specific implications of this remark—that culture is wholly independent of biology, that the human brain creates ex nihilo, that constraints are severe limitations of "visions" and "potentialities"—would take more space to address than I have room for, though I'll return to the first of them momentarily. What I draw attention to here is the general assumption underlying all three, the assumption that, along with the equation of biology with determinism, props up the constructivist faith. That assumption, very simply, is that the natural is the good. The reasoning (wholly "unconscious," in the most untechnical sense of that word) seems to run this way: If the differences currently observable between the sexes, to which we owe the patriarchy, are "natural," then nature is careless of individuals and their "visions"; but nature is, as the author of those individuals, by definition good; therefore, the differences must be "learned." Never one to betray the heart that loves her, Bleier's nature is, like Mohanty's "rationality," the underpinning of a faith (and an idea of culture) that has suffered a wanton perversion. The male-contrived "subject-object split" is the source of all our woe: it is to "harmony" and "holism" (as Hilary Rose urges [72]) that science must return—but to a holism, I assume, that keeps biology out of the whole. "It seems to me," writes Norman Holland, in one of the few books of literary criticism I know of to draw upon recent cognitive research,

> [that] the sciences of our age have for many decades outmoded the simple split of subject and object or the simple process of signifiers' signifying. These are flat earth theories that look incontrovertibly commonsensical—until you try to detail them or fit them into other knowledge. We need to get beyond these nineteenth-century models. (175)

In one important respect, at least, feminist criticism has "gotten beyond" the nineteenth century, and that is by exposing, in the "hard" sciences as well as the "soft," the insidiousness of male bias. In genetic theory, in primatological study, the tendency for male scientists to assume male-centered structures, to build models upon foundations of dominance and overt aggression, has been challenged very provocatively by feminist argument. The feminist historian Evelyn Fox Keller has long championed the work of Barbara McClintock, whose much-questioned research on transposable elements (popularly known as "jumping genes") finally won her a Nobel Prize in 1983. The female primatologists, who now number in the scores, have virtually redefined crucial aspects of primate cultures, emphasizing, as Donna J. Haraway has remarked, "matrifocal groups," "long-term social co-operation," and "flexible process" (*Primate Visions* 19) where their male colleagues had seen little or none. Male bias has typically been given a historical genesis, with Descartes and Bacon as pivotal figures, although the chief defense of this line of reasoning, Carolyn Merchant's *The Death of Nature*, also tracks the bias to the ancient Greeks. But to do so seems to rob "history" of much meaning. There's a more parsimonious explanation for the genesis, I think, an explanation that has an important bearing, not only upon the general argument of this chapter, but also upon the nature of human perception and cognition as a whole. I'd like to join the maternalists in proposing that female (and not "feminist") epistemology differs profoundly from that of the male.[27] It does so because of the comparatively different "selection pressures" that produced that "sexualized organ," the brain.

If we are to take seriously the implications of human evolution, we must acknowledge, as Michael Ruse does (and as Lorenz did before him), that the foundations of human knowledge are to be traced to strategies of survival. That they are rooted in an unmediated apprehension of the world has long been thoroughly discredited. As Mary E. Hawkesworth reminds her readers in a review of feminist epistemological theory, "A fact is a theoretically constituted proposition, supported by theoretically mediated evidence and put forward as part of a theoretical formulation of reality" (550). In Popperian terms, all genuine reasoning is deductive reasoning, in which the truth of the conclusion is implicit in the truth of the premises. Does this therefore suggest that so-called scientific reasoning is a mere shuttling of wisps in the void, the fabrication of a vast skein of meaning that (as a misreading of Thomas S. Kuhn would have it)[28] is displaced by another with each "paradigm shift"?

I think not. The "truth of things" in all of its wholeness and baldness must forever elude the human mind, but that mind has been so constituted by its encounter with those things—it is in fact an emanation of them—that it necessarily perceives and thinks in adaptively elucidative ways. In other words, the "theoretical mediations" of scientific reasoning, though unable to uncover anything like absolute truth, allow the human thinker to apprehend and manipulate reality in ways advantageous to immediate (but not necessarily long-term) survival. Hence the universality of induction, mathematical logic, the principle of parsimony.[29] Ruse illustrates this idea by proposing scenarios for a typical "proto-human":

> A tiger is seen entering a cave that you and your family usually use for sleeping. No one has seen the tiger emerge. Should you seek alternative accommodation for this night at least? How else does one achieve a happy end to this story, other than by an application of those laws of logic that we try to uncover for our students in elementary logic classes. . . . Analogously for mathematics. Two tigers were seen going into the cave. Only one came out. Is the cave now safe? Again: you have to travel across a plain to get to your hunting grounds. You can only walk a limited distance in this heat. Should you set off now? Should you wait until tomorrow? Should you plan to camp out for the night? And so forth. The proto-human who had an innate disposition to take seriously the law of excluded middle, and who avoided contradictions, survived and reproduced better than he/she who did not. The proto-human who innately preferred "2 + 2 = 4" to "2 + 2 = 5" was at a selective advantage over his/her less discriminating cousin. (162)

In short, the world as perceived is the world *survived*. And it should therefore come as no revelation that the world as perceived by a dimorphic species, whose very dimorphism attests to sexually differentiated strategies of survival, should be a world *differentially* perceived. The male everywhere sees dominance and aggression because, in his distant proto-human past, it was in his adaptive interests to do so.[30]

The usual objection of feminist thinkers is that such interests—as much "scientistic" as male, we are told—lead to destructive violations of the world and that, if that world is to be rescued from what Michel Serres has called (with Gallic extravagance) the "thanatocracy," the notion of knowledge as an extension of *domination* must be wiped from the human slate. But, as Paisley Livingston has pointed out, such assumptions are merely capitulations to the myth that the natural is the good. "It strikes me," he writes in *Literary Knowledge*,

> that those who castigate science's presumed instrumental and dominating attitude toward nature are necessarily using the concept of nature in a normative rather than descriptive manner; nature is "the good," it or She is "in order" as things are, and it is mankind's acquisitive and instrumental attitudes that initiate violence. But does not this assumption merely perpetuate the myth of the Garden? (110)

Every species on the earth is a species that has been impressed by natural selection, as it were, into a posture of mastery:[31] at the very least, an organism must maintain a "sense" of itself as distinct from the environment that surrounds it, must establish an originary relationship of binary opposition between itself and the world. It fell anciently to the male of our species, I would argue—to the hunter, defender, and contestant of women—to develop a sensitivity toward this sort of imperative to an unusually high degree. He couldn't foresee how successful (and destructive) his mastery of the world would become, of course, but it's idle to propose that the relinquishment of control will somehow set things right.

That his vision, however inimical to world (or female) interests, survives robustly today is a perhaps lamentable but inescapable fact about modern life. It is also one of those facts upon which any unsentimental politics (as well as any unsentimental criticism of art) must be founded. The emotionally motivated human animal is a behaviorally conservative animal—though certainly not one completely impervious to correction. To the politically sensitive I may seem to have been building a case for a kind of quietism here: in the face of a nature afflicted with phylogenetic inertia, we can only fold our hands and wait to declare that *la commedia è finita*. Such, essentially, is the subtext of sociologist Steven Goldberg's *The Inevitability of Patriarchy*, a book with which I am, in most points but this, in generally substantial agreement.[32] But neither the politics nor the art that I envisage (and know) is so despairingly passive. I began this chapter with a vulgar anecdote; I'll draw toward a close with a vulgar analogy (or homology, to be more precise). No less than much of my behavior is my body the relic of a hominoid past: my armpits give off an acrid stench; my appetite leads me to store more fat than I either want or need; I wake up each morning with a faceful of prickly hair. And every day I meet the politics of my body with resigned but determined resistance: I shave, I diet, I apply Old Spice. In none of this do I deceive myself into thinking that I am "changing" myself (or the world). I am simply muddling through, as best I can, impressed (as I am not when I gape before inner visions of a rosy-hued New Society) with the necessity of *always staying alert*, of living every minute as a reflective labor that cannot ever relax its vigilance. The political life is endless work, grounded, as it is, in certain morally questionable instincts.

So, too, human culture. Breuer offers a crisp formulation: "Instincts in man are . . . emotional tendencies which form the basis for cultural superstructures in specifically human forms" (134).[33] Thus, given my argument: the (thanatocratic?) "patriarchy"—but a patriarchy with the powers of self-criticism. For if rationality is not, as Mohanty argues, the foundation of sociality, it is surely, however weakly, an instrument of (at least) legal equality. Which is not to imply that it is opposed to what Hume called the human "passions."

> "Reason" [I quote Mary Midgley now] is not the name of a character in a drama. It is a name for organizing oneself. When there is a conflict, one desire *must* be restrained to make way for the other. It is the process of *choosing which* that is rightly called reasoning. (*Beast* 258)

The human desire to form passionate and respectful attachments (to "bond," as an ethologist would say) is as strong as the equally instinctive human desire to dominate. Culture is the record of our complex and shifting allegiances between these imperatives and others.

But it is not an opaquely random affair, as it often appears to those for whom no Archimedes fulcrum offers a *point d'appui*. Human life, as I shall argue in Chapter 2, is a structure of intelligible allegiances and rivalries—of binary oppositions, once again—that have coalesced into a socially functional system of dynamically constrained ambivalences.[34] Its operations obey a generally adaptive logic, however obscure its local vagaries, and its coherence may be said to describe what Earl W. Count called the "biogram," the behavioral grammar of our species. To say it has a grammar is to imply that, for all the richness of cultural inflection (that is, of our behavioral syntax) human culture in its global manifestation is a structure of loose constraints. The notion that both culture and the human "subject" are completely plastic entities, susceptible of being bent into any shape that history or language pleases, is an absurdity that we may summarily dismiss. Such a notion requires a tabula-rasa mind, and that sort of mind, as Ruse observes, "demands a brain with a great deal of useless capacity"; its "total receptivity" would require a cranial cavity probably "several times larger than the one we now possess," and it would always be a dangerous instrument, since "one or two wild thoughts could steer [us] straight into maladaptive oblivion" (141–42). It is not merely fortunate but inevitable that our genes (in E. O. Wilson's much-quoted and memorable phrase) "hold culture on a leash" (*On Human Nature* 167). Otherwise, a certain strain of Pauline Christianity, with its loathing of the body and sex, could have put an end to the whole human experiment some two thousand years ago.

Of course, literally conceived (and how else is one to conceive it?), a tabula-rasa mind is simply an impossibility. *Any* mind that survives in the world must be prepared for that survival: it must begin its life endowed with the equivalent of what Edelman calls a "primary" neural "repertoire." Ornstein offers an amusing illustration:

> To give Locke's ideas a test, I went to an office-supply shop and bought a piece of writing paper and let it sit on my desk for a couple of weeks. And I talked and sang to it. I told it to do all sorts of things. I gave it food, I gave it water, I read to it the works of Descartes, I gave it the works of Freud, I tried to get it to talk, I tried to take it for a walk. I put it in my car to see whether it could recognize the ocean as well as the mountain.
>
> The paper was unable to do any of these things. (*Evolution* 68)

Wilson and Charles Lumsden have in fact demonstrated that, even if a "blank-slate" species were a possibility, natural selection would inevitably favor some genetic types over others, thereby rendering that species, within a very few generations, a genetically directed one (13).

Biology counts. How much it counts has come as a surprise even to the geneticists themselves. Recent studies with twins and triplets have led "to two general and seemingly remarkable conclusions concerning the sources of the psychological differences—behavioral variation—between people: (i) genetic factors exert a pronounced and pervasive influence on behavioral variability, and (ii) the effect of being reared in the same home is negligible for many psychological traits" (Bouchard et al. 223). Heritability has been found to be as high as 50 percent (sometimes higher) for traits and conditions including activity level, anxiety, criminality, divorce, dominance, extraversion, homosexuality, intelligence, manic-depressive psychosis, novelty-seeking, obesity, personal autonomy, political attitudes, schizophrenia, sociability, substance abuse, values, and vocational interests.[35] Based on the results of his Louisville Twins Study, the late Ronald Wilson hypothesized that "behavioral development is guided by a genetic strategy analogous to that for biological development" (qtd. in Holden 600). Such conclusions are justifying the "quiet revolution" that, in Robert Cairns's words (58), has, since the early 1970s energized the behavioral sciences—a revolution often associated with the word "sociobiology," though "evolutionary psychology" is currently the phrase under which the majority of the revolutionaries most openly and willingly march. Fittingly, perhaps, since that phrase acknowledges what E. O. Wilson has called "the philosophical legacy of the last century of scientific research," and it foregrounds, as the manifesto of the revolutionary program, "the essential first hypothesis for any serious consideration of the human condition" (*On Human Nature* 1–2).[36]

To the extent that art as mimesis is a response to that condition, the criticism of art has, I think, the responsibility to come to terms with both the legacy and the hypothesis. "No excuse remains," Mary Midgley writes, "for anybody in the humanities and social sciences to evade the challenge of Darwin and treat social man as an isolated miracle" ("Rival Fatalisms" 34). The last twenty years or so have seen not so much evasion as self-satisfied and self-congratulatory ignorance—have seen, moreover, a willful enthrallment with the notion that *all* foundationalism in the interpretive disciplines is both misguided and corrupt.[37] And so "theory" has drifted blimpishly across the critical landscape, buoyed up by thin hot air (mostly French), nosing this way and that according to whatever politically sanctimonious (foundationalist) enthusiasm seizes the hierophantic pilot of the hour. (An enthusiasm for "antifoundationalist" difference and deferral is of course a foundationalist enthusiasm.) And at all our elbows, as it were, a reproachful little black dog sits. He knows the hierophant for the fraud he is, smelling, in his smell, and sensing, in his moods and more animated accesses, a comrade, a *semblable*, a *frère*. We are all what we are because that little dog knows us, and what he knows should be the beginning of a true account of art.

2

"Me against My Brother; Me and My Brother against Our Cousins; Me, My Brother and Our Cousins . . .": The Genetic Construction of Sociality

Natural selection dictates that organisms act in their own self-interest. They know nothing of such abstract concepts as "the good of the species." They "struggle" continuously to increase the representation of their genes at the expense of their fellows. And that, for all its baldness, is all there is to it; we have discovered no higher principle in nature.
—Stephen Jay Gould (opponent of sociobiology),
Ever Since Darwin: Reflections in Natural History

It would be hard to find a clearer example of an analysis of biological objects in terms of the systems sciences rooted in military combat, competitive sexuality, and capitalist production. . . . The disquieting aspect of all this is that sociobiologists can and have correctly predicted insect caste distributions with these analyses.
—Donna J. Haraway (opponent of sociobiology),
Simians, Cyborgs, and Women: The Reinvention of Nature

He knows, beloved creature, that Iris Murdoch the theorist is, at best, in possession of a half-truth. "That human beings are naturally selfish," she writes in *The Sovereignty of Good*, "seems true on the evidence, whenever and wherever we look at them, in spite of a very small number of apparent exceptions" (78). Her authority for this pronouncement—she calls it "modern psychology"—is Freud. Unfortunately, she is not alone in her respect for that authority. Freud's analysis of human motivation and behavior has come to exert an overwhelming, if often unrecognizably insidious, influence on contemporary Western thought—a fact that Murdoch's own novels both resist and attest. Harold Bloom, who quarrels with so much of that thought, at least in its academic manifestations, has no reservations about Freud's preeminence: "Freud," he declares in *The Breaking of the Vessels*, "has usurped the role of the mind of our age, so that more than forty years after his death we have no common vocabulary for discussing the works of the spirit except what he gave us" (63). And that vocabulary includes few words (outside the category of the "neurotic") for the unselfish, the self-effacing, the altruistic.

"His Majesty the Ego": the phrase seems to sum up the revolutionary new way that Freud gave us to look at ourselves—but that way, let me begin by saying in critique of the prevailing thought, was hardly original with Freud himself. It was derived, essentially (and somewhat selectively), from Darwin. The founder of psychoanalysis, as Frank J. Sulloway demonstrates in his brilliant book on Freud, was a "crypto-biologist," a "principal scientific heir of Charles Darwin" (5), who had argued in his *Origin of Species* that all organisms "struggle" to maximize their fitness and that natural selection "works solely by and for the good of each being" (428). (The more complex Darwin, who wrestled with the enigma of animal altruism, was largely ignored by Freud.) Ironically, Sulloway goes on to identify Freud as "a major forerunner of the ethologists and sociobiologists of the twentieth century" (5), presumably because of the importance that evolutionary considerations play in both of their closely related disciplines. But, as I shall suggest during the course of this chapter, it is a mistake to associate what has been called "the Modern Synthesis"—and to associate sociobiology, especially—with our nineteenth-century Freudian inheritance. Despite what either of my epigraphs may first imply, sociobiology provides a perspective upon human life that offers a serious (and exciting) challenge to the assumptions of psychoanalysis and of many other fashionable currents of academic and popular thought. And yet, though its formulation was announced over twenty years ago in E. O. Wilson's magisterial *Sociobiology* and it is now being mainstreamed rapidly in the biological and even some of the social sciences, sociobiology has, to date, made no significant impact on the humanities. Of course part of the reason that it has failed to do so can be explained by the current political climate: sociobiology is generally, if erroneously, assumed to support—through its alleged defense of "biological determinism"— conservative political agendas, and so, although many of its conclusions, as we shall see, sit comfortably with those of the deified Marx, it is regarded among the students of the liberal arts with almost universal suspicion.

But its theory has been widely misrepresented, and the scientific integrity and utility of that theory have been very widely underappreciated. It is, first, crucial to understand that, far from insisting upon the "determinism" of behavior (or, like ethology, its relatively stereotypical invariance), sociobiology stresses its flexibility, often analyzing it in terms of cost-and-benefit strategies and (at least in the hands of its best practitioners) taking pains to respect its complexity. A second and equally crucial point has to do with the ultimate unit of selection in its theory of social interactions. That unit is not Darwin's individual organism—or what we'll occasionally refer to as the "phenotype"—but, as the title of Dawkins's *The Selfish Gene* makes clear, the individual gene.[1] "Evolution," Dawkins argues in *The Extended Phenotype*, "is the external and visible manifestation of the differential survival of alternative *replicators*. . . . Genes are replicators; organisms and groups of organisms are best not regarded as replicators; they are *vehicles* in which replicators travel about" (82). The "survival of the fittest," therefore, has less to do with the survival of individual organisms than with the survival of genes and of aggregates of genes: *of entities that are transvehicular.*

It is the drive toward "inclusive fitness," defined as the success of an individual in assisting its genes (or, more accurately, their copies or "alleles") through both present and future generations, *largely irrespective of the fate of the vehicle,* that has, as we shall see, both new and profound implications for the understanding of human behavior. But, before turning to those implications, we must deal with one other problematic point, and that is a terminological one. Dawkins's gene is "selfish," of course, in a metaphorical sense alone. The usage, implying to some a volitional tenacity on the part of DNA (and a corresponding ruthlessness in its vehicles), has caused serious and damaging confusions. Robert Trivers, one of the most important theorists of sociobiology, has suggested, as a more proper phrase, the "self-promoting" or "self-benefiting" gene ("Sociobiology" 38), but these alternatives, to which anthropomorphic projections still cling, are really not much better. The "selfishness" of genes, like the concept of evolutionary "competition" itself, should be understood as Dawkins defines it above: as "the differential survival of alternative replicators," usually (though not always) through the differential adaptive success of their phenotype(s). To interpret it in any other way is to spring the trap into which Murdoch stumbles when she concludes that human beings (like, presumably, other organisms in the Darwinian struggle for life) are constitutionally, "naturally," selfish.

Even Dawkins himself thinks otherwise. "To the extent that I am interested in human ethics (a rather small extent)," he has written, "I disapprove of egoism. To the extent that I know about human psychology (again, a rather small extent), I doubt if our emotional nature is, as a matter of fact, fundamentally selfish" ("In Defence" 558). His modesty may strike some as ignorance (elsewhere in the same article he protests that he is "not even very directly interested in man" or in "the ethics of one particular, rather aberrant, species" [556]), but his doubt threatens no serious contradiction to the theory of genic selection. *A "selfish" gene does not necessarily imply a selfish organism, although it typically implies a self-serving one for which altruism—and other unselfish behaviors—may be entirely compatible with its interests.* R. D. Alexander summarizes the argument, drawing out its philosophical implications, in his *Darwinism and Human Affairs:*

Despite its philosophical impact, Darwinian evolution did not initially provide the solution to the age-old conundrum of whether humans really are
hedonistic individualists or group altruists. Only knowledge of genes could
tell us that, in fact, they are both and yet neither. They seem to be individualists because each individual tends to behave according to his separate
genetic interests, but each individual actually and literally uses or gives his
life for others, *who carry the copies of his genes*. . . . Now we can proceed from the
knowledge that the unity of the individual derives from the ability of the tens
of thousands of separately heritable genetic units making up its genotype to
act in all of their separate interests equally by dispensing altruism to other
individuals on the basis of the *probability* that such individuals carry any
particular one of the genes of the altruist. . . . This I regard as a general theory
of the individual, and as a theory of human nature. (56–58, paragraphing
simplified, first emphasis mine)

The theory represents, as John Hurrell Crook has called it, with a discernment
unremarked by the humanities, a "major shift in our comprehension of man"
(*Evolution* 152).

And in our comprehension, of course, of woman. For the first thing the theory
does is account for the ambivalent relationship of the sexes. Their mutual attraction
is essential for offspring (and thus the perpetuation of their genes), but theirs is an
attraction of the genetically different, with separate, even divergent, interests. The
difference begins, at least on the cellular level, with the gametes, the male sperm
and the female egg. Humans are "anisogamous" (the gametes of the two sexes
are unequal in size) and so have been disposed, in their sexually differentiated
reproductive strategies, to fundamentally different behaviors: solicitude from the
female toward her few large eggs in which a great deal of energy has been
invested; prodigality from the male of his numerous small sperm, each of which
represents a (fairly expendable) fraction of his overall reproductive costs. Careful
preservation and wide distribution of those gametes thereby characterize their
respective strategies, and, as David M. Buss has recently shown, the strategies
are reflected, cross-culturally, in what men and women value in their mates. Cues
that signal "resource acquisition" (that is, signs of a healthy earning potential,
of ambition and willingness to work) are more important to women than to men,
while those having to do with "reproductive capacity," signaled by youth and sexual
attractiveness in general,[2] are more valued by men than by women. These findings
support Robert A. Hinde's conclusions, based upon earlier research: "Thus we see
that . . . observed social attitudes and behaviour are in line with the presumed
desiderata of early human history—namely that it is in the male's interests to
fertilize as many females as possible, and to play only a limited role in child care,

whereas female reproductive success depends on the adequacy and competence of a male protector."

"And in so far as he takes that role," Hinde continues, "the male must be sure he is not being cuckolded" (129). In this he is at a distinct disadvantage by comparison with many primate kin. For unlike, for example, the female chimpanzee, whose genital and mammillary swellings give clear signs of receptivity and lactation, the human female has evolved a number of traits that confuse her reproductive status. Her continuous sexual receptivity, her concealed ovulation, her perennial pendulous breasts, her ability to achieve (or simulate) orgasm—all of these characteristics, once thought to have evolved "epigamically" as attractions for the opposite sex, are now interpreted by a number of theorists as early tools of sexual/political manipulation (Hrdy, *Woman*; R. Smith). In an evolutionary "game otherwise heavily weighted toward male muscle mass," as Sarah Blaffer Hrdy describes it (*Woman* 187), the female evolved subtle strategies to forge ties with as many male consorts as possible, thereby offering all of them "some probability of having sired her offspring" (157) and so some advantage in extending them care.[3] She could forge those ties only if, for each of them, the fact of paternity were uncertain, a state of affairs made possible by her cryptic ovulation, by her apparently promiscuous sexuality, by her liberation from the estrus cycle and from obvious signs of maternal care (for example, lactation).

The advantages lay in keeping the male off-balance. "But such advantages," writes Hrdy, "were not granted to females in a vacuum":

> once again the ball was tossed back into the other court. To keep women (and their sexuality) in check, husbands and their relations (and perhaps especially property-owning families) devised cultural practices which emphasized the subordination of women and which permitted males authority over them. (*Woman* 187)

Thus was born the patriarchy, with all of its attendant institutions: sequestration of women, clitoridectomy and infibulation, the legally sanctioned "double standard." But Hrdy's conclusions should not be read too literally. Behind her phrase "devised cultural practices" lies a tangle of determinate forces. Only a sex predisposed to dominance and aggression (and with the "muscle mass" necessary to carry out its intentions) could, as I proposed in Chapter 1, come to institute such "practices": and that is a sex that is motivated by more than vulgar visions of power. It is motivated, for one thing (and even more vulgarly), by universal male sexual jealousy.

In an important and frequently cited paper on the subject, Martin Daly, Margo Wilson, and Suzanne J. Weghorst argue that sexual jealousy is not only a transhistorical and pancultural phenomenon but a peculiarly male "complex," as well. For, "although both sexes experience jealousy, just what they experience evidently differs":

> Shettel-Neuber, Bryson, and Young . . . had students describe their own probable behavior in a jealousy-inducing situation portrayed on videotape. Men considered themselves likelier to become angry, drunk, threatening, and aroused than did women, and likelier to start going out with others. Women, on the other hand, were likelier to anticipate crying, feigning indifference, or striving to increase their attractiveness. Teismann [and Mosher] . . . solicited the reactions of American undergraduate dating couples to a hypothetical jealousy-inducing situation and reported that men focused on possible sexual contact of their partner with the rival male while women were primarily concerned with their boyfriends' expending time, money, and attention upon the rival female. (18)

Such reactions support the hypothesis that, "while women may be expected to be jealous of their mates' allocation of attention and resources, they should not be so concerned with specifically *sexual* fidelity as men" (12). They also explain why jealousy is so prominent a motive in homicide and wife abuse and why "fear of male violence constrains the behavior of countless women the world round" (17).

It's upon emotional substrates such as these that cultural practices are devised. For men, this often means the "mixed tactics" of polygyny or of adulterous facultative monogamy, wherein they "pair-bond with one or more females by high investment, and opportunistically (more or less promiscuously) mate with other females" (R. Smith 602). For women, it means the widespread practice of "hypergamy": "marrying up," in nontechnical terms.[4] For both it means making do with a much-less-than-ideal mate. Buss remarks, perhaps overcautiously, that "all 37 societies in [his] study placed tremendous value on *kindness-understanding* and *intelligence* in potential mates; these characteristics were among the four most highly ranked in all 37 societies, and it is reasonable to characterize them, provisionally, as species-typical mate preferences" ("Sex Differences" 42). We might even say that these are species-*specific* preferences: they characterize only the *human* animal. Only the human male would like his spouse to be intelligently understanding about his adulteries (whether committed in reality or, as an American president put it famously, in his heart), and only the human female would like her spouse to be intelligently kind—and ruthless. The philosopher Agnes Heller dilates upon this latter point in a way provocatively suggestive of its influence upon culture as a whole:

> Whenever men do make efforts not to feel and behave in the old "masculine" way and whenever women expect them to change their emotional habits, this happens only within the framework of the family or occasionally in

man-woman relationships in general. But no attempt at change is made and no expectations for such a change are developed on the level of sociopolitical activity. Here the traditional male stereotype prevails unchallenged. Wives may require their husbands to be emotional, nonauthoritarian, playful in the family, but they want them to be authoritarian, strong, tough, competitive and earnest in all other areas of social life. They could not even love a man behaving differently[,] that is in an "unmanly" way. (qtd. in Eibl-Eibesfeldt, *Human Ethology* 286)

The result is a familiarly divided animal, usually trying his clumsy best to satisfy both Nature and his mate (or, if not his mate, his conscience). His task is complicated by the fact that Nature finds its instrument—its goad for his ambition, his assertiveness, his shows of strength—*in* his mate, while finding there as well its own opponent.

That marriage (what Loyal Rue calls "the most densely concentrated arena of reciprocal altruism there is" [220]) is often an uneasy alliance, marked by transgressions, propitiations, and refinements of manipulation, follows rather obviously from all this. What does not follow is that the alliance (I address here the cynicism of inexperienced youth) is necessarily a cruel or an unhappy one. For many couples, both the rewards of that alliance and the bonds of their affection prove more powerful than egoistic interests, and, for all, the eye of foresight makes possible life-dramas of intelligently minimum risk. It is in the nature of specifically human relationships that the actors can imagine the consequences of their actions, and that knowledge very profoundly affects the whole tenor of human exchange. To a far greater extent than any other primate, the human being is a master of ceremony, circumspection, and tact. "One of the basic principles of affiliative strategies," writes Irenäus Eibl-Eibesfeldt,

arises directly from the human knowledge of the power relationships with one's partner. This means that we behave in such a way as to prevent a loss of face for either the partner or oneself. The combination of positive self-presentation and appeasement, the veiled form of demands, self-deprecation as a friendly act of submission in gift-giving, and other unique aspects of friendly interactions are the immediate results. (*Human Ethology* 522)

For husband and wife, for whom it's generally advantageous to maintain a balance of power, the strategies are often indirect. For parent and offspring—to whose relationship we now turn—this needn't (at least on one side of the equation) be the usual state of affairs.

To the too-curious mind this may seem to be explained by the close genetic interests of the agents. A child inherits 50 percent of its genes from each parent, and sociobiological theory (and Rousseauian wisdom) might lead us to expect plain dealing from such commonly endowed interactants. But, as Trivers has argued in a celebrated paper—and as any parent could tell us—the parent-offspring relationship is neither straightforward nor free of either conflict or deceit, even in its earliest stages. Over matters such as the onset of weaning, the amount of parental care alloted to the infant (as opposed, for example, to that conferred on a sibling), the degree to which egoistic impulses are to be indulged in the latter or its altruistic tendencies encouraged, parents and offspring can be expected to disagree. "According to the theory presented here," Trivers writes in "Parent-Offspring Conflict," "socialization is a process by which parents attempt to mold each offspring in order to increase their own inclusive fitness, while each offspring is selected to resist some of the molding and to attempt to mold the behavior of its parents (and siblings) in order to increase its inclusive fitness" (125). Such manipulation extends, as Trivers observes, even into the maturity of the child. And thus the familiar (but often misinterpreted) maladjustments or mistakes of adult life: the son or daughter who chooses a mate by criteria largely determined by a parent, or who relinquishes the desire for family or children in order to stay home and help "tend the nest." A disturbed sexual infancy has less to do with such behaviors than the success of a parent or parents in pursuing the "selfish" interests of a gene.

But, as in much of the interaction between the parents themselves, the behaviors are, for the most part, "unconscious." Just as the jealous husband need never know that his wrath has been occasioned by an evolved uncertainty of paternity, so the child (and the parent) need never realize that, "in [a] species in which kin-directed altruism is important, parent-offspring conflict may include situations in which the offspring wants *less* than the parent is selected to give as well as the more common situation in which the offspring attempts to garner *more* than the parent is selected to give" (Trivers, "Parent-Offspring Conflict" 127). In effect, the cost-benefit calculations have already been done by evolution, and the result is, even from life's earliest weeks, a psychologically responsive organism of extraordinary subtlety and sophistication, prepared by its emotional sensitivity and authority to pursue its own inclusive fitness.

Which means that its naive skills of manipulation are usually a good match for its parents'—and a formidable match as that organism matures. "At any stage of ontogeny," Trivers writes, "in which the offspring is in conflict with its parents, one appropriate tactic may be to revert to the gestures and actions of an earlier stage of development in order to induce the investment that would then have been forthcoming. Psychologists have long recognized such a tendency in humans and have given it the name of regression" ("Parent-Offspring Conflict" 122). (Eibl-Eibesfeldt adds that such a tendency may be termed "neurotic" only if it begins to rule one's functional life [*Love* 152].) It is probably on this "regressive" tendency that the affects of courtship are based. In fact, Erving Goffman has argued—like Midgley (*Beast* 136), though from a non-evolutionary point of view—that, "given this parent-child complex as a common fund of experience, it seems we draw on it in a fundamental way in adult social gatherings":

> The invocation through ritualistic expression of this hierarchical complex seems to cast a spate of face-to-face interaction in what is taken as no-contest terms, warmed by a touch of relatedness; in short, benign control. The superordinate gives something gratis out of supportive identification, and the subordinate responds with an outright display of gratitude, and if not that, then at least an implied submission to the relationship and the definition of the situation it sustains. (73)

Observations like these have encouraged many ethologists to maintain that cooperative behavior and sociality in general have evolved from this earliest of affiliative bonds. Eibl-Eibesfeldt is, as I noted earlier, the most eloquent spokesman for this position, contending that "only with the appearance of parent-offspring signals, infantile appeals, and the corresponding affectionate responses behavior became available that permitted adults to create friendly and affectionate relationships" (*Human Ethology* 167). Certainly this explains the relational key in which much of human interaction unfolds. It explains, too, why the family is generally the center of gravity of our social and emotional life.

For, however conflictive the relations among parents, offspring, and siblings may be, the fact remains that all three share more genetic interests than with any other organism. And both sociobiological theory and anthropological evidence argue the universal primacy of those interests. As W. D. Hamilton explains in his seminal paper "The Genetical Evolution of Social Behaviour, I," humans (like all nonclonal organisms) reside in the middle of kinship networks of concentrically diminishing investments and returns: "To express the matter more vividly, in the world of our model organisms, whose behaviour is determined strictly by genotype, we expect to find that no one is prepared to sacrifice his life for any single person but that everyone will sacrifice it when he can thereby save more than two brothers, or four half-brothers, or eight first cousins" (21). The anthropologist Marshall Sahlins (who has taken the trouble to denounce sociobiological theory in a book-length diatribe) expresses the same idea when, in a diagram of reciprocal social relations that are maintained in "primitive" cultures, he locates Ego's "house" at the center of several concentric circles, that house closely tied by "generalized" (or largely nepotistic) bonds to the "lineage sector" outside it; beyond, linked to Ego by ever-weakening strains of reciprocity, lie the village, the tribe, then the "intertribal sector" (reproduced in Alexander, *Darwinism* 57). Even among peoples who reckon their lineages in ideological ways, there is, through the phenomenon of "complementary filiation," invariably a system of nepotistic provision for close consanguineous kin. The anthropologist Donald E. Brown explains:

> This term [complementary filiation] was coined to refer to a phenomenon found repeatedly in societies that ideologically reckon kinship either matrilineally or patrilineally. In either case, in spite of the prevailing ideology of descent, an individual has strong sentimental ties to those (usually close) genetic kin who are not ideologically reckoned as kin, i.e., some close genetic relatives through the mother in a patrilineal society, through the father in a matrilineal society. (105)

Far from the merely historical phenomenon that Philippe Ariès has claimed it to be, the "family"—as a group of close kin united (though not always in the physical household space) by sentimental affiliation and solicitude—long predates the appearance of *Homo sapiens* and, as a "unique and seemingly irreplaceable" phenomenon (Johnson and Earle 315), will probably outlast all of the political alliances that human history can devise.[5] It was doubtless within the family that hominid etiquette first appeared: the sharing of food, though it has been recorded occasionally among reluctant chimpanzees, is, when regular and voluntary, a sophisticated phenomenon of social exchange that has little strong precedence among the apes. (Even today such sharing, intuitively calibrated, serves as a marker of fondness and respect: we offer coffee to our acquaintances, writes sociologist Saul Feinman, and dinner to our bosses and friends.)[6] The forms of feeling and the manners of reciprocity both evolved within the family matrix; they did so largely as a distinctively human way of responding to the drive for inclusive fitness—for the ensuring, through the survival of now and future kin, the propagation of a multivehicular gene.

Which may prompt us to wonder how extrafamilial reciprocity ever appeared in primate affairs. If the gene is mindlessly "selfish," how could the social hominoid have evolved?[7] Trivers offers a carefully developed illustration in his classic paper on the subject, "The Evolution of Reciprocal Altruism":

> One human being['s] saving another, who is not closely related and is about to drown, is an instance of altruism. Assume that the chance of the drowning man['s] dying is one-half if no one leaps in to save him, but that the chance that his potential rescuer will drown if he leaps in to save him is much smaller, say, one in twenty. . . . Were this an isolated event, it is clear that the rescuer should not bother to save the drowning man. But if the drowning man reciprocates at some future time, and if the survival chances are then exactly reversed, it will have been to the benefit of each participant to have risked his life for the other. Each participant will have traded a one-half

chance of dying for about a one-tenth chance. If we assume that the entire population is sooner or later exposed to the same risk of drowning, *the two individuals who risk their lives to save each other will be selected over those who face drowning on their own.* (39, my emphasis)

The last idea is both radical and crucial: what Trivers is implying by his verb "selected" is that it is legitimate to speak of "a gene for altruism," much as one speaks of a gene for brown eyes. And it would follow that its vehicle, the human organism in this instance, is, to the extent that such a gene could find expression, biologically disposed to unselfishness. That "altruism" is "heritable" in so-called lower animals is suggested by the behavior of the grouper fish, which, although reared alone in laboratory seclusion (and so deprived of the instruction of experience), will not eat the cleaner fish with which it lives naturally in symbiotic reciprocity—while snapping up all the other small fish in its tank (Trivers, "Evolution" 45). And such astonishing findings seem applicable to man. Recently the neurologist Antonio Damasio has found specific brain lesions in patients who seem unable to distinguish right from wrong. "They clearly understand what killing is," Damasio has told a *Science* reporter, "and they know it will land them in jail. But they don't feel it in the flesh" (Palca 813).[8]

They are without "empathy," as a psychologist would say, and "what shared genes are to the biology of altruism," in the words of Simon Fraser's Dennis Krebs, "empathy is to the psychology of altruism" (104). It is, in fact, the mediators of altruism that have been selected by evolution ("What evolution selects for is not *behavior*," correctly observes moral philosopher James Q. Wilson; "it only selects for *mechanisms* that produce a behavior or predispose an animal to it" [126–27]), just as the latter has selected, for the grouper fish, not forbearance but a response to visual cues. And empathy (or perhaps sympathy) is the chief candidate for altruistic mediation. Nancy Eisenberg and Paul A. Miller, in a recent reexamination of the literature, conclude that "empathic responding is an important source of prosocial (including altruistic) behavior" (91). Earlier, Martin Hoffman had distinguished such responding from a need for social approval: what Hoffman calls, generally, "helping behavior" is offered most readily when no witnesses are present; the help is "more or less automatic," and, though the subject's relief may be the only reward, the helper needs no other reinforcement (126). "These findings suggest," writes Hoffman, "that humans may be built in such a way that what happens to others is at times as motivationally significant as what happens to themselves" (127). But since empathy evolved as a fitness-maximizing strategy for "a gene" residing in a group-living phenotype, it can be expected, like most psychological mechanisms, to be loosely calibrated according to costs and benefits. Indeed, Hoffman suggests this is so: there is evidence that people "respond more altruistically to others who resemble the self than to those who are different" (132). Like the phenomenon of assortative mating, whereby humans apprently "detect and prefer genetically similar others as marriage partners" (Rushton and Nicholson 45), this instinctive kind of rough-and-ready discrimination implies that the gene looks after its own.

As it must in a system of relations in which "cheating" is always a temptation. "The human altruistic system," writes Trivers, "is a sensitive, unstable one."

> Often it will pay to cheat: namely, when the partner will not find out, when he will not discontinue his altruism even if he does find out, or when he is unlikely to survive long enough to reciprocate adequately. And the perception of subtle cheating may be very difficult. Given this unstable character of the system, where a degree of cheating is adaptive, natural selection will rapidly favor a complex psychological system in each individual regulating both his own altruistic and cheating tendencies and his responses to these tendencies in others. ("Evolution" 56–57)

In brief, we must view humanity's whole development of psychological complexity as a response to its social adaptation. Not only did empathy evolve as a consequence of that sociality, but so did the nuances of social responsiveness, both pro- and anti-, as well. Gratitude, guilt, the need for social approval, all bind us to a sense of reciprocal duty (in ways exquisitely sensitive to "personal" reward); anger, indignation, "moralistic aggression"—sometimes escalating to acts of revenge— protect us from the "cheat." And on top of this system of emotional controls rests the deliberative machinery of the neocortex. With its infinitely greater repertoire of deceptive tactics than that of vervet monkey or chimpanzee (Cheney and Seyfarth; Jolly), *Homo* may smile, and smile, and be a villain, to the advancement of its adaptive agenda. But (like Hamlet and unlike the most wily chimp) its ambitions are usually checked, when they are not "repressed" altogether, by the unblinking eye of conscience. This is the eye of what Adam Smith called "the man within the breast," a man who represents the interests of the Other. For James Q. Wilson, who offers the most thoughtful contemporary analysis of "the moral sense," that "man" functions as a "core self," one that is "not wholly the product of culture," and that evinces "both a desire to advance our own interests and a capacity to judge disinterestedly how those interests ought to be advanced" (11).

Wilson lists the prosocial sentiments through which conscience makes its adjudications: empathy/sympathy, a sense of fairness, feelings of duty, the intuited need for self-control. But is there a single sentiment underlying their exercise, an ancient mechanism that precipitated this complex of feelings in the face of social necessity? Fred H. Willhoite Jr. has, in fact, proposed a phylogenetic source for all of "the emotions that may have evolved as regulators of the competitive and cooperative relationships involved in networks of reciprocal altruism" (247). Envy, "a pan-human phenomenon, abundantly present in every society, and present to a greater or lesser extent in every human being" (Foster 165), evolved, suggests Willhoite, as a psychological "weapon" to ensure that neither the cheat nor the cheated feel a maladaptively delusive sense of prosperity. Envy spurs the cheated to seek reparation from the cheat; fear of envy (and the guilt that it gives rise to) checks the ambition of the cheater. Although this is a seductively elegant hypothesis, it seems to me unlikely that envy is at the "source" of reciprocity, since other social primates form reciprocal altruistic networks and yet envy is the possession of a self-conscious creature, capable of imagining scenarios of proprietorship or revenge that lie beyond the restricted horizons of the alloprimates' here and now. It's likely, then, that its emergence in human affairs closely paralleled the emergence of speech, by which narratives of those scenarios could be constructed, refined, and rehearsed in consciousness, then stored in memory for retrieval at an opportune time. As both evolved in tandem, the hominid system of social reciprocity grew more and more complex and subtle, acquiring, eventually, a ritualistic dimension: both the rhetoric and the gift-giving that are common to all cultures appeared to exalt and to symbolize the system of morality to which envy had given birth. And as human relations became more abstract, they became perforce more vulnerable to exploitation from the bearers of gifts and of language.

Especially after both had been sacralized. Arguing that "religion has not merely been important but crucial to human adaptation," anthropologist Roy A. Rappaport has speculated that "the evolution of language and of the idea of the sacred were closely related, if not indeed bound together in a single mutual causal process" (23). Whatever the first impetus for religious thought—the need for cosmic intelligibility, for mystification of human mortality, for explanation of rituals originating in what Dudley Young calls "the ecstasies of love and war"—the sacred must soon have become an indispensable tool for the regulation of social affairs. What the Greeks called *theoi*, the "powers," for example, could be persuaded to bestow gifts upon the humanly deserving—but only if the latter obeyed divine law. And so with the "sanctification" of civic discourse, the conferring of truth-status upon moral propositions by appeal to transcendent authorities, social leaders found themselves possessed of a potent instrument of control:

> Through the invocation of unquestionable propositions concerning spirits whose very existence cannot be verified, or falsified, the purpose of a higher-level system . . . is made to appear to one of its subsystems . . . to be its own purpose. . . . In slightly different terms, sanctity helps to keep subsystems in their places. (Rappaport 36)

But it also ensures that, to a certain extent, those "higher-level" systems are answerable to the lower. "Sanctified" discourse is obscure discourse, often ambiguous, sometimes unintelligible, and it is necessary that it remain that way: "It is important, if evolution [that is, cultural change] is to take place, that what is accepted as unquestionably true be clearly and definitively understood by *no one.* Thus, the concept of the sacred not only may allow but may even encourage organizational change in response to changed circumstances and at the same time provide continuity through such changes" (Rappaport 40).

As Rappaport implies, the rise of increasingly complex theocratic societies was contingent upon an earlier evolutionary development, also with its source in the social web: the emergence of hierarchical status. Many anthropologists would deny that hierarchy emerged as an "evolutionary" development since it had obviously, they would argue, a "cultural" source. Margaret Power, Helen Fisher, and Alexandra Maryanski and Jonathan H. Turner have all emphasized the likelihood that early hominid horde-groups resembled the bands of today's "immediate-return" foragers; that, like the "carnivalesque" networks of wild chimpanzees, the social structure of those groups was loose, flexible, and fluid; and that only with the coming of horticulture, then agriculture, were the bars of the "social cage" at last forged. Fisher even singles out the implement that decisively clapped—at least from the woman's point of view—the lock on the newly fashioned hasp: the plow. "With the introduction of the plow," she writes, "much of the essential farm labor became men's work"; "women lost their ancient honored roles as independent gatherers, providers of the evening meal." And "soon after the plow became crucial to production, a sexual double standard emerged. . . . Women were judged inferior to men" (279).

Much of this may be true (although Fisher, like Lerner, oversimplifies the developments),[9] but the myth of the Garden meretriciously clings to all three of these theorists' accounts. Hunter-gatherers, for example, are often said to be "egalitarian," but the word carries much more freight, for anthropologist as well as layman, than it very clearly should (see Chagnon). It seduces Power, for example, into a portrait of the Kalahari "Bushmen" that bears little relationship to the reality of their lives. They are a "gentle, friendly, harmless" people who value "peace and harmony"—a people who lived a "free nomadic foraging life," in a state of "complete independence," until the intervention of European colonialism in the early 1960s (18, 14). Robert J. Gordon's *The Bushman Myth,* grounded in extensive archival research, tells a somewhat different story:

> Bushmen emerge as one of many indigenous people operating in a mobile landscape, forming and shifting their political and economic alliances to take advantage of circumstances as they perceived them. Instead of toppling helplessly from foraging to begging, they emerge as hotshot traders in the mercantile world market for ivory and skins. They were brokers between competing forces and hired guns in the game business. Rather than being victims of pastoralists and traders who depleted the game, they appear as

one of many willing agents of this commercial depletion. Instead of being ignorant of metals, true men of the Stone Age, who knew nothing of iron . . . , they were fierce defenders of rich copper mines that they worked for export and profit. . . . [I]gnorance of archival sources helped create the Bushman image that we, as anthropologists, wanted to have. (11)

But, even if we were willing to accept Power's description of the !Kung and their culture at face value, we are still left to struggle with our skepticism toward her principal thesis: that "the fundamental adapted form of social organization of human and chimpanzee is egalitarian" (250). "Fundamental" suggests, of course, "authentic,"[10] as if other forms of organization are corruptions of this Edenic way of life. But all human behaviors, as I noted in Chapter 1, are stimulus- and context-specific, and the "adapted forms" of those behaviors fall within what E. O. Wilson calls the "scales" of response that unite, probabilistically, the possible extremes. For very few cultures, especially today, is the old !Kung system of organization an implementable state of affairs: "Human foragers," Power writes, "are normally free to exit from a situation which even hints at tension, and they usually do so" (20). It is (or at least was) natural for the !Kung to deal with inevitable conflicts of interest by licensing distance between disputing parties; it is just as natural for sedentary peoples to entrust disputes to arbitrating bodies in which they more or less willingly invest authority. The !Kung themselves now do the same: since giving up much of their mobility, many look to local Bantu chiefs to arbitrate their disagreements. They regard those chiefs as their (dominant) "protectors," who in turn call them, familiarly, "their" Bushmen (Yellen 105).

The erection of hierarchy is as "natural" a behavior as the avoidance of conflict once was for the !Kung: "natural" because it is a fitness-enhancing response to the environmental conditions that give rise to it. And, as the !Kung example suggests, those conditions are not necessarily related to either horticulture or agriculture— or to amassed wealth or to capitalism in general or to any of the reasons typically invoked to explain them (although all of these reasons, together or singly, may constitute a sufficient cause).[11] The "carnivalesque" chimpanzees, who are neither horticulturalists nor agriculturalists, who neither manufacture nor use plows, and who neither amass wealth nor regulate their affairs through an abstract system of economic exchange, are never without a dominance hierarchy, either in the wild or in captivity. Wild male chimpanzees, writes Frans de Waal, the primatologist best informed about their behavior, "dominate all females . . . and compete fiercely over rank and sexual partners" ("Chimpanzee's Adaptive Potential" 248). And, as with the !Kung, curtailment of their mobility, with their confinement in zoos, results in even more marked displays of hierarchy, since the frequency of their aggressiveness increases (de Waal, "Chimpanzee's Adaptive Potential" 248). So with their human counterparts. If the initial (not "fundamental") conditions of human life were such that hierarchies were not a necessity, only the most self-deluded of human apologists would argue that those conditions have remained unchanged. "Near the end of this decade," as the popular press has noted, "mankind will pass a demographic milestone: for the first time in history, more people will live in and around cities than in rural areas" (Linden 31). What this will mean inevitably for the majority of human beings are greater crowding and greater anonymity of social exchange, both of which invite conflict—and hierarchy. Fisher, Maryanski and Turner all celebrate the freedom and mobility of modern life, but, as I shall emphasize in the section that follows, *Homo* has apparently lost as much as it has gained in its triumphant march toward Western emancipation.

About one aspect of social organization it has stubbornly remained unenlightened, and that is in its propensity to rank-order its groups by age. Even among the !Kung who are still attached to traditional "immediate-return" foraging, hierarchy is an unquestioned fact of extended-family life. Sons and sons-in-law are expected to obey if a father asks them to go hunting, and if, in fact, the father accompanies the party, he is acknowledged to be in command (Marshall 357–58). In all cultures known to history and ethnography, "age stratification"—in the words of anthropologist Nancy Foner—ensures that "structured inequality" is woven deeply into the social fabric (ix). The inequality is "a systematic product of the way rewards and roles are allocated in each society," their allocation usually benefitting "the active and alert old" (240). Especially in nonindustrial cultures, old men are typically at the top of the age hierarchy: they govern large families, control material resources, exert power over kin and community members, acquire ritual authority, enjoy respect from the young for their wisdom and experience. In almost all social systems (including those of the West), the young "must wait their turn" (240).

To the extent that human beings can be expected to apportion rewards and roles among themselves (and that, at least today, is a very great extent) hierarchical organization seems inescapable. When they must share them as part of an extrafamilial contract, hierarchy is a certainty among the non-nomadic moderns, since "conflicts of interest," writes Laura L. Betzig, "exist in all human groups" (21). As the recent changes in !Kung culture illustrate, such hierarchy makes life stable and predictable, while inevitably erecting a ladder of rank. To those who see shades of the prison bars descending (or ascending, to sustain the previous metaphor), Eibl-Eibesfeldt offers a well-considered reply: "Rank striving (success striving) is opposed to egalitarianism, so any [modern] system that maintains equality as [its] ideal must of necessity be repressive" (*Human Ethology* 307). Maoist China, the now-defunct U.S.S.R.—both espoused "equalization" of the masses by powerful, high-ranking elites. Both ensured that "the climbing maneuver," in Joseph Lopreato's phrase (110), was restricted to the few, the reliable, the already well placed. And both castigated individual pride, that "carrot" encouraging social success, "motivating the individual to seek high status and hence to gain access to the material rewards associated with social position" (Weisfeld 282). In the West, egalitarianism means—at least the well-placed tell us—that the climbing maneuver is an exercise that may be enjoyed (or suffered) by all.

But it's an easier climb if you're male, to begin with, since *Homo* is like its great-ape kin, for which male dominance is the rule.[12] Certainly the male's jealous need to sequester the female has a great deal of bearing here (see Wilson and Daly's harrowing exposition in "The Man Who Mistook His Wife for a Chattel"), and his greater strength and aggressiveness, as I suggest above, translate need rather easily into decision. But the ease with which he ascends in hierarchical rank is not simply a result of his sexism. "The male," psychiatrist Virginia Abernethy announces, after surveying the evidence for hierarchies among women, "more often than the female is emotionally fulfilled by the hierarchy per se" (132). Which is not to say that women are without either the talent or the ambition for success; on the contrary, "hierarchical structures and lines of authority are more likely to be used by a woman exclusively in pursuit of a goal, so that the status aspects of hierarchy, including secrecy and strict protocol, are less likely to be elaborated by a woman than by a man" (Abernethy 132). Women work best, Abernethy concludes, in a so-called lattice structure, which circumvents hierarchical processing and deals with problems as they first arise. In both this and the male style of cooperative organization, we can see evidence for Doreen Kimura's speculation that the division of labor in early human life led to differentiated behavioral adaptation. For a "lattice structure" ensures the most efficient organization of domestic duties— duties (among which child care figures prominently) to which the labor, if not the lives, of *Homo*'s ancestral women were probably very largely confined.

"It takes," writes Abernethy, "considerably greater interpersonal skills to op- erate in a lattice-type organization" (131). And so it should not be surprising that women are, in interpersonal terms, for the large part the more sensitive sex.[13] Popular wisdom has long told us such things; women's language, according to sociolinguist Deborah Tannen, implicitly tells us the same. Women use "rapport- talk," signaling support, confirming solidarity, indicating they are following a conversation; "for most men, talk is primarily a means to preserve independence and negotiate and maintain status in a hierarchical social order" (77). But it would be a mistake to polarize these behaviors too dramatically. Many women are as comfortable in a hierarchy as most men seem to be (and it takes only one of these women to head a corporation—or state). Many men, on the other hand, find it often advantageous to adopt typically "female" social strategies. High-ranking primates are not always the strongest but the most "charismatic" of their group. This means that they, like the "alphas" in a chimp unit-group, attract the attention of their subordinates: they seem singular, somewhat alien, they excite fear and respect, they are vital, lively, and charming. They also (if we may judge, like R. D. Masters, from the photographs of our political leaders) "display submissive behaviors similar to that observed in children shortly before submitting in a conflict" (Eibl-Eibesfeldt, *Human Ethology* 313). They behave, in the words of Eibl-Eibesfeldt, describing the wifely comportment of every male dream, "particularly 'obligingly'" (*Human Ethology* 313).

By such (not necessarily calculated) mimicry, the leader becomes all things to all men—even the ostensible subordinate of those whom he and his satellites control. Not that subordination is without its rewards. "Lower ranking individuals," writes Eibl-Eibesfeldt, "enjoy protection and are removed from decision making"; they find "security" in their subordination and are encouraged by their successes to take risks leading to more achievement, and thereby to self-assurance and promotion (*Human Ethology* 301–03). But it's the rare leader who is willingly displaced. As Lionel Tiger and Robin Fox observe, in a pioneering account of the human primate's behavioral repertoire, animals "strive for dominance because they want to be dominant. A dominant animal moves more freely, eats better, gets more attention, lives longer, is healthier and less anxious, and generally has a better time than a lowly and peripheral animal" (28). In these days of the supernation-state, not all of these remarks apply (Does Bill Clinton still subsist on fast food? With his "approval rating" dropping, is he having a good time?), but the psychological mechanisms that evolved to incite domination—feelings of pride, of excitement, of well-being, which all follow in the wake of attention paid—still fuel the climb to the top.

For the gorilla or baboon, say Tiger and Fox, the stakes are simple: "While all males get a chance to copulate, . . . the more dominant get a [better] chance to breed.[14] This is the point around which the whole social system revolves: who does the breeding?" (28). It is a point that has been complicated by human evolution, for, "as society increased in density and complexity, sexual dominance ceased to be much of a genetic issue" (28). Tiger and Fox define the fundamental nature of the change:

> Power became divorced from the control of the genetic future of the population, and fastened instead onto the control of material goods and the symbolic future. The leaders could not ensure that they controlled the future merely by peopling it with their own offspring; they had to ensure that their offspring controlled the future by having the monopoly on wealth and power. (37)

Which reminds us that dominance is not only a male phenomenon but usually an intergroup one as well: to dominate means to set human factions at variance with one another; it is to establish groups within groups, to give birth to "minorities," all with needs and ambitions of their own. And it is, of course, to defend "dominant" interests, in crude or politic ways: if women are the most obviously impeded in the climbing maneuver, the minorities are not far behind.

But, before rushing precipitately into Karl Marx's arms, let us recall the genesis of this oppression. The control not of production but of *re*production is the original motive for hierarchical structures, and so, as we should readily expect, the formation of intensely competitive groups not only commonly occurs among primates in general but is easily incited within human populations, usually irrespective of the age of its members and often for very trivial reasons. The research of Henri Tajfel and his colleagues has suggested how minimal are the conditions under which human groups divide and square off against each other, sometimes over the most arbitrary of differences. In one experiment, a group of Bristol schoolboys broke up into two competing factions, each professing preference for one painter over another; later they distributed their rewards according to group-membership status, even though this practice reduced the sum available to the whole (J. Turner). "It seems that quite small criteria," writes Crook, in summary, "are used to create distinctions between 'us' and 'them' and that these distinctions arise very easily and naturally in any group" (*Evolution* 391).

They are aided in their emergence by various tactics for group maintenance, both to encourage intragroup solidarity and conformity and to sharpen the opposition, perceived or imagined, between the in-group and the (one or more) out-. "Badging" draws an in-group's members together, with common dress and idiosyncratic behaviors, with passwords and slogans, shared values and ideals; harassment of the deviant ensures that cohesiveness is maintained, through teasing and ridicule or, if neither proves effective, through verbal and physical abuse. And of course all join in abusing the out-group. One of the most effective of their tools is stereotyping, which is not always negative but always, in the words of Heiner Flohr, a "response to practical problems of living" (195). The stereotype usefully dichotomizes phenomena, defining their characteristics by reference to group identity and ignoring the variant individual. This implies, contrary to enlightened opinion, that the stereotype indeed offers truth of a sort,[15] but it's a truth that is easily betrayed. For group identities can be not only confused with individual characteristics but interpreted or evaluated or even "constructed" in unflattering or detrimental terms (and so a comparatively and generally low activity level in a group becomes "laziness" among all of its members). It's by operations such as these that "social distances" are created, maintained, and justified, especially when the interests of two groups meet and clash. As Donald T. Campbell points out in his "Stereotypes and the Perception of Group Differences," the (negative) stereotype seems not only to capture the "essence" of an out-group, at least in the eyes of the "naive in-grouper," but also to account for the psychological distance that it puts between the two: "The out-group's opprobrious characteristics seem . . . to fully justify the hostility and rejection [that the in-grouper] shows toward it" (825).

The real facts of the matter are, of course, the other way around: "Causally, first is the hostility toward the out-grouper, generated perhaps by real threat, perhaps by ethnocentrism, perhaps by displacement" (Campbell 825). If we may believe Irwin Silverman's recent analysis, it's possible to simplify Campbell's list, since ethnocentrism is, by Silverman's assessment, "primarily a consequence rather than a cause of intergroup strife" (218). An ethnic group is (among other things) an alliance group, united in the cause of its members' mutual interests. "It seems plausible," writes Silverman,

> that selection would have favored plasticity in these formations, inasmuch as individuals and/or groups with maximal options could achieve the most adaptive arrangements in response to variable situational factors. Racism, here defined as a-priori interpersonal affinities beyond direct kin, would, naturally, impose constraints on plasticity and limits to options. In the terms of one prominent paradigm (Maynard-Smith and Price, 1973), racial tolerance, confronted by racial intolerance, would have evolved as the *Evolutionarily Stable Strategy*. (217)

This is a politically attractive—and so seductive—argument, but it takes no account of the conditions of the environment in which the "plasticity" at issue "evolved." The "environment of evolutionary adaptedness" probably offered *little* variation in the "situational factors" that would have selected for such plasticity. In other words, the Ice Age hunter-gatherer was a preeminently parochial specimen of humanity; the alliances he forged (a "she" here may be superfluous) doubtless went no further than the tribal group. And, under such conditions, a warm ethnophilia would have been the best group adhesive, a robust xenophobia the best group defense. "The animal rule," as Robin Fox reminds us, "is basically the same: Trust the familiar, suspect the unfamiliar."

> In the animal and early-human case, this would have been literally true: The familiar would have been "of the family," relatives of a similar phenotype. Recognition would have been easy. In the human case, when other than family groups came into contact, some means of identifying "us" and "them" (however defined) would have been necessary. The differentiation of languages would have at first served this purpose, but one doesn't always get a chance to hear a stranger speak. So distinctive markings, scarification, paint, hairdos, and so forth would have come into play to make the distinctions obvious. . . . Of course, when one crosses significant phenotypical boundaries (e.g., to other skin colors), nature again does the job for us. ("Prejudice" 146)

But it's a "job," of course, that has lost its function in the multicultural late twentieth century, and so the psychological mechanisms that evolved in its favor—distrust and unease in the company of the "alien"—must be overridden by the cost-and-benefit sensitivities of the diplomatic neocortex. When they are not, and when "nature" (that is, feelings) addresses the world beyond the in-group with the authority invested in it by the naive, the result is what is justifiably called savagery. For, to the extent that an ethnic group today cultivates "fixed responses," drawing sharp lines of demarcation between itself and other groups, it is, in E. O. Wilson's words, "the enemy of civilization" (157). It is the fanaticism that ethnocentrism generates (almost always in the service of political and economic interests) that is the force behind war and "acts of aggression"; Freud's vague "aggressive instincts" have, aside from their obvious instrumentality, very little to do with the matter. It's also ethnocentrism that explains tribal territoriality, not an "instinct" but a tendency, more accurately, which begins as a stubborn defense of resources, then leads to the erection of an "invincible center," and ends with an emotional attachment to a place (Lopreato 120–29; cf. Dyson-Hudson and Smith). Even as the ethnocentrist is dreaming of conquest of the out-group's power and wealth, he or she clings to the home, the neighborhood, the motherland, as to the place where the real "human being" (in the phrase that most tribes adopt as their name) resides.

2

But we're modern, enlightened—I hear Coulmier's words from Weiss's *Marat/Sade* forming in the back of my readers' minds: what I've been describing are "traditional" peoples and hardly the educated of the industrialized West, with its studied respect for minority interests, its empowerment of women, its fluidity and mobility, its weakening of kin ties, its moral monogamy, its *rationality*. Where is any sign of the selfish gene in the small families of the United States, for example, in which fewer and fewer children have seemed—at least until very recently—increasingly to be the rule?

The question presupposes the kind of hard-wired determinism that I rejected at the beginning of this chapter. The gene can be said to pursue inclusive fitness only within particular environmental constraints: and those constraints have been altered radically by the technology of the industrial age. To consider the case of the family in particular: as an *economic* organization it has become, in sociologist Pierre van den Berghe's words, "both less important and less permanent" (170). Modern society organizes its people in numerous kin-atypical ways (political parties, professional groups, school grades, bridge clubs, and so on) and it has taken over the functions of both education and production that, at least before the Industrial Revolution, were traditionally assumed by family members. As a consequence, the family has shrunk, since "the most glaringly obvious limitation to family organization in a society where the system of production is outside the home and where market conditions, changing technology, changing skills, shifts in regional development and a multitude of other conditions require constant relocation, is *size*" (van den Berghe 172–73). To reduce its size and so become "more movable, more flexible and more responsive to outside constraints," the Western family adopted three fitness-encouraging strategies:

> 1. It adopted neolocality as the main rule of residence, thereby shedding all or most of the relatives outside the nuclear family.
> 2. It eliminated polygamy, *de facto*, and increasingly, *de jure*, as well. Countries, polygamous until recently, are shifting to compulsory or at least preferential monogamy as they begin or hope to enter the industrial era. . . .
> 3. It reduced its fertility to levels approaching zero population growth— even somewhat below in some countries. (van den Berghe 173)

Curiously, the Western family, as van den Berghe observes, now resembles the mobile and flexible family units of hunter-gatherer peoples. But, whereas the !Kung live (or lived, more precisely) a pared-down existence because of the meagerness of their resources, the modern nuclear family—at least of the comfortable middle-class and above—does so because of their great abundance. "In the space of a couple of generations," van den Berghe writes, describing the triumph of twentieth-century medicine and the efflorescence of material prosperity, "there was a sudden and unprecedented increment in things *worth living for*" (181).

It's this last change that has had the profoundest impact upon modern human existence. For, with the sanctification of everyday life by our engines of secular pleasure, we have, quite unconsciously but understandably, betrayed the genes that bore us:

> We have been programmed to love ourselves, directly, and indirectly in our children and relatives, because that is how our constituent genes were selected in the first place. Genes that had this effect in their carriers were selected for. But human consciousness now turns that self-love against the genes. We use the proximate mechanisms of genetic selection, including sexual behavior, not only as means to the end of gene reproduction, but as ends in themselves. We proclaim, in effect, that we love the entire assemblage of genes we call "me" better than our genes taken separately, and that therefore we are going, in some circumstances, to gratify that "me," even

at the expense of reproducing our genes. Our genes may be theoretically eternal, but we know that we are highly ephemeral; therefore, we want to make the best of our short lifespan, especially now that we have a good deal to live for. (van den Berghe 182–83)

In short, we've grown oversolicitous toward those vehicles in which our genes "travel about" and careless of the interests of the genes themselves. But we must keep in mind that the vehicles are products of eons of evolutionary selection, selection that a mere two hundred (or two thousand) years of cultural change and enlightenment will not very easily invalidate. Of course, attempts at deconstruction have been steady and deliberate, usually accompanied by jubilant encouragement from the troops on the progressive front lines. The poststructuralists are only the latest in a long list of utopians ("man is only a recent invention, a figure not yet two centuries old, a new wrinkle in our knowledge, and . . . he will disappear again as soon as that knowledge has discovered a new form"—I quote, of course, that ass Foucault [*Order* xxiii]) to announce that man is dead.

For what the genes want to make of our short life span—and what, more important, they have evolved in our brainpans to encourage our collusion in their design—is not always to personal taste or satisfaction. Ironically, for example, the twentieth-century woman, whose efforts to escape domestic confinement have worked the deepest changes on our social structure, is still a victim of primate praxis. "Despite large structural changes in the economy," writes Victor R. Fuchs in a definitive report for *Science*, "and major antidiscrimination legislation, the economic well-being of [American] women in comparison to that of men did not improve between 1959 and 1983" (459).[16] And, for all the wonder-working miracles of kitchen technology, some of the burdens of the home have grown heavier. "Gone are the relatives," notes Eibl-Eibesfeldt astutely,

aunts, grandparents, and caring neighbors and their older children, who in earlier times (and in rural areas today still) would provide essential relief by attending to smaller children and providing emotional outlets for stimulation and conversation. Contacts with same sex members of the same age bracket are also lacking. In traditional societies, men and women spend many hours of the day with members of the same sex, with obvious enjoyment. . . . It is in modern society that marriage partners are so limited to each other. This affords the opportunity for deepening relationships but can also lead to difficulties in the form of strain, habituation, or irritation since the spouse cannot fulfill all the social needs of his [or her] partner. (*Human Ethology* 285–86)

There is a sad surreptitiousness about modern life: men "bond" both in reality and in its mirror, the sitcom, with self-conscious irony and unease; they talk a good game about pitching in with the housework, but, as sociologist Arlie Hochschild has revealed, in her study of San Francisco Bay area folkways, the modern working woman still tends the babies and the broom.[17]

And the intransigencies of the gene are fully evident in the larger spheres of contemporary life. The state may try hard, in its ceremonial occasions, in its symbolizations, in its evocations ("our forefathers") of the ties that bind, to unify its polity, but the interests of its elements will always conflict, making "justice" a provisional and fluid concept that shifts with the power structure (Johnson and Earle 318, 322–23; Alexander, *Darwinism* 236–37). And so intricate and sprawling has that structure become that it is often very easy for the advantageously placed to manipulate it for private ends. Examples abound at all levels of government. (And let us not speak of academic politics. Let us not speak of academe at all.) Add to this sense of injustice a diffuse fear and guilt, born of the depersonalization of our social exchanges and the weakening of our ties with family and friends, especially with parents and siblings, and the familiarly Kafkaesque angst of our age begins to find its focus. Emotionally and psychologically, ours is the disquiet of the late-Pleistocene hominid thrust into a crowd of alien bipeds-on-the-make and dependent on the kindness of strangers. And now, as members of the polluted "global community," we are being asked to extend our sympathies to the foreign, the far-flung—the unborn, even—as an inducement to clean up our mess. But the genetic vehicle is dragging its feet. "Man," as anthropologists Sherwood L. Washburn and Robert S. O. Harding observe, with a regrettable fidelity to the evidence, "has evolved to feel strongly about few people, short distances, and relative[ly] brief intervals of time. These are the dimensions of life which are still important to him" (qtd. in Ike 231).

All of which is to imply that, not only is our "rationality" a severely limited faculty, but that it achieves whatever identity it has through its respect for— its opposition to or alliance with—the inclinations of our "instinctive" life. We are fairly stable and predictable creatures, with an identifiable "human nature," because we are servants of the gene. Without its suasions, inducements, and predispositions, we would indeed be those plastic "indeterminate subjects" that poststructuralist "theory" claims that we are. We can put this differently by saying that we are children of the "Darwinian unconscious," concealed in the labyrinth of the hominid mind. It's an animal very different from Freud's savage beast: it acquired much of its cunning not in savagery but in civilization, as an adaptation to both the opportunities and the constraints of very early hominid group life. But what cannot be too strongly emphasized is that it is a "normal" adaptive faculty: it solves problems in accordance with what was anciently a functional program, not in response to a lurid scenario played out between a mother and her infant son.

Not that it is any less distorting of the so-called real world than Freud's multivolumed fiction. As Shelley E. Taylor and Jonathon D. Brown have observed, considerable research evidence suggests that overly positive self-evaluations, exaggerated perceptions of control or mastery, and unrealistic optimism are characteristic of normal human thought. Moreover, these illusions appear to promote other criteria of mental health, including the ability to care about others, the ability to be happy or contented, and the ability to engage in productive or creative work. (193)

The gene-machine is most efficient, in other words, when it is most thoroughly self-deluded, serenely bearing its molecular residents through the rubble of the war that is life. To fight that war most successfully, it needs to keep its motives dark, even (and most obscurely) to itself. "I suggest," writes Alexander, "that the separateness of our individual self-interests, and the conflicts among us that derive from this separateness, have created a social milieu in which, paradoxically, the only way we can actually maximize our own self-interest and deceive successfully is by continually denying—at least in certain social arenas—that we are doing such things. . . . The result, I believe, is that in our social scenario-building we have evolved to deceive even ourselves about our true motives" (*Darwinism* 134).

"Sincerity" is what we call that result, the most sublimely ironic of human adaptations that natural selection has devised. Sincerity assures us that its possessor is operating, not out of opportunistic self-serving calculation, but out of the spontaneity of his or her "heart." It's the one quality that seems indispensable to human character—and (at least according to the Romantic aesthetic) to the highest of human art. "Fake that," goes the advice to the young actor, "and you've got it made." The old joke bristles with an uncomfortable wisdom in light of Alexander's remarks:

It is not difficult to appear sincere if one is sufficiently ignorant about his own motives to believe in fact that he is a just, moral, ethical person with mandates from Heaven for whatever particular actions he may feel are necessary or profitable to carry out. For an individual who must carry out all of his actions within a social group of one sort of another, sincerity is an invaluable asset. ("Search" 97)

So, too, finally, is the conviction that one's orders are one's own. The Murdochian vision of Freudian man with which I opened this chapter is, however, "depressing" a picture of humanity (her word), still a rather reassuring one. If Freudian man is "selfish," he is selfish by and for himself alone. It should now be apparent that when I say "self-serving" I mean "gene-serving," in an almost technically literal sense. And perhaps the most powerful of all human adaptations (or cherished of human illusions, if you will) is the human being's passionate

conviction of completely self-determining autonomy. This sociobiological theory demystifies in a particularly uncompromising way, and for this it will for a
long time seem an "antihumanism" about which, even and perhaps most especially to those who are now enamored of the word, all discussion should remain
closed.

On Discourse and the Darwin Machine: The Matter and the Chatter of the Mind

To a great extent, the philosophy of mind has pitched its inquiries without concerning itself (except anecdotally) with the body or the brain.
—Gerald M. Edelman, *Bright Air, Brilliant Fire: On the Matter of the Mind*

In the previous two chapters I offered an account of the human being as an anthropological *object*, as a probabilistic figure whose behavior may be said to betray a kind of biogenetic grammar. In this chapter I'll take up the human being as *subject*, as a locus of sophisticated cognition and agency; I do so, however, not from the standpoints most familiar to literary theorists, of psychoanalysis and Continental philosophy, but from those of experimental and developmental psychology, especially as they have been informed by recent research in the neurological sciences within the general framework of evolution theory. Much of what I shall have to say would strike the clinical psychologist as very familiar indeed; some of it, particularly about the role of narrative in both reasoning and enculturation, would have a slightly more speculative ring. But almost none of it, from what I can judge as a spectator of the critico-theoretical scene, seems to have penetrated to the luxuriant forests of Lacanian fantasy or Foucauldian delirium that currently supply the lumber for subjective model-building among most "advanced" students of the humanities. I'll therefore risk an occasional trafficking in the trite, and even a banality or two; I hope, however, that by the end of this chapter the banal will have been transfigured by my larger argument so that those issues at the heart of today's literary controversies—especially the relationship of the "self" to language—will have received a little light.

We must begin with the infant, and we must begin by divesting it of all Freudian garb. So we are urged by Daniel N. Stern, who, since the early 1970s, has been revolutionizing the field of infant psychology by revising so-called psychodynamic theory to accord with actual behavioral research. That research (which is still ongoing) has produced a picture of early infancy that contrasts sharply with received psychoanalytic accounts. Whereas influential Freudians like Margaret S. Mahler still cling to the idea of a slowly individuating neonate, beginning life in an "autistic" phase in which "the 'I' is not yet differentiated from the 'not-I'" (9), Stern has argued that all observable evidence points to the contrary. "Infants," he writes in *The Interpersonal World of the Infant: A View from Psychoanalysis and Developmental Psychology*,

> begin to experience a sense of an emergent self from birth. They are predesigned to be aware of self-organizing processes. They never experience a period of total self/other undifferentiation. There is no confusion between self and other in the beginning or at any point during infancy. They are also predesigned to be selectively responsive to external social events and never experience an autistic-like phase. (10)

The infant shortly after birth is alert and seeking stimulation: Aristotle would have said it is striving to realize its "entelechy." "Workers who have studied the development of the brain," writes neurobiologist Carla J. Shatz, "have found that to achieve the precision of the adult pattern, neural function is necessary: the brain must be stimulated in some fashion. Indeed," she continues, "several observations during the past few decades have shown that babies who spent most of their first year of life lying in their cribs developed abnormally slowly" (61). It is for human contact *outside* the crib that the neonate is adaptively prepared. The infant is responsive to the smell of its own mother's milk; it shows a preference for the human voice over other sounds and for symmetry on the vertical plane ("characteristic of human faces" [Stern 40]) to symmetry on the horizontal plane. It clearly enters life under the sway of what Eugene d'Aquili has called the "cognitive imperative": the drive by which the "mind rises to meet the phenomenal world" (Laughlin, McManus, and d'Aquili 166). Not only does it behave consistently as "a separate, cohesive, bounded, physical unit, with a sense of [its] own agency, affectivity, and continuity in time" (Stern 10); it actively forms and tests hypotheses about the things and events that surround it. It remarks samenesses and differences, invariances and discrepancies, showing an instinctive need to apprehend its experience as (in Mihaly Csikszentmihalyi's words) "a unified, manageable, rule-bound task" (189). "Infants from the beginning," Stern declares, in opposition to classic psychoanalytic dogma, "mainly experience reality. Their subjective experiences suffer no distortion by virtue of wishes or defenses, but only those made inevitable by perceptual or cognitive immaturity or overgeneralization" (255).

It may be useful to pause for a moment over Stern's use of the word "reality." He isn't implying, of course, that infants (or children or adults) experience anything like unmediated apprehension of the world. All our perception—and, in turn, all our cognition—is, as Mark Johnson reminds us in a book to which we'll have occasion to return, inescapably *human* through and through (*Body* xi). Which is to say that it is subject from the beginning to the filtering and organizing structures of human consciousness. The phenomenon now known as "center-surround antagonism," by which neural cells exhibit discriminatory responses to stimuli through a dynamic interplay between excitation and inhibition,[1] is in large part responsible for the "boundedness" of our perceptions. The brain-mind's tendency, early noted by Gestalt psychologists, to delimit those perceptions as "figure" and "ground" makes attention and therefore cognitive mastery possible. Our attention is, moreover, operationally selective, since, by the functioning of particular receptor cells, information from one sensory modality or location in the environment is given prominence over that of another; thus we can react to sounds while ignoring sights or tune out our neighbors' conversation in a restaurant.

And apparently we enter the world with sophisticated preconceptions about its properties:

> For example, contrary to the Piagetian notion that infants must 'learn' the object concept, recent research has shown that (at least) as early as 10 weeks—an age at which the visual system has only just matured—infants already have a sensorily-integrated concept of objects as entities that are continuous in space and time, solid (two objects cannot occupy the same place at the same time), rigid, bounded, cohesive, and move as a unit. (Tooby and Cosmides 71)

The human being (and I include, by that phrase, the human infant) is "designed" by nature to tease order from its experience. In part it is discovering regularities that are inherent in its surround (as Roger N. Shepard has argued that it is evolutionarily disposed to do); in part it is, rightly or wrongly, deducing them. It half-perceives, to invoke the inevitable phrase, and half-creates the world.[2]

That its practices carry naturally over into adulthood is suggested by our techniques of categorization, definition, and cross-modal association. The psychologist Eleanor Rosch has, for several years, argued that "human categorization should not be considered the arbitrary product of historical accident or of whimsy but rather the result of psychological principles of categorization" (27)—principles that early engage the human perceiver, emerging from facts about both the world and the mind. The first is that "information-rich bundles of perceptual and functional attributes occur that form natural discontinuities," and the second is that, when "basic cuts in categorization are made at these discontinuities," they are made by a perceiver who apprehends in species-typical ways and whose ability to make them is "determined by many factors having to do with the functional needs of the knower interacting with the physical and social environment" (31, 29).

The result is a system of "prototypes," by which is meant "the clearest cases of category membership defined *operationally* by people's judgments of goodness of membership in the category" (36, my emphasis). For an American resident of the Lower Forty-Eight, the sparrow is more prototypical of the category of "bird" than, let us say, the penguin, and so those birds that share the sparrow's attributes fall most unambiguously into the class. Although an Inuit or a Yanomamö tribesman categorizes according to exactly the same principles, his prototypes and therefore his categories are, doubtless, somewhat different.

The example emphasizes that both perception and cognition are functionally interactional processes and that (in Rosch's words) "inseparable from the perceived attributes of objects are the ways in which humans habitually use or interact with those objects" (33). Linguist George Lakoff and philosopher Mark Johnson, taking their cue from Rosch, have also argued that, contrary to the "objectivist" view of categorization, according to which entities are classed by reference to purely inherent properties, categorization is, for human beings, "primarily a means of comprehending the world, and as such it must serve that purpose in a sufficiently flexible way" (122). This means that there need be *"no fixed core* of properties" that are common to all of the members of a class; there need only be what Wittgenstein called workable "family resemblances," those that can (and usually must) be established in interactional ways: "Thus the interactional properties relevant to our comprehension of chairs will include perceptual properties (the way they look, feel, etc.), functional properties (allowing us to sit), motor-activity properties (what we do with our bodies in getting in and out of them and while we're in them), and purposive properties (relaxing, eating, writing letters, etc.)" (123). Such modes of human comprehension, at once complex yet cognitively automatic, have evolved to serve what Rosch claims to be the basic function of categorization: the providing of "maximum information with the least cognitive effort" (28).

The infant is born innately disposed to sort out its sensations in this way,[3] but it is also disposed to unify those sensations, in order to constitute its world as a whole. This it accomplishes through "amodal perception," the instinctive ability "to take information received in one sensory modality and somehow translate it into another sensory modality" (Stern 51). Experiments initiated in the early 1970s have suggested that—again, contrary to Piagetian theory—infants do not identify a single source of sensations through independent processing and "reciprocal assimilation" of its diverse stimuli: they do not, in other words, learn "nippleness," for example, by first sucking a nipple, then looking at a nipple, then associating, by virtue of simple proximity, the two separate schemata that result. For them, "haptic" (that is, tactile) sensations *automatically* can be translated into visual terms, so that even blindfolded infants can distinguish a nipple they have been sucking from another of a different shape. And such translations are not restricted to touch and sight. Infants are able to cross-transfer sound intensities to light intensities, auditory temporal patterns to visually presented temporal patterns, even the sounds of the human voice to the sight of the lips actually producing them. "We can only conclude," writes T. G. R. Bower (in words that would not have surprised Charles Baudelaire), "that in man there is a primitive unity of the senses . . . and that this primitive unity is built into the structure of the human nervous system" (qtd. in Laughlin and d'Aquili 56).

Psychologist Lawrence E. Marks, who has made the most thorough investigation of this phenomenon, including its literary manifestations as synesthesia, argues that cross-modal processing "is a direct and economical, a salient and compact mode of childhood cognition," one that "may play an important transitional role in the sharpening of modes of information processing" (102). He emphasizes its "transitional" quality because, as he observes, "it may be superseded by the more abstract representations embodied in the linguistic mode of cognition" (102). There is, in fact, good evidence to suggest that, while synesthesia "is common in children," it "often diminishes or disappears when child grows into adult," although the cross-modal analogies that it excites "remain very much alive" (102).

We'll presently turn to that "linguistic mode," but before we do so it's important to stress what Marks's last sentence merely implies: that perception and cognition, especially for the prelinguistic infant, are inescapably *affective* processes. "You cannot show the observer a wallpaper pattern," writes one of the founders of experimental psychology, E. B. Titchener, "without by the very fact disturbing his respiration and circulation" (qtd. in Berlyne 113). And infants are, in their sensitivity to stimuli, like most curious mammals of any age: below a certain threshold they will seek stimulation; above that threshold, avoid it. It is often sought for its own reward, as play and other exploratory behaviors are sought for the pleasure they offer "in themselves." D. E. Berlyne has isolated several properties of stimulus patterns ("collative" patterns, to use his word, alluding to the necessity of collating two or more sources of information to determine the intensity of the property) that are particularly conducive to "arousal." Up to a certain point, a stimulus invites attention and interest (at least in the cognitively average perceiver) by being novel, surprising, complex, ambiguous, and/or puzzling. A pattern informed by such properties "induces a certain amount of disorientation and cannot be assimilated immediately," but, insofar as it stays beneath the threshold above which disorientation arouses fear and flight, it will hold out a certain "promise of success" for the perceiver seeking to assimilate it. "In other words," Berlyne concludes, "such a pattern has some internal structure waiting to be apprehended and redundancies, similarities and other relations among its elements that take some time to be recognized" (215). The connection of such "collative" stimuli with sophisticated human art has, since Berlyne's findings began to appear, of course often been remarked.

For the student whose notions of subjectivity have been nurtured by the "linguistic turn," it may seem disorienting that my discussions to this point—of categorization, of cross-modal processing, of perceptual/conceptual discrimination—have implied little role for language. But the fact of the matter is that language, although anciently responsible, as I shall suggest, for how all human brains are neurologically "wired," now intervenes modestly, if at all, in the early atomization or amalgamation of experience into discrete and manageable units.[4] As Rosch suggests, the tendency to categorize is simply the extension of an innate predisposition to group sensations and perceptions; Marks has concluded, on the basis of several lines of evidence, that "linguistic mediation of the cross-modal transfer seems extremely unlikely" (25); and almost all psychologists are now in agreement that concepts—by which we "make judgments based on recognition of category membership or integrate 'particulars' into 'universals'" (Edelman, *Remembered Present* 141)—are acquired (as chimpanzees acquire them) prior to the acquisition of language.

And no less than Mahler's "autistic" or "symbiotic" infant, adrift in an undifferentiated sea of unknowing, the prelinguistic Lacanian "subject," whose "imaginary" world is an esemplastic plenum, has been utterly discredited by empirical research. The infant is, from birth apparently, neurologically prepared to enter a world of "difference." Contrary to what was believed as recently as twenty years ago, the brains of newborns seem to be functionally asymmetrical: by three months they show right-hemisphere bias in perceiving familiar faces holistically; even earlier they exhibit a similar bias in their response to musical notes, while they suggest left-hemisphere bias in their response to human speech. "Clearly," write Dennis L. Molfese and Jacqueline C. Betz, in a summary of the most recent research, "some speech discrimination abilities seem to be lateralized from birth" (186).

2

The implications of the lateralization of the human brain seem to be far-reaching. Although skeptical in general of the visionary claims of, say, the early work of Robert Ornstein (for whom the split between the right and left hemispheres seemed to explain the gulf between East and West), most neuroscientists now seem to agree that the "two brains" are distinguished by important, if sometimes elusive, differences in styles of information-processing. Some of the most intriguing of those differences involve the relationship of language to emotion and motivation. Damage to the right hemisphere often results, for example, in verbally articulate but emotionally and inventively lame speakers. Their intonation is flat and their delivery is insufficiently forceful; they have trouble gauging the emotional tone in the speech of those with whom they're conversing. When confronted with an imaginative or playful stimulus, they seem mentally lead-footed and humorless, assigning literal meanings to metaphorical statements and inappropriate endings to cartoon-strips (Springer and Deutsch 185, 186). There is, moreover, evidence that the "verbal" left hemisphere,[5] which seems so deficient in affect and wit, is capable of "tyrannizing" over its "subordinate" counterpart.

In a fascinating set of experiments conducted by M. S. Gazzaniga and J. E. LeDoux, a "split-brain" patient, whom they call "P. S.," his hemispheres separated by commissurotomy, was presented visually with two disparate images, one to each separate hemisphere, and asked to choose two picture-cards from an array before him that was relevant to what he had seen. Then P. S. was asked to "explain" his choice in verbal terms.

When a snow scene was presented to the right hemisphere and a chicken claw was presented to the left, P. S. quickly and dutifully responded correctly by choosing a picture of a chicken from a series of four cards with his right hand and a picture of a shovel from a series of four cards with his left hand. [Recall that the right hemisphere governs the left hand's response, and vice versa.] The subject was then asked, "What did you see?" "I saw a claw and I picked the chicken, and you have to clean out the chicken shed with a shovel." . . .

In trial after trial, we saw this kind of response. The left hemisphere could easily and accurately identify why it had picked the answer, and then subsequently, and without batting an eye, it would incorporate the right hemisphere's response into the framework. While we knew exactly why the right hemisphere had made its choice, the left hemisphere could merely guess. Yet, the left did not offer its suggestion in a guessing vein but rather as a statement of fact as to why that card had been picked. (148–49)

These results suggest that, although the operations of the right hemisphere (in general, associated with holistic, nonanalytic, and imagistic thought) may be responsible for much of human behavior, that behavior tends to be interpreted by the "dominant" hemisphere in plausible, however erroneous, verbal terms: "It is as if," write Gazzaniga and LeDoux, "the verbal self looks out and sees what the person is doing, and from that knowledge it interprets a reality" (150).

More recently, Gazzaniga has found fresh evidence for this conjecture, now concluding in his book *Nature's Mind* that "the special capacity to make an inference about both internal bodily states and external actions of ourselves and others seems, when fully developed, to reside in the left hemisphere of humans, and is called 'the interpreter'" (113). Whereas the right hemisphere "can possess an extensive auditory and visual lexicon and sometimes even speak" (130), it has poor syntactical and logico-inferential skills and is unable to articulate its intuitions:

in Gazzaniga's scrupulous and felicitous phrase, it "can be critical without being knowledgeable" (130). Not surprisingly, the "interpreter" is impatient of such mute wisdom, and may be prone to ignore it altogether. Such conclusions support the observations of psychiatrist David Galin, for whom the "two brains" may exhibit dichotic functioning: in moments of apparent "disconnection," the left governs consciousness, the right behaving as a "repressed" unconscious, in which mental events "can continue a life of their own" (575).

For Gazzaniga and LeDoux, maturation is usually synonymous with the emergence and gradual dominance of what they call the "verbal self." Such a self—recall the image of the young Helen Keller, one hand held under a running pump while the sign for "water," tapped out in the palm of her other hand, began quelling her raging mind—is a locus of enabling conceptual stabilizations. Although visual imagery (of which Keller was of course deprived) may also help effect such a locus, language, as psycholinguist Ray Jackendoff explains, "can stabilize a much wider range of concepts."

> Linguistic structures are the only peripheral levels with distinctions that correspond (albeit sometimes only roughly) to basic conceptual elements such as the type-token distinction, predication, negation, and hypotheticals; they are also the only ones that can pare away all features from a concept other than the bare identity expressed by the pronoun *that*, and the only ones that can explicitly encode affects (such as *true* and *false*). Thus, language is the only peripheral faculty that can stabilize the kinds of concepts we most strongly associate with logical reasoning. (324)

Jackendoff calls language a "peripheral" faculty because, as I noted earlier, in stressing the priority of concepts, "language is not a medium of thought, only conceptual structure is" (325). What language enables the thinking subject to do is to encode concepts syntactically and phonologically for the sake of objective inspection ("as new 'objects' in their own right") and for stable storage in memory, probably including both short- (or "working") and long-term. (It has also, of course, obviously, communicative functions, an issue that I would like to reserve for the third section of this chapter.) Jackendoff is not oblivious to the "pitfalls" of linguistic encoding, phenomena about which every student of Ferdinand de Saussure is particularly well informed: linguistic discriminations can lead one "to believe in sharp distinctions where there is really continuity between the ranges of concepts. . . . Moreover, since the language is not always systematic in assigning one word per concept, one is sometimes led to conflate two or more concepts that ought to be differentiated for the purposes at hand, because they happen to be associated with the same word" (323–24).

But, whereas Jackendoff tends to emphasize the conceptual advantages of linguistic stabilization, it is Stern who most dramatically underscores its experiential deficits. Amodal global experience, for example, through which the world of the prelinguistic subject is grasped and unified, is "fractured" by the advent of language. Stern offers an extended illustration that seems worth quoting at length:

> Suppose we are considering a child's perception of a patch of yellow sunlight on the wall. The infant will experience the intensity, warmth, shape, brightness, pleasure, and other amodal aspects of the patch. The fact that it is yellow light is not of primary or, for that matter, of any importance. . . . To maintain this highly flexible and omnidimensional perspective on the patch, the infant must remain blind to those particular properties (secondary and tertiary perceptual qualities, such as color) that specify the sensory channel through which the patch is being experienced. Yet that is exactly what language will force the child to do. Someone will enter the room and say, "Oh, *look* at the *yellow* sun*light!*" Words in this case separate out precisely those properties that anchor the experience to a single modality of sensation. By binding it to words, they isolate the experience from the amodal flux in which it was originally experienced. (176)

His subsequent speculation recalls Gazzaniga and LeDoux's conjectures about the gradual dominance of the "verbal self": "What probably happens in development is that the language version 'yellow sunlight' of such perceptual experiences becomes the official version, and the amodal version goes underground and can only resurface when conditions suppress or outweigh the dominance of the linguistic version" (176).

Such reflections may make it easy to adopt the facile assumptions of post-Romantic cliché: that language has alienated the human subject from both the body and the so-called natural world; that language (despite the priority of concepts) effectively "speaks" the self, and so on. But these are premature conclusions. As the remarkable work of Lakoff and Johnson—and, more recently, of Mark Turner—suggests, it is in fact the body that articulates the structure of both conceptual and, subsequently, verbal thought. This idea was first elaborated with rigor in their collaborative (and unpretentious) *Metaphors We Live By*, and it has since been refined in Lakoff's *Women, Fire, and Dangerous Things: What Our Categories Reveal about the Mind* and in Johnson's *The Body in the Mind: The Bodily Basis of Meaning, Imagination, and Reason*. Briefly, they argue that "our ordinary conceptual system, in terms of which we both think and act, is fundamentally metaphorical in nature" (*Metaphors* 3). In other words, we think *necessarily* in metaphorical (or, to use Johnson's more inclusive word, "imaginative") structures when we conceptualize our world. This is not to say that *language* constrains our thought: on the contrary, like Jackendoff and other students of consciousness, Lakoff and Johnson insist that metaphor is "primarily a matter of thought [that is, conceptual activity] and action and only derivatively a matter of language" (153). In fact, language is stamped, semantically and syntactically, by the metaphoricity of our conceptual structures.

Common among those structures are spatial orientations for mood-states, quantities, values: to be happy, for example (because erect posture means mastery), is almost invariably to be "up" ("That *boosted* my spirits"); to produce more of a thing is, like heaping up objects, to elevate its number ("My income *rose* last year"); to avoid the socially taboo is to assume dominant values and so to reside respectably on the heights ("She has *high* standards"). Space is invariably conceptualized as a container ("There's a lot of land *in* Kansas"); an activity is a substance ("How did Jerry *get out of* washing the windows?"); an event or action is an object ("Are you *in* the race on Sunday?"). Theories are buildings ("Is that the *foundation* for your argument?"); ideas are organisms ("She has a *fertile* imagination"), products ("His *intellectual productivity* has decreased in recent years"), commodities ("That idea just won't *sell*"), resources ("He *ran out of* ideas"), money ("Let me put in my *two cents' worth*"), cutting instruments ("He has a *keen* mind"), fashions ("What are the new *trends* in English criticism?"). As all of these examples (drawn from *Metaphors*) make clear, *the immaterial and the elusive are habitually expressed through the material and the physically interactional.* Moreover, such strategies seem to be woven into the very texture of language itself. A study by Susan Lindner, for example, of verb-particles with *up* and *out* in English has shown that, "in contrast with the standard view that they represent unrelated semantic atoms," they can be explained systematically by a small number of "prototypical schematic structures" covering nearly all cases of the some 600 constructions under review (Johnson, *Body* 32). Lindner's findings indicate, for example, that "our IN-OUT schemata emerge first in our *bodily* experience," specifically, "in our perception and movement" (Johnson, *Body* 34).

Although Lakoff and Johnson begin by emphasizing the "purely cultural" origins of such metaphors, they are soon led to assert that the "domains of experience" in terms of which understanding usually takes place "seem to us to be *natural kinds of experience.*"

These kinds of experiences are a product of

> Our bodies (perceptual and motor apparatus, mental capacities, emotional make-up, etc.)
>
> Our interactions with our physical environment (moving, manipulating objects, eating, etc.)
>
> Our interactions with other people within our culture (in terms of social, political, economic, and religious institutions)

In other words, these "natural" kinds of experience *are products of human nature.* (117–18)

And because our schemata are *human* schemata, they rest on an anthropocentric epistemology. Lakoff and Johnson speak of a "rejection of epistemological foundationalism" in describing their own philosophical orientation (181), but it is clear that such a rejection does not mean for either of them the embrace of a radical cultural relativism. "Though there is no absolute objectivity," they write,

> there can be a kind of objectivity relative to the conceptual system of a culture. The point of impartiality and fairness in social matters is to rise above relevant *individual* biases. The point of objectivity in scientific experimentation is to factor out the effects of *individual* illusion and error. . . . [P]ure subjective intuition is not always our only recourse. Nor [do] . . . the concepts and values of a particular culture constitute the final arbiter of fairness within the culture. There may be, and typically are, transcultural concepts and values that define a standard of fairness very different from that of a particular culture. (193–94)

Just as the pursuit of truth is a search for metaphors of progressively more sophisticated functional applicability to what we have come to know as the world,[6] so the movement of cultural history is a movement through successive metaphorical approximations of idealized human relations. I say "idealized" rather than "ideal" in order to include conceptualizations—communism, fascism, or Nazism, for example—that enjoy ephemeral, though ardent, allegiances. The fact that such aberrations are always still possible should suggest the essential difference between social and scientific "truth": the gains of science (its conceptual, not ethical gains) are in the main progressive, as our increasingly complex technology implies; those of politics, provisional only. And understandably so, since the latter is the art of apportioning power—which is to say, of devising metaphors to legitimate its negotiations among the inevitable inequalities of the governed. "The most fundamental values in a culture," Lakoff and Johnson observe, "will be coherent with the metaphorical structure of the most fundamental concepts in the culture" (22). But since cultures are never completely homogeneous, neither are the structures that undergird them: "because things are usually not equal, there are often conflicts among these values and hence conflicts among the metaphors associated with them" (23). In a sense it may be accurate to say that the metaphors both promote and deny those conflicts, since it is partly a function of metaphors to hide certain aspects of the concepts they express. If time is money and not a stream, one doesn't have the leisure, as Thoreau thought he had, to go a-fishing in it. On the other hand, the creative potentiality of metaphors—the fact that they may be extended in unaccustomed ways, or that they may be engendered ab ovo as a new way of grasping the world (the mind as computer, for example)—ensures that their limitations are neither crippling nor insuperable.

If there is resistance to thinking in these terms about human conceptualization, that resistance may be attributed, at least in part, to what Lakoff and Johnson call "the fear of metaphor," which they associate with a fear of "the imagination" (191). It is such fears as these that appeals to "rationality" are usually intended to allay. And yet, as both theorists argue, "since the categories of our everyday thought are largely metaphorical and our everyday reasoning involves metaphorical entailments and inferences, ordinary rationality is therefore imaginative by its very nature" (193). Moreover, so-called rational argument, being merely a form of verbal struggle, is invariably structured by a martial metaphor, specifically the metaphor "argument is war." Whatever the forum—a learned journal, an academic conference, a newspaper editorial—"rational persuasion" is the art of defending a position, which means defeating an opponent, explicit or implied, and doing so by recourse to the usual tactics of assault: invoking authority, challenging authority, intimidating, insulting, evading issues, belittling, flattering, and so on. The academic may be more subtle in the deployment of these tactics than the average man on the street, but he or she inevitably deploys them. In fact, the more trenchant and memorable his or her argument, the more likely it is that those tactics have been exploited with skillfully daring impunity. The human animal is an animal that has evolved to think, as it were, with the body, and such thinking usually entails a subversive respect for the system that motivates the body's attachments, aversions, and aggressions: the emotions. Thus Johnson's answer to Kant's grand project ("how imagination can be both formal *and* material, rational *and* bodily"): "there is no unbridgeable gap between these two realms in the first place" (*Body* 168).

Not that the "verbal self" betrays no struggle to dissociate itself from the emotive. One example of its doing so has already been suggested by Gazzaniga and LeDoux's experiments. To understand fully just when and why this dissociation usually takes place, we must consider the role of narrative in human thinking and reasoning. But that necessitates a consideration of human relationships and so a turn from cognitive to social concerns.

3

Again I shall begin with the infant, particularly with Stern's observation that its life "is so thoroughly social that most of the things the infant does, feels, and perceives occur in different kinds of relationships" (118). Those relationships have structure from the beginning. Jerome Bruner has concluded, after decades of study of human development, that "we come initially equipped, if not with a 'theory' of mind, then surely with a set of predispositions to construe the social world in a particular way and to act upon our construals" (*Acts* 73). In other words, we are endowed at birth with "a primitive form of folk psychology" (*Acts* 73), prepared to attribute to (and read from) others expressions of emotions—expressions that, in turn, reveal desires, beliefs, intentions.[7] Language enters the scene much later. In fact, the child (like the mature chimpanzee [Jolly 238–46]) has mastered various communicative functions and intentions—indicating, labeling, requesting, misleading—long before language makes them verbally communicable.[8] Bruner indeed goes further to suggest that, "looked at naturistically, it would seem as if the child were partly motivated to master language in order better to fulfill these functions *in vivo*" (*Acts* 71). And he summarizes his argument in a way that recalls our earlier remarks about concept-formation: "the acquisition of a first language is very context-sensitive, by which is meant that it progresses far better when the child already grasps in some *prelinguistic* way the significance of what is being talked about or of the situation in which the talk is occurring" (*Acts* 71).

How the child grasps that significance is illustrated dramatically by Stern's discussion of "attunements." "Attunements" is the name Stern gives to episodes of "affective intersubjectivity" that occur between adult (usually parent) and child during moments of caregiving and play. Such episodes arise precisely by virtue of the infant's capacity for cross-modal processing: or as Stern puts it, "the capacities for identifying cross-modal equivalences that make for a perceptually unified world are the same capacities that permit the mother and infant to engage in affect attunement to achieve affective intersubjectivity" (156). Usually the modalities that are "crossed" in attunements are verbal (on the parent's part) and gestural (on the infant's), but in all instances the communicative "matching" that results is a matching of affective (that is to say, of proto-intentional) states. Stern offers several examples:

> • A nine-month-old boy bangs his hand on a soft toy, at first in some anger but gradually with pleasure, exuberance, and humor. He sets up a steady rhythm. Mother falls into his rhythm and says, "kaaaaa-*bam*, kaaaaa-*bam*," the "*bam*" falling on the stroke and the "kaaaaa" riding with the preparatory upswing and the suspenseful holding of his arm aloft before it falls.
>
> • An eight-and-one-half-month-old boy reaches for a toy just beyond reach. Silently he stretches toward it, leaning and extending arms and fingers out fully. Still short of the toy, he tenses his body to squeeze out the extra inch he needs to reach it. At that moment, his mother says, "uuuuuh . . . uuuuuh!" with a crescendo of vocal effort, the expiration of air pushing against her tensed torso. The mother's accelerating vocal-respiratory effort matches the infant's accelerating physical effort.

• A ten-month-old girl accomplishes an amusing routine with mother and then looks at her. The girl opens up her face (her mouth opens, her eyes widen, her eyebrows raise) and then closes it back, in a series of changes whose contour can be represented by a smooth arch ($\frown$). Mother responds by intoning "Yeah," with a pitch line that rises and falls as the volume crescendos and decrescendos: "Y$\overset{\frown}{\text{ea}}$h." The Mother's prosodic contour has matched the child's facial-kinetic contour. (140–41)

It's important to distinguish the behavior of the adults in these three episodes from merely imitative behaviors. There is, in fact, no attempt on their parts to *duplicate* the child's behavior since such duplication would simply maintain "the focus of attention upon the forms of the external behaviors" (142). The point of the attunement is the indication of a sharing of an intentional state *by appeal to the quality of the feeling that is instinctively associated in the infant's mind across two different modalities of perception or sensation.* Here is where the "primitive folk psychology" with which the infant enters the world begins to achieve sophistication.

Unfortunately, it is also where the origin of what Trivers calls "parent-offspring conflict" can be dated with unequivocal confidence. For attunements may not only be calculatedly "selective"; they may be "misattunements" as well. By such intersubjective economies is the child's intentional life given shape. Stern relates the case of Sam and his mother, who

was observed characteristically to just undermatch the affective behaviors of her ten-month-old son. For instance, when he evidenced some affect and looked to her with a bright face and some excited arm-flapping, she responded with a good, solid, "Yes, honey" that, in its absolute level of activation, fell just short of his arm-flapping and face-brightness. Such behavior on her part was all the more striking because she was a highly animated, vivacious person.

In our usual fashion, we asked her our routine questions—why she did what she did when she did it the way she did it—for each such inter-change. . . . [W]hen asked if she had intended to match the infant's level of enthusiasm in her response to him, she said "no." She was vaguely aware of the fact that she frequently undermatched him. When asked why, she struggled toward verbalizing that if she were to match him—not even over-match, but just match him—he would tend to focus more on her behavior than on his own; it might shift the initiative over from him to her. . . .

When the mother was asked what was wrong with the child's being relatively more passive or less initiatory than she at this life phase, she revealed that she thought he was too much like his father, who was too passive and low-keyed. . . . She was the one who infused enthusiasm into the marriage, decided what to eat, whether to go to the movies, when to make love. And she did not want her son to grow up to be like his father in these ways. (211–12)

However successful such tactics may be in channeling the drives of the child ("One of the fascinating paradoxes about her strategy," Stern writes, "is that, left alone, it would do exactly the opposite of what she intended" [212]), it doubtless has an effect on what Stern calls the "evoked companions" of both infancy and childhood. Such companions are composite memories of "self-regulating others" that offer the affective experience of "being with others" when the infant or child is alone. "Prototypic memories," the companions "represent the accumulated past history of a type of interaction with an other" and "serve a guiding function in the sense of the past creating expectations of the present and future" (115).

Behind the most important of such companions stand C. G. Jung's archetypes. It may seem curious, in a book that has been so inhospitable to Freud, to encounter this concession to Jung, but, as Anthony Stevens correctly observes, in his synthesis of ethology and analytical psychology, "whereas many of the original concepts of Freud have been superseded, those of Jung are just beginning to receive [in developmental psychology] the attention they deserve" (142). Jerome Kagan agrees, noting that "perhaps Jung's deepest insight, which Freud may not have understood," was that most of the explanatory concepts of psychoanalysis ("libido," for example) had a merely culturally circumscribed legitimacy, and that the scientific mind of Freud's day was all too eagerly prepared "to describe psychological qualities with an energy metaphor" (*Unstable Ideas* 98). Although, like Darwin, the early Jung had no knowledge of the genetic basis of organismic behavior, he was led to posit behavioral templates (to revert to a more promising metaphor) for the newborn human infant in much the same manner that Lorenz and Tinbergen hypothesized "fixed behavior patterns" in the graylag goose or gull. The archetype, he wrote in his foreword to M. Esther Harding's *Woman's Mysteries* (1949),

is not meant to denote an inherited idea, but rather an inherited mode of psychic functioning, corresponding to the inborn way in which the chick emerges from the egg, the bird builds its nest, a certain kind of wasp stings the motor ganglion of the caterpillar, and eels find their way to the Bermudas. In other words, it is a "pattern of behaviour." This aspect of the archetype, the purely biological one, is the proper concern of scientific psychology. (XVIII.518)

Of course, the "biological" in the human infant is never unmediated by the "cultural"—the learned—and the archetypes manifest their polarities (the "good" and the "terrible" mother, for example) and acquire what Jung called their "feeling-tones" through the child's actual experience of being in the world. In Stevens's words, "the archetypes of the phylogenetic psyche are actualized in the complexes (pathological or normal as the environment disposes) of the ontogenetic psyche, and tend to maintain the individual on whatever developmental pathway he [or she] is already on" (144). In short, the "evoked companion" (to return to Stern's terminology) is an ontogenetically prototypical memory superimposed upon a phylogenetically archetypal one.

The work of John Bowlby and of the "attachment" theorists offers the most convincing argument for such inherited structures. Building upon classical experiments with nonhuman animals, such as those of the Harlows with rhesus monkeys, which were shown to have a need for maternal proximity that was independent of a "reinforcing" reward of food, Bowlby proposed in the late 1950s that mothers and infants are attached by *instinct*—that the child's tie to parent is simply "the human version of behaviour seen commonly in many other species of animal" (183). Infants, in other words, are biologically prepared to form "archetypal" relations with their caregivers, typically with their mothers. That this relational (as opposed to imagistic) aspect of the archetypes had been primary for Jung himself is suggested by his remarks in "Psychological Aspects of the Mother Archetype" of 1938 (revised 1954):

> Again and again I encounter the mistaken notion that an archetype is determined in regard to its content, in other words that it is a kind of unconscious idea (if such an expression be admissible). It is necessary to point out once more that archetypes are not determined as regards their content, but only as regards their form and then only to a very limited degree. A primordial image is determined as to its content only when it has become conscious and is therefore filled out with the material of conscious experience. Its form, however, as I have explained elsewhere, might perhaps be compared to the axial system of a crystal, which, as it were, preforms the crystalline structure in the mother liquid, although it has no material existence of its own. . . . The archetype in itself is empty and purely formal, nothing but a *facultas praeformandi*, a possibility of representation which is given *a priori*. The representations themselves are not inherited, only the forms. (IX.1.79)

Earlier in the same essay he notes—importantly, for discussions of art—that "in the products of fantasy the primordial images are made visible, and it is here that the *concept* of the archetype finds its specific application" (IX.1.78, my emphasis).

Jung once remarked that there are as many archetypes "as there are common situations in life" (Stevens 53), and, indeed, the "evoked companions" of infancy and childhood are not the only "self-regulating" structures tied to the phyletic memory.

If, as the findings of developmental genetics argue, there is a general "blueprint" for human life, according to which physical as well as behavioral changes appear as an individual matures over time, we should expect certain archetypal "images" to cluster about recurrent life-events—especially as those events were experienced in the species' formative Pleistocene past. Early dependency in infancy, self-assertion and courtship in youth, marriage and childbearing in maturity, retrospective vision in old age—these are the major experiential nodalities that have spawned the images that stalk the mind: woman as Child, Maiden, Mother, and Medium; man as Child, Hero, Lord, and Wanderer. And because (as I indicated in Chapter 2) those nodalities are invariably conflictive ones, marked by the pull of competing interests, the images are all stamped by ambivalence.

The Child is the *enfant terrible*, an "unholy" boy, in Jung's words (IX.1.159), savage in the pursuit of its own interests. Or, on the other hand, it is a cherub, pliant to the wishes of its parents. The Mother is of course the "great" or "terrible" mother; the Medium—woman possessed of the authority of age—is a powerful muse or witch. Man as Lord is either tyrant or protector; as Wanderer, is (like the Winnebago Trickster) ambiguously sage or fool. Even Maiden and Hero have antithetical aspects: when Maiden is Brünnhilde, faithful to her rock while Siegfried sallies forth to "do deeds," she is the male's companion in her benevolent aspect; when, Circe-like, she binds him to watchful domesticity, she is *la belle dame sans merci*. As for the Hero, he is either saint or seducer—passionate Siegmund, loyal to Sieglinde, or incorrigibly philandering Don Juan. In brief, the *facultas praeformandi* of human social life disposes the organism to both approach and avoidance, and so the latter, like the cognitive animal that I introduced in the opening section of this chapter, may be said to be an organism of natural divisions. Eibl-Eibesfeldt suggests the consequences of these developments for human sociality in general: "In addition to general rules resulting from characteristics of human perception, the motivational structure of man, especially his ambivalence toward others, determines the course of social interactions" (*Human Ethology* 522).

Those interactions have evolved into exquisitely modulated negotiations between Ego and the ambivalently apprehended other. And one of the chief instruments of those negotiations, perhaps expressly evolved for that purpose, is of course human language. An irony, from a certain point of view. We have already noted how language may be said to fragment the infant's perceptual world; Stern adds that it is also responsible for the atomization of the self as moral agent. The gestural assertion is, in the language-learner, quickly understood to be subordinate to the verbal, and this may be so because of the human insistence upon "accountability" in social exchange.

Because language is so good at communicating what, rather than how, something happened, the verbal message invariably becomes the accountable one. A year-old-boy was angry at his mother and in a fit of temper, while not looking at her, brought his fist down hard on a puzzle. Mother said, "Don't you yell at your mother." She would have been very unlikely to say, "Don't you bring your fist down like that at your mother." (Stern 181)

What the gesture expresses, in effect, may come to be ignored and denied. And significantly, Stern adds, "what is deniable to others becomes more and more deniable to oneself" (181). Thus with language is born the tendency (as the dichotic dissociations of the brain suggest) to split the self into what Jung called Persona and Shadow, the former the repository of the legitimately accountable, the latter of the furtively "repressed." Which is to say that, while language permits "mutually negotiated meanings" (Stern 170), it does so between agents who are in part strangers to themselves, often advancing their interests with displays of verbal integrity while their Shadows brandish clubs in speechless threat.

Such self-deceptive tactics, as we have seen Alexander insisting, are essential for social success. For if "accountability" is the desideratum of all members of the social system, "deniability" is what ensures that each can participate without exciting in fatal ways the others' envy. Of course the potentiality for deniability is inherent in language itself, with its ambiguities, equivocations, circumlocutions, and sheer vaguenesses. It is also inherent in nonverbal behaviors, including those closely tied with speech. William Labov and David Fanshel have analyzed intonation from this point of view:

The lack of clarity or discreteness in the intonational signal is not an unfortunate limitation of this channel, but an essential and important aspect of it. Speakers need a form of communication which is deniable. It is advantageous for them to express hostility, challenge the competence of others, or express friendliness and affection in a way that can be denied if they are explicitly held to account for it. If there were not such a deniable channel of communication and intonation contours became so well recognized and explicit that people were accountable for their intonations, then some other mode of deniable communication would undoubtedly develop. (qtd. in Stern 180)

Perhaps the most remarkable development of human communication has been the evolution of a verbal medium by which the deniable (and the denied) can be *turned into* the accountable. That medium is narrative, a globally pervasive and perhaps prototypical way of reasoning about social affairs. Jerome Bruner suggests, in a provocative recent book, that the child masters grammar in a certain "order of priority" because of the "'push' to construct narrative" sequences (*Acts* 77).[9] There is probably, he argues a "human 'readiness' for narrative" that is responsible for "conserving and elaborating" its universal logic (*Acts* 45). For that logic functions as a kind of cultural adhesive, making it possible to deal "simultaneously"—if paradoxically—"with canonicality and exceptionality" (*Acts* 47). The "canonical" is what a culture legitimizes as "the expectable and/or the usual in the human condition" (*Acts* 47); the "exceptional," of course, marks an (often individual) deviation from that set of behavioral norms. And "while a culture must contain a set of norms," Bruner writes, "it must also contain a set of interpretive procedures for rendering departures from those norms meaningful in terms of established patterns of belief. It is narrative and narrative interpretation upon which folk psychology depends for achieving this kind of meaning" (*Acts* 47).

Narrative is an indispensable instrument of social negotiation because of the inherent ambivalence of human relations. Bruner offers an illustration, instancing the parent-offspring conflictual bond:

> The child, in the nature of things, has his or her own desires, but given her reliance upon the family for affection, these desires often create conflict when they collide with the wishes of parents and siblings. The child's task when conflict arises is to balance her own desires against her commitment to others in the family. And she learns very soon that action is not enough to achieve this end. Telling the right story, putting her actions and goals in a legitimizing light, is just as important. Getting what you want very often means getting the right story. . . . But to get the story right, to pit yours successfully against your younger brother's, requires knowing what constitutes the canonically acceptable version. A "right" story is one that connects your version through mitigation with the canonical version. (*Acts* 86)

Narrative thereby performs a host of important functions. It, first, brings the young effectively *into* a culture, sharpening their sense of both the canonical and the exceptional and of the legitimate ways of reconciling the two. It also "equips these young children with a more discerning empathy," allowing them, for example, "to interpret for their parents the meanings and intentions of younger siblings who are trying to make a case for themselves—especially when there is no conflict of interest involved" (*Acts* 87). Narrative thereby serves "a peacekeeping function" (*Acts* 50): it presents, dramatizes, and explicates "the mitigating circumstances surrounding conflict-threatening breaches in the ordinariness of life" (*Acts* 95). In doing so, it makes life significant and meaningful, "framing" or "schematizing" its important events (and thereby "indexing" them for memory), drawing order out of what Bruner calls the "murk of chaotic experience" (*Acts* 56). This last is an apparently essential function, since events that lack indexical properties are simply not remembered. "A story is useful," writes Roger C. Schank of the Institute for the Learning Sciences, "because it comes with many indices":

These indices may be locations, attitudes, quandaries, decisions, conclusions, or whatever. The more indices we have for a story that is being told, the more places it can reside in memory. Consequently, we are more likely to remember a story and to relate it to experiences already in memory. In other words, the more indices, the greater the number of comparisons with prior experiences and hence the greater the learning. (11)

It is this pedagogical aspect of narrative that Bruner emphasizes most. And yet his own remarks about the heterogeneity of culture suggest another face to his subject. Earlier on he paraphrases James Clifford's *The Predicament of Culture*, noting that "cultures, *if they were ever homogeneous*, are no longer so, and . . . the study of anthropology perforce becomes an instrument in the management of diversity" (*Acts* 27, my emphasis). That diversity, he adds, creates "conflicts in commitment, conflicts in values, and therefore conflicts about the 'rightness' of various claims to knowledge about values" (*Acts* 29). He is therefore later led to concede that the narratives that bind the individual to culture "may not represent a consensus" (*Acts* 96)—a concession that seems logically destructive of the concept of canonicality itself. If there are *many* "connecting stories" in a culture, the sum of which never achieves consensual status, then the "canonical" is a much more elusive category than Bruner tends to imply.

What is needed, of course, is some consideration of audience. A narrative that "mitigates" between a child and parent may not do so between the child and peer. And, even when agents of the same age are involved, narratives on the same theme may assume radically different forms depending upon the participants' race, sex, and class. The "canonical" through which narrative negotiates reconciliation is, in short, highly context-sensitive. Which is to say that, while one narrative may succeed among a certain group of auditors, it may baffle, bore, or anger another. The destabilizing element is antagonism born of human ambivalence, particularly as it atomizes human communities into ever smaller self-interested groups. Bruner explicitly regards such antagonism as symptomatic of a "breakdown" in culture (*Acts* 96). And yet, as his own quotations above suggest, *no* culture is—or apparently has been—exempt from the divisions that subvert canonicality. There exist or have existed cultures, certainly, in which there is little *evidence* of dissent, but in such cultures public acts of narrative seem relegated, either by strong force of custom or by governmental force, to the socially prominent and dominant—to the tribal elders, for example, or in the old Soviet Union to the KGB.

The more actively engaged that most members of a culture are in elaborating and construing its narratives, the more ambiguous will those narratives be: the line between the "exceptional" and the "canonical" (as "multiculturalism" has shown) will become harder and harder to draw. Bruner identifies ambiguity—he elsewhere equates it with interpretive necessity—as a defining characteristic of narrative, but he does so because he assumes that all narratives must have a narrator and that all narrators are "subject to the vagaries of intentional states" (*Acts* 54). But, aside from the questionable status of the premise (I shall later argue that drama is narrative), ambiguity as a phenomenon of narrative accounts seems to go rather deeper than that. Ambiguity can ensure that a narrative may be read as legitimizing diametrically opposed interests; it can ensure, in short, that human ambivalence, by which is acknowledged both conflict *and* consensus, is given its most articulate expression and freedom of play. In fact, the "purer" the narrative—the more successfully it restricts itself to Bruner's categories: presentation, dramatization, explication—the more successfully will it resist *explanation* and so reside more elusively in the realm of the ambiguous. The implications of this idea for both art and adaptation will form part of the subject of Chapter 4, but, before moving on to what might be described as the mind's antinarrational posture, it may be useful to develop a "definition" of narrative in what Rosch would call prototypical terms.

The prototypical narrative either exhibits or may be reconstructed as a sequence, usually shadowed by what Frank Kermode calls its "doppelgänger" causality ("Secrets" 80). Sequence is, according to Bruner, its "principal property" (*Acts* 43), and it indeed may be the only narrative property beyond dispute. Specifically human narratives involve human actors in their events: even if no human being appears and a narrative construes the happenings of dogs and cats, it is implicitly understood to have a bearing upon human affairs, if not to be "about" human beings altogether. (The case is apparently different for chimpanzees, who prefer to watch films of other chimpanzees [Sagan 119], unable—or unwilling—to extrapolate narrative logic from films about human beings.) This suggests another characteristic commonly attributed to narrative, at least of the human kind: that it is both concrete and emblematic. Narrative (I quote Bruner) "must 'ascend to the particular,' as Karl Marx once put it. Once it achieves its particularities, it converts them into tropes: its Agents, Actions, Scenes, Goals, and Instruments (and its Troubles as well) [Bruner is drawing upon Kenneth Burke's terminology] are converted into emblems" (*Acts* 60); that is to say, into symbols of transpersonal significance. A nature documentary—about the life of a pair of lion cubs, let us say—may therefore draw upon narrative *techniques*, such as the indispensable one of sequentiality, but it cannot be comfortably classed as narrative proper because it lacks this invitation to abstraction. The lion cubs remain, stubbornly, lion cubs, and their pawing and tousling has no significance outside itself.

The wary reader will have realized that we have begun to elaborate a paradox: narrative resists "explanation" and, at the same time, also invites it. Once narrative particularities are converted into emblems, they begin to dispel ambiguity. But it may be useful, in fact, to back up and reconsider the legitimacy of including generalization as a narrative property. Broadly speaking, what motivates narrativic generalization is precisely what engenders the metaphors we live by: the drive toward conceptual stabilization. And at this point I suggest that the narrative and the conceptual are antithetical impulses (if, in practical terms, inseparable ones), representing two different ways of apprehending reality: *What metaphor often is for the conceptual world, narrative is for the social one.* And, "while we can capture," in Mark Johnson's words, "certain aspects of our experience via concepts, models, propositions, metaphors, and paradigms, only narrative encompasses both the temporality and the purposive organization at the general level at which we pursue overarching unity and meaning for our lives" (*Moral Imagination* 171).[10] Narrative is not, as many theorists have maintained, so much "story" as an innate *way of knowing*, essentially as prelinguistic in its operations as conceptualization has proven to be. Only when narrative thought is *re*-presented, usually through the usefully (if meretriciously) stabilizing medium of language, does it acquire the "ambiguity" that I have ascribed to it; it is then that social relationships are crystallized—in the terms of Jung's provocative metaphor—into the notoriously intractable binary oppositions that characterize the *images* of the archetypes. Just as fantasy precipitates archetypal figures from the *facultas praeformandi*, so representation precipitates ambiguity from the narrative logic by which we intuitively negotiate our social lives.

The priority of narrative to language, the fundamental nature of narrative thinking, and the centrality of that thinking in the conduct of our daily affairs are all suggested by what Freud christened famously the "dreamwork." His terminology I think we can still retain, although much of the theory of *The Interpretation of Dreams* has been discredited by recent research. Contrary, for example, to Freud's hermeneutic emphasis on oneiric punning (and to Lacan's highly dubious—if intelligible—assertion that "the Unconscious is structured like a language"), the tendency of scientific dream theorists today is to underscore the preverbal quality of dreaming. Language-like "sleep thinking" is indeed a common phenomenon, more common, in fact, than dreaming itself, but such thinking is not accompanied by the "sensory illusions" that are the hallmark of the dream. And those illusions are obviously not language-generated. Other mammals, of course, exhibit REM sleep, and dreaming cats relieved surgically of locomotor inhibitions have suggested by their behaviors that they hallucinate the same movements and encounters in physical space that the dreaming human being experiences (Winson 46–47). Although verbal behaviors may appear in dreams, what is usually more prominent is the dreamer's sense of an unmediated immediacy of sensation. The *experience* of the dream is largely *pre*-representational: events seem not to be reviewed or recalled but to be endured directly by the dreamer. And they are endured in narrative, that is to say sequential, form.

Given the ill-assorted material that often makes up the dream, there is no obvious reason why this should be so. Neither is it self-evident why the dreamer should suffer its incongruities of sequence—the odd shifts of locale, the metamorphoses of actions and goals, for example—with such familiar equanimity.

The most parsimonious explanation is that it is simply "natural" for the brain to cast social episodes (as dream episodes usually are) directly into narrative form. And so predisposed is consciousness, apparently, to sequential logic in daily life—to the expectation that *contiguity* means *congruity*—that *affectively* the dreamer endures logical dislocations with little psychological strain. It is only when the dream is re-presented, first in memory, then perhaps in a verbal account, that ambiguity inevitably surfaces (*"somehow* the floor changed to the ceiling"), even as, for the dreamer, the affective "naturalness" of the experience remains.

Some confirmation of these speculations can be found in the work of J. Allan Hobson, director of the Laboratory of Neurophysiology at the Massachusetts Mental Health Center. Dreaming, Hobson proposes, echoing other dream theorists, is a form of primitive information-processing, probably having evolved (although Hobson does not stress this) to screen and sort material for long-term memory.[11] Since the processing is being done under abnormal conditions ("the space-time dimensions of the external world are absent; multiple sensory channels are activated in parallel; and attentional processes are impaired" [218]), the *form* of the resultant operations is aberrant. Space and time become elastic and variable, personalities unstable and protean. And yet, even under the "adverse working conditions" of REM sleep (214), the brain is "so inexorably bent upon the quest for meaning that it attributes and even creates meaning when there is little or none to be found in the data it is asked to process" (15).

Although Hobson suggests that "the brain-mind may need to call upon its deepest myths to find a narrative frame that can contain the data" (214), it is equally possible to conclude that the narrative frame *is* the brain-mind's "deepest myth." Narrativizing is what the dreaming brain does to make sense of the social world; in that form it may activate exploratory negotiations with other subjects— subjects that, significantly, retain the intentional states of "folk psychology" in waking life. The "others" that one encounters in dreams are motivated (however obscurely) by beliefs, desires, and goals: affectively, in other words, they are like the intentional self, which is prepared, therefore, to negotiate relations with an instinctive savoir-faire. But the meaning-making mind is already at work at re-presenting their significance. Hobson (like Freud) isolates a feature in dreams "that could be described as an abnormal fluidity between opposites, resulting in a heightened ambivalence that amplifies the ironies of human existence" (280). Such an amplification is presumably in the interests of educating the dreamer, exciting his or her reflective sensitivity to the narrated social scene.

It's likely that animal dreaming is in narrative form, but what Michael Carrithers calls "narrativity," the capacity to cognize long narrative structures,[12] seems typical of the human animal alone. (REM sleep in the cat, perhaps significantly, is of relatively short duration [Winson 44].) The world of the nonhuman primates, Carrithers argues, is one "whose temporal horizons are very close and which does not . . . suffer the burden of a laboriously planned future or a long remembered past" (307). By contrast, human beings exist in a temporal web of "ramifying complexities, complexities extended through social rather than physical space and unfolding in an event-filled rather than abstract time" (309), and their survival has depended upon their having evolved a capacity to negotiate those complexities.

> It is this capacity which I want to designate as narrativity, a capacity to cognize not merely immediate relations between oneself and another, but many-sided human interactions carried out over a considerable period. We might say: humans understand *characters*, which embody the understanding of rights, obligations, expectations, propensities and intentions in oneself and many different others; and *plots*, which show the consequences and evaluations of a multifarious flow of actions. Narrativity, that is, consists not merely in telling stories, but of understanding complex nets of deeds and attitudes. (310)

Carrithers adds that narrativity is not "a strictly or narrowly linguistic skill, though it is certainly entwined with linguistic skills in adult humans at present" (313). It is, rather, an "active competence" (313), one "essentially connected to conation and emotion," and only secondarily "a mental capacity for representation" (316). The cognitive theorist Simon Baron-Cohen, who uses the word "mindreading" for the same capacity, makes a strong case for its being an "innate" endowment: "we are born understanding social chess," he writes in his book *Mindblindness*, "or at least we have many of the basic principles that we will need in order to make sense of and take part in the game. We have some key neural mechanisms that allow us to 'see' the solution to a social situation intuitively" (19–20).

The extent to which narrativity is an "innate" human competence and the extent to which it may be developed by "learning" are both suggested by the experience of the so-called autistic personality. "At one time," writes the developmental biolinguist John L. Locke, "autism might have been attributed to the misbehavior of parents or other environmental factors, but there is now reasonably good evidence that autism is associated with abnormal brain morphology and cell structure" (316–17), both of which, in cases unconnected with prenatal risk, are traceable to genetic defects.[13] Also, although popularly associated with disorders of speech, autism, as the well-known neurologist Oliver Sacks has noted in a recent article on the subject, embraces "a wide range of phenomena and symptoms" ("Neurologist's Notebook" 106). Some autistics are highly intelligent and develop complex verbal skills: indeed, the focus of Sacks's article, Temple Grandin, has written an autobiography, earned a Ph.D. in animal sciences, won a place on the faculty at Colorado State University, and published more than a hundred scholarly papers.

But, though verbally deft, Grandin remains narrativically unsophisticated. In an interview, Sacks asks her about Shakespeare's plays:

> She was bewildered, she said, by Romeo and Juliet ("I never knew what they were up to"), and with "Hamlet" she got lost with the back-and-forth of the play. Though she ascribed these problems to "sequencing difficulties," they seemed to arise from her failure to empathize with the characters, to follow the intricate play of motive and intention. She said that she could understand "simple, strong, universal" emotions but was stumped by more complex emotions and the games people play. "Much of the time," she said, "I feel like an anthropologist on Mars." (112)

To overcome her ignorance, she has built up "a vast library of experiences over the years . . . like a library of videotapes, which she could play in her mind and inspect at any time—'videos' of how people behaved in different circumstances" (112). These she played—and, in her mid-forties, still plays—over and over again in order to "learn, by degrees, to correlate what she saw, so that she could then predict how people in similar circumstances might act" (112). In this enterprise she has also repaired to books and newspapers, "all of which [have] enlarged her knowledge of the species" (112). But hers is an emotionally impoverished knowledge: "With farm animals," she says, "I *feel* their behavior. . . . With primates I intellectually understand their interactions" (121). She still misses what puzzled her in childhood: "an exchange of meanings" with which other children were adept, "a negotiation, a swiftness of understanding so remarkable that sometimes she wondered if they were all telepathic" (116). She will always be deficient in narrativic competence.[14]

In summary, narrative is a form of thinking that is inseparable from the affective interests of human narrators (and their audiences) and that, while resisting, during the course of representation, conceptual—or "intellectual," as Grandin would say—translation into the emblematic, converts intuitively negotiated social interactions (that is, those that we are genetically prepared to apprehend through the competence of narrativity) into spectacles that are resonant with ambiguity and ambivalence. That it is perhaps *the* prototypical form of human reasoning has been proposed by Trinity College's Dan Lloyd. Lloyd concludes his fascinating *Simple Minds* by compiling a taxonomy of human error in both deductive and inductive reasoning.[15] From well-known tendencies of experimental subjects, he adduces that logical error has its source in quite particular and recurrent deficits: subjects routinely fail to look for (or ignore) disconfirming evidence of hypotheses; they are "averse to thinking about samples of groups, and hence, about [statistical] frequencies"; they formulate their principles of explanation in a post hoc manner ("apparently, most people do not know what principles they apply when they reason") (227). These (and other) tendencies can be explained, Lloyd argues, by an appeal to a narrative model of essentially *preconceptual* thought. First, narrative is fundamentally affirmative—"Kafka tells us that Gregor Samsa was transformed into a giant insect, and not that he was not transformed into a water buffalo" (219)—and thus the human reluctance at disconfirmation: "narrative neglects negation" (227). Narrative also deals typically with the singular and the concrete, accounting for the fact that comparatively few people are adept at probabilistic thinking. Narrative, finally, entails a deeply intuitive logic: "there are no explicit principles in the inner narrative. Psychotales move from event to event without explicit covering laws" (227). Most "reasoning" is therefore, in retrospect, a kind of representation as explanation: the superimposition of meaning upon a set of events that is uncomfortably *conceived* as ambiguous—events that are managed in everyday life by little more than intuition alone. "In sum," writes Lloyd,

> I propose that the primary patterns of reasoning are narrative patterns. If narrativity defines the primary psychodynamics, is there a secondary counterpart? We are, after all, able to see how our reasoning fails, so there is in us some capacity to judge our narratological leaps by some other standard. What is that standard? Logic, of course. The emerging big picture is one that stands standard psychodynamics on its head: The primary psychodynamics is narrative, and the secondary psychodynamics is rational. The role of the secondary psychodynamics, accordingly, is not to prune the burgeoning fruits of unrestrained primary psychodynamics, but rather to correct it. (228)

And how, exactly, is narrative "corrected"? In part by being robbed of affective power. The move from narrative to so-called pure logic entails a usurpation of bihemispheric thinking by the primarily "verbal" self.[16] Lloyd points out that, whereas "narratives can comprise representations of all forms (including, for example, pictorial representations)," only language "is capable of readily presenting negation and universal generalization, both requirements for a general capacity for logical reasoning" (230). Logical cognition is "accordingly exclusively language-like, while narrative cognition can employ both languagelike and nonlanguagelike metarepresentations" (230). Lloyd concludes by offering an explanation for the often remarked phenomenon that, while narrative is a universally invariant form, "rational"—that is, analytical—systems may diverge widely from culture to culture:

> The distinction between narrative psychodynamics and rational psycho-dynamics reflects the conjecture that the latter is a heuristic overlay, con-straining, correcting, and extending the basic narrative apparatus. The rational system arises through the explicit learning of rules of reasoning. Those rules govern (as well as describe) the system when it is operating as a

rational system. Accordingly, if cognition is culturally relative, that relativity will be more conspicuous in styles of explicitly rational thought. (230)

Lloyd emphasizes that the distinction that he is drawing between these two types of cognition arises "only at the representational level" and that the "same neural network, if it is sufficiently complex, could realize any of the . . . systems from moment to moment" (230). It's to be expected, in fact, that the analytical system should intercede rather frequently in both the generation and reception of narrative, if only to resolve the ambiguities and ambivalences that are born of the representative act. Thus the "tyrannizing" that I noted earlier, of the verbal over the nonanalytic self. Thus, too, perhaps, the occasional revolts on the part of the "subordinate" hemisphere, resulting in a momentary overthrow of both narrative and logic alike.

I'm alluding to the so-called extraordinary mental states: of trance, ecstasy, and what Mihaly Csikszentmihalyi calls "flow." Neuropsychologist Barbara W. Lex has suggested that trance states are cultivated in ritualistic ceremonies as a way of gaining access to right-brain functions and of subverting the authority of the "dominant" hemisphere (144). Both ecstasy and "flow," too, seem to tap those functions: the first offers a sense of holistic vision and of release—however brief—from reflexive thought; the second enables those engaged in "autotelic" activity to surrender the self-consciousness of ordinary cognition. "Autotelic" is a word used by Csikszentmihalyi (from the Greek *auto,* "self" and *telos,* "purpose") to describe activities that require "formal and extensive energy output" but that provide "few if any conventional rewards" (10). Chess-playing, rock-climbing, rock-dancing, and surgery are all activities that induce autotelic "flow," a state described by Csikszentmihalyi as "beyond boredom and anxiety": "In the flow state, action follows upon action according to an internal logic that seems to need no conscious intervention by the actor. He experiences it as a unified flowing from one moment to the next, in which he is in control of his actions, and in which there is little distinction between self and environment, between stimulus and response, or between past, present, or future" (36). In flow, there is an erosion of "dualistic perspective": the actor is aware of his or her actions "but not of the awareness itself" (38). One of Csikszentmihalyi's rock-climbers expressed it with an image: "You become a robot—no, more like an animal. . . . There is a feeling of total involvement. . . . You feel like a panther powering up the rock" (43).

As Csikszentmihalyi has shown with experimental subjects, quasi-flow states are common in everyday life. Called "microflow" experiences, they include such noninstrumental activities as chatting and joking, fiddling with objects, daydreaming, talking to oneself, playing music in one's head, humming, whistling, chewing gum. When deprived of such experiences, Csikszentmihalyi's subjects reported feeling tense, hostile, angry, irritated, and in general "extremely" debilitated (169). He was therefore led to conclude that microflow is not only a necessary recreative part of life but also "a form of microcreativity," and that choosing "how to pattern experience" through its activities "could be the most simple and most basic manifestation of the creative process" (169).

Apparently in the "higher" states of full flow and ecstasy, creativity entails something very like a radical reconstitution of mental "grasp." In the course of her exhaustive analysis of ecstatic states, Marghanita Laski observes that "in these experiences we have a loss of the normal sense of relationships by which we assess our perceptions and a regaining of that sense of relationship in improved form," and she concludes that "ecstatic experiences are manifestations (probably exaggerated manifestations) of processes facilitating improved mental organization" (280).

That the nonanalytic and synthesizing tendencies of the right hemisphere play an important role in this organization is suggested by the usual sorts of stimuli that "trigger" the ecstatic response. In Laski's subjects, sublime natural scenery was the most common trigger, followed by tonal music. It should be obvious why the former, with its holistic power, should stimulate right-hemisphere cognition. As for the latter, it's been known for several years that the appreciation of the emotionally melodic is for the most part right-hemisphere-dependent; in fact, "melodic intonation therapy" has been developed to help brain-damaged patients recover from certain speech deficits when their right hemispheres remain intact. Such patients, suffering typically from Broca's aphasia, having good comprehension but poor speech production, are taught to sing word sequences, which are gradually inflected into "normal" speech. "It is presumed," write Sally P. Springer and Georg Deutsch, in their compendium of hemispheric research, "that the intact right hemisphere learns the phrases this way and, as a result, develops more language production skills that compensate, to a degree, for the left-hemisphere deficit" (185). Such conjecture emphasizes the flexibility of brain functioning, but it also underlines the usual division of labor: verbal skills generally the province of the left hemisphere; melodic judgments that of the right.

As the psychologist Michael C. Corballis observes, in his book *The Lopsided Ape,* "the picture of hemispheric duality in humans that emerges [in clinical research] is not very different from the popular account of the left hemisphere as more analytic, rational, and propositional, and the right as more holistic, intuitive, and appositional" (273). This being the case, the "improved mental organization" that ecstasy seems to provide must result from a relaxing of conceptual constraints: like the shaman, as Laughlin, McManus, and d'Aquili describe him, the ecstatic "immerses" himself mentally in "a broader, more destructured phenomenal field" (341). Such a field typically functions, like flow, to discourage "dualistic perspective," so that the division between subject and object is (as all mystics claim for their experiences) phenomenologically obliterated.

In that field, representation is of course impossible (though *presentation*—sensation, perception—is not), and, indeed, in what Laughlin, McManus, and d'Aquili describe as "Polyphasic Void Societies," there are adepts who court an escape from representation (more specifically, from its attendant ambiguities) in "the realization of a phase of consciousness beyond any phenomenal reality" (294). A paradoxical quest, quite obviously, since all consciousness (as Husserl rightly assures us) is consciousness *of* something. And yet the fantasy of transcending the very font of representations—that is, of consciousness itself—seems persistently endemic to the human enterprise. One ethnographic survey has reported that 89 percent of 488 societies show some form of institutionalized trance or dissociation experience (Dissanayake, *What* 155). Some cultures, such as the North American Hopi, seem conceived to approximate an uninterrupted "flow."

But for the literate modern of the industrialized West, neither flow nor trance nor (certainly) ecstasy, apart from that purchasable by drugs or alcohol, is anything more than a rare experience. Of Laski's subjects, mostly artists and professionals of the British upper-middle class, 50 percent claimed to have experienced ecstasy fewer than ten times in their lives; only seven (of the fifty-eight total) "claimed the experience in hundreds or constantly" (43). What the modern learns to cultivate is "microflow," the TV tuned to a soothing white noise as the mind gathers wool among its bric-a-brac. In such moments, perhaps just beyond both boredom and anxiety, it enjoys representation as self-presentation, the vague trickle (or treacle) of associative drift. Here, in effect, is the unexamined life, relaxed from its habitual organizing structures—a life that is, for most of the unfussy species, apparently quite comfortably worth living. It sets the self adrift upon the stream of consciousness rather than forces its hand to the rudder. And, momentarily at least, that self is dispersed among the flotsam and jetsam that swirl through the current.

4

That the mature brain-mind is a massive parallel processor, ordinarily "involving," in the words of philosopher Owen Flanagan, "coordination of disparate neural areas" and yet lacking a "thought center" (39)—what Daniel Dennett calls a "Cartesian theater"—where everything "comes together" for a mental audience: this is the picture that has won widespread acceptance among both neuroscientists and theorists of consciousness. As such a processor (or "Darwin machine," as neurobiologist William H. Calvin describes it), it is engaged, moment by moment, in the reception and review of mental contents, a sifting that yields, in Dennett's formulation, "something *rather like* a narrative stream or sequence, which can be thought of as subject to continual editing by many processes distributed around in the brain, and continuing indefinitely into the future":

Contents arise, get revised, contribute to the interpretation of other contents or to the modulation of behavior (verbal and otherwise), and in the process leave their traces in memory, which then eventually decay or get incorporated into or overwritten by later contents, wholly or in part. This skein of contents is only rather like a narrative because of its multiplicity; at any point in time there are multiple drafts of narrative fragments at various stages of editing in various places in the brain. While some of the contents in these drafts will make their brief contribution and fade without further effect—and some will make no contribution at all—others will persist to play a variety of roles in the further modulation of internal state and behavior and a few will even persist to the point of making their presence known through press releases issued in the form of verbal behavior. (*Consciousness* 135)

What I have been referring to as the "self" is a concatenation of those narratives that "persist to play a variety of roles in the . . . modulation of internal state and behavior." Elsewhere Dennett calls the self the "center of narrative gravity," and describes it as "strings or streams of narrative [that] issue forth *as if* from a single source" (*Consciousness* 418). In the microflow of the couch potato, the illusion has been relinquished, and the drift of the mind—to use Dennett's word (*Consciousness* 113)—"precipitates" a polyvocal babble from the subject.

As the metaphors of the foregoing paragraph imply, the primary medium of consciousness is language, at least as Dennett conceives the stream of thought. For him, consciousness is an "emergent" phenomenon, "largely a product of cultural evolution that gets imparted to brains in early training" (*Consciousness* 219). The "self" may consequently begin to seem (especially in light of how Dennett describes it, as an ebullient "Joycean machine" [*Consciousness* 220]) a mere signifier at play upon the field of the Word, since the narratives that swarm to its gravitational center are necessarily consciousness-derived and (as I earlier argued about narrative ambiguity) the heterogeneity of all cultural interests would ensure in the mature (that is, nonparochial) subject a Bakhtinian heteroglossia in those narratives. But even Dennett rejects the notion that language "constructs" the thinking subject, thereby "liberating" it to linguistic play. "It is plausible," he writes, "to maintain that the details of a natural language—the vocabulary and grammar of English or Chinese or Spanish—constrain a brain in the manner of a high-level programming language. But this is a far cry from asserting the dubious hypothesis that such a natural language provides the structure *all the way down*" (*Consciousness* 302).

The very fact that there *is* a "structure," a *center* of "narrative gravity" for the self, suggests that those narratives that "persist to play a variety of roles" emerge both through and by virtue of nonverbal constraints. And those constraints are, in all probability, not very "largely" cultural. Flanagan points out that "many features of consciousness—its streamlike character, the core emotions, perceptual sensitivities in the five modalities—are most credibly thought of as having a genotypic specification" (84–85).[17] And the most familiar of its properties, its likeness to a "stream," derives not merely from the linear flow of language. "The stream of thought," writes philosopher John Searle, "contains not only words and images, both visual and otherwise, but other elements as well, which are neither verbal nor imagistic. For example, a thought sometimes occurs to one suddenly, 'in a flash,' in a form that is neither in words nor [in] images" (128).

In short, although knowing "who one is," as Flanagan concedes, apparently "requires a narrative" (193), it need not require a *verbal* narrative (though the "verbal self," as I have noted, is very hard to supersede), nor should that narrative be assumed to emanate from a matrix of cultural "discourses" alone. Clearly the self's center of narrative gravity is to be found in that infinitely variable behavioral predisposition popularly known as "temperament." Ornstein implies as much:

> It is a constant hope that we're rational and that a judicious component of the human brain controls and orchestrates this parade of talents. Unfortunately for those who hold such a view, but fortunately for the biological survival of the organism, the commanding, controlling mental operating system (which might be called the self) is much more closely linked with emotions and the system of automatic bodyguards than with conscious thought and reason. (*Evolution* 152–53)

Just as the soul selects its own society, then shuts the door, so temperament selects those narratives of self most congenial to its operations, and silences other voices.[18] Of course the selection is a dynamic, always ongoing process, early complicated by the fact that all narratives, to a greater or lesser extent, imply social negotiations with other subjects. For this reason Flanagan distinguishes between "two different aims of self-representation, which in the end are deeply intertwined":

> First, there is self-representing for the sake of self-understanding. This is the story we tell to ourselves to understand ourselves for who we are. . . . Second, there is self-representing for public dissemination, whose aim is underwriting successful social interaction. . . . [T]he strategic requirements of the sort of self-representing needed for social interaction, together with our tendencies to seek congruence, explain how self-representation intended in the first instance for "one's eyes only," and thus which one might think more likely to be true, could start to conform to a false projected image of the self, to a deeply fictional and farfetched account of the self. (196)

The juxtaposition here of "farfetched" and "deeply fictional" is, I think, instructive. Flanagan is implying that, however "fictive" the self may be, some of its narratives of self-representation are more expressive of its gravitational center than others. The self, in other words, is not a "mere" fiction, as so many poststructuralist theorists have claimed. Much in its narrative repertoire is admittedly borrowed, so to speak, not new, since "it invariably draws on available theoretical models about the nature of the self in framing its reflexive self-portrait" (Flanagan 197). But to liken selves to fictional "constructs," to porous and protean figments of myth-making that various discourses merely "author" into being, is to ignore the whole issue of temperamental constraints, of the "characteristic dispositions," as Flanagan calls them, that "we reveal in social life" (206). And it's also to ignore the thirst for "congruence" that drives us to unify our selves. "The Darwin machine itself," notes Flanagan, "favors minimal cognitive dissonance and maximal integration at the level of conscious thought and action guidance (harmony at the top may well belie all sorts of disagreement and competition among lower-level processors)" (200). A unified self flourishes on a simple argument: in the practical world, it works.

How deep is the need for it is suggested by cases in which the sense of a self has been lost.[19] In *The Man Who Mistook His Wife for a Hat*, Sacks describes a man he calls Jimmie G., his long-term memory destroyed by alcoholism, who has become "a man without a past (or future) stuck in a constantly changing, meaningless moment" (28). Reduced to "a sort of Humean drivel" (35), to "mere disconnected, incoherent flux and change" (30), his inner life now seems so impoverished and incoherent that he denies at most times that he feels alive. Significantly, it is only when mood or emotion can succeed at involving him in a series of events—while churchgoing, gardening, or singing, for example—that Jimmie can reclaim his sense of self. When Sacks once observed him participating in the Mass, Jimmie seemed completely "absorbed in an act, an act of his whole being, which carried feeling and meaning in an organic continuity and unity, a continuity and unity so seamless it could not permit any break" (38). Sacks's words very strongly suggest that, while narrative constitutes the conscious self and provides its (multifarious) "meaning," the "center of gravity" of that self lies in the "feeling" that ensures its coherence.

That verbal narrative alone is tragically insufficient in "constructing" that crucial coherence is dramatically illustrated by A. R. Luria's account of his patient Zasetsky, a Russian soldier who lost his memory to a bullet in the brain. After decades of attempts to regain his identity by a conscious effort to recover his past, he made the discovery (in Luria's words) that "proved to be the turning point: writing could be very simple" (72). Zasetsky embarked upon the heroic project of reclaiming himself in an act of pure narrative inscription. He has produced over three thousand pages of manuscript, the memories emerging from his automatic writing with apparent veridicality—but, despite his great effort to decipher and organize them, to give them the temporal sequence of a life, he has never regained a sense of self. The verbal narrative is not enough: "This strange illness I have," he confides to his notebooks, "is like living without a brain" (145). The book of himself, although tirelessly elaborated, has turned out to be less than worthless— an alien account of an alien being, forever in pursuit of the enduring center that would unify the whole.

Zasetsky's loss of that sense of unity is of course not a fatal impairment: he can still function as a being in the world; only meaningfulness has vanished from his life. He is like the research chemist that Sacks describes who, because of a tumor affecting both frontal lobes (the neurological seat of "selfhood," apparently [Ornstein, *Evolution* 153]),[20] found "the world reduced to a facetious insignificance":

> "Of course," she said, with a chemist's precision. "You could call them ["left" and "right"] *enantiomorphs* of each other. But they mean nothing to *me*. They're no different from *me*. Hands . . . Doctors . . . Sisters . . ." she added, seeing my puzzlement. "Don't you understand? They mean nothing to me. *Nothing means anything* . . . at least to me." (*Man* 117)

Apparently, then, without a sense of self, human beings have little *incentive* to function in the world. But it is not immediately clear why consciousness, and hence selfhood, evolved in the conduct of life at all. For if a sense of self is not crucial to behavioral functioning, consciousness may, at times, be inimical to it: new research has validated Hamlet's conclusion that thinking too precisely on th'event can obstruct its consummation (Wilson and Schooler). As the case studies of neurosurgeon Wilder Penfield suggest, complex goal-directed behaviors may be accomplished without consciousness of any kind:

> Attacks of epileptic automatism show clearly the automatic, complex perfor-mance of which man's computer is capable. In an attack of automatism the patient becomes suddenly unconscious. . . . Patient B. was subject to epilep-tic automatism that began with discharge in the temporal lobe. Sometimes the attack came on him while walking home from work. He would continue to walk and to thread his way through busy streets on his way home. He might realize later that he had had an attack because there was a blank in his memory for a part of the journey, as from Avenue X to Street Y. If patient C. was driving a car, he would continue to drive, although he might discover later that he had driven through one or more red lights. (38–39, paragraphing simplified)

Evidence such as this has led some theorists to conclude that consciousness is merely an "epiphenomenon," a "collateral product" of the body's functioning (as Thomas Henry Huxley put it) that does no work itself.

Both Flanagan and Searle have recently challenged this position, Flanagan contending that "consciousness facilitates performance on many activities, despite being not absolutely necessary for these activities" (139). And Searle takes a stronger line: "Normal, human, conscious behavior has a degree of flexibility and creativity that is absent from the Penfield cases. . . . Consciousness adds powers of discrimination and flexibility even to memorized routine activities" (108). But it may not be "consciousness" that provides these advantages. Searle and Flanagan are both conflating consciousness with what Derek Bickerton calls "off-line thinking," to which properly should be ascribed the "flexibility and creativity" that Searle sees as typical of conscious thought. Consciousness, Bickerton argues, is "essentially dual in nature" (154): its operations may be ascribed to two now-overlapping faculties, which he calls "Consciousness-1," concerned with "on-line" thinking, and "Consciousness-2," concerned with reflective "off-line" thought. Consciousness-1 is possessed by many (if not most) organisms, since it is synonymous with those various powers of sensation or perception that enable their possessors to respond to their environments in fitness-enhancing ways. Such systems are "on-line" processors because they "mediate between a nervous system and the rest of nature" (129). The Penfield cases offer human examples of typical on-line thinking, unusual only in the respect that his patients performed their tasks without any awareness of the processing (or the tasks). Off-line thinking, which seems to be unique to the human species, "involves computations carried out on more lasting internal representations of . . . objects [in the external world]. Such computations need not be initiated by external causes, nor need they initiate an immediate motor response" (90). Theoretically, as Bickerton points out, consciousness is no more necessary for off-line thinking than it seems to be for on-line, but, for reasons that still elude the theorists, it has emerged as the usual medium for such thought: Consciousness-2, which "is merely consciousness of Consciousness-1" (153), is the familiar, often fretful, result. Bickerton sees its emergence in evolutionary history as the crucial event in the making of *Homo sapiens sapiens*:

Until that moment, ever since the first protozoan wiggled away from an aversive chemical, interactions between organism and environment had been governed by two principles: "If something important happens, do something about it" and "If nothing important happens, save your energy." Now there was an additional principle: "If you see something that might be important, do nothing right now, think about it, and maybe you can do something later on." This third principle would change the world utterly. (57)

What off-line thinking made possible for the human being was, not only the creativity of reflective thought, but also the "scenario-spinning" (to borrow William Calvin's word) of narratives in consciousness. In other words, the intuitions of narrativity, which preceded all the thinking of "Consciousness-2,"[21] could now be *represented*—articulated in mental and verbal and dramatic narratives—thereby facilitating the management of those "social dramas" so potentially disruptive to culture. If Bickerton is right, the birth of language was the key: off-line thinking was born of its acquisition; more specifically, it was born of the refinement of a "protolanguage" (still the language today of children under two, as well as of educated chimpanzees) by the organizations of syntax. With the "rewiring" of the brain for syntax, perhaps through the mutation of a single gene, a "neural workspace" (96) was cleared for those "conceptual structures" to which Jackendoff and others credit our cerebration.[22] This account, as Bickerton notes, stands "the conventional wisdom on its head: instead of the human species['] growing clever enough to invent language, it . . . view[s] that species as blundering into language and, as a direct result of that, becoming clever" (40).

Clever and irredeemably self-conscious. But the latter is not to be completely deplored. For all its incessant, sometimes distracting, chatter, the stream of thought through what Bickerton calls Consciousness-2 has the power of carving new troughs in the old beds that channel our seeing, knowing, doing. Like language, to which it owes not only its origins, apparently, but much of its "computational" medium, off-line thinking can offer imaginative possibilities—of concept, behavior, emotional orientation—that are completely alien to the temperament of the thinker. And it can offer them with impersonally dramatic persuasiveness. Although Dennett goes far toward demolishing the "Cartesian theater," that hypothetical mental space before which we sit to behold its spectacles with Hamlet's now-proverbial "mind's eye,"[23] he cannot demolish its illusion, and I am sure he would never try to do so. For the illusion is crucial for the work of off-line thinking, in both its conceptual and narrative strains: with such thought, a curtain is lifted upon an actor in the head, often to discover that he or she is speaking of things undreamt of in the beholder's philosophy. Thus the often-lamented self-estranging effect of off-line mentation; but thus, too, its creative interventions. For that thinking makes possible the sort of operations that seem to baffle the disciples of Foucault: by countering the "I" with an "other," it permits *objectivity*, and permits it of a body that, as a preprogrammed gene-machine, can aspire to it only by a wonderful paradox. In doing so, it gives birth to strange monsters—to such thoughts, for example, as poststructuralism spawns. But it also disposes that body to the reception of spectacles of sophisticated provocativeness and utility.

In short, to the spectacles of reflection, and art.

Part II
The Book

4

"What Is Art For?": Narrative and the Ludic Reader

> *Joyce's first question when I had read a completed episode or when he had read out a passage of an uncompleted one was always: "How does Bloom strike you?"*
> *Technical considerations, problems of homeric correspondence, the chemistry of the human body, were secondary matters.*
> —Frank Budgen, James Joyce and the Making of Ulysses

1

The picture that is emerging of the human subject is, then, complex but fundamentally coherent. That subject is a seeker and maker of meaning first of all—not because it is a bourgeois capitalist, or a hegemonic sexist, or even a benightedly retrograde humanist, but ultimately because it is a gene-driven organism that has evolved to live by its wits. What all of the foregoing chapters have argued, broadly, is that the models of human development, motivation, and behavior that are prominent in contemporary (that is to say, poststructuralist) literary theory should be abandoned in favor of an evolutionary one. Carroll succinctly identifies the deficiencies of those models: "By taking Derridean semiotics and Foucauldian discourse theory as a matrix within which to synthesize the obsolete linguistics of Saussure and Jakobson, the obsolete psychology of Freud, and the obsolete sociology of Marx, poststructuralism has generated an ever more complex system of rhetoric altogether detached from empirical study, whether of evolutionary research or of standard social science" (27). The "subject" as merely a signifier signifying or the locus of so-called infantile fantasy or the ensemble of its social relations, however sophisticated by poststructuralist inflection, is a highly dubious artifact of largely ill-informed rhetoric, corresponding only accidentally and very imperfectly to the human being that empirical research describes. It may be useful, at this point, to recapitulate some of the chief nodes of the latter's development.

It is born alert and responsive to its natural social world, prepared prelinguistically to negotiate that world in species-typical ways, which is to say that it is both a cognitively precocious and a naively anthropocentric creature. It is innately disposed to process its sensations with cross-modal economy and efficiency, a fact that enables it to establish, with what Stern calls "attunements," emotionally vibrant intersubjective bonds. Those bonds, in turn, mature within the loose constraints of a general genetic program—the "archetypes"—through which the developing organism accommodates its singularities to the curve of the social world. Always its cognitive compass is the body, that brittle and vulnerable gamete-bearer for which its huge brain anciently evolved: all its categories as well as its conceptualizations are erected upon a scaffolding of the needs, limits, and relationships, defined both ontogenetically and phylogenetically, of the omnipresently physical and emotional *Moi*.

With language come both a consolidation and a tesselation of its social bonds—and the fret and creativity of "off-line" thought. Language, usefully if impoverishingly, sharpens the edges of its conceptualizations, distills many of its interpretive possibilities into the "verbal self," and encourages an often socially advantageous, if psychologically disturbing, split between Persona and Shadow. In its massive contribution to the subject's self-consciousness, it shatters the amodal sentience of infancy, thereby strengthening in the adult the nostalgic allure of the "extraordinary" mental states of ecstasy, trance, flow. Preserver and destroyer, language extends immeasurably the subject's social and cognitive reach, thus giving the human adaptive advantages that well justify its unique classification as *hominidae*; but it does so at considerable psychic cost. Not only does language exert a certain tyrannizing force upon its unwitting speakers, but, in its formidable powers of specification, it opens up a field of "accountability" from which those speakers are very often wise to seek escape. Like the mute narratives of consciousness itself, language is as much an instrument of ontological and ethical commitment as it is of communication, recall, and conceptual control.

But the subject has evolved, as the last chapter proposed, a competence that allows it to justify its commitments, a competence that several theorists have dubbed "narrativity." For narrativity in the human animal, as opposed to that in the alloprimate mind, is a competence subject to immense enrichment through *Homo*'s off-line ability to narrate. "Nature, not art," writes Barbara Hardy, "makes us all story-tellers" (vii): it does so by having bestowed language upon its most gregarious, albeit wary, of apes. Just as a humanity without language seems an impossibility (when deprived of it, human groups will develop a language of their own over the course of a mere two generations [Rosenfield 109]), so a human consciousness, a speaker, a culture without narrative is nothing less than unimaginable. Narrative is, in Roland Barthes's words, simply "there, like life itself" (252); and, although it is not, as Fredric Jameson declares, "the central function or *instance* of the human mind" (*Political Unconscious* 13), it is certainly *among* the mind's central manifestations.

And just as "life itself," as I have argued, is disposed in terms of a behavioral grammar, so narrative, too, has a grammar—the same—that is both pancultural and transhistorical. Earlier theorists (Propp, for example) have generally approached that grammar from what we may call a Skinnerian standpoint, assuming that the minds of fictional agents are Black Boxes, as it were, and deducing the "morphology" of their narratives from the transposable fragments of their actions. A more fruitful approach, I am proposing, is to view all minds, both real and fictional, as "Darwin machines" (of variable sophistication), engaged in the project of negotiating and making sense of their physical and social worlds.

Crucial to this approach, however, is the acknowledgment that those worlds are not completely synonymous with the environments in and for which the Darwin machine evolved. The grammar of narrative is consequently fraught with the same ambiguities—arising from the same social ambivalences—that distinguish the biogrammar itself. Male versus female, self versus kin, kin versus non-kin, group versus group—these gene-bred antagonisms are embedded in a social life that is always demanding (through gene-bred imperatives) their resolution. Thus the insuperable ambivalences of the species. Tragedy, I shall argue, is a meditation upon the destructive effects of those ambivalences, specifically of their antagonistic aspects; comedy exploits those ambivalences as a source of incongruity, inviting the spectator to take pleasure in *Homo*'s own paradoxical allegiances.

But narrative offers more than meditation or amusement, of course: it serves as an instrument of social adaptation and, as such, ensures the Darwin machine a way of transcending its own anachronistic biases. Although narrativity seems initially to be grounded in those biases (as I shall demonstrate when we turn to stories by young children), narrative, which works to refine its operations (and to "carve out" what Edelman calls the "secondary neural repertoire") has at least the potentiality to encourage and develop sophisticated ethical sympathies in its audiences, speaking, for example, through tragedy and romantic comedy, of the necessity of restraining the asocial will. As essentially an enculturating agent, narrative has also, as I shall suggest, a demonstrably age-sensitive appeal, doing its most useful and efficient work on the young seeking a place in their culture. And it works best when the conceptualizing tendencies that all audiences bring to the clarification of its drama is restricted to large issues of genre, allowing the intuitions uninhibited play in the act of refining narrativity. This I hope to demonstrate in the last chapter of this book, a chapter dedicated to a novelist whose conceptual (that is, philosophical) sophistication is sometimes at odds with her own narrativic discernment.

But we must first give some attention to that special creature for whom narrative is sung, spoken, written, or performed—often addressed, with the convenience born of a modern bias, as "the reader."

2

How does narrative commend itself to that reader? As much else does to the human animal: through his or her emotions. When it is operating most efficiently, it engages the body in a powerfully affective embrace. What psychologist Victor Nell calls the "ludic reader" feels rapt before narrative—fiction, nonfiction, the tug of the imaginative current is what matters—the effects of which on the nervous system are clearly measurable. There is an onset of tension (or it is "focused," perhaps, as Hans and Shulamith Kreitler argue [22]): muscles in the forehead, beneath the chin, and around the mouth subtly contract; both breathing and heartbeat tend to quicken; the skin's electrical activity (recorded in lie-detector tests) increases—all signs of organismic arousal. Then arousal declines precipitously when the reading is laid aside. "The powerful reward value," writes Nell in conclusion, "associated with a sudden drop in activation level (after sex, or when a climber reaches a mountain peak) . . . seems applicable to the ludic reader" (191).

The experience of arousal that Nell describes makes good sense for the participants of narrative intercourse as Bruner has elucidated its dynamics. If one of narrative's principal functions is to mitigate conflicting interests, it's to be expected that both parties, at any point in the exchange, be prepared to fight or flee. But how a purely *imaginative* engagement in narrative can arouse, even excite, inspire fright or exhilaration, continues to perplex the aesthetic theorist. Kendall L. Walton, in one of the most recent addresses of this issue, can only conclude that, when his hypothetical Charles quakes with "quasi fear" as a green slime bears down on him from a movie screen, it is only "fictional in Charles's game that he fears a slime" (246), since Charles knows the slime does not exist and so cannot be a genuine object of fear. "Charles does not imagine merely *that* he is afraid; he imagines *being* afraid, and he imagines this *from the inside*" (247). This last formulation seems closer to the truth, but its air of odd abstraction, of its interposing what smack of deliberative operations between Charles and the cinematic slime, may have its source in Walton's own inability to define what it means to imagine.[1] Well into the text of *Mimesis as Make-Believe*, a note informs us that Walton finds plausible "the old idea that there is no such thing as the way the world is in itself, that things as they are conceived by one or another sentient being may be all there is" (99 n). He can therefore conclude that "fictionality," which is to say the imagining of a world by "one or another sentient being,"

> has nothing essentially to do with what is or is not real or true or factual; that it is perfectly compatible with assertion and communication, including straightforward reporting of the most ordinary matters of fact, yet entirely independent of them; that it is not essentially the product of human action nor paradigmatically linguistic; and that fiction is not parasitic on "serious"

discourse or nonfictional uses of symbols. These results, unexpected though some of them are, flowed easily from the simple intuition that to be fictional is, at bottom, to possess the function of serving as a prop in games of make-believe. (102)

If that sentient being, my reader, is human, he or she will balk at a number of these conclusions. For the act of imagining, as Walton himself insists, means the projective *participation* in games of make-believe; it means imagining "from the inside" of fictional egos. (The ludic reader is "absorbed," in Nell's words, in the space of the narrative world.) And such imagining is possible for the human being only in specifically human terms. "Virtually all stories," observes Robert Scholes, "are about human beings or humanoid creatures. Those that are not invariably humanize their material through metaphor and metonymy" ("Language" 206). And so, although it is theoretically possible to imagine oneself to be a groundhog, say, or a mole, in doing so one can only imagine how a human being would think and behave in the animal's circumstances: thus the Kafkaesque cogitations of "The Burrow." The act of imagining, I am insisting, has a necessary connection with the "real" (though not, as I shall argue, with the factual); more specifically, it is both the product and the parasite of human action, if by "action," of course, we denote both inner and outer processual affairs. It is because the world is *not* merely the solipsistic dream of one or another sentient being but, rather, the artifact of an evolutionary logic that has, on the one hand, spawned species that are adaptively alien to one another and, on the other, evolved conspecifics that compete most effectively when they are alert to the implications of each other's behavior that the human imagination is both as constrained and as emotionally empowered as it is. Imagining—what A. L. Cothey calls the "active capacity for envisaging and contemplating possibilities" (150), or what the neurobiologist William Calvin calls, more simply, "scenario-spinning" (83)—is a spontaneously natural human act, inseparable from the real world of human action and, as such, should be expected to be invested with affective salience. As Richard J. Gerrig has recently argued, "many criterial properties of narrative worlds emerge directly from the ordinary and obligatory operation of basic cognitive processes," and, "in some sense, all a reader must do to be transported to a narrative world is to have in place the repertory of cognitive processes that is otherwise required for everyday experience" (239). To make as much as Walton does of the "fictionality" of Charles's experience is to misdirect the reader about the source of his emotion.[2] For, as Nell observes, in enumerating the "paradoxes" of narrative engagement, the pleasures of the imagination do not originate in the "fictional" nature of the exchange (50).

On the contrary, the fundamental fact about every work of art is that it reifies the imaginative experience of the participant in order to confer significance upon those emotional effects that quite naturally accrue to the engagement. Like those spheres of human action to which it is often compared (and with which it is doubtless contiguous), play and ritual,[3] art demarcates itself from the quotidian world through what Ellen Dissanayake calls a "making special." But, whereas play rarely produces either an artifact or a vision of significant perdurability, and ritual rarely relaxes its ties with the narratively familiar and the sacred, art does both, elevating its objects and its acts to a still-profane realm that is qualitatively different (in its "timelessness," for example) from the mundane and everyday. "Reality," writes Dissanayake, "or what is considered to be reality, is elaborated, reformed, given not only particularity (emphasis on uniqueness, or 'specialness') but import (value, or 'specialness')—what may be called such things as magic or beauty or spiritual power or significance" (*What* 92). Dissanayake makes a strong case for the selective value of "making special" in human affairs: "making special (as, say, embellishing, repeating, or performing a particular act with virtuosity) might well have originated as a demonstration of the wish or need to persuade others (and oneself) of the efficacy or desirability of what was being done." And "when allied to life-serving activities—tool manufacture, weaponry, ceremony—elaboration (as reinforcement) would enhance survivorship" (*What* 104). What Dissanayake is suggesting is that art emerged as a reification of the ordinary imaginative act: as the investing of significance in the "off-line" envisaging of possibilities—and, by extension, in the instruments through which (magically or otherwise) those possibilities could be realized—through its demarcation from the practical world. In this emergence, at least one literary theorist has identified the "uniqueness" of the human species: "It is our specialization to create worlds to be tested against sensory experience, as it is the mole's to dig and the bird's to fly" (F. Turner, *Natural Classicism* 17).

The ways in which art generally has announced its "making special" have long been recognized by theorists of aesthetics. The Russian Formalist Viktor Shklovsky was one of the earliest to observe that art "defamiliarizes" its materials. "The purpose of art," he wrote in *Theory of Prose* (1925), "is to lead us to a knowledge of a thing through the organ of sight instead of recognition. By 'enstranging' objects and complicating form, the device of art makes perception long and 'laborious'" (6). The result is contemplative "distance," as Thomas G. Pavel has more recently maintained: "Creation of distance could well be assumed to be the most general aim of imaginary activity: the journey epitomizes the basic operation of the imagination, be it realized as dreams, ritual trance, poetic rapture, imaginary worlds, or merely the confrontation of the unusual and the memorable" (*Fictional Worlds* 145). But there clings to this idea (as Pavel himself realizes) a certain odor of modern bias. That the "goal" or "aim" of art is the encouragement of contemplative detachment in the perceiver is an idea little older than some three hundred years and preeminently a notion of the industrialized West. Art defamiliarizes for preliterate peoples (as it did, presumably, for their artisan ancestors) *in order to* accomplish its goal. And that goal is rarely disinterestedness. "The known nonliterate societies seem to differ sharply from ours," writes the anthropologist Daniel J. Crowley, "in their greater proportion of practicing artists, higher integration of art into everyday life, and perhaps greater concern on the part of the artists with the social and sociological implications of their work" (326). Thus Pavel's "important, ineliminable intuition": "namely that literary artifacts often are not projected into fictional distance just to be neutrally beheld but that they vividly bear upon the beholder's world" (*Fictional Worlds* 145).

The apparently universal function of defamiliarization is both to invest the artwork or experience with "specialness" and to tease the beholder into engagement with its world by the arousal induced by novelty. And the process of defamiliarization often begins even before the work or experience is encountered. The engagement with art is usually prepared for by what psychologists of aesthetics call "set": expectations are attuned to the specific nature of the encounter, and the participant is inducted into the specialness of the experience by various contextual cues. As Hans and Shulamith Kreitler observe, "The traditionally ostentatious decorations of opera and theater halls, the solemn atmosphere of museums, the formal dress of orchestra musicians, the elaborate frames of pictures, and formerly the cover and bindings of books bear witness to age-old endeavors to produce in the audience of art a special and festive mood" (263). Such endeavors invest the occasion with perceptual and, hence, cognitive significance, leading the participant to expect a certain "repleteness" from the experience (Winner 7), both in the whole and in all its details. "Set" is essentially the management of attention, a management that encourages as well as facilitates "the meaningful elaboration of stimuli" (Kreitler and Kreitler 259). Like aesthetic "distance" and the defamiliarizing properties of poem, dance, or epic, "set" enables the bracketing of art so that its commentary upon the world may seem saturated with recoverable significance.

As I shall argue later at greater length, that significance is rarely grasped by the purely analytical mind. It emerges, at least in the literary arts, including the (ostensibly) non-narrative poem, from an exercise of its audience's narrativity. Thomas M. Leitch, in an often penetrating study of fictional discourse, has suggested that the point of fiction—a point we may extend to all of art—is to *display* a state of affairs. The display is an ambiguous or "problematic" one (26), for reasons that surfaced in the previous chapter, but it's brought into resolution less by reasoned analysis than by the operations of the audience's intuitive competence to make sense of the human world. "We might distinguish," Leitch concludes, " . . . between the audience's narrativity, which *fills in* the connections required to make sense of agents and incidents by establishing the relations and imputing the motives which give them significance, and the discourse's narrativity, which *fills out* a given series of states of affairs by providing the details that make the audience's narrativity necessary and rewarding" (40). The focus is always upon the human scene, even if that scene (as in a Robbe-Grillet novel) seems completely bereft of characters. When it is replete with them, either as independent figures on stage or page or as the presiding intelligence of a poem, the temptation is usually irresistible to forge with them ties of subtle and elusive psychological complexity, ties that range (and shift) from intense empathic identification to amused or disgusted detachment.

For Leitch, such ties may excite false expectations: "characters," he insists, "cannot be explained in the same way human behavior as such is explained, because characters differ from people in being incompletely specified (how many characters are said to have armpits?) and intentionally intelligible, as human behavior is only among highly histrionic people or people performing for an audience" (158). But there are a number of problems with these distinctions. First, as Jonathan Culler has pointed out, it is part of the usual "narrative contract" that the "order of the notable" will be observed by the primary organizing consciousness—that is to say, by the storyteller or author. "When a text behaves," Culler writes, with reference to Robbe-Grillet's *La Jalousie*, "as though the reader were not familiar with tables set for dinner—when it presents descriptions without regard for the 'order of the notable'—the reader must assume that it is trying to tell him more and has difficulty in discovering what in fact is 'the matter in hand' " (*Structuralist Poetics* 196). Similarly, any text that specifies that its characters have armpits would generate more perplexity than illumination. (And how completely "specified" are human beings in life? Do we reserve judgment that an acquaintance is truly human until we have seen his or her armpits with our very own eyes?) That characters are, as Leitch argues, "intentionally" intelligible is an idea that I'll take up toward the end of this chapter. Suffice it to note here that people in life, often despite their intentions, are, for the most part, more intelligible than Leitch implies. It's on this point that Paisley Livingston rests his argument about the "rationality" of human life (we may, I think, more accurately refer to its "intelligibility") both inside literature and out:

> it is plain that in their daily affairs, women and men constantly interpret themselves and each other as persons having conscious desires, beliefs, and intentions to act. People think that it is often possible to distinguish between cases where someone does something intentionally and cases where behaviour is not under intentional control. Moreover, these attributions of mental states to other agents are not tentative and purely speculative, but involve serious practical commitments. Every time we take a flight in an aeroplane, or step into the cross-walk before an approaching automobile when the traffic signal has just given us the right of way, we are implicitly wagering that other people's behaviour will conform to any number of complex constraints on perception, inference, and action. (*Literature and Rationality* 2–3)

In short, their sharing what has come to be called "folk psychology" ensures all its agents an intelligible world.

Leitch's difficulty with character seems to have its origins in his insistence that it is merely a literary "trope." Like Culler and Northrop Frye, for example, who both argue that "lifelike" characters are essentially "literary constructs," owing their consistency, in Frye's words, "to the appropriateness of the stock type which belongs to their dramatic function" (172), Leitch regards character merely as an "invention," adding that "the debate over the status of the human subject [that dominates much poststructuralist theory] is largely irrelevant to character as a trope or conceptual category" (148). "Character has been invented repeatedly," he writes (149), instancing specifically the emergence of Euripidean "psychology" out of the unreflective agents of Aeschylus.

> Here then is a formula for the historical emergence of character: When the bonds joining the individual to the larger communities and ideals of worship, religious belief, and kinship have become tenuous enough to make piety a matter of choice rather than a requisite of personal identity, then it becomes possible to speak of character as a distinctive trope for human identity. Character is not to be confused with identity; people always and everywhere have an identity, whether or not they consider themselves individuals, and there is nothing necessarily more authentic, or even more individualistic, about defining people with reference to their emotional and sexual desires than with reference to their pious allegiances. Moreover, piety remains a constitutive element in all characters, even those in which it is partially eclipsed; if it did not, we could not make sense of any characters whose emotions and whose immediate situation were different from our own. (153)

A rigorous, if ultimately perplexing, argument. Leitch is certainly correct in asserting that "primitive" characters—Aeschylus's, for example—are defined (in a sense) by "piety." Every agent in the *Oresteia*, for example, "acts in accord with the wishes of his or her patron deity," and, indeed, "no one ever does anything" in that trilogy that "he or she believes to be wrong" (152–53). But Aeschylus's characters can, in fact, feel guilt—can feel themselves burdened with a "polluted" conscience—even though they are completely confident (as they always are) that their actions are ethically unimpeachable. Thus Agamemnon's reported outburst, pregnant with anguish and apprehension, before the sacrifice of Iphigeneia:

> Obey, obey, or a heavy doom will crush me!—
> Oh but doom *will* crush me
>   once I rend my child,
>   the glory of my house—

a father's hands are stained,
blood of a young girl streaks the altar.
Pain both ways and what is worse?
Desert the fleets, fail the alliance?
No, but stop the winds with a virgin's blood,
feed their lust, their fury?

(206–15)[4]

It is in speeches like this that we understand Agamemnon, not as an unreflective agent of Zeus's commands, but rather as a father and a commander of his fleet. When he decides the issue in favor of the alliance, one (very typical) masculine allegiance has taken precedence over his almost equally powerful—and pathetic— need to spare his daughter's life. Agamemnon is intelligible to a modern audience because the latter, in however peripheral or diminished a way, shares the Greeks' emotional world. (The views of an older generation of critics seem to me intuitively on the mark: "Man has grown," writes Oscar Mandel in his witty and shrewd *Definition of Tragedy*, "no new emotions since Homer's day" [9].) Leitch seems to think, as the last two sentences in his "formula" make clear, that piety and the emotions are to be distinguished from each other, but even the vague definition that he borrows from Kenneth Burke—of the "pious" as loyal to the "sources of their being"—suggests that they are in fact indistinguishable. For the modern, piety *means* emotional allegiance, and, when we try to make sense of Homer or Aeschylus, we look to their characters to behave as human beings—that is, to behave as creatures who share with us the human emotional repertoire.

As Leitch himself admits, all "tellable" characters—that is, characters of inter- est, whose "display" is not exhausted by thematic function—"are based ultimately on identification" (162). And such identification is not possible if a character can't be conceived as a hypothetical being in the world, however grotesque, idiosyncratic, or mysterious a being. Empirical studies have confirmed that "the concepts and techniques used to describe people in general and literary figures in particular do not differ in any major respect" (Kreitler and Kreitler). Specifically, as Jerome Bruner has suggested, a "tellable" character, like people in life, is apprehended "as a Gestalt, not as a list of traits that account for particular actions. And the Gestalt seems to be constructed according to some sort of theory about how people are" (*Actual Minds* 38). That "theory" we've encountered in both Bruner and Livingston: it's the "folk" conviction that people can be expected to act out of desires, beliefs, and intentions, all of which operate with at least functional consistency and coherence. Even the now-no-longer-new *nouveau roman* depends, as Culler takes pains to point out, "on the[se] traditional expectations concerning character which the novel exposes and undermines" (*Structuralist Poetics* 231).

And the observation may be extended beyond character. In general, it is impossible to address any work of art completely innocent of expectations about coherence or meaning—impossible because human beings had evolved to decipher the text of the world long before they became readers of Robbe-Grillet. All mature readers approach a literary text with what I have called an intuitive competence, the most fundamental demand of which, in Culler's words, is "the demand for sense" (*Structuralist Poetics* 123). Meeting that demand is a matter of "naturalizing" the text, of bringing it "into relation with a type of discourse or model which is already, in some sense, natural and legible" (*Structuralist Poetics* 138). That "in some sense" is important for Culler. A reluctant structuralist in all his books, he resists any suggestion of the "coextensiveness" of competence with the so-called individual subject: literary competence is the precipitate, so to speak, of a "series of conventions, the grids of regularity and intersubjectivity," and "the empirical 'I' is dispersed among these conventions which take over from him in the act of reading" (*Structuralist Poetics* 258). But the oppositions implicit in these remarks are incompatible with Culler's own powerful sense of the ubiquity of the meaning-making drive. "We are born into a world of meaning," he writes, "and cannot even shun its demands without thereby recognizing them" (*Structuralist Poetics* 252). There can be, therefore, no fundamental discontinuity between "the empirical 'I'" (whatever that is) and the "conventions of reading," those "grids of regularity and intersubjectivity." It is only because Culler, like the Lévi-Strauss whom he chastises, has little appreciation for the mind as an *adapted* faculty, that he can declare, in his most guarded and deliberative moments, that such a discontinuity exists.

And since the mind's "primary psychodynamics" (Lloyd's phrase) is narrative, it seems natural to conclude, with Alexander Argyros (223), that narrative is not simply the basis of literary competence but the "deep grammar" of literature itself. Leitch makes it clear how superficial is the distinction between narrative and the arts of the stage and screen: "Since narratives are tellable only insofar as they are realized through a given medium of discourse, and since there is no reason to limit the medium to a verbal diegesis which would exclude films, dance, and pantomime, the distinction between mimesis and diegesis becomes tangential to the problem of narrative ontology" (40). Even lyric poems might most fruitfully be regarded as "holographic fragments of larger, ghost narratives that they presuppose and develop" (Argyros 224). All "literary" genres seem fundamentally dependent on what Ellen Winner calls a "story grammar" (269); that is, all elicit (and most satisfy) expectations of sequence, coherence, and probability.[5] Indeed, it seems likely, as Scholes has suggested, that the conventions of narrative "are too deeply rooted in human physical and mental processes to be dispensed with by members of this species" and that "even the most devoted practitioner of anti-narrativity" cannot completely do without them ("Language" 208).

Modern narrative theorists tend to interpret this necessity in characteristically modern terms. From Walter Benjamin through Sartre and Kermode, narrative has been seen as what Peter Brooks calls "the discourse of mortality" (*Reading* 22): it gives shape and point to the lives of creatures condemned to living in "the middest" (Kermode, *Sense* 7) and does so by keeping those creatures ever mindful of their sense-determining ends. For other theorists, narrative alleviates the paralyzing ennui of modern life: "Stories and histories," writes Paul Hernadi, "and other narrative or descriptive accounts help us to *escape boredom and indifference*—ours as well as that of other people" (199). And for still other writers—here, Ursula LeGuin— the escape sought in narrative is from the oblivion of death itself: "Why do we tell tales, or tales about tales. . . . Is it because we are so organized as to take actions that prevent our dissolution into the surroundings?" (194). But narrative preceded the modern sensibility, with its somewhat tedious egoism and anxiety, and it seems to have done so, as Bruner suggests, primarily as a form of social contract. And so it still functions, according to anthropologist Victor Turner: as part of the "social dramas" of human life.

What Bruner describes in developmental terms, Turner describes in cultural ones:

> a social drama first manifests itself as the breach of a norm, the infraction of a rule of morality, law, custom, or etiquette, in some public arena. This breach is seen as the expression of a deeper division of interests and loyalties than appears on the surface. The incident of breach may be deliberately, even calculatedly, contrived by a person or party disposed to demonstrate or challenge entrenched authority—for example, the Boston Tea Party— or emerge from a scene of heated feelings. Once visible, it can hardly be revoked. Whatever may be the case, a mounting crisis follows, a momentous juncture or turning point in the relations between components of a social field—at which seeming peace becomes overt conflict and covert antago- nisms become visible. Sides are taken, factions are formed, and unless the conflict can be sealed off quickly within a limited area of social interaction, there is a tendency for the breach to widen and spread until it coincides with some dominant cleavage in the widest set of relevant social relations to which the parties in conflict belong. (146)

It's usually in the "third phase" of social drama, a phase called by Turner "redress," that the conflict is "sealed off" and the "contagious spread of breach" (147) is halted. This phase marks a "liminal time, set apart from the ongoing business of quotidian life, when an interpretation *(Bedeutung)* is constructed to give the appearance of sense and order to the events leading up to and constituting the crisis" (152). Bruner would say there's an attempt to reconcile the extraordinary with the canonical; for both him and Turner, that reconciliation is made possible by narrative. The interpretation is conferred "by *looking back* over a temporal process: it is generated in the narrative constructed by lawmen and judges in the process of cross-examination from witnesses' evidence or by diviners from their intuitions into the responses of their clients as framed by their specific hermeneutic techniques" (153). And Turner concludes:

> The social drama, then, I regard as the experiential matrix from which the many dramas of cultural performance, beginning with redressive ritual and juridical procedures and eventually including oral and literary narrative, have been generated. Breach, crisis, and reintegrative or divisive outcomes provide the content of such later genres, redressive procedures their form. (154)

Turner's argument accords remarkably well with that of John E. Pfeiffer, who sees in the paintings from the Upper Paleolithic, preserved in the caves of Lascaux and elsewhere, the earliest of attempts to control a social crisis through the narratives[6] of visual art:

> The Upper Paleolithic saw a coming together of bands for mass hunting and other purposes, the formation of band societies, local and seasonal aggregations which put a strain on our limited capacity for getting along with one another. Judging by analogous situations in recent times, conflict soared under conditions of increased population density, and one of the most effective ways of keeping conflict under control was the invention of a special kind of coming together, ceremonial meetings [focused upon the art-decorated caves] designed specifically to promote group solidarity. (228)

But we needn't retreat to Lascaux or Altamira (or the recently discovered treasures of the Chauvet cave) for evidence of the early social function of narrative. There is general agreement among scholars of oral literature that epic, for example, serves an initiatory role: Eric Havelock in particular has stressed that the Homeric epics, taught by old to young, compiled "a digest of attitudes, beliefs, behavior patterns, and customs encoded in the exemplary actions of their heroes" (J. Foley 5)— heroes who suffered extraordinary ordeals the more dramatically to exemplify the canonical. Loyal Rue has recently emphasized the cohesive function of myths as a whole: "cultural myths are powerful means of cooperation because they function to integrate the domains of human interest into a comprehensible narrative unity and to safeguard the culture against an influx of meanings that might otherwise disrupt social coherence" (207).

It's precisely this capacity to "safeguard" traditional values that makes narrative so suspect today. But not only is value inseparable from all narrative ("Could we ever narrativize," asks Hayden White, "*without* moralizing?" [23]), but it is also, as I shall argue in the section that follows, most compelling both physiologically and cognitively in the period of what is now called early adolescence, when its auditors and readers are most susceptible to its "truth." This confirms, then, the assertions of Bruner and Turner, that narrative helps ensure the cohesiveness of a culture by bringing the potentially disruptive in line with social norms. But it's important to stress the difficulty of that enterprise—and the narrative ambiguity that it consequently encourages: like religious discourse, narrative may seem most efficacious and "special" when it can be pressed into the service of irreconcilably divergent interests; when it, in the words of Roy A. Rappaport, is "definitively understood by *no one*" (40).

And of course narrative—literature, more narrowly—has many other functions, a number of which I'll specify in the following section. The great range of those functions explains why most of my argument has been couched in the deep grammar ("narrative") of literary art. For "literature" should be understood as not simply a canon (or anticanon) of "great" (or "interesting") verbal work. It includes nonsense rhymes and fairy tales, popular song lyrics and supermarket novels, TV scripts and comic books. And its "audience" is as protean a creature: not only is it divisible into many different "cultures," which may or may not enjoy strong narrative links; it shows different needs and "competences" at different ages, at least in the literate West. Most recent academic discussion has focused upon the "cultural" divides and appropriations, including those of gender and class, that are so evident in the operations of all literary discourses. In the next section I concentrate on the functions of literature as they are demarcated by reader age: in the process, my case for the evolutionary origin of those functions will, I hope, be strengthened, and a necessary distinction among the three voices of literature—those of author, audience, and species—will finally be introduced. The voice of the species, I shall argue, is what we hear most resonantly in mimesis.

3

As early as two years of age, children can invent rudimentary narratives. Their first stories are not very coherent: action is elliptical and the import is obscure; "characters" often appear out of nowhere, participate in (or suffer through) one or two events, then vanish, or transmogrify into someone or something else, or initiate another series of actions, sometimes in contradiction to the first. These stories often have the appearance of crude palimpsests through which a number of potentially coherent narratives seem to be competing for elaboration at once. Evelyn Pitcher and Ernst Prelinger provide hundreds of specimens in their *Children*

Tell Stories, from which I reproduce one by a two-year-old boy and another by a two-year-old girl:

> "Stanley F.": Horsie went up the mountain. Then the horsie ran away through the woods. He gets lost. He came through a little bit of woods, but he got lost. Then he got through the woods and fly like a bird up in the sky. Then he fell and broke his knee. Then somebody shoot him. Then he flew like a bird and fell down and broke his other knee. (33)

> "Laurie W.": A kitty—he's not a bad boy. He didn't go to school. He went out the front door and banged it and it went to pieces. A long big turtle came. He splashed the kitty all broken. (37–38)

As they get older, children tell increasingly coherent stories, and more daring ones as well. Their "utilization and mastery of space" grow surer as the characters go out into "fantastic and abstract" locales; they begin to endow those characters with greater "internal complexity" as well as a more sensitive capacity to be affected by events; and they make significantly more inventive use of "fantasy and imagination" (159).[7] But by the age of five, when their stories seem to achieve full coherence, socialization has begun to curb invention: "Five-year-olds," writes Louise Bates Ames, "tend to have trouble in telling stories chiefly because of their strong drive to tell stories they already know, such as 'The Three Bears' " (393).

Two aspects stand out starkly in young children's stories, at least in those of the several hundred Connecticut preschoolers who have contributed to the meager studies that we have. Like the cartoons and fairy tales that fascinate children, they are filled with catastrophe—sometimes violent conflict—and they manifest gender differences in their tellers to an obviously high degree. "Even very young children," Ames observes, "tell . . . tales of violence and disaster for the most part with great relish" (356). Like the victims in the stories that I've quoted above, people and animals fall down, break their necks, get hit by choo-choo trains, get "hurt on a big cigarette lighter," crash, tumble, are bitten by horses and scratched by cats and stung by bees, go "boom," get shot and bumped and spanked, lose their fingers on railroad tracks. This stimulates much dark talk from Pitcher and Prelinger about "unconscious wishes striving for expression and fulfillment" (216–17), but a prosaic non-Freudian explanation seems to me the more plausible and preferable. In the recklessness of play (and with the heedlessness of inexperience), children are in fact often disaster-prone, but they can rehearse with "relish" real or imagined distresses for the same reason that adults enjoy, say, the movies of Bergman: they can have the pleasure of the emotions that accompany loss or injury while remaining certain that they will suffer the real effects of neither.[8] Their narratives are, in effect, rehearsals of possibility, rehearsals—very often amusingly extravagant ones—that are stimulated by imaginative rewards. They are preparations, quite obviously, for encounters not only with the guileless but ubiquitous hazards of the world but also with agents, both human and monstrous, whose interests oppose their tellers' own.

It's in these latter narratives that the sexes begin clearly to differentiate themselves, often in ways that "social conditioning" cannot very easily explain. Boys invent stories in which boys and men (except for Mommy's occasional appearance, female characters are rare) act violently against each other.[9] "Whereas the girl includes such characters as firemen, police, and farmers along with nurses and waitresses, the boys allude only to what men might do" (171). And what they do with improbable but rabid frequency is fight. After describing a bizarrely catastrophic end of the world (a house had come "over to the movie, and then crash again!"), a three-year-old "Upton S." concludes:

> Then another world came, and they fighted to another war. Then the war came into the house. And they had a big fight in the house. They knocked down the chairs and tables and candles. And then police came and put them in jail and they had to stay forever and ever. Then the war was all gone and then there was coming for night. (52–53)

Often, as here, boys' narratives "pit opposing forces in death": good and evil are matched in "organized warfare"; there is a concern that "bad witches" (among other wicked powers) be checked in their malevolence, and a "sense of duty" motivates the boy to take part (181, 202).

This is all in marked contrast to stories by young girls. Although the girl seems to take a much greater interest in the young boy's world than the boy takes in the girl's, her style of engagement with either arena is significantly dissimilar to the boy's. "Almost as many girls as boys speak of aggression," as Pitcher and Prelinger observe, "[but] there are differences in the quality of the described aggression" (177):

> Among the girls, even shooting is not so likely to be synonymous with violence or death. An Indian boy, in a gallant gesture, shoots a bear to get a coat for his girl friend—and he is promptly rebuked by another Indian, who says the bear is his friend. (First he kindly heeds a squirrel's request to spare his life, and decides not to kill a skunk because of his smell.) A horse shoots an owl with a gun, then they shake hands and become friends. (178)

Nor is death likely to be associated with warfare: often for the girl it is just "something that *happens*, with no particular association of good or bad" (182). And when an accident occurs, the girl's interest is not, as it is for the boy, upon "the calamity for its own sake," but rather upon cure and recovery (186). Indeed, the "theme of *Sociability*—a concern with friendship and pleasure from interpersonal relationships, a mention of friend, friendship, or friendliness—is more frequent among the girls, and indeed can so dominate a story that everyone must become friends" (204). As Carol Gilligan has famously suggested, the girl's sense of morality differs from the boy's: she is more "personally involved in her judgment of what is good or bad" (199), tending to see her characters, not as stereotypical Right- or Wrongdoers, but as vivid and realistic individuals with whose personalities and experiences she feels sympathy (170). Finally, while the boy is at home among vehicles and machines—rockets, trucks, fire engines—the girl finds her interest in "personal or household equipment" (173). She is early assuming the domestic robes (or shackles, if you will): "it is obviously the girl who markedly identifies with the female role of cook and hostess" (203), and it is only she who refers "to love, courtship, and marriage" (188).

If it is kindergarten, as Vivian Gussin Paley has declared, that is the "triumph of sexual self-stereotyping" (ix), the process has begun, if we may extrapolate from these studies, very early in the toddler years. And narratives, especially the mute Ur-narratives of developing consciousness, probably play a large role in this process: from their palimpsest of possibilities, children gradually sort out those strands best conducive to a stable sense of self. Of course the dominant (often sexist) narratives of their culture—narratives that, as I've suggested, have a genetic source—figure obviously and prominently in this enterprise; but it's the child's individual temperament and the conditions under which it develops that will stamp this self-fabrication with "personality." In any case, the child's "invented universe," half-borrowed, half-new, is the "matrix that provides the structures," in J. A. Appleyard's words, "in which [his or her] consciousness matures" (13).

When that universe becomes less an invented than a received set of possibilities and the child is no longer "player" but reader, socialization by the so-called wider world begins in narrative earnest. At school, reading becomes "an intensely social activity," what Appleyard calls "the collective task of absorbing the culture's lessons," by which children "slowly build up repertoires of the structures and motifs that are conventional" (48)—not only "in the world of literature" that widens before them but also in the culture that gives that world value. But at the same time that it inducts the child into mainstream-culture values, it is developing the capacities of minds predisposed for narrative (and hence moral) instruction. Narrative and its values are not *imposed* upon the child; there is complicity from the beginning on the part of a reader to construe the world in narrative terms. And not complicity only, but strong emotional incentives to do so: reading gives most children a great deal of pleasure—pleasure that persists into their teenage years. A 1979–80 U.S. survey of the National Assessment of Educational Progress reported that more than half the nine-year-olds included in its canvassing read for their enjoyment every day

(Appleyard 99). These are Nell's true "ludic" readers, the preadolescent boys and girls who get utterly "lost in a book."

What is the attraction of books at this age? It's not of course what professors of English emphasize: the ludic reader tends to inhabit a wholly transparent text. "You get the feeling you're not reading any more," one of Nell's older subjects reports, "you're not reading sentences, it's as if you are completely living inside the situation" (238). Like the Flaubert that Jonathan Culler describes, who reads (actually misreads) Shakespeare's *King Lear* in order to "set [himself] dreaming" (*Flaubert* 173–74), the ludic reader courts absorption and trance:

> One study of comic-book readers discovered that children who are fans (distinguished from moderate readers or those indifferent to comics) often could not even recall the plots of comic-book stories they had just read. What satisfied them apparently was being absorbed in a mood or "aura," escaping into a world where they could imagine themselves as powerful heroic figures. . . . Nell reports a vivid case of "reading gluttony": a text gobbler who speed read books hoping that he could forget them so as to be able to have exactly the same experience when he read them again. (Appleyard 86)

Theirs is the absorption of John Gardner's hypothetical book-bound brotherhood: "we have the queer experience of falling through the print on the page into something like a dream, an imaginary world so real and convincing that when we happen to be jerked out of it by a call from the kitchen or a knock at the door, we stare for an instant in befuddlement at the familiar room where we sat down, half an hour ago, with our book" (112–13).

That book, for the preadolescent, is for the most part undistinguished fare: it's usually a tale in a formula series of mystery and/or adventure. Bobbie Ann Mason has described how the discovery of the Bobbsey Twins books affected her at the age of eight: "It is my impression," she writes in *The Girl Sleuth,* "that I went straight to my favorite chair with a sack of hard candies and didn't get up for three years, after reading all forty of the series at least a dozen times each" (29). Her experience seems to be fairly typical, especially of young readers with high IQs: according to a number of surveys and studies prior to 1980, the so-called juvenile series—variously featuring Tom Swift, the Hardy Boys, Nancy Drew, as well as more recent heroes and heroines—comprise "the most popular books read by fifth, sixth, and seventh graders" (Appleyard 84). And, apparently, they are read again and again for the "aura" that they create. These are books in which the readers themselves occupy the center stage of the action, those in which it may be said that the reader's "voice" is most loudly heard.

The characters are merely types, defined more by action than an interior life; the plots are fairly simple and repetitive. In a sense, the "juveniles" are extremely conventional books, since, as Mason complains, from the perspective of adulthood, they merely perpetuate naively the sexist, racist, and materialist values of a white upper-middle-class culture. But they are unusual in that their central figures are always "at least psychologically parentless" (Appleyard 76), apparently a device by which each reader is invited emotionally into the narrative. Their value lies in their offering that reader an imaginative avenue of autonomy and agency. The prominence of a single archetype in these books—"of the powerful or clever hero or heroine"—suggests, as Appleyard has persuasively argued, "that a main reward of reading fictional stories at this age is to satisfy the need to imagine oneself as the central figure who by competence and initiative can solve the problems of a disordered world" (59). Not only is the reader, then, being educated in the mainstream culture's values; he or she is emotionally rehearsing a role in the management of "social dramas." The preadolescent reader is making a transition from "a world organized largely as a dream to a world imagined in terms of action" (Appleyard 71), and is projectively seeking a place there.

Once having passed into adolescence itself, the reader still wants to be "involved" in fiction but also demands of it two other things: it must be "realistic" (to describe it with his or her word), and it must stimulate the reader to "think." As we would expect of fiction that "involves" an adolescent, favorite books are those in which gender differences are most marked and which include sensitive protagonists of the same sex as the reader and what Nell calls "positive themes" (121).[10] Although Appleyard interprets the need for "realism" as an indication of the reader's shift from "participant" to "onlooker," from whose vantage reading "is a process of attending to the representation of imagined events and of evaluating their significance and the adequacy of their representation" (108), the words of his respondents suggest a rather different possibility. "A story is praised," Appleyard observes, "because it is 'true,' 'normal,' 'like how people really act,' 'valid,' 'something that's not like a fantasy'" (107). And one student notes, "That's what I like about Dickens. For example, in *David Copperfield* you get . . . you can identify with him because you know all his feelings and how he identifies with each situation" (108). Clearly, the demand for "realism" is simply another way of expressing the adolescent's continued wish for an emotionally engaged role. Appleyard prepares us for this conclusion toward the end of his discussion of preadolescent readers:

> Their growing self-consciousness about their own inner states, their contra-
> dictory and unresolved feelings, and their confused thoughts find no mirror
> in the underdeveloped characters of adventure stories, certainly not in the
> eternal juveniles of the series books. So they look for stories about people
> who are not simply good or bad, stories about intentions and motives and

points of view and how they might conflict even in well-meaning people. In short, their own role as readers changes and the attitudes toward stories that satisfied them as juveniles no longer work for them as adolescents. (87)

They now need protagonists who share their confusions, not so much because they have come to occupy a spectatorial point of view but because such protagonists draw them into the world of the book.

It is usually *after* they have entered and left that world that adolescent readers begin to "think." Again, what is apparently implied by that word has little to do with aesthetic contemplation: "the most obvious meaning," writes Appleyard, "is that the reader reflects about the characters, their motives and feelings, and how these do or do not resemble his or her own motives and feelings" (111). But, even more important, the reader reflects upon the writer's role in the mediation of this process. Whereas younger readers show little interest in the writers of their books (who created the Bobbsey Twins?), adolescents discover that their books have authors, and "begin to think of the writer as someone like themselves, with a point of view, speaking out of his or her experience, saying something to the reader about the way the world is" (Appleyard 119). Indeed, as most teachers of adolescents can attest, for them much of the "interpretive" process is simply the recovery (or imputation) of what the author "says." For all the rebelliousness of the teenage years, adolescents are humbly deferential before the writer; and his or her voice—whether inferred or overheard, in asides, in prefaces, in the letters that modern editors append conveniently to their texts—very quickly tends to become their primary interpretive authority.

Probably at no other stage in a reader's maturation is the writer as shaman a more powerful myth. This is less obvious today among American teenagers than it was twenty or thirty years ago—maybe because today's adolescents seem to read less for pleasure than their own teachers did during their tempestuous Sturm und Drang. A film like Oliver Stone's *The Doors* recalls the fervor of being young— and a reader—in 1965: then it was de rigueur for all adolescent visionaries to apprentice themselves to the shamans of the Word, to Jack Kerouac or Arthur Rimbaud. Today when a critic like Charles Altieri pleads for the recovery of "the *force* that writers intend by their efforts as artists and interpreters of action" (1), he is speaking on behalf (though he may be appalled to learn it) of youth like Jim Morrison everywhere.

"Reading for enjoyment," Appleyard writes, "typically reaches a peak in the junior-high-school years and drops steadily from the ninth grade onward" (99). He offers no explanation for this provocative phenomenon, perhaps because he sees it as a self-evident consequence of the anti-intellectualism of his subjects' culture and of a system of education, produced by that culture, that tends to equate learning with coercion. But it may useful to put his findings within a broader context, to integrate them within the evolutionary perspective that informs the central argument of this book. To do so is of course both risky and speculative, since most of the research (certainly all of the interviews) from which Appleyard has drawn his general conclusions reflect trends among American readers from about the middle of the present century. But because man (including the American adolescent) has grown no new emotions since Homer's day, it seems legitimate to extrapolate from the experience of his readers to speculate that narrative may have generally an age-sensitive appeal. Such an extrapolation seems to me all the more legitimate in light of the transgressive practices of the "ludic reader": what Appleyard suggests gives young readers pleasure are books that would excite most teachers' dismay. Comic books and Nancy Drew mysteries, *Love Story* and *Brian's Song*—these belong to the popular underworld, despised and neglected by the trustees of literature, and, if they survive and continue to appeal to readers, they do so *contra culturam*.

Narrative seems to be experienced as most valuable and absorbing precisely at the point when, in "primitive" cultures, the child becomes woman or man. Just prior to that point, narrative enthralls him or her, as we've seen, as a participant, inviting reader (or listener) into an imaginative world in which ordeals are suffered in order to safeguard conventional values under siege. Then, at or near the point of graduation, when the "preadolescent" crosses the pubertal divide, the participant also seeks actively the counsel of a teacher, a wise man or shaman who may direct his or her steps on the road to ethical wisdom. It seems unlikely to be pure accident that readers mature in this way. Nor is it coincidental that reading for pleasure often declines in the adolescent years, sometimes dropping off further in later life (Nell 24), or even ceasing altogether (Appleyard 181). Like most other life-sustaining human behaviors, reading or storytelling is probably linked to a general genetic program of development, a program that encourages the behavior when most efficacious, allows it to lapse when unneeded. In other words, humans are "wired" not only for narrative comprehension but also for the emotionally induced reception of narrative—and the cultural enfranchisement that it makes possible—at a "sensitive" point in their lives.

Which is not, of course, to argue that narrative is simply a tool of enculturation. Like many other adaptive mechanisms, narrative seems to serve collateral functions, if in elusively covert ways. As I've suggested in my discussion of the preschool child, narrative may be instrumental, through its "scenario-spinning" capacities, in the conceptual stabilization of early selfhood. Schank has emphasized its age-independent value in encoding information for storage in memory. Even the literary theorists whom I earlier cited offer plausible explanations of its power and appeal. If it is received with less pleasure in adulthood than in youth, it is respected much more seriously for the provocativeness of its "display." And sometimes, in fact, for the older "ludic reader," it continues to exert its absorptive spell.

The adult's reading pleasure, however diminished, persists because of the very versatility of literature. Adults are, to quote Appleyard, "pragmatic" readers, seeking to satisfy often disparate interests, and so it should not be surprising that their diet is varied, ranging from Stephen Duck ("The Thresher Poet") to (he needs no introduction) Stephen King. Nell reports that, among his experimental subjects, it was a doctoral candidate writing a dissertation in English who read the highest percentage of "trash" (5). He therefore concludes that the "elitist" distinction between "lowbrow" and "highbrow" classes of readers does not, in effect, exist. Adults may read to reinhabit old stereotypes; to court new, perhaps socially inhibited sensations; to exercise their meaning-making tact and ingenuity; to "comfort" themselves, as Appleyard suggests, with images of experience and "wisdom" (15). On the whole, however, for the pleasure-seeking reader, the "trash" appears to predominate—and does so for psychological reasons. "For three of [my] four discussants," Nell writes,

> fear is an especially salient emotion—fear of social and sexual rejection, of maltreatment, and of separation from the sources of security. For them, one of the principal uses of reading is for the fine control of fear, in order to master it by experiencing its gooseflesh but not its terror, to know that the fear is self-induced and under one's own entire control. They explore these issues indirectly, with little insight, but at length. (244)

Sadly but not surprisingly, the majority of these fearful readers are women, of the so-called introverted type (Appleyard 155, Nell 254). From a study of such readers in a midwestern city, Janice A. Radway concluded that it was not only the thrill of print-inspired gooseflesh but also the tug of consoling fantasy that addicted them to the romances they consumed. These books, the familiar bodice-rippers of supermarket fame, all promise their consumer that, "if she learns to read male behavior successfully, she will find that her needs for fatherly protection, motherly care, and passionate adult love will be satisfied perfectly" (149).

Ironically, the anxieties that are palliated in such fantasies seem exacerbated by much "serious" modern literature, and the common reader often hastens from it in retreat. "It may be," as Appleyard observes, "not only their own problems that adult readers want to turn away from, but also the kind of fiction that, with its complicated narrative methodology, ironic perspective, and lack of clear resolution, makes the problems it deals with seem as intractable as those of readers' own real lives" (165). The "skepticism to which our adult sophistication condemns us is wearying": we "long for safe places," Nell aptly adds—"a love we can entirely trust, a truth we can entirely believe" (56). Most readers for pleasure listen for voices of assurance: voices that assure because they are familiar ones, speaking from within the trite but consoling fantasies of the self or from within the wells of shamanic wisdom.

But some attend to neither of these voices. Significantly, Appleyard seems to dwell upon the response of a fifty-year-old teacher of literature, a man who reads, in his own suggestive phrase, for "records of human experience." He is "fascinated" by the ways in which literary works are connected to the lives of their authors, but he seems most preoccupied by what he, those authors, and the rest of the world share. Appleyard quotes him at length:

> I don't read literature for wisdom, as I once did. I think a lot of undergraduates become English majors because they have this feeling that novels and poems can teach them about life or change the quality of their moral experience better than other things can. And I find that to be less and less true. . . . There's some way that I think that . . . I feel that . . . I've really become much more . . . conscious of the fallibility of an author. (172)

He counsels, on the other hand, a different way of reading: "I would connect the story with [the author's] life, but I would also enjoy it . . . in a way that I don't think people can do very well, if they haven't had [a similar] experience, or if they haven't set up some kind of sensibility that would respond to it" (173). And so, concludes Appleyard, "though the author of a work of fiction may be no source of wisdom about the world for this reader, the work itself is a record of human experience that moves him because he can recognize himself, even his fallibility, in it" (173). This is a reader attending to the voice of the species—the voice, I've suggested, of mimesis.

To claim today a mimetic dimension for literature will strike many, of course, as naive: structuralism exposed that particular fallacy. For Barthes, for example, the function of narrative was never "to 'represent'"; it was "to constitute a spectacle still very enigmatic for us but in any case not of a mimetic order" (294). Like the Marxists for whom, say, the realistic novel is merely a concatenation of "signifying systems"—"linguistic, literary, semiotic" (Belsey 49)—Barthes dismisses literary referentiality as merely the "babble" of the stereotypes and *idées reçues* that make up a particular and quite arbitrary "code." It should be clear by everything I have said up to this point how profoundly I disagree—or, perhaps more accurately, how mistaken I believe Barthes (and his disciples) to be in assuming a discontinuity between "intelligibility" and mimesis (see Barthes 294 n). "Codes" there are, of course, and "signifying systems," but they are all bound up intimately with both the social dynamics and the cognitive practices that are more or less common to all human beings. In one very important sense I agree that it is not the function of literature to "represent": mimesis as a record, more or less "factual," of "states of affairs" in the actual world (as the imperfect "copying" that Plato decried) plays only a trivial role in literary representation. As Auerbach demonstrated a full fifty years ago, "reality" in literature embraces gods and demons, offers unimpeded access to human consciousness that interlocutors in the "real world" can never know. What is "real" in mimesis is not the factual; it is what Aristotle called, with a kind of technicality made intelligible by the context of his philosophical system, the "universal."

The Greek word for poet (*poiētēs*) means "maker," and, for Aristotle, art imitates nature (as James Joyce realized) by producing a structure, as nature does. Anticipating Jung's archetypes by some two thousand years, Aristotle contended that form is immanent in all materiality, that all of life, including human life, evolves toward fulfillment of its "entelechy" or purpose, through fruition of which it achieves form. So, too, the poet's conception, which comes into being as artful structure. But it can achieve that structure, its formal coherence, only by attaining cognitive significance. John D. Boyd puts the matter succinctly in *The Function of Mimesis and Its Decline*:

> *What is made* can be coherent only in being a *thing of meaning*. . . . Only with difficulty can they be spoken of in relative isolation. Attempts to speak of them by categorical application of Aristotle's hylomorphism, as "matter" and "form," as what is determined and what determines the other, tend to confuse a complicated situation. In some instances this has led to the fallacy that separates "form" and "content" in different ways, reflecting on the one hand the Platonic concept of imitation as "copying," and on the other the formalism of T. E. Hulme and the formalism which some find in the Chicago Aristotelians. If one does wish to speak of matter and form in a poem or play, it can only be by way of analogy. The cognitive and structural elements of mimesis both determine and are determined by one another. (131–32)

What mimesis then achieves, in Richard Courtney's words, is "a double but not a copy" of the world (42), germinating from the structures of human life[11] and finding its entelechy in what Roger Frye used to call (though with different import) "significant form." Because its object is *human* life ("those who represent," we read in *The Poetics*, "represent people in action" [2]), its province is neither the factual nor the reportorial but what Aristotle calls appropriately the "universal." "A universal," he explains, "is the sort of thing that a certain kind of person may well say or do in accordance with probability or necessity" (12).

With one important change, we may adopt such notions for all representational literary art: its *province* need not confine itself to the "universal," but its *intelligibility* wholly depends on it. Art may violate Aristotelian decorum and show us, in Clytaemnestra, Medea, or Hedda Gabler, what the *Poetics* finds improbable, a "manly" woman (19), but the actions of such a character are both intelligible and significant because they are read, as it were, through the scrim of its "kind," defined by sex, age, and (in both the widest and the narrowest senses of the word) occasion.

Such a formulation answers the objections of critics like Bradley Berke: "It should be obvious," Berke writes in his *Tragic Thought and the Grammar of Tragic Myth*, "that any conception of mimesis as the imitation or representation, in explicit terms, of 'normal' or 'probable' characters, actions, or situations is totally inadequate. One does not meet a Hercules or a Siegfried every day in the street, nor does one hear of parricides, of incests, or even of saintly acts very often" (23). But even an "improbable" character may behave with probability, and, when it doesn't, the departures are understood *by reference to the probable.*

To take Siegfried as an example (I assume Wagner's character is meant): Like men everywhere in so-called primitive cultures, Siegfried is a weapon-maker and a hunter; like the young in such cultures, he shows his valor by doing extraordinary "deeds"; with Mime he insists upon the privileges of rank, privileges that accrue (as they do for modern adolescents) to both his physical skills and good looks; with other men of worth he declares a *Blut-Brüderschaft*, the sign of a bonding in loyal allegiance; and so on. In explanation of his less "universal" behaviors, we may of course repair to Wagner's culture. Siegfried's fidelity to Brünnhilde is of a High Romantic kind, violated (probabilistically?) by a supernatural potion that sends him into the arms (via a familiar late-nineteenth-century conceit) of the dark and undeserving Other Woman. And his behavior never rebukes our sense of the probable even when he hears directives in bird song: that song propels him (appropriately, after a *rite de passage*) to a mate and not, sobered, home to Mime, there to apologize for his insensitivity toward a dwarf. When, on the other hand, he behaves *improbably*, showing supernatural strength and skill, for example, it is by reference to *human* powers that his extraordinary gifts are made intelligible—and significant.

"We all have a sense of the probable," writes Gardner (117). It's a sense that arises from those paradigm scenarios that educate the young in the practices of their culture, but it's also a sense that is easily enlarged by cultural encounters for which they are pedagogically unprepared. Not only can other cultures be addressed through the biogrammatical regularities that are universal in human life (as the example of Siegfried suggests); they can be understood through the operations of what Tooby and Cosmides call the "human metaculture":

> There is certainly cultural and individual variability in the exact forms of adult mental organization that emerge through development, but these are all expressions of what might be called a single human metaculture. All humans tend to impose on the world a common encompassing conceptual organization, made possible by universal mechanisms operating on the recurrent features of human life. This is a central reality of human life and is necessary to explain how humans can communicate with each other, learn the culture they are born into, understand the meaning of others' acts,

imitate each other, adopt the cultural practices of others, and operate in a coordinated way with others in the social world they inhabit. (91)

Earlier, I called this "conceptual organization" a capacity for narrativity: without such a capacity, neither human life nor human art could exist. And because art demands its ceaseless operation, all literature, as Boyd writes, is "essentially mimetic" (xvii), relying as it does upon the reader's attempt to descry an intelligibility in human affairs. The narrative of action does this most obviously, in equating "being alive," as Leitch observes, "with a sequence of purposive, discrete, consequential, morally significant decisions" (143). But narratives of stasis extend as irresistible an invitation, insofar as they concern (as, to be "tellable," they must) human intelligences reflecting with more or less typicality upon an inescapably anthropocentric scene.

And what are the fruits of mimesis? Why does Appleyard's interviewee find more pleasure in its spectacle than in the offerings of authorial wisdom? Most theorists are inclined to attribute "knowledge" to narrative, that generatrix of representation: W. J. T. Mitchell gestures toward this tendency when he observes, in his brief foreword to On Narrative, that "the idea of narrative seems, as several contributors to these pages note, to be repossessing its archaic sense as *gnārus* and *gnosis*, a mode of knowledge emerging from action, a knowledge which is embedded not just in the stories we tell our children or to while away our leisure but in the orders by which we live our lives" (ix–x). But "knowledge" may be a misleading word. Leitch points out that inconclusive narratives, those of soap opera, for instance, in which "synthesis or integration is indefinitely withheld" (75), are as absorbing as those with a beginning, middle, and end. In them, certainty recedes as twists of plot multiply, thereby leaving Leitch to conclude that "narrative may be only incidentally a mode of analytic or semiotic knowledge" (75). But unarguably it is a mode of some cognitive reward. Maybe the practicing novelist can make the necessary distinction: fiction, writes Gardner, "deals in understanding, not knowledge" (135).

> Though the distinction between knowledge and understanding may seem abstruse, it is one we recognize in everyday speech: I can "understand" you, having *felt* the coherence of your speech, gestures, and behavior, but we all agree that no human being can really "know" another one. If I say I "know" you, I mean I know some of the classifications which help to identify you: your name, features, occupation, age, religious persuasion, and so on. (139)

As Gardner is suggesting, narrative "understanding" is (to use my own word) a more or less intuitive process. He best illustrates that process when he describes a parlor game that was a favorite of the Iowa Writers' Workshop members back in the 1950s. Called "Smoke," its object was to stimulate questions about an unnamed figure until his or her identity was finally revealed. The most important rule was that the possibilities had to be narrowed through metaphor: "What kind of smoke are you?" "What kind of weather are you?" "What kind of insect?" The answers, says Gardner, built "a stronger and stronger feeling of the character" (118) until the name was shouted out. And he adds: "There is obviously no way to play this game with the reasoning faculty, since it depends on unconscious associations or intuition; and what the game proves conclusively for everyone playing is that our associations are remarkably similar" (118–19).

It also "proves," of course, that such an understanding, accessed by metaphor (the computer term seems impersonally appropriate in this context), draws heavily upon right-hemisphere cognition. As I argued previously in Chapter 3, narrative is a *bi*hemispheric mode of grasping the world, engaging both the verbal sophistication of the left hemisphere and the holistic faculties of the right. What is even more germane to our present discussion is that narrative as a purely *imaginative* way of thinking seems unmanageable for that hemisphere specialized in analytical thought. Ellen Winner has summarized the evidence for narrative dysfunction in right-hemisphere-impaired subjects. They show, she says, "an unwillingness to accept [a] story on its own terms and to respect the boundary between fiction and life":

> For instance, upon hearing a story about a fireman, one patient insisted that the story was "incorrect." The reason given for this odd statement was that the story mentioned an alleyway, and alleyways, he explained, could not be located near a firehouse. Similarly, commenting on a part of the story describing a little girl who sneaked a ride on the fire engine, the patient insisted that this was an impossible occurrence. (344–45)

Like a French neoclassical critic adhering fanatically to "the rules," such a patient takes the mimetic for the "factually" referential instead of recognizing it as the mode in which behavioral probability necessarily plays the largest part. To see it as the latter is, in effect, to acknowledge that mimesis (quite literally) exacts full engagement of the mind. And how crucial is such engagement for human understanding is suggested by another set of findings that Winner cites:

> In one story, a boss decided to give a lazy hired hand a raise. While normal people as well as those with left hemisphere damage found such a statement odd and recognized that it was at variance with the description of the employee as lazy, those with right hemisphere damage did not react in this way. Moreover, in retelling the story, they related such elements as faithfully as they did the canonical elements of the story. (345)

In short, what Gardner calls "understanding," which he sees, I think properly, as the most valuable effect of mimesis, is a process that exercises the whole of a reader's mental life. As such, it offers satisfactions—not least of which is the temporary demotion of the reigning verbal self—that are denied to more purely analytical thought.[12] At the same time, it encourages the sympathetic sharing of other lives; more specifically and importantly, it encourages sympathy and respect for the "improbably" *possible*, for the extraordinary "Trouble" of aberrant humanity that disturbs the canons of its world.[13] Ibsen's Hedda acquires intelligibility and significance by being seen through the lens of the probable; her actions acquire pathos (if they do for the spectator) by the sympathies they excite for her fate. And this enlargement of what David Novitz calls "empathic belief" (120) seems also to accompany the creative act. Again, I turn to the writer himself for an account of how character is conceived:

> Much of what a writer learns he learns simply by imitation. Making up a scene, he asks himself at every step, "Would she really say that?" or "Would he really throw the shoe?" He plays the scene through in his imagination, taking all the parts, being absolutely fair to everyone involved (mimicking each in turn, as Aristotle pointed out, and never sinking to stereotype for even the most minor characters), and when he finishes the scene he understands by sympathetic imitation what each character has done throughout and why the fight, or accident, or whatever, developed as it did. (Gardner 109)

As this passage makes clear, such a process is more a matter of *discovering* motivation than of inventing (I return to Leitch's phrase) "intentionally intelligible" characters. The successive drafts through which most writers go (Gardner mentions Tolstoy's work on *Anna Karenina*; we could also mention Shakespeare's on *Hamlet* [Sams]) often attest to the intuitive nature of this process, and the sometimes puzzling judgments writers make of their characters suggest how tenuously it is linked to "intentionality." Joyce may have intended Buck Mulligan to be tiresome, but many readers find Stephen to be more so; when Racine informs us in his preface to *Phèdre* that "vice" is in that play "painted in colours which render its deformity recognizable and hateful" (23), we're led to suspect him either of disingenuousness or of an unaccountable naïveté. If the teller can with confidence be separated from the tale, it's the latter that, as Lawrence said, should have our trust.

Without it, readers' sympathies are constricted or misdirected, and what narrative does best is to educate those sympathies. It can induct those readers into a human scene that is free, in the words of the aesthetician Ivy Campbell-Fisher (as quoted in Susanne Langer's masterwork, *Mind*), of distracting "entanglements with contingency" (88). Understanding is easier in literature than in life because the reader has been relieved of physical involvement and can rehearse the dynamics of human transactions with both emotional intensity and detachment. Another writer, Murdoch, has put literature, for this reason, at the center of all cultural practice: "The most essential and fundamental aspect of culture," she writes in *The Sovereignty of Good*, "is the study of literature, since this is an education in how to picture and understand human situations" (34).

In the "purest" of narratives (that is, those that resist "knowledge," which we may define for our purposes as the *conceptualization* of understanding) the reader may enjoy a kind of negative capability, moving imaginatively and sympathetically from ego to ego, "without any irritable reaching after fact or reason." Such mobility may offer the keenest of pleasures, unbinding him or her from the moral contract and permitting the expression, within the dreamtime of reading, of those crudities of which circumspection robs the selfish gene. So we may account for the surprising confessions of some of our most ethically high-minded of writers and readers—of Shaw, for example, on *Man and Superman*. "All my characters," he writes, "pleasant and unpleasant,"

> are all right from their several points of view; and their points of view are, for the dramatic moment, mine also. This may puzzle the people who believe that there is such a thing as an absolutely right point of view, usually their own. It may seem to them that nobody who doubts this can be in a state of grace. However that may be, it is certainly true that nobody who agrees with them can possibly be a dramatist, or indeed anything else that turns upon a knowledge of mankind. Hence it has been pointed out that Shakespear had no conscience. Neither have I, in that sense. (26–27)

To write—and to read—"without conscience" is to apprehend the represented world quintessentially as an adult. Appleyard defines this best: "what is most characteristic about mature adult thinking is that it is grounded in polarities of experience, that it juggles contingencies and partial truths, that it deals in fragile and provisional certainties, and that it therefore has a dialectical character rather than the logical clarity of formal-operational thinking" (175).

But all dialectic, of course, tends toward synthesis, and narrative can be "pure" in only a hypothetical sense. Few writers and still fewer readers can resist the temptation to conceptualize, especially in the face of a verbal art. Verbal processing is predominantly a left-hemisphere function, perhaps dooming literature to ratiocination, even to that tedious intellectual aridity exhaled by most contemporary literary "theory." But whatever the ultimate neurological connections, narrative inevitably invites generalization, and does so, most simply, as Appleyard suggests, "because the structure of narrative mimics the quest for meaning" (174). To "move" from beginning to end is to imply, at least to the mind psychologically "set" for significance, some sort of sense or rationale to the movement: an answer to the question "Why?" Consequently, narrative is, as narratologists have argued, "metonomy in the search to become metaphor" (Brooks, *Reading* 106). Such a search is a veering toward the Scylla of mimesis, toward the dark cave of knowledge that arrests understanding, transforming display into authorial oracularity, bihemisphericity into laterality. This is obviously the course of the interpretive act, and suggests why every "reading" of a literary text is always already a misreading.

If its Scylla is knowledge, the Charybdis of mimesis (as Kant would have inferred) is the inarticulate sublime. Literature as one of the "extraordinary" experiences, inciting not knowledge but ecstasy and trance: this represents, for more than one writer and reader, a retreat from both the impoverishments of conceptualization and the often frustrating elusiveness of understanding. Such a literature (as in Artaud's theater) respects the verbal for its somatic effects, seeking through expletive and incantation and pure noise and song, through immersion in the rhythms and textures of poetry or in an exalted and hypnagogic prose, a return to what John Eccles calls the "animal mind," to that proleptic right-hemispheric processing that predates all sophisticated thought. Here Dionysus is the presiding genius; his Boswell, Longinus and his critical line. It's on the whole a peculiarly "decadent" phenomenon, exercising an appeal born of despair over Homo's inability to make sense of its own meaning-making mind. As such, it is the province of the névrosés of literature, of those sophisticated primitives so enthralling to youth and, not uncommonly, to the critics of academe. Its prototypical hero is obviously Des Esseintes, the artist/reader of Huysmans's Au rebours who triumphs as an artisan with his orgue à bouche and who thrills to the deconstructive wit of Mallarmé. His progeny in the twentieth century is, to put it mildly, legion: and to the aestheticizing of narrative for which it is responsible we owe most that is antithetical to mimesis.

But this last formulation may not be quite accurate: it's the motive behind the aesthetic impulse that's most responsible for that hostility. As our century gropes its way to a deconstructive close, skepticism about all knowledge has lain waste to the concept, if indeed not the practice, of what is usually called representational art. In the foregoing, I have suggested that that skepticism is misplaced: that it is the product of a kind of thinking about the "real" that has been derived uncritically from Platonic categories and so is subject, as literary theorists do not tire of pointing out, to charges of "naive essentialism." Where the real resides is between the display of a text and the narrativity of the attentive subject; there the probable erects its sense-making coordinates to effect an understanding akin to knowledge and rapture but ultimately subtending and transcending both.

But "understanding," admittedly, needs further refinement. Because it entails, as Gardner points out, essentially affective apprehension, it is, like all other artifacts of emotion, a highly "situation-dependent" phenomenon. And so the best way to delimit its elusive dynamics is by reference to those arenas of imaginative experience that stand in greatest contrast to each other. For the West, that means tragedy and comedy.

5

Tragedy: The Ape Gets Serious

[Tragedy] shows us the greatest misfortune, not as an exception, not as something occasioned by rare circumstances or monstrous characters, but as arising easily and of itself out of the actions and characters of men, indeed almost as essential to them, and thus brings it terribly near to us.
—Arthur Schopenhauer, *The World as Will and Idea*

In "Shakespeare in the Bush," the 1966 article that the textbooks call a "classic of anthropology," Laura Bohannan sets out to show—again in the textbook phrase—"the way in which different cultures provide distinct and separate worlds of meaning for those who have learned to live by them" (Spradley and McCurdy 21). At first armed with the confidence that "human nature is pretty much the same the whole world over," Bohannan had resolved to "prove *Hamlet* universally intelligible" (Bohannan 21, 23) by telling its plot to the Tiv, the tribe that she and her husband, Paul, describe in their contribution to the ethnographic survey of Africa, published by the International African Institute, as "by far the largest pagan tribe in Northern Nigeria" (Bohannan and Bohannan 9). The undertaking is a failure: midway through the recital, Bohannan concludes that, although *Hamlet* is obviously "a good story" to her listeners, their corrections, embellishments, and typically Tivian interpretations make it "no longer . . . quite the same story" to her (Bohannan 29).

Indeed, much is unrecognizable. Having no belief, as Bohannan puts it, "in the survival after death of any individuating part of the personality" (25), the Tiv must impute old Hamlet's reappearance, as well as Hamlet's madness and Ophelia's drowning, to witchcraft ("Only witches can make people drown. Water itself can't hurt anything. It is merely something one drinks and bathes in" [Bohannan 29]). Happy polygynists, they are astounded by old Hamlet's having had only one wife ("How . . . can he brew beer and prepare food for all his guests?"), and they exclaim with satisfaction when they hear of Claudius's marriage to Gertrude, for in their country also "the younger brother marries the elder brother's widow and becomes the father of his children" (Bohannan 25, 24). It's obvious to them that it was Laertes himself who practiced sorcery on his own sister, since selling her body to the witches was his only way of covering his fines for brawling and of settling his gambling losses in Paris. *Hamlet*, they conclude, is not unintelligible, just badly in need of correct interpretation, and when next Bohannan tells the Tiv "more stories" of her country, she must allow the elders, to whom *Hamlet* has been recounted, to instruct her "in their true meaning, so that when you return to your own land your elders will see that you have not been sitting in the bush, but among those who knew things and who taught you wisdom" (Bohannan 31).

Part of the problem is, of course, the smugness that infuses those last few lines. Inviting the elders of the Tiv to interpret *Hamlet* is a little like inviting Polonius to do so: there is a general air of consternation that one so young as the eponymous hero is undertaking to set things right. (Among the Tiv that consternation is deepened by perplexity, since they cannot understand, as Polonius can, the Anglo-Saxon respect for the warrior, around whom, according to Tacitus at least, cohered the English ancestral tribes.) In some respects—European monogamy, for example— the Tiv are wrestling with something of a departure from the more universal cultural norm; in others, such as their "pagan" skepticism about a Catholic afterlife, they are closer to the beliefs of the American undergraduate than the latter are to the pieties of the Renaissance. In general, as this last remark may suggest, one of the largest stumbling blocks is the difference in "rational" systems that inform the Tiv and Shakespearean worldviews. For the post-Petrarchan Shakespeare one can plausibly go "Mad for . . . love" (2.1.82); for the Tiv "only witchcraft can make anyone mad, unless, of course, one sees the beings that lurk in the forest" (Bohannan 27).

Dan Lloyd's previously met hypotheses have prepared us for this difference: "if cognition is culturally relative, that relativity will be more conspicuous in styles of explicitly rational thought" (230). More conspicuous, that is, than in styles of narrativity. And, in fact, when we set the Tiv's narrativic understanding next to Shakespeare's, we are more apt to be struck by their overlap than by the contrasting sense of their constructing "distinct and separate worlds": what is "probable" for the Tiv in narrativic terms is in large part probable for the Elizabethans. We can begin with the obvious things shared between them, things that, however obvious, are nevertheless profound.[1] The Tiv and the Elizabethans both communicate in a language, and, though different, both languages are translatable by virtue of referential identities and near-identities (a tree is a tree in Tivland as well as in Hamlet's Denmark) and of regularities that are inherent in all human grammars. Both peoples are sensitive to extraverbal communication (and so Bohannan can detect in the tone of one of her listeners "that insincere, but courteous, agreement one extends to the fancies of the young, ignorant, and superstitious" [26]). As that parenthesis implies, their psychological systems are exactly the same: they both share a universal "folk psychology" that attributes desires, beliefs, and intentions to human beings, and both assume that persons are usually "readable" in consistent and understandable ways. (Indeed, if our remark about the Tiv's "smugness" is accurate, they are readable largely in *identical* ways.) Finally, both regard the emotions with profound respect, as providing, as de Sousa suggests that they do, the "framework" within which the world is perceived. "Tiv think (*ben*)," write the Bohannans, "perceive or understand (*kav*), and know (*fa*) with the heart (*ishima*)" (82).

Their hearts dispose them to familiar expectations—that is to say, to bio-grammatical ones. They take it for granted that Shakespeare's Denmark, like the compounds of Tivland, is under the political sway of its "elders"; that those elders are (more or less perceptibly rank-ordered) males; that the most influential among them "should be a man of sincerity and integrity" but that he may very well have attained to eminence "through force of character, intimidation, a talent for intrigue and bribery"; that he is a man to be as much feared as respected; and that "the industry, general behavior, cleanliness, and the whole moral atmosphere" of his compound/kingdom "depend to a large extent on [his] character" (Bohannan and Bohannan 32, 18)—or, as Shakespeare puts it, majesty "is a massy wheel / Fix'd on the summit of the highest mount / To whose huge spokes ten thousand lesser things / Are mortis'd and adjoin'd" (3.3.17–20). Women they expect—and find—to play a negligible role in Elsinore's political life: it's the men who (like Claudius) furnish "safe conduct to passers-through," who act "as arbitrators in quarrels within their lineage and between strangers," who sit "on moots," and who act "as spokesmen, representatives, and leaders in external affairs and, as unusually influential elders, in all internal affairs" (Bohannan and Bohannan 36). It's the men, too, who set the marriage laws, forbidding certain unions (as Polonius forbids that between Ophelia and Hamlet), though they are sometimes defied by headstrong youth (Bohannan and Bohannan 28).

At one point during Bohannan's recital, she is enjoined to respect the "ge-nealogical details" of her account (24); to the Tiv, as in fact to Hamlet himself, kin are supremely important. Their living arrangements visibly calibrate that importance: "A man lives closer to his full brother than he does to his half-brother, and closer to his half-brother than to his father's brother's son" (Bohannan and Bohannan 17). Enmity, too, "is stated in genealogical terms": "To strike a close agnate is a moral offence for which one's agnates may justifiably bewitch one. To get into a fight with a non-Tiv is sometimes foolhardy, but certainly not immoral" (Bohannan and Bohannan 25, 26). Consequently, Bohannan can rely on their being suitably shocked by Claudius's fratricide (25). (She is caught off-guard by their disapproval of Hamlet's scolding of Gertrude—an understandable reaction on their part, especially since her narrative fails to foreground the play's Hamletic point of view.) And nowhere do the Tiv ever question the revenge motif of the play: revenge is a perfectly natural response to the unprovoked killing of kin,[2] although "Hamlet [should] have called the elders to settle the matter," since affairs of such importance are "not for youngsters" (Bohannan 28, 24).

As for the world outside that of close-kin ties, it is, morally, of more slippery terrain. "Age-mates"—Hamlet and Horatio are Shakespeare's equivalents, as well as Rosencrantz and Guildenstern, Hamlet's "excellent good friends" (2.2.229)—"are supposed to be on a footing of friendly equality" (Bohannan and Bohannan 48), but corruption can easily creep in. Even "in-laws are fair game" when it comes to exploitation (Bohannan 23), the Tiv showing no scruples about forging documents (one thinks of Hamlet's doctoring of Claudius's commission to send Rosencrantz and Guildenstern to their deaths) in order to ensure their own personal gain. To regulate relationships in the wider world, the Tiv, like Claudius, resort to legal treaties, which include "general rules of almost exaggerated hospitality" (Bohannan and Bohannan 30): any Tiv can understand Claudius's courtesy to Fortinbras, even though the latter once menaced the land. In short, both Shakespeare and the Tiv are acutely sensitive to the rules of reciprocity (as well as their violations) that always govern human non-kin affairs.

And they are sensitive, as well, to the rites of sociality. "We'll teach you to drink deep ere you depart," says Hamlet to Horatio (1.2.175), and the Tiv are eager to offer the same hospitable instruction to Bohannan: *Hamlet* is told in an atmosphere of beery celebration. And where there are stimulants, there are of course dancing and singing: the "heavy-headed revel" that offends the ascetic Hamlet who listens on the ramparts as Claudius "takes his rouse" (1.4.17, 8). "By midmorning," writes Bohannan, describing those days between harvest and field-preparation when the Tiv, at their leisure, hear out her tale, "the whole homestead was singing, dancing, and drumming" (22). And amid such revelry and conviviality, it comes as naturally to the Tiv to exchange old stories as it does for Claudius and his court to amuse themselves with the "Murder of Gonzago." Clearly classicists in aesthetic matters (for them "storytelling is a skilled art" [Bohannan 23]), the Tiv demand a "proper style," one that anchors Bohannan's text in both the authority of age and the anonymity of myth: "Not yesterday, not yesterday," she feels compelled to begin, "but long ago, a thing occurred" (23).

This opening line suggests that the Tiv share one more thing with Shakespeare, indeed with all narrative artists: the intuitive sense that the raison d'être of narrative is to deal with departures from the canonical. Like many peoples, sophisticated and "primitive," the Tiv "can always produce particular circumstances to explain any exceptions although they can give no reason for the common observance" (Bohannan and Bohannan 17). Laura Bohannan assumes that this explanatory failure—the Tiv's resorting to a formulaic "That is the way it is done, so that is how we do it"—is merely "their favorite way of fobbing off my questions" (25). But, as Bruner has argued, "it is only when constituent beliefs in folk psychology are violated that narratives are constructed," and, "when things 'are as they should be,'" such narratives "are unnecessary" (*Acts* 39–40).

But, for all their behavioral similarities (what I earlier called the "overlap") to the figures in Claudius's court, the Tiv are unable to construct a narrative that seems adequately responsive to *Hamlet*. They are unable to do so chiefly, I think, because they lack Shakespeare's sense of genre. The "old stories" that the Tiv exchange are apparently of the same generically "mixed" type that most non-Western cultures produce: to the Tiv "tragedy" and "comedy" are unaccustomed categories. That being the case, they can assign ignoble motives to characters in a drama that Aristotle has led us to find *spoudaia*, a word that he uses to mean both "serious" and "good." Thus, Laertes is not above drowning his sister and selling her body to the witches, and he is prevented from doing so only because Hamlet, "the chief's heir, like a chief, does not wish any other man to grow rich and powerful" (Bohannan 30). Without a sense of genre, the Tiv must fall back upon those narrative explanations that are most relevant to their social world, and these are explanations obviously less equal to the exalted motives of Shakespeare's tragic figures than to the opportunistic strategies of comedy.

Which is not to concede that tragedy has little connection with real life, Tivian or otherwise. As I shall later argue, tragedy acquires logically both verisimilitude and social function among highly populous peoples: it is really not a genre that the Tiv need cultivate, living as they do, at least of the late 1960s, in smallish compounds of 140 people or less (Bohannan and Bohannan 17). But this is a speculation for the end of this chapter; at this point we should simply register the observation that *Hamlet* for the Tiv is not a "serious" action, at least in accordance with the fullest meaning with which Aristotle invested the word. And here at the brink of our own inquiry into the genre, we should note that "seriousness" was for Aristotle its central, perhaps definitive, characteristic.

The relevant paragraph is well known:

> Tragedy is a representation of a serious, complete action which has magnitude, in embellished speech, with each of its elements [used] separately in the [various] parts [of the play]; [represented] by people acting and not by narration; accomplishing by means of pity and terror the catharsis of such emotions. (7)

Richard H. Palmer, who has recently published an "analytical guide" to tragedy and tragic theory, complains that, "with the exception of the vague and undeveloped use of *serious*, no element before the final semicolon occurs uniquely in tragedy" (21). Indeed, this seems to be definition according to *genus* and *differentia*, the "seriousness" of the genre being its distinctive trait. But that seriousness, as I suggest above, is not "vague and undeveloped"; it had quite specific connotations for Aristotle. An action was tragic if its characters were "good," meaning that they were admirable, both socially and morally ("comedy prefers to represent people who are worse than those who exist, tragedy people who are better" [3]). An antonym of *spoudaios* is also "laughable," and it is in this sense—that their actions are not laughable, at least for the better part of their drama—that modern tragic heroes are still *spoudaioi*. Willy

Loman and Raskolnikov[3] may lack both the social and moral stature of, say, Oedipus or Hamlet, but neither is, over the main course of their "actions," laughable, and the seriousness with which they're regarded ensures them (if nothing more) the *candidacy* of genuinely tragic stature.

The centrality of this attitude that we take toward the characters, though obvious, cannot be overemphasized. As the rest of the *Poetics* makes clear, tragedy, in Aristotle's estimation, can be more or less perfect depending upon the principles of its construction—upon whether it describes a turn from good fortune to bad rather than from bad to good (both are possible [14, 16, 24]); whether it is "complex" rather than "simple," utilizing both reversal and recognition (as the best tragedies, like the *Oedipus*, do [14]); whether it offers a "unified" rather than "episodic" plot (the latter may still produce tragedy, but of the "worst" kind [13]); whether its hero is of "intermediate" virtuousness who falls through *hamartia* (not the only type possible, but requisite for "the finest tragedy" [16])—but no action that is not *spoudaia* can be tragic. And the sense of *spoudaia* as "not laughable" seems primary. Tragedies "should not" show "wicked men [passing] from misfortune to good fortune" (16), but it's clear, in fact, that they *may* do so (the *Alcestis* has been interpreted in this way) and still remain tragedies if the laughable has little role.

But the latter class of tragedy is the "most untragic of all," for "it is neither morally satisfying nor pitiable nor terrifying" (16). Which brings us to the element after Aristotle's final semicolon: the much-discussed *katharsis* of tragedy. That there is a sense in which *katharsis* may legitimately be retained as part of a "definition" of the genre is an argument that I'll make farther along in this chapter. For the moment I'd like to probe the nature of the emotions that tragedy has been traditionally supposed to excite. Pity and fear, of course—a pairing whose "oddity," in Oscar Mandel's words, "is exceeded only by the strangeness of the flood of commentary it has caused these last two thousand years" (62). Confident that "there can be little objection today to keeping it out of the definition," Mandel goes on to "disallow *any* given emotional consequence as a requisite for tragedy" (62).

> The complexity of our emotional state at the conclusion of a work, and the great number of different possible complexities, make it impossible, in the end, to agree with any critic who undertakes to inform us in a few, striking words, what emotional effect tragedy shall produce. From tragedy that crushes to tragedy that exhilarates a gamut not merely of single notes can be struck, but an endless number of chords. (69)

But Aristotle himself seems to have been aware of the range of possible responses. When he turns to a discussion of "reasoning in tragedy," he notes that, of the several effects of tragic rhetoric, one is "the production of emotion," and then lists examples in a parenthesis: "pity, terror, anger, etc." (25). The famous "pity and fear" may be merely a synecdoche; they obviously do not exhaust the tragic repertoire. But the *range* of emotion that tragedy excites is, as Aristotle clearly understood, less important than the *kind*. There is a "pleasure," he writes, that "is more particular to comedy" than to tragedy—when, for example, "the bitterest enemies . . . exit as friends at the conclusion, and nobody kills anybody else" (17). The emotions of affiliation, he instinctively realizes, do not consort with tragic seriousness (although tragedy, as I shall later argue, *implicitly* valorizes such emotions), and this is a conclusion with which Mandel would agree.

Why the affiliative emotions join "the laughable" as proper "pleasures" of comedy is a question for my next chapter; here it should be sufficient to observe that both imply a kind of mastery that is alien to the tragic posture. Tragedy calls up the agonistic emotions (anger, fear) as well as those, like pity, for example, that suggest a yet-to-be-mastered "working-through" of suffering or painful spectacle. Unlike comedy (as we shall see), tragedy typically engages the spectator in a kind of emotional *process*, either as it transpires between two or more characters or as it defines the dynamic relationship between a character and the spectator proper. There may be moments of processual resolution, as when Gloucester, after his "leap" from the "dread summit" in *Lear*, expresses his resolve to master "Affliction," or when Oedipus serenely delivers himself to the gods in the *Oedipus at Colonus*, but such moments strike a modern reader as the more proper stuff of comedy. When they round out a narrative, as in the last example, they seem to be violations of genre, and so for plays like the *Ion* of Euripides, which is a tragedy by Aristotle's definition, a term like "tragicomedy" seems the appropriate epithet.

For—again as Aristotle intuits—suffering most properly concludes tragic process, a *pathos* that is more kinetic in its effects than it is emotionally arresting. From tragedy we leave the theater "moved," as most spectators are wont to say; from comedy we leave (the French word seems appropriate) *contents*.[4] And this effect is ultimately a consequence of tragic "inevitability": at least since the Middle Ages, tragedy has been inseparable from catastrophe, or from grave suffering relieved only by death (Leech 2). "Set" by this expectation, spectators of tragedy are always in a position of Brechtian enlightenment; they know that Oedipus is doomed from the start. And, possessed of such knowledge, they must invest their interest, not in the outcome of the action, but in what I have called its process: the emotional dynamic that suspends spectatorial mastery by encouraging engagement and empathy. When we smile upon hearing Oedipus pronounce a curse upon Laius's murderer, we are momentarily relinquishing that empathy to behold him mastered by our knowledge, as it were; when we experience a response, on the other hand, compounded of admiration, pity, and fear, we are tempering that knowledge with empathic understanding. And tragedy is most characteristic, most "morally satisfying," I shall argue, when it sustains just that sort of engagement. Thus the "tragic poet," who, in Northrop Frye's words, "knows that his hero will be in a tragic situation," must exert "all his power to avoid the sense of having manipulated that situation for his own purposes" (211). The more obviously manipulated the situation, the more powerful will be the spectator's temptation to assume a position of knowing mastery, and the less compelling will be the invitation to enter the empathic contract. Bad tragedies, as a result, seem comic.

All of which suggests that the "seriousness" of tragedy is synonymous with its power to evoke empathy. It's because this is so that the spectacle of a "wicked" man's passing from misfortune to good fortune is the "most untragic of all." We can go further and say that such a spectacle cannot be witnessed—at least by the psychologically average spectator—with any seriousness at all; although identification may be possible with a "wicked" character, that is, one whose exploitativeness is unjustified or capricious or (unlike, say, Macbeth's) unqualified by reluctance or remorse, it is, for reasons I shall offer when we turn to comedy, always accompanied by a smile. In other words, unless the tragic hero shows a modicum of integrity, his or her "action" will be perceived as comic by the spectator who is seeking empathic identification. (Recall the black comedy of *Richard III.*) Thus the inappropriateness of the Tiv's reading of *Hamlet:* their assuming that Hamlet plots with self-promoting cunning is plausible from a general point of view, but not from a generic one.

So although, as Mandel writes, "a criminal as well as a saint can be the protagonist of a tragedy," he or she must command—to use Mandel's terminology—"our earnest [unsmiling] good will [that is, empathy]" (138). Beyond that, there seem to be few requirements that the tragic hero must meet—requirements, at least, on which theorists can agree.[5] Robert Heilman, whose distinctions between tragedy and melodrama will prove useful to my own discussion, insists that tragedy has nothing to do with "innocence and victims" (21 n), an opinion that Mandel shares; but Frye describes the hero of his "first phase" of tragedy as one who is dignified with "courage and innocence"—"a stag pulled down by wolves" (219). (For Frye *The Duchess of Malfi* is first-phase tragedy, "and certainly one of the greatest in English literature" [219]; for Heilman the *Duchess* is not tragedy at all, merely an example of the "drama of disaster" [61].) Heilman, like many other theorists, insists on the hero's self-awareness, and quotes Henry James with approval ("we do not care . . . for 'what happens to the stupid, the coarse, and the blind,' but only for 'what happens to . . . the really sentient'" [294]); Mandel argues confidently, on the other hand, that empirically "tragedy offers three possibilities: *first,* the actor proceeds throughout with full lucidity, knows more or less completely what to expect, and is not surprised by his own misery; *second,* the actor proceeds with hope of success, unaware of the doom which his purpose necessarily entails, and only recognizes the truth and the horror when it is too late; and *third,* the protagonist proceeds in ignorance, suffers in ignorance, and dies in ignorance" (148). My own position on these matters must emerge gradually over the course of this discussion, but there is one much-vexed issue with which we can deal summarily, and that is the pseudoproblem of the hero's "free will."

Mandel exposes the factitiousness of the problem with customary trenchancy: "To be the 'puppet' of one's own desire—with desire itself the 'puppet' of one's total psychic history—that is free will" (121). In other words, the fulfillment of desire is the goal of all agents ("We experience the absence of freedom only when our desires are thwarted—usually from the outside" [121]), but desire itself is the production of the "total psychic history" of the desiring subject and so, arguably, the mere "puppet" of that history. But included in that history is the acquisition of "off-line" thought, upon whose stage, as I have argued previously, moral choices may be rehearsed by "scenario-spinning," and all but the deviant in narrativic competence (about whom later I'll have more to say) may fret their little hour upon that stage. Aristotle puts the matter more tersely: "Character is that which reveals decision, of whatever sort" (9). Tragic action may be (for, say, Oedipus or Macbeth) *fatalistic* in the tracing of its design, but it is never *deterministic:*[6] both Oedipus and Macbeth reveal "decision."

Some tragic theorists, following Hegel obviously, have seen in the hero's revelation of decision a definitive necessity of the genre. Tragedy, in this view—it is Heilman's, most notably—is fundamentally *about* decision, and decision between two opposed allegiances within the psyche: "There is a pulling apart within the personality, a disturbance, though not a pathological one, of integration. The character is not 'one,' but divided" (Heilman 7). And it is divided because of competing desires. Tragedy "means not simply 'painful,' as in popular usage, but requiring a choice between counterimperatives of such authority that one has to act faultily and yet cannot feel that he could act more wisely" (Heilman 10). This is, in general, a compelling perspective, and one that is applicable to many tragedies, particularly to those of the neoclassical stage; but clearly it is not applicable to all. Its limitations are apparent when Heilman turns to Oedipus: "Oedipus wants to obey imperatives but is betrayed by the riotous impulse. . . . Oedipus strenuously seeks to escape the father-murder foretold for him, but the impulse that betrays him is an ego-serving violence that he lets fly as if it were a right" (11). Quite apart from the fact that the "tragedy" of the play is made to hinge upon revelation, not incident, we have additional difficulty in accepting this reading because of the defensibility of Oedipus's "violence." (One thinks here of Corneille's puzzlement, attendant, in his case, upon the neoclassicists' equation of *hamartia* with "moral error": "Aristotle gives as examples [of ideal tragic heroes] Oedipus and Thyestes, in which case I do not understand his thinking. The first seems to me not to make any error, although he kills his father, because he does not know him and because he is only disputing the right of way, like a man of mettle, against an unknown man who has attacked him with the advantage on his side" [89].)

It's now common practice among theorists of tragedy to stress what Michelle Gellrich calls "Aristotle's distinct bias against a conflictual understanding of character and action" (18). In Gellrich's Nietzsche-inspired poststructuralist perspective, "the conflicts of dramatic tragedy defer the stability of a center that secures order" (xiii), and the *Poetics* is obviously founded on a metaphysics that "affirms the rule of . . . order" (102). But, despite whatever biases of which Aristotle may be guilty, the *Oedipus*, his model of the perfect tragedy (and by anyone's definition a good example of the genre), can very well be defended as a "nonconflictual" action. Geoffrey Brereton has done so, arguing patiently in his well-conceived *Principles of Tragedy* that, although rich in irony and in dramatic contrast, the *Oedipus Tyrannus* does not turn upon conflict. There is certainly conflict within the play—between Oedipus and Tiresias, Oedipus and Creon, and so on—but the "fall" of Oedipus is not its consequence:

> There is no struggle in the hero's mind. . . . There cannot be, because he is not aware of the disparity ["between the world as he wishes and believes it to be and the world as it is"] until it is far too late to do anything but submit. We cannot even say that he beats against the walls of a trap, since he does not know that he is in one. We witness his suffering or anguish, but only at the end, in the prolonged recognition. It is not the anguish of a man torn between two alternatives, but the agonising contemplation of a disaster which has already occurred. Here we have a tragic hero in an indubitably tragic situation which does not entail conflict. (86)

Tragedy, Brereton (I think rightly) concludes, does not necessarily *demand*—at least to drive the tragic machinery—the "decision" that the actions of its heroes "reveal"; tragedy is, instead, more generally about "the nature and sources of power" (which may or may not engage the hero in conflict) "as it affects the human subject" (117). Frye describes it similarly: "The tragic hero is very great as compared with us, but there is something else, something on the side of him opposite the audience, compared to which he is small. This something else may be called God, gods, fate, accident, fortune, necessity, circumstance, or any combination of these, but whatever it is the tragic hero is our mediator with it" (207). In thus "mediating" between the audience and the power that he or she confronts, the hero is often ensnared in conflict, since conflict—as well as the other staples of tragic action: irony, recognition, acts of retribution—makes "the serious exploration of power" possible, and so "it is therefore virtually certain that one or more of [these elements] will be present in any embodiment of tragedy in a verbal art-form" (Brereton 126). And, in whatever terms the exploration is conducted, even, as at the end of the *Oresteia*, in terms of a conflict between supernatural agents, its bearing will be upon the human scene; like all art, tragedy is, in Brereton's words, "always human-centered" (272).

When the "power" resides therefore outside the human actor, it tends to assume, generally, one of two familiar forms. Either it is a representation of what is extraordinary in nature, of an inexplicable departure from everyday process, or it represents what is "unknown" about the actor itself, specifically its anonymous emotional imperatives and their mysterious irresistibility. The Artemis who raises the improbable crosswinds in the Chorus's first ode of the *Agamemnon* is an example of the former. Also the gods of the *Oedipus Tyrannus* (whom I'm convinced were conceived by Sophocles much as Milton conceived his Christian God, as divinely omniscient but morally guiltless in the affairs of human beings) may be and usually are regarded (at least by generations of earnest undergraduates) as similar kinds of powers: those that "explain" how the most blameless of intentions can lead to catastrophe. Examples of "gods" of the second type, as externalizations of desire and passion that bear a metaphorical relation to our insistent sense of the strange autonomy of emotion, are of course legion in tragedy. From the Furies of Aeschylus, which represent, in Mandel's words, "convenient higher sanctions for a human drive [for vengeance] which brooks no gainsaying" (123), to the Aphrodites who inflame the many Phaedras into forbidden but all-mastering lust, the gods have represented the human emotions as both fearful and divinely alien, often blocking their victims' power of appeal to other, perhaps more clement, deities (the so-called gentler passions) and so depriving them of "rationality."

It's because we intuit this relationship of supernatural power to human systems of explanation and feeling that we can still respond to ancient tragedy with a full measure of involvement. But it is also why the supernatural seems a dispensable element of the genre. "Whether [Racine's] Phedre," writes Brereton, "was brought to the brink of the slope by Venus, a supernatural entity, by the aberrations of her ancestors, by her own personal erotic proclivities or even, on the shortest view, by the 'fault' of her husband in leaving her unhusbanded in the company of her stepson, the result is still a tragedy." (And he adds: "We quote this in disproof of the widely held view that tragedy is 'numinous' by nature" [273].) What is indispensable is the sense that the hero is "brought to the brink of the slope" by a power that is larger than him- or herself. When that power is not enfigured as a "god" (or as one of the secular equivalents mentioned by Frye: fate, accident, fortune, and so forth), it is—and I think I can state this without qualification, given my discussion of emotions as "metabeliefs"—emotion itself. It need not be one of the destructive passions (Antigone's is not such an emotion), and it need not, as Heilman thinks, reside in the hero in conflict with other "counterimperatives" (Antigone's is not a conflicted psyche). But it must be of a kind and magnitude that the stakes seem important in the behavioral game—of a sort that can, and must, result in tragically "inevitable" ruin. Of that sort only the antagonisms of the biogram can offer sufficient depth and intractability, and it is with such antagonisms, I propose, that tragedy is chiefly concerned.

Antigone offers perhaps the richest example in the whole of the tragic literature. Creon's opening lines delineate the antagonism that Hegel would see as central: between the claims of the family and the claims of the state ("non-kin," in its simplest designation). "Whoever places a friend [*philos*, which also means "relative"] / above the good of his own country, he is nothing," Creon maintains, "I have no use for him," and the Chorus—"of old Theban citizens"—expresses no disagreement.[7] "The state," as anthropologist Robin Fox writes, in a provocative essay on the play, "abhors kinship":

> To put it another way, from the state's point of view, the highest level of kinship group it likes to see is the nuclear family, which is in fact the lowest level of operative kinship group possible that is compatible with effective reproduction and socialization of the young. To be exact, this could be done by the mother-child unit with the state as provider. But this is not the state's aim, and in fact causes it a great deal of trouble—viz. the welfare system. . . . But note also that the state usually dislikes intensely the idea of the male supporting several mother-child units, i.e., polygyny. . . . [T]he state frowns on the possibility of the growth of large kinship units and actively discourages it. . . . The paradox then is that, in promoting the nuclear family, the state (or church) is paring kinship down to its lowest common denominator while appearing to support basic "kinship values."[8] ("Virgin" 144–45)

To Antigone such values are paramount—and they embrace, to her ruin, individuals outside the "nuclear family," the grown brothers who fell in their contest for Thebes. And if, for both Sophocles and his fifth-century audience, the civic sentiments of Creon and the Chorus translate easily into divine imperatives, Antigone's bond to her kin does likewise: in fact, that same Zeus to whom Creon piously appeals as his "witness" in this affair is described by Creon himself as a Zeus "who defends all bonds of kindred blood" (736). Both the emotional bonds of kinship, in short, as well as those of reciprocity, have been sacralized in Sophocles's culture, and when Antigone oscillates between respect for the laws of the sacred gods and respect for the person of her brother, she is making a distinction without a difference.

We may do well to emphasize the nature of that respect. Antigone does not die, in the words of H. A. Mason, "for love but for a bond" (47): "she feels identified with her *philoi*"—her brothers—"so close is the complex they form" (56).[9] As well they might, for both are in fact genetic extensions of herself. This helps explain the famous lines in her much-disputed farewell song, a passage that some modern editors continue to excise as an interpolated textual "corruption":

> Never, I tell you,
> if I had been the mother of children
> or if my husband died, exposed and rotting—
> I'd never have taken this ordeal upon myself,
> never defied our people's will. What law,
> you ask, do I satisfy with what I say?
> A husband dead, there might have been another.
> A child by another too, if I had lost the first.
> But mother and father both lost in the halls of Death,
> no brother could ever spring to light again.
>   (995–1004)

Commentators have seen contradictions in these lines. "They are certainly," Bernard Knox complains, "a total repudiation of her proud claim that she acted as the champion of the unwritten laws and the infernal gods, for, as she herself told Creon, those laws and those gods have no preferences, they long 'for the same rites for all'" (45). But they are not such a repudiation; they are simply an admission that only in this case will she defend those laws with her life. Knox's second criticism also seems unjustified. Noting that these lines have their source in a story by Herodotus, in which a Persian noblewoman saves her brother's life with "words that are unmistakably the original" of Antigone's, Knox argues that the speech "would be fully appropriate only if Antigone had managed to save Polynices's life rather than bury his corpse" (46). But, to her mind, she *is* saving his life—saving it "for glory down among the dead" (31), where he will join his "great growing family" (981).

The important point, of course, is that Antigone is not reasoning out her position, at least as "reasoning" is usually understood. That position has been prepared by natural selection, meaning that the emotional options among which she must choose have already been invested with a certain relative weight. In the "environment of our evolutionary adaptedness," the valuing of a brother over a (hypothetical) child or husband would make perfect fitness-enhancing sense, especially since that environment permitted little optimism with respect to the ravages of infant mortality and few expectations about long-lived conjugal bliss. (In Sophocles's Greece, of course, not much had changed.) In standing with her brother, Antigone is thinking with a primitive's heart,[10] but the circumstances hardly favor such thinking. Not only is she up against powerful civic sentiment, but she confronts a king who fears that his dominance is threatened, and threatened by his "natural" inferior, a woman.

For "as the action develops," Knox remarks accurately, "the favorable impression created by Creon's opening speech is quickly dissipated" (41). At the Chorus's suggestion that the gods were behind the first attempt to bury Polynices, he erupts

in fury, fingering "certain citizens" as "the instigators" (328, 333). "From the first,"
he cries, they

> could hardly stand the spirit of my regime,
> grumbling against me in the dark, heads together,
> tossing wildly, never keeping their necks beneath
> the yoke, loyally submitting to their king.
>
> (329–32)

When Antigone is brought before him, he expresses immediately his determination
to keep her neck beneath that yoke, to "break" her as one breaks "proud, rebellious
horses" (532–33). And then he shows his ugliest side: "I am not the man, not now:
she is the man / if this victory goes to her and she goes free" (541–42). By the end
of their interview, at Ismene's entrance, he has completely lost sight of his citizens'
welfare and is fighting for his interests as the dominant male: "While I'm alive," he
contemptuously declares, "no woman is going to lord it over me" (592–93).

With his son, he will put those same interests first. "Are you coming now,
raving against your father?" he asks Haemon, and, when the latter shows eagerness
to defer to paternal "wisdom," Creon praises him for his obedience:

> That's how you ought to feel within your heart,
> subordinate to your father's will in every way.
> That's what a man prays for: to produce good sons—
> households full of them, dutiful and attentive.
>
> (713–16)

Haemon of course proves to have a mind of his own. With exquisite courtesy and
tactful control, he pleads with his father not to be "quite so single-minded, self-
involved" (789): "Oh give way. Relax your anger—change!" (804). But it is by just
such urgings that Creon is stiffened in his resolve. First expressing his incredulity
that he is to be "schooled by a boy" (814), he next declares himself superior to all
of Thebes: "The city is the king's—that's the law!" (825). "This autocratic phrase,"
as Knox observes, "puts the finishing touch to the picture Sophocles is drawing
for his audience: Creon has now displayed all the characteristics of the 'tyrant,' a
despotic ruler who seizes power and retains it by intimidation and force" (43).

In this reading of the play (which can offend only by the slavishness of its
fidelity to the dialogic actions of the text), *Antigone* seems to assume the complexion
of what Heilman would call a "drama of disaster" or, in more general (albeit
nonevaluative) terms, catastrophic "melodrama." Neither Antigone nor Creon is a
conflicted figure; each is what Heilman calls "essentially 'whole.'"

This key word implies neither greatness nor moral perfection, but rather an absence of the basic inner conflict that, if it is present, must inevitably claim our primary attention. Melodrama accepts wholeness without question; for its purposes, man's loyalties and his directions are neither uncertain nor conflicting. He is not troubled by motives that would distract him from the outer struggle in which he is engaged. He may indeed be humanly incomplete; but his incompleteness is not the issue. It is in tragedy that man is divided; in melodrama, his troubles, though they may reflect some weakness or inadequacy, do not arise from the urgency of unreconciled impulses. In tragedy the conflict is within man; in melodrama, it is between men, or between men and things. (79)

But if *Antigone* is not tragedy then nothing is, and so Heilman conscripts its heroine into the ranks of the conflicted by highlighting her disloyalty to the state (9)—a disloyalty about which she shows no concern and for which the Thebans, according to Haemon's account, think she "deserves a glowing crown of gold" (782). *Antigone is* tragedy, but its conflicts are not "within man," or within woman, for that matter: they are, more precisely, within the *species*. The play, as George Steiner points out, expresses "the principal constants of conflict" in human life (231): man versus woman, parent versus offspring, self and kin versus the non-kin community.[11] These conflicts, indeed, create psychological divisions, but neither in *Antigone* nor in other tragedies is it the psyche of the hero that's necessarily divided: the divisions are in the sympathies of the audience itself. The ambivalence attendant upon all human relationships is evoked and sharpened by the tragic spectacle, and the more intense the ambivalence, as Aristotle understood, the more poignant is the *pathos* of tragedy: "when sufferings happen within friendly relationships, e.g. brother against brother, son against father, mother against son or son against mother . . . —these are what must be sought after" by the tragedian (18).

Underlying this ambivalence are the emotional inclinations that encourage allegiances to the agonistic poles. And if *Antigone* skirts melodrama, it is not because the characters are—in the somewhat homegrown terms of Heilman's psychology— "essentially 'whole,'" but because Creon in particular has relinquished his power of choice in shifting allegiances. The male-centered society for which Sophocles wrote would doubtless have been more ambivalent about this relinquishment than most modern audiences are likely to be. Certainly, the men among the spectators would have felt the power of the emotions that drive Creon over the brink of ruin. "Oh, it's hard," he says when finally persuaded to lift his sentence on Antigone, "it's hard, / giving up [*eksistamai*: literally, standing away from] the heart's desire" (1229). But, when he returns from the tomb immediately after the catastrophe, hugging his dead son's head in his arms, he knows that he has been destroyed by the "god" of his own rancor:

Then, it was then,
when the god came down and struck me—a great weight
shattering, driving me down that wild savage path,
ruining, trampling down my joy.

(1402–05)

In recovering what our folk psychology would call his emotional "balance," Creon recovers narrativic competence, that evolved ability (in Tooby and Cosmides's words) to "interpret social situations correctly" (110). And his "recognition" (which, for many readers, makes him the central figure of the play) thereby delivers him, as well as *Antigone*, from melodramatic singleness of vision.

The example is an instructive illustration of Heilman's own conclusion: that tragedy and melodrama make up "two contiguous and complementary realms which fluctuate between an impulse to partial fusion and an impulse to total independence" (88). Keeping them separate can often prove, for the theorist, a futile and profitless enterprise, especially when the focus is on intergroup competition and the "hero" is not one but many. Is Cervantes's *Siege of Numantia*, for example, tragedy or melodrama? Following much the same trajectory as *Antigone*, the play concerns the second-century beleaguerment of Spanish Numantia by troops under Scipio Africanus. Scipio's opening lines express his heartsickness over the ravages of "such a long and monstrous war" (101), but, like Creon, he soon bares an efficiently ruthless will: rejecting an embassy's offer of a settlement, he resolves to "dig a deep ditch round the town / And with insufferable famine finish / Them off" (108).[12] The siege reduces the Numantines to desperation, and they propose a duel between the best champions of both armies to end "this stubborn strife" (129). But Scipio, eager for the fame that will follow upon a victory costing none of his soldiers' lives, greets the offer with derision. When he enters Numantia after the ravages of the siege, he finds no one left alive, the strong having murdered their weaker compatriots to rob him of his triumph. At which point comes the *anagnorisis*:

Could it have been, by chance, that in my breast
My savage arrogance, pregnant with their doom,
Had left no room for clemency at all?
And is my character, by chance, an alien
To that benignity which every victor
Should use to deal with a defeated foe?

(156)

But the lure of identification with the victimized group proves to be too strong for Cervantes (or maybe for his commercial sense), because, following upon these lines, a young boy appears from a tower in which he had hidden to escape the slaughter, and, in heroic defiance of Scipio's offer to surrender to him and "live free" (157), he hurls himself from the ramparts, thereby "level[ing]" Scipio's victories "to the ground" and perhaps vanquishing his tragedy by melodrama. Group loyalties seem naturally to invite such handling (at least before the conscience-riven twentieth century, with its Ireland, its Algeria, its Vietnam), but some tragedians are successful at resisting the lure. Certainly Euripides is, in his *Trojan Women*, forcing his spectators to confront in the suffering of the conquered their own poisonous depths of vindictiveness. And in John Osborne's *A Patriot for Me*, a brilliant but neglected modern specimen of tragedy, the oppressiveness of both groups in which Redl must live—the treacherousness of the gay world and the suffocation of the straight—is delineated with an objectivity that may itself be said to be the distinguishing mark of the genre.

How willing we are to allow the melodramatic vision to "corrupt" this objectivity is really a kind of index of how we regard the function of tragedy. "Definition" here, in other words, is, as we saw in Chapter 3, an interactive enterprise, erected upon the scaffolding of human needs to which the defined must offer a sufficient response. Is tragedy to traffic with "innocence and victims"? It depends upon whether the "combative" response seems appropriate to the tragic vision. For combat is, as Heilman points out, what melodrama imaginatively incites in its spectators: it encourages "a unity of feeling" that gives those spectators "competitive strength against things or persons" (99). The opponent in that combat need not always be a villain seized by hatred or cruelty—an Iago, for example, or (insofar as he is unredeemed by his belated recognition) a Creon or Scipio. As the "middle plays" of Ibsen suggest, the enemy may very well be a comic figure. The Aslaksen whose motto is "everything in moderation" in *An Enemy of the People*, the egocentric Hjalmar who drives Hedvig to her suicide through his fidelity to the "Claim of the Ideal," even the thick-witted Jörgen Tesman, whose fondness for his house slippers and his maiden aunts condemns Hedda to a life of genteel banality—all these represent forces of victimization against which the audience is invited to rebel.

Tragedy, on the other hand (we'll adopt Heilman's distinction), has a different function, chiefly because it is usually predicated upon a different conception of character. The antagonist of melodrama is oblivious to the social rights and claims (or sometimes, as in the case of Ekdal or Tesman, to the beliefs and desires) of other agents; he or she has a deviant narrativic competence and can excite neither empathy nor (consequently) ambivalence. In tragedy, when full competence is not manifested by the hero, it always seems imminently recuperable. Macbeth may steep himself deeply in blood, but he does so in full knowledge of his criminality; Lear may foolishly give up his crown while expecting to retain "all the additions to a king," but he will come to find that "unaccommodated" man smells vulnerably of mortality. Which suggests that, if tragedy is to be purged of the melodramatic strain, "self-awareness" must be a requisite of its hero: such awareness implies, not so much an understanding of the *self*—Ibsen's Hedvig commits suicide with full knowledge of her motives, though in her immaturity she can't be said to be self-aware—as an understanding of generally *human* potentialities. To be self-aware is to exercise a narrativic competence that is equal to both the ambitions and the obligations of the social animal. And it's precisely in the exercising of that competence that the tragic hero can be differentiated from the villain and the fool.

Because its hero is possessed of such competence, Heilman (among others) is led to conclude that tragedy is about "the inevitability of the avoidable":

> An "accident" takes on the coloring of tragedy when it is morally avoidable and when we look at it in such terms. The *morally* avoidable accident can be guarded against not by better equipment and new electronic devices, but by a state of mind which is anterior to all technical practices, that is, an adequate sense of reality. (30)

That sense I have been calling narrativity. And tragedy functions to refine its operations, chiefly, I think, through the empathic identifications that are synonymous with tragic seriousness. This is the process to which Aristotle may have been alluding in his cryptic reference to *katharsis*, at least in the opinion of Richard Janko, a recent editor of the *Poetics*:

> Just as, in Aristotle's moral theory, we become good by habitually doing good, so too by feeling emotion appropriately (towards the right object, at the right time etc.), we become habituated to having the right emotional responses. . . . Now poetry offers an obvious way in which we can learn these responses without the hazardous process of undergoing in actuality the experiences represented in poetry. By responding emotionally to the representation, we can learn to develop the correct emotional responses. Aristotle says precisely this about music, *in which he includes poetry*, at *Politics* VIII 5.1340a14–25.[13] (Aristotle xviii, paragraphing simplified)

Whether or not this represents Aristotle's thinking, it accurately accords with what psychologists of the emotions have suggested about their role in learning. As we saw in Chapter 1, an emotion "indexes" an experience in memory, and, when a similar experience is encountered by the agent, it may be engaged on the basis of the success or failure that followed upon the actions earlier motivated by the emotion. The emotions, in short, are not "purged" by tragedy; they are actively courted and entertained, even and most especially the "painful" emotions. For in literary representation, as Janko implies, the emotions are not experienced as painful: the suffering to which they refer is recognized as fictional and so their cognitive content is robbed of its sting.[14] The (pleasurable) affect, in the meantime, remains, both as index and incentive, to attend to the spectacle.

And in this way the spectator is educated by tragedy. We can recapitulate, in summary, the requisites of the process: (1) empathic identification with the tragic hero, identification encouraged both by the impending disaster, which cues spectatorial attention to the conduct of the plot instead of its (predictable) outcome, and by the narrativic competence, potential or complete, through which the hero manifests his or her integrity; (2) ambivalence over the emotional allegiances to which the hero has pledged his or her conduct, resulting for the audience in a preparedness for instruction about their social and psychological consequences; and (3) vicarious endurance of the tragic catastrophe, which, through being indexed in memory by the "painful" emotions, arms the spectator with the heightened narrativic competence to turn the "inevitable" into the avoidable. All of this may be called—to borrow a word from Chapter 4—a process of "understanding." And the *conceptualization* of this understanding need not be a part of the process. Understanding results not in *ideas* about social action (that way lie what Stephen Dedalus would have called the abstruosities of ethical philosophy) but rather in the spinning of scenarios about it. Understanding, in short, fertilizes the imagination, in the dreams of which begins responsibility.

But there is a rather large class of tragedies in which responsibility seems irrelevant, tragedies in which the catastrophe is *unavoidable*. Sophocles's *Oedipus* is of this class: it is difficult to say how the *pathos* of that play can have been avoided by responsible action. (Although my students unfortunately are always trying to tell me: Oedipus should have stayed at home.) A better example may be Corneille's *The Cid*. Here we have a tragedy in which the suffering of the protagonist is brought on clearly by biogrammatical conflict—Chimène must choose between honoring the paternal tie or marrying her lover, who has killed her father in a duel—but, as in the *Oedipus*, the "action" of the play merely sets up the dilemma, and that dilemma is one over which Chimène has no control. And so how does the spectacle of her moral paralysis function in any but a voyeuristic way?

A recent article by the Nobel Laureate Herbert A. Simon, who is professor of psychology and computer science at Carnegie-Mellon University, may help to provide an answer. Simon suggests that one of the evolved mechanisms for social selection and successful altruism among human beings is "docility," a general receptivity to social learning, which "contributes greatly to fitness in the human species" (1665). The better disposed to be taught is an individual, the more genetically "fit" he or she tends to be. But such a disposition may be "taxed" by the culture: the docile may be encouraged to dispense acts of altruism far in excess of their own personal gain.[15] And, as the culture itself grows more functionally cohesive, its enculturated may or may not prosper. Although Simon does not say so, such a model of selection is probably most applicable to "modern" populous nation-states: when the mechanisms (like empathy) regulating the face-to-face interactions that characterize the reciprocity of small social groups break down in the facelessness of impersonal exchange, the cultural "taxation" of which Simon speaks becomes an indispensable social adhesive.[16]

As should be evident from much of my previous discussion, tragedy of what I'll call the avoidable type implicitly valorizes the affiliative behaviors, including the altruistic ones. Although "the center of tragedy," as Frye points out, "is in the hero's isolation" (208), its moral sentiments always reside with those instincts that Freud collectively called Eros, instincts whose object is "to bind together." To the extent that it valorizes an opposition between the protagonist and some part of the social world, a literary action is, properly, "melodramatic"; to the extent that it suggests that that opposition is self-destructive to the hero who willfully enjoins it, it attains to the candidacy of a tragic action. (Some works may be read both ways, of course: Ibsen's Hedda may be seen as a Dionysian victim, hounded to suicide by a dull Apollonian world, or as a fearful woman unable to love, whose self-serving manipulations of Ejlert Lövborg entangle her in her own web.) The formal qualities of tragedy proper—its seriousness, its hero of clear narrativic competence who is destined for suffering or death—work to dispel the ambiguity that I have suggested is inherent in narrative itself, and to induce in the audience an emotional receptivity to the cultural instruction that Simon describes. Hence, "avoidable" tragedy is one cog in the cultural "mechanism" of human social selection.

And what I have called "unavoidable" tragedy probably functions as another. *The Cid*, the *Oedipus Tyrannus*—both can have but one meaning for their spectators: "the sky," in the words of Antonin Artaud, "can still fall on our heads" (79). In this sort of tragedy, we enter a world, as Frye eloquently describes it, "in which existence is itself tragic, not existence modified by an act, deliberate or unconscious. Merely to exist is to disturb the balance of nature" (213). It's a world that humbles by its resistance to human dominance and that proclaims its superiority to all acts of the responsible will. Its effect can be only to chasten the self-importance, the unwarranted optimism, the pride in mastery that tend to characterize the self-deluding but well-functioning human gene-machine. And in bringing its pride low (the cliché seems vindicated against one's will), tragedy ensures that machine's docility for a state that functions best when its citizens know "terror and reverence." The words are Athena's at the end of the *Oresteia;* the whole passage, in which she establishes trial by jury at the court of the Areopagus, has immediate bearing on my argument. She is addressing the citizens of Athens:

> Worship the Mean, I urge you,
> shore it up with reverence and never
> banish terror from the gates, not outright.
> Where is the righteous man who knows no fear?

The stronger your fear, your reverence for the just,
the stronger your country's wall and city's safety.
(709–15)

When the *Oresteia* was first produced, around the middle of the fifth century
B.C., the population of Athens had grown far beyond the number that Hippodamas
had thought ideal for a polis. [17] And it may be no accident that tragedy matured as
an institutionalized art form over those years in which Attica became a populous
power. Although it struggled to ensure a system of face-to-face governance, the
Assembly, which admitted every eligible adult (male) citizen, was much too large to
avoid the anonymity and corruption that in all nation-states breed discontent. And
where there is discontent, there is, of course, political disunity, at least in ostensibly
free-speaking democracies. The development of tragedy as a state-nurtured genre
and the inclusion of the form in religio-civic ceremonies may have been a small but
significant contribution to the overall coherence of the culture. Certainly tragedy
has best thrived in cultures in which political strength has been well consolidated:
Periclean Greece, Elizabethan England, the Bourbon Sun-King's France. And it
has appealed naturally to those aristocrats (in both blood and spirit) for whom
literature offers the "people" a *consolatio mortis*.

As mimesis, it hardly presents a full picture of life; it, rather, inscribes what
Mandel calls "tragic facts" onto the soul of the receptive spectator:

Death with its inevitable victory over effort is then the first tragic fact. The
second tragic fact is a socio-psychological one: the very act of living in the
society of others brings with it—unavoidably, "naturally"—friction, hate,
misery. The tragic purpose is the desire, or rather the need, to live among
one's kind. (163)

In pursuit of that purpose, it underscores with its form the elusive difficulty of
the enterprise; the "inevitability" of its *pathos* seems largely a metaphor for the
ineradicability of human conflict and of the immanence of disaster in human affairs.
But even as it insists upon that ineradicability, it is instructing its audience in the art
of social action as it's delimited by insuperable agonistic constraints. To comedy
will be consigned the vicarious pleasures of eluding and overreaching their limits.

6

Comedy and the Relaxed Open-Mouth Display

The angelic and the diabolic . . . move along parallel lines.
— Charles Baudelaire, "The Essence of Laughter"

But what of Dionysiac revelry, and of the birth of tragedy from what Aristotle calls cryptically "the leaders of the dithyramb" (6)? George Steiner responds to this best: "To locate the sources of western drama, of all theatrical arts anywhere, in ritual, in mimetic ceremonies of a liturgical-civic character, is to focus on a late and formal phase." And he concludes that "the original source of the dramatic lies in the paradox of conflict" (234).[1] It's a paradox that antedates all conceptual expressions of it. Thus the confusion of a logic like Gilbert Murray's that engrafts the tragic action—the fall of the hero—upon the decline of sun and seasons. It seems much more likely that early *Homo* latched upon the spectacle of the natural cycles as both explanation and justification of the primordial agon: the displacement of one *alpha* male by another. Conflict (like feeling) was first; there then followed, in the minds of big-brained creatures growing ever more conscious of the history of themselves, a narrative in which both natural and sacred precedent emerged to legitimize their social transactions. The usurper triumphed not only by "natural" legitimacy, as the spring inevitably overpowers the winter, but also by virtue of being a god. (And, if the narrative was to be convincing, it had to be consistent, which meant that the defeated was divine as well.) From this point, all manner of elaboration was possible: the "gods" were not two, but essentially one, a Year-Spirit who was, in Murray's words, "first new and then old, first pure and then polluted" (65), but who rises from his sickness, mutilation, and death in a theophanic glory. Then, like all "memes" (Richard Dawkins's word for cultural "replicators," which multiply themselves like genes [*Selfish Gene* 192]), this narrative combined with other myths, and the resultant theology (which inspired, admittedly, the "late and formal" phases of drama) gradually floated free of its source.

But we err to confound the two, either for tragedy or for comedy. Francis Cornford, following out Murray's speculations, goes back only so far, as Murray does, as the late elaborations, concluding that the "ritual" of comedy, like the theophany of tragedy, arises chiefly from "the renewal of life in spring" (15). Frye reaches a slightly more sophisticated conclusion. For him, comedy comes from ritual, with its source in the seasons, but beneath spring's tubers clutch Freudian roots: "The fact that the son and father [of romantic comedy] are so often in conflict means that they are frequently rivals for the same girl, and the psychological alliance of the hero's bride and the mother is often expressed or implied" (180). What I am suggesting is that we seek out a source in neither the "mythic" nor the (spuriously) fantasmatic of *Homo*'s early conceptual life, but in its—largely prelinguistic—"social dramas," the most important of which for the narrativizing male was the perennial contest for dominance. Surely that contest is more plausibly behind what Frye calls the "total *mythos* of comedy" than Freud's dubious Oedipal drama. Boy is blocked from getting girl, not because he and his father are "frequently" rivals, but because the girl is of the sort that promises no extension of his father's inclusive fitness. New Comedy (which provides, in Frye's words, the formulaic "basis for most comedy" [163]) throws this aspect of the plot in relief: the girl in question is of disreputable origins—a slave girl, a "flute girl," an orphan or waif—and it's not until it's discovered that she's of a "good" family that the hero receives her hand.

Certainly the *resolution*, at least of romantic comedy, translates the action to a conceptual plane, since that resolution seems born of an insistent male wish (and a wish, significantly, of the usurper): that the hero of New Comedy should get his girl, often irrespective of what that girl should want or think or feel. Roman theatrical convention tended to ensure that she had little say in the matter: in the *Phormio*, for example, the play by Terence that seems most representative of New Comedy as a whole, neither the girl nor the love-interest of the young hero's friend ever puts in an appearance on the stage. Later comic dramatists (Shakespeare, most familiarly) will smite both partners with a passion, but how fundamentally superfluous is such motivic scrupulosity is suggested by modern successes in the older vein—Mike Nichols's film *The Graduate*, for example, whose Elaine has the tractability of doll or dream. Such pieces work because comedy has, I think, precisely the opposite of that appeal described epigrammatically by Horace Walpole: The world is a comedy, not to those that think, but in fact to those that feel. Unlike tragedy, which encourages scenario-spinning, exercises of consciousness that its Creons neglect, comedy forestalls the thoughtful response. "Comedy usually moves toward a happy ending, and the normal response of the audience to a happy ending is," as Frye writes, "'this should be'" (167). The affiliative spectacles that conclude most comedies—where "the bitterest enemies . . . exit as friends, and nobody kills anyone else"—arouse (for reasons that I'll offer later) a pleasure that recoils at analysis. Unions in comedy can be flimsily motivated; they're sufficiently justified by the feeling they excite.

For the medieval audience, as Nevill Coghill has argued, the affiliative spectacle of comedy was primary. A comedy was not (as it was earlier for Aristophanes, or would later be for the moralists of the Renaissance) a show inviting "corrective" laughter, but "a tale of trouble that turned to joy" (4). So Dante conceived his *Commedia:* "Comedy," he wrote to his dedicatee, Can Grande, "begins with the harshness of some affair *(asperitatem alicuius rei)* but its matter ends happily *(prospere)* as appears by Terence and his Comedies" (qtd. in Coghill 5). Shakespeare, writes Coghill, continued the tradition, implying in his plays that—*pace* Ben Jonson— "the harmonious is the normal, the attainable," and that "life is a union in love, not a battle of self-interest waged by the rules of an expedient ethic" (13). Perhaps because of the authority that Shakespeare (thus interpreted) wields in the English-speaking world, this view has entered some of our most influential theory—Frye's, for example, in which comedy primarily (in T. G. A. Nelson's words) "moves towards joy, reconciliation, and new beginnings," and in which "the element of laughter" is underplayed: "at times [the *Anatomy of Criticism*] seems to merge comedy into the related mode of romance" (2). Indeed, not only does Frye emphasize the festivity of comedy, its "tendency . . . to include as many people as possible in its final society" (Frye 165), but he also imagines that "society" as transcendently, mythically "new" (163), an assertion that seems applicable to only a minority of comic texts. True, hero and heroine bring their youth to their union, but this rarely raises a new heaven or a new earth. Frye's view (and Coghill's on Shakespeare, as I shall argue) illustrates the seductiveness of the feeling with which comedy concludes, a seductiveness that robs the spectator of the power of analysis that may make something rather different of the comic world.

But we must approach our subject crabwise. If we are to understand fully the comic denouement, we first should investigate the nature of the response that, like the happy ending, seems a sufficient (though not necessary) determinant of comedy: the laugh or, relatedly, the smile. About laughter—and humor, a slightly separate issue—a great deal has already been written, of course, but much, if not most, of it can be set aside, especially that produced by literary critics. As Paul Lewis points out in his *Comic Effects,* "in our time, the study of humor in literature continues to be shaped by two dated and, therefore, limiting methodologies. On one side are critics who derive their conceptual frameworks from an early universalist theory that has been either discredited or subsumed in the past thirty years. On the other side are critics who see no reason to refer to humor research or theory at all" (2). And then there are critics who concoct theories of their own, usually on the authority of native instinct or of a "philosophical" thinker more current and "advanced" than Hobbes or Kant or Freud. And so George McFadden formulates an "essence of the comic" by standing Bergson on his head: "The essence of the comic . . . is founded in a being that shows the power of continuing as itself, substantially unchanged, while overcoming a force or forces that would substantially alter it" (12). Or John Morreall proposes a new "formula" for laughter that exceeds in comprehensiveness all previous theories, and that will long stand as a triumph of the self-evident: *"Laughter Results from a Pleasant Psychological Shift"* (39, capitalization and emphasis in original).[2] Or Susan Purdie brings Lacanian dogma to the task of explicating what Freud called the "joke-work": "joking paradigmatically involves a discursive exchange whose distinctive operation involves the *marked* transgression of the Symbolic Law" (5). And so forth.

The persistence of this sort of theorizing about comedy—theorizing that merely flirts with empirical fact (if it flirts with it at all)—is illustrated by the most recent contribution in the theoretical lists, Dana F. Sutton's *The Catharsis of Comedy*. Its discussion quickly gravitates toward one of the bibles of literary theorists, *Jokes and Their Relation to the Unconscious*. Sutton is perceptive enough to admit Freud's considerable shortcomings: "in its expressed form, Freud's theory is liable to accusations of being unclearly stated, difficult to understand, needlessly complicated, and generally implausible." ("Even within the framework of orthodox psychoanalytical theory," he adds, "it does not seem like a particularly successful piece of reasoning" [29].) But he goes on to salvage from his own critique what he calls "a certain highly valuable residue" in that theory (29). This is Freud's notion of "psychic energy" that is "vented" by the laughing subject. "Someday," writes Sutton, "a description of laughter can be devised to which a physiologist, a psychologist, and a literary critic can subscribe with equal enthusiasm. Such a theory, I am sure, will contain some component roughly equivalent to 'the discharge of psychic energy' to describe laughter's subjective effect" (19).

I, on the other hand, am sure that it won't. The model of the mind emerging from the cognitive sciences (and especially from the cognitive neurosciences) over the last twenty years or so seems to give little support to Freud's hydraulic metaphors and, specifically, to such notions as "psychic energy." As for his specific idea that humor results in a "free discharge" of "liberated energy" (151), an idea derived from the fantasticated operations of his pseudoscientific "cathexes" and their "undoing," it has not stood up to empirical testing.[3] Arousal is *increased*, not decreased, by humor, and it's possible that laughter results directly from this increase instead of causing the subsequent decline (McGhee 16, 22). Still less support does all this promise to Sutton's own final conclusions: that laughter is a "purgative," relieving the spectator of various "bad feelings" and encouraging an attitude of "disdain" toward its "targets," generating thereby "a kind of antitoxin that inhibits the target's capacity to induce bad feelings in the future" (44). The argumentative contortions in defense of this position are rather painful to witness.

First, we're told that, "very much in the spirit of homeopathic medicine, it is necessary to impose a careful limit on the size of the [inoculatory] dose"—in other words, on the intensity of the "bad feelings" evoked by the comic target.

If this were not done, there would exist the danger that the bad feelings evoked by the surrogate might prove too strong to be purged effectively. Under these conditions, comedy would backfire and have the counterproductive effect of making the spectator feel worse rather than better. The presence of ridiculousness [defined previously as "the quality that makes things strike us as funny" (38)] is one of what will prove to be a number of comic strategies to ensure that this does not happen. (42–43)

And yet earlier we have been informed that *tragic* catharsis (which is credited with the same homeopathic effects) "produces pleasure" in the spectator (10), though it obviously does nothing to moderate the "dose" of its *pathos*. Why, then, should the "bad feelings" evoked by comedy (which for Sutton include pity and fear) threaten to make the spectator feel worse rather than better?

Contradictions like this tend to plague the argument. "There are various specific ways," Sutton declares with confidence, "in which the spectator can feel superior to surrogates," and one is through the "moral deficiency of comic characters" (57). But, immediately, this ground begins to crumble: "Moral deficiencies that mark characters on the comic stage," we read two pages later, "are many and various, but since we are not always invited to pass a negative judgment on these qualities, it is not self-evident that their presence is always calculated to induce an attitude of superiority in the spectator" (59). This scruple should not detain us, however: after another thirty pages it is simply forgotten and the reader is assured with a "certainly": "Certainly, fraud, pretense, and hypocrisy are moral shortcomings; and so here is one way in which the spectator can perceive the target . . . as inferior to himself" (91).

Nagging doubts about the *central* thesis must be evaded in a footnote. "Obviously," Sutton writes toward the end of his book,

> satire teaches us to disdain and dislike its targets, or more precisely the moral deficiencies its targets embody, and so presents a parallel to those components of comedy's ridicule process that perform a similar function. But whether there is any element of purging bad feelings seems questionable: what bad feelings could these be? So is there any such thing as satiric catharsis? (115 n)

Thus the note concludes. We're not really encouraged to answer the question because an answer will level the whole edifice. If it is yes, there *is* such a thing as a satiric catharsis, then Sutton must concede that the purging of bad feelings has nothing to do with it. If it is no, there is no such thing as a satiric catharsis, then he must concede that satire is not a species of comedy. Neither concession can be made, of course, and so, after a glimpse into the argumentative abyss, the reader is summoned out of the note into the more authoritative text, much as a sightseer who's wandered too close to a chasm is called back by the guide who is eager to repair his own lapse in responsibility.

But the alert reader would have long entertained suspicions about this guide's authority. Is laughter really a purgative of "bad feelings"? What sorts of bad feelings are being "purged" by the spectacle of Chaplin's making his hard rolls dance? or by one of Kramer's frenetic entrances on *Seinfeld*? or by Garth's addressing an enormous and elaborately festooned cocktail in the interview scene of *Wayne's World*? And why assume that characters in comedy are always regarded with "disdain"? The wit, as I shall argue, is a staple of comedy, and the humor it excites is not always disdainful—not always at the expense of a stooge. Roseanne needn't denigrate her admittedly numerous targets for her one-liners to have their effect. Finally, what *is* it that makes things strike us as funny? To call it "ridiculousness" is like explaining fire by phlogiston: wherein lies the ridiculousness of the ridiculous?[4]

To answer these questions, we must give Freud a wide berth, as we must to the other philosophers of comedy (to me Freud is more philosopher than psychologist). In keeping with my practice throughout this book, I'll approach laughter and smiling—universal reactions of human beings to specifiable classes of stimuli—as *evolved* responses of an apparently adaptive kind. I'll argue that they both have a provocative phylogenetic history, a history that may, in part, be recuperated from a study of *Homo*'s close primate kin. And I'll assume that the most reliable findings on laughter (and smiling, as well as the humor to which both are a response) are those that are *cumulative* in the advancement of our knowledge, which is to say, those that have been winnowed by the self-correcting labors of responsible scientific research.

Of all the comic theorists with whom literary critics are acquainted, Bergson comes closest to a plausible theory of laughter, mainly because he develops the latter along ostensibly adaptationist lines. But Bergson was working with group-selectionist assumptions, that is, notions of adaptation as benefiting the group in direct, and not merely secondary, ways. Laughter, he writes, "pursues a utilitarian aim of general improvement" (73); it expresses "a special lack of adaptability to society" (146) and counters it with a social "corrective," singling out and repressing "a special kind of absentmindedness in men and in events" (117). Evolution doesn't proceed in this way, however: selection ultimately benefits the gene, and functionally it usually benefits the phenotype; its benefit to the group is an incidental affair. So while Bergson often happens upon valuable observations, his conceptual framework is basically flawed. All the new findings argue for an approach to the subject along rigorous (that is to say, contemporary) evolutionary lines. The fact, for example, that laughter "disturbs one of life's most basic . . . activities," causing "a consistent and complete disruption of the usual physiological respiratory cycle," leads William F. Fry Jr. to conclude that it has survived in the human behavioral repertoire for *phenotypically* adaptive reasons (23, 24).

Some of those reasons can be suggested by reference to the homologues of laughter in the chimpanzee. Darwin noted in his *Expression of the Emotions* that, "if a young chimpanzee be tickled . . . a . . . decided chuckling or laughing sound is uttered" (132–33), and modern ethologists have linked these vocalizations, as well as the "relaxed open-mouth display" with which they're accompanied, to the "mock-fighting and chasing involved in social play" (van Hooff 217). Human infants exhibit the same kind of responses to tickling, play-chasing, mock-attacking, and also peek-a-boo. The "themes" of these games, observes Thomas R. Shultz, are "abandonment by the . . . caretaker in the case of peek-a-boo and predatory attack in the cases of tickling and chasing" (33). The arousal they excite—not to be confused with Sutton's "bad feelings," since, within a certain context and below a certain threshold, that arousal is experienced as pleasurable—has evolved to counter these threats to survival. Indeed, even today, the response of a tickled infant can sometimes tremble upon an expression of distress: it "can easily erupt into crying," Shultz writes, "if the arousal is not reduced" (33)—or recontextualized. It's recontextualized through the assurance that the threat is not real, an assurance conveyed by the smiles and predictable movements of the caretaker. And from this conceptual shift follow pleasure and laughter, signaling acknowledgment by the infant that the game is just a game. (But an adaptively valuable game, nevertheless: the playfully responsive infant is an alert, well-exercised, and so fitness-promoting infant.)

Why the smile should serve as effective reassurance may, again, be answered by the primatologist. Its origin is, doubtless, the "bared-teeth display," which in primates has both a vocalized and an unvocalized manifestation. The vocalized display (which in humans persists in the baring of teeth during fits of screaming or shouting in rage) is a reaction to "some threat or strong aversive stimulation": in monkeys it "may be regarded as a preparedness to bite, should the attacker suddenly advance," and so may be assumed to have developed in the "higher" primates "into a signal of general frustration and excitement" (van Hooff 213, 214, 215). The "silent bared-teeth" face or "fear-grin," however, communicates submissiveness in most higher primates, and its display, in some species, from dominant to subordinate suggests that it may function "as a reassuring signal or even as a sign of attachment in these species" (van Hooff 215). Human smiling probably originated in this particular display, evolving into a general "invitation to bond" (Pollio 221), a gesture as useful between human strangers as between infant and caregiving adult.

Although laughter and smiling, as the foregoing suggests, seem to have had different origins, both "have converged to a considerable extent in *Homo*" (van Hooff 212). In some situations, obviously, they are not interchangeable:

Fig. 2. At top, relaxed open-mouth display of crab-eating monkey; below, bared-teeth display or "fear grin" of rhesus macaque (drawings by Priscilla Barrett, the first after van Hooff); in Hinde 89. Reprinted by permission of Cambridge University Press.

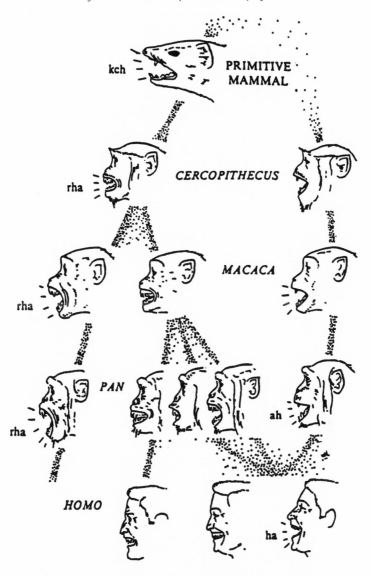

Fig 3. The phylogenetic development of laughter and smiling as suggested by homologues in existing members of the phyletic scale leading to *Homo*. "On the left is the speciation of the *silent bared-teeth* display and the *bared-teeth scream* display. The *silent bared-teeth* display, initially a submissive, later also a friendly response, seems to converge with the *relaxed open-mouth* display (on the right), a signal of play" (van Hooff 237). Reprinted by permission of Cambridge University Press.

the smile suggests "sympathy, reassurance, or appeasement" (van Hooff 227) less ambiguously than does the laugh. But often smiling seems a kind of "low-intensity laughter" (van Hooff 227), especially in the nonsocial contexts for which both have evolved. In nonhuman primates, the facial displays and vocalizations that I've described seem restricted to social negotiation and play, but in humans they have been extended to acts of mastery involving the physical and cognitive domains as well. Howard R. Pollio sums up the relevant developmentalist theory:

> From both a theoretical and an empirical standpoint . . . the earliest smiles produced by the infant and responded to by the mothering one usually function as signals of bonding; they both request—and confirm—the bond between infant and adult. Although the smile continues to have this meaning (and effect), certain theorists such as Kagan (1971)—and Piaget before, and McGhee (1979) after—have attempted to interpret smiling as a sign of rudimentary understanding brought about by an infant's growing ability to assimilate an originally unfamiliar event to an existing schema. Under this interpretation the smile means: "I've understood or mastered something I originally found strange or puzzling." This smile of recognition, or mastery, signals the end of a problem and thereby seems more related to a triumphant laugh than to the bonding smile that often transpires between the younger infant and his or her parent. (221)

Shultz proposes that this "pleasure in mastery represents a primitive stage of humour" (30), since humor theory based upon empirical research now recognizes the importance of mastery in dealing with the incongruity of jokes.

But before taking up joking and wit in general, we should pause over the paradoxes of the ethological findings. Both laughter and smiling seem to have evolved out of signals inseparable from agonistic encounters, the laugh closely tied to predatory attack, the smile to displays of both defensiveness and fear. Both emerged, in other words, from protective responses, which preserved the organism (and so advanced its interests), and yet both evolved into "*nonagonistic* signals" (van Hooff 230, my emphasis), the laugh into a pleasurable acknowledgment of safety during bouts of boisterous "mock-aggression or play" (van Hooff 235), the smile into a gesture of friendliness and appeasement. Both are ways of either expressing or inviting a form of social relation that allows one superordinance or autonomy (that is, mastery) without risking the injury or defeat of conflict. And both are, suggestively, close to anger and tears. Mary K. Rothbart's "model for laughter" (which owes much, as she acknowledges, to the theory of Berlyne that we've encountered in a previous chapter) explains why the closeness of the relationship still holds. Any sudden, intense, or discrepant stimulus may lead, she observes, to laughter or smiling, but, if the stimulus is such that it's judged to be dangerous, then fight-or-flight responses usually ensue: if not avoidance or anger, then perhaps tears of distress. "Incongruities experienced in a safe or playful setting" can lead, on the other hand, to arousal and approach (38); and a resolution of the discrepancies—physical, visual, verbal—will subsequently result in laughter or smiles.

Apparently the element common to all laugh-inducing situations (at least when the response is so-called enjoyment laughter) is the presence of a *masterable* descrepancy or incongruity, whether of a social or of a cognitive kind.[5] This has long been acknowledged by humor theorists, but only recently have the concepts that are central to the hypothesis acquired precision and sophistication. In a 1992 article in the journal *Humor,* the cognitive psychologist Giovannantonio Forabosco offers some of the most important refinements to date: "A stimulus is incongruous," he suggests, "when it differs from the cognitive model of reference" (54), that model approximating what I called earlier, in describing Eleanor Rosch's theory of categorization, a categorical "prototype." "Generally speaking," Forabosco observes, "a cognitive model does not define characteristics given in a predetermined way; rather it delineates the field of variation within which the characteristics of the stimulus must fall in order to be perceived as conforming and hence congruous" (54–55). So just as different cultures have different prototypes—a "pet" is a dog for a resident of Pennsylvania, a dove or a fish for a Thai—so those cultures (as well as the subcultures within them, and the age-groups within the subcultures) will have different models of reference for processing "discrepant" stimuli. But all cultures (and ages) will process those stimuli in exactly the same way. As in the generation of mental categories, the perception of an incongruity and its resolution (or "mastery") by an alternative "congruence criterion" occur both unconsciously and more or less instantaneously: "the congruence aspect," Forabosco writes, "is not normally brought to the awareness of the subject: it remains, as it were, in the background, almost like a mental net protecting the subject from cognitive 'recklessness'" (58). Furthermore, congruence and incongruity are grasped "in a uniconfigurational way": "we might say that at the end we have a *congruent incongruity*" (58, 59). The adaptive advantage of assimilating incongruities into diverse behavioral and cognitive systems—and, in doing so, extending intellectual reach—accounts, undoubtedly, for the pleasure of this paradox or, in plainer terms, the funniness of a joke.

Comic "thinking" is averse to Aristotelian logic (since *A* is both *A* and not-*A*), and so, not surprisingly, as we remarked earlier, it's apparently the province of the right side of the brain. Theorist Paul E. McGhee points out that "data from the limited number of humor studies completed with individuals with right- or left-hemisphere damage are consistent with the view that it is the right hemisphere that performs the insightful integration of the key elements of information that must be meaningfully linked before the humor can be understood and appreciated" (30). Predictably, given this lateralized processing, men and women react differently

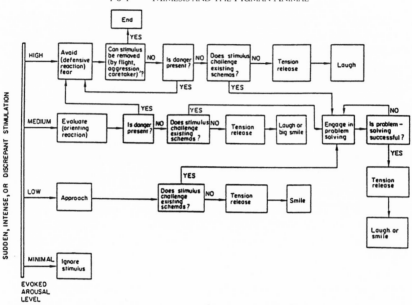

Fig. 4. Mary K. Rothbart's model of laughter. "Schematic representation of affective response to sudden, intense, or discrepant stimulation" (Rothbart 39). Reprinted by permission of John Wiley and Sons, Ltd.

to humor, women monitoring their own laughter more closely before making a judgment about funniness, perhaps a "manifestation of a general trend toward females taking their own expressive reactions into account in making judgments about events" (McGhee 23). Even more significant is McGhee's suggestion that, because humor is processed by the hemisphere that lacks what Gazzaniga calls an "interpreter," there may be some substance to "the common observation that trying to analyze or explain humor interferes with funniness" (32). Similarly, there may be substance to Freud's familiar claim that the "unconscious" is plumbed in humor—if we adopt the suggestion in Chapter 3 that equates right-hemisphere processing with unconscious thought. Humor offers a way of bringing to light, not an "infantile type of thought-activity" (170), but antagonisms inherent in the biogram (and perhaps deeply imprinted on the more "primitive" hemisphere) that reasoned—that is, left-brain—analysis would usually pronounce unworthy of their professors. Thus the easy gravitation of humor toward sexist and ethnic jokes; thus, too, the incompatability of firmly held values with humor that seeks congruence in their shameless (but often witless) transgression. "Take my wife . . . please!" is not funny to a female Significant Other.

But to insist, as some theorists do, that humor is "fundamentally" transgressive (or liberating) is to simplify a complex issue. "Joking," as Lewis writes, "can not only express but also support and advance destructive ideologies and political programs."

> On the other hand, as [Lawrence] La Fave and [Roger] Mannell have shown, in other circumstances ethnic jokes can be harmless or socially beneficial. Sociologists of humor have demonstrated that we cannot conclude *a priori* that humor in general is harmless, or liberating or oppressive. . . . Insofar as the sociological study of humor is now based on the observation that humor serves many social functions, an awareness of sociological research can give the student of comedy not "one idea of laughter" but a complex sense of the multiple uses of humor . . . : a sense that humor can be innocent, in Freud's sense of the word, or tendentious, hostile or benign, oppressive or revolutionary, that it can support or undermine accepted norms, that it both highlights and dismisses incongruities. (39)

Comedy, also, can be and do these things, and to hold it accountable to a "truth" about life is an obviously misguided project. "*Comedy*," we're told (in italics, of course), "*is an amusing, relatively discontinuous action concerning success and failure in social relations and culminating in a judgment whereby the 'divine average' triumphs over the exceptional or peculiar*" (McCollom 7). The first part of that sentence seems reasonable enough (although there are many comedies that are neither amusing nor discontinuous, and "physical comedy"—say, Chaplin on rollerskates—needn't be about "social relations"), but that comedy culminates in the triumph of the "average" is a judgment of doubtful validity. In what sense, for example, is Ubu Roi "average"? And, if he is not, are the plays in which he appears not comedies? Again: comedy is "the joyous consciousness of our finitude, the capacity to be amused at what holds us in check" (Gutwirth 190), but rogue comedy, I shall argue, achieves its effects by exceeding the "finitude" of human powers. When the incorrigible Jim Dixon walks off with the girl at the end of Kingsley Amis's *Lucky Jim*, his escape from limitations is exhilaratingly complete, offering a vision of Effrontery Untrammeled and Unbowed.

  If comedy is to be approached with descriptive precision and not merely prescriptive, or proscriptive, force, we should confine our discussion to its indisputable determinants: its humor and the tendency of its hero to triumph. Even so we should realize that just one is sufficient: sentimental comedy (such as Steele's *The Conscious Lovers*) can be completely devoid of humor, and dark comedy, though full of it, can be careless of its principals (recall Rosencrantz and Guildenstern from Stoppard's play); yet both kinds of representation are respectable claimants. But a work can't lack humor *and* a rewarded hero and still be a called a comedy. As *Lucky*

Jim illustrates, that hero and his girl may stand alone at the conclusion, especially in modern examples of the genre, many of which seem to show an affinity with the romantic polarizations of melodrama. (And even Shakespeare does not share Frye's anxiety about the inclusiveness of the denouement: not only is Shylock self-exiled, as Frye points out, from the final festivities of the *Merchant,* but so is dour Jacques of *As You Like It;* and the pathetic Malvolio of *Twelfth Night* exits famously swearing a revenge.)

And, just as it is difficult to find a single tendency in the dramatization of the hero's triumph (the title-character of the film *Charlie Bubbles* escapes what Dante would call the "harshness" of his affairs in a magically providential hot-air balloon), so, too, is it impossible to defend, for "laughing" comedy, every instance of humor as thematically apt. Frye finds such aptness in comic disguise, calling it preparation for "a movement from illusion to reality" (169), but tragedy is equally obsessed with such movement, and disguise is rarely a recourse of its characters. Clearly, disguise, among the conventional comic confusions—mistaken identity, misunderstandings of all sorts, messages and letters and tokens that go astray, farcical maneuverings in ill-lighted quarters, encounters with animals, sight gags and sound riffs—is important primarily for its incongruity, specifically for a type of incongruity that (unlike the serious dissembling of a villain—say, Edmund's in *King Lear*) seems harmless and so subject to the mastery of laughter by an audience that is cued to its playfulness. Of course the inventive writer will graft these incongruities to character and/or to theme, but comedy can be successful—at least efficiently amusing—in bald-faced defiance of both: a late episode of *Cheers* saw Carla dropped repeatedly down the well of a pantry dumbwaiter, a piece of business essentially unconnected to character (Rebecca would have been a more likely victim) and mute with respect to thematic development, but a funny bit nevertheless.

The scene as a whole suggests how important is cuing to the audience's reception of comedy. Cuing may be thought of as an extension of "set": in comedy we're not only set for humor, but cued in various semiotic ways to regard the (perceived or imagined) spectacle now as playfully, whimsically fictive, now as seriously engaging and "real." In a fictive spectacle, no harm is possible, and so, although Carla is apparently dropped from a height that would cripple a human being, her stylized shriek and the context of mayhem—general, improbable, but infectious—assure us that a *character,* not a person, has been victimized. But she's a much beloved character, and so she must survive—unlike the minister who dies quietly in the episode and whose body is bundled from place to place in an effort to conceal his demise. It was, doubtless, scenes like these that led Bergson to conclude that "the comic demands something like a momentary anesthesia of the heart" (63–64). But I think we can refine that judgment: first, it is *laughter,* not "the comic," that is a sign of constrained feeling, although we needn't agree that, in Bergson's words, an *"absence of feeling . . .* usually accompanies laughter" (63).

Laughter is an expression of the pleasure of mastery, of what Hobbes called, rightly, "a *sudden glory* arising from some sudden *conception* of some *eminency* in ourselves" (46), although that eminency is not necessarily a social one. "The comic," on the other hand—comedy, more generally—may admit of other feelings, and, even in the presence of comic "types," we may experience a considerable range of emotions as we oscillate between identification with or empathy for a character and detachment encouraged by a sense of our "eminency." The minister of *Cheers* had no time for ingratiation, given the perfunctoriness of his on-camera life; his death, therefore, seems of little consequence, permitting the incongruities of his mortification (so affectively unreal) to delight.[6]

Here we have a case of visual incongruity, of a corpse inconveniently encumbering the pantry, an incongruity "mastered" by the implicit concession that an encumbrance is an encumbrance, dead body or what-have-you, and that it must be shifted like any other eyesore if the party is to be a success. (But, as Forabosco notes, this is "congruous incongruity": the encumbrance remains stubbornly a corpse.) When we turn from situation to character in comedy, we remain within the paradigm sketched out above, but we can introduce a greater orderliness into our discussion by classifying comic characters according to type. Frye's is the best-known of these classifications, but his categories seem to me both eccentric and confused. His enthusiasm for Aristotle sends him to the *Ethics*, as well as to the anonymous *Tractatus Coislinianus* (sometimes argued to be a summary of *Poetics II*), and from these he derives four types that fall, suspiciously, into the symmetry of "two opposed pairs": the *alazon* (impostor) and the *eiron* (self-deprecator) oppose the *bomolochos* (buffoon) and the *agroikos* (churl) (172). The "self-deprecator" he associates with the hero of comedy, since "the dramatist tends to play him down and make him rather neutral and unformed in character" (173)—although how this diminution relates to self-deprecation is not immediately clear. Nor is it clear why the go-betweens of comedy (the sharp slaves of Plautus and Terence, for example) should be classed as self-deprecators as well. When we turn to Frye's buffoons and churls, we find that both of them can be described as fools: then we read, puzzlingly, that "often . . . the churl belongs to the *alazon* group," since in comedy "all miserly old men" are churls (176). Finally, a fifth type is smuggled into the argument, "a character we may call the plain dealer, an outspoken advocate of a kind of moral norm who has the sympathy of the audience" (176).

These categorical confusions can be avoided, I think, if we restrict the types to just those characters that elicit laughter (or the smile), conceding that others, like the mouthpiece or author's "advocate," are not exclusively *comic* types. So restricted, the types reduce to a simple four (and no Greek names are necessary): the fool, the wit, the rogue, and—in the case of romantic comedy—the hero.[7] But it may be best to regard them, not as types, but as centers of gravity to which characters are drawn and around which, temporarily or permanently, they coalesce, often in motley states of hybridization. It's rare to find pure examples of the four: the fool, for example, is often witty (or "wise"), the rogue is sometimes identical with the hero; a character may begin as a rogue but be proven a fool, like Volpone or Tartuffe. And it's possible—even usual in the modern sitcom—for a character to drift in and out of "type": Falstaff (in the hands of an intelligent actor) is not solely defined by his comic persona(e). For the sake of clarity, however, I'll discuss each type as a behavioral potentiality with both purity and persistence. I should emphasize that I'm dealing with conceptual categories, not literary figures (Lear's Fool, for example) in which hybridization has already taken place (like Erasmus's Folly, Lear's Fool is wise). If this is kept in mind, I'll be forgiven some of the simplifications involved in sharpening and delimiting the categories.

The fool is perhaps the most important of the types, since his (or her) blunders often serve to clarify the norms of the comic spectacle. Usually it's the fool who actively "blocks" those norms, as Orgon blocks both the lovers' union and the concomitant restoration of common sense throughout the first four acts of *Tartuffe*. Frye suggests that the absurdity of such a character results from "what Pope calls a ruling passion" and that his or her function "is to express a state of what might be called ritual bondage" (168). All fools, like Orgon, are addled by obsession, and the movement of the play is toward delivery from their bondage, toward "a kind of moral norm, or pragmatically free society" (169). But the example of Orgon should give us pause. He's obsessed, it is true, but his obsession is a symptom, not the cause, of his absurdity. When his eyes are finally opened to Tartuffe's hypocrisy, his reaction is not to throw off his shackles, but to chain himself blindly to another illusion: "Enough, by God!" he cries to Cléante (here in Wilbur's elegant translation), "I'm through with pious men: / Henceforth I'll hate the whole false brotherhood, / And persecute them worse than Satan could" (Molière 301). Because he seems such a vital creature, modern readers have been eager to account for his weaknesses in psychologically determinate ways: he's a repressed (and so fantasmatically enfevered) homosexual; he's a "narcissist" fleeing "ontological insecurity" (Riggs 38); he's a tyrant who is punishing his family "for possessing what he feels himself to be losing: youth, gaiety, strong natural desires" (Wilbur 161). All of this may be true, but the most plausible explanation is that he is a fool, and that fools are incorrigibly stupid.

Such are the blocking figures in Roman comedy, usually characters as free of a "ruling passion" as they are of intelligence. How is it, for example, that old Theopropides, the *senex* in Plautus's *Mostellaria*, is so easily duped by Tranio, his slave, into believing that his house is haunted? The answer: Theopropides is a fool, and fools can be expected to be credulous. He suffers fundamentally from what Bergson calls a *"callousness to social life"*: "Any individual is comic," Bergson suggests, "who automatically goes his own way without troubling himself about getting into touch with the rest of his fellow-beings" (147). When he is *put* in touch with them, as Theopropides is, he is unable to "read" them with precision or skill. We can translate this into narrative terms: as the villain of melodrama is narratively deviant, indifferent to the social rights of the victim, so the fool of comedy is narratively incompetent, unable to detect the stratagems by which he or she is duped by the rogue.

The fool lacks *mastery*—a mastery measured not only by its defense against roguery but also by the norms of the fictive world with which his or her behavior is incongruent. Which is to say that foolishness unattributable to mere narrative incompetence is always a relative affair, and that what is foolish in one play or novel (by the reckoning of its norms) may be genuinely admirable behavior in another. It's not difficult to find in many comedies, for example, various boobies who are the fools of books, but in Aldous Huxley's wicked *Antic Hay*, we encounter in Casimir Lypiatt a stupidity derived from an ignorance of T. S. Eliot ("Look down on Mexico, Conquistador," runs a typical line of his fervid doggerel: "Land of your golden dream" [47]).[8] *Any* set of norms is in fact possible in comedy, and any fool may be found to violate them, since stupidity, the fool's defining malady, may be chalked up to any cause. Oversophistication or undersophistication, lack of constraint or too much control, contempt for the average or its divinization—all are possible targets in comedy, and a fool may be imagined for each of them.

The foolishness can take various forms, of course. Lypiatt's is verbal, part of a lively history of linguistic incompetence, from the turgidity of Aeschylus in Aristophanes' *Frogs*, to the baffled entanglements of a lost Lou Costello as he stumbles through "Who's on First." The issue is mastery, or the fool's lack of it, and so any aspect of the fool's experience is subject to his or her omnivorous bungling—the physical, the verbal, the social, the imaginative. (As an example of the latter, there is Kirby Groomkirby from N. F. Simpson's play *One Way Pendulum*, who conceives the project of teaching speak-your-weight scales to sing the "Hallelujah Chorus." Once instructed, they'll all be transported to the North Pole, where a crowd will gather to hear them. The listeners will be asked to jump on cue; the impact will tilt the earth on its axis; the ensuing Ice Age will cause thousands of deaths, and bring out mourning attire—gratifyingly for Kirby, since he is fascinated by black clothing.) The pleasure of the spectator lies in perceiving the bungling both as possible and as incongruous: possible because the fool is "out of touch" (even Aeschylus occasionally nods), incongruous because the spectator is narratively savvy, or sympathetic—for the nonce—with the norms. (Children, significantly, find an absurd movement funny only after they have mastered the movement themselves [Levowitz 113].) It's from, then, a certain spectatorial remove that the fool's calamities are entertained, a detachment bespeaking the viewer's own eminency as much as his or her sense of the harmlessness of the scene.

Not so, I think, with the wit. Part of the pleasure in beholding a wit work is in imagining the mastery of the character as one's own. While the fool incarnates all manner of incompetence, the wit enjoys total control. Like the fool's, his or her world is interactively various, and various are the wits that control it. The physical wit is an acrobat or juggler: a Chaplin, for example, who's a Brummell of his bowler or suave balletic genius of his cane. (Usually, however, this wit is a hybrid, a fool that is a wit by inadvertence: Harold Lloyd of course always comes to mind, dangling spiderishly from his clockface and mastering the precariousness *malgré lui*.) As for the wits of the verbal, there are no purer examples than the characters of *The Importance of Being Earnest*; in them wit acquires a kind of bizarre self-sufficiency, unalloyed to the vulgarity of psychological motive ("You see, [my diary] is simply a very young girl's record of her own thoughts and impressions, and consequently meant for publication" [73]). Less exaltedly, we can repair to the sitcom, where the fools seem, unfortunately, to be getting rarer and the rogues have all but disappeared (Dabney Coleman's much-missed Buffalo Bill crowned the type with short-lived glory) but the wits survive enfeebled though undaunted. Murphy Brown doesn't have the style of Lady Bracknell, but she has the wit's characteristically assured savoir faire. Somewhat less common are wits of the imagination, although Stoppard, at least in his early work, seems fascinated with the type: in *Jumpers* it makes an appearance as Archie, whose philosophy is that "no problem is insoluble given a big enough plastic bag." Dandy, magician, acrobat, Archie is close kin to those shadowy wits with whom the artist is often romantically allied: Shakespeare's Prospero, Nietzsche's rope-dancer, the confidence men of Melville and Mann.[9] But in these figures the humor (if it is present) is greatly attenuated, a legacy of the artist's ambivalence about art, and about the humanity that aspires to its crafty perfection.

The social wit enjoys its most vital life in classical and Renaissance comedy: there it's enfigured as the go-between, the willing servant, the wily slave, the Celestina of Spain's early Golden Age drama, the *architectus* of Plautine intrigue. As the so-called first *zanni* of *commedia dell'arte*, it tends to control the entire comic action, keeping the lovers on tenterhooks, duping fools, foiling rogues, then making all come out right in the end. Of all the comic types it seems the most fantastical, since its motives are often obscure, even perverse. Of course the slave of Roman comedy and the Spanish *gracioso* are both driven by fear and a concern for their livelihood, but later incarnations, like Dorine of *Tartuffe*, seem to abet the lovers' interest in defiance of their own. That they're born as the fulfillment of a (usually male) wish is suggested by the magical milieu of Puck and Ariel, "the two clearest examples of the type in Shakespeare" (Frye 174), and in keeping with their general fantasticality, they are usually of uncertain or indeterminate origin, having (like Murdoch's charismatic Julius King, whom we'll meet in the following chapter) neither discoverable parentage nor kin. As literature becomes more realistic (and its social context more egalitarian) this type is endangered, reduced to the clever Jeeves of Wodehouse's stories, or to the spunky maid, like Shirley Booth's Hazel.

But we have a need for the type, and so we find for it contexts other than those that traditionally obtain between master and servant or slave: Eddie Murphy's inventions in *Beverly Hills Cop* are some of the most brilliant of its later avatars, even though Justice is the only master it serves.

In most of these characters there's an admixture of the rogue, and it may be tempting to class the latter as simply a subtype of the wit. But I think that the rogue deserves a class of its own, not only because rogues are not always witty (Tom Arnold's roguery in "The Jackie Thomas Show" smacked more of the fool than the wit) but also because the rogue, as I shall argue, rouses in the spectator a more complex response than detachment or identification. The defining characteristic of the rogue is gross selfishness: unlike the social wit, which survives in serving others, however incidentally, mercenarily, or reluctantly, the rogue works for him- or herself alone; the rogue's name—"Volpone," "Sergeant Bilko," "Lex Luthor"— often suggests contest or predation. If the social wit sometimes seems a fantastical creature, the rogue seems an unnervingly possible one. It satisfies, not the hunger of easy access to the girl, of social harmony or the triumph of justice, but the more modest thirst for exploitation. The rogue is, in the terminology of the evolutionist, a "cheat" at the banquet of life. (In Roman comedy, the banquet is often literal, and the rogue who sits down to it a "parasite.") If he or she can get something for nothing—or for the small effort that it takes to be adopted by a rich man, or to pretend a deathbed agony and bilk the would-be heirs—then neither the intelligent nor the foolish is immune from victimization. The rogue can be utterly ruthless in swindling others, and yet still retain the appeal of a comic type.

How it can do so is partly explained by the playfulness of comedy as a whole. The rogue's aggressiveness is *mock*-aggressiveness, a fact that is signaled by the cues of a text or, in the case of performance, of an actor. The incongruity of his or her criminality is resolved, therefore, by its apprehension as a game. But the appeal of the figure runs deeper, I think, than its power to evoke incongruity: the rogue holds out a certain attraction to the spectator, as one who can turn the social scene to his or her wanton advantage. Having silenced that voice that tells us how far we can go without incurring intolerable risks (what Alexander calls the voice of conscience), the rogue slips by both shame and guilt to savor the fruits of audacity. When those fruits are stolen from the mouths of fools, there is little scruple in our laughter, since the fool's misfortunes, as I earlier suggested, are viewed from a superior vantage. When the intelligent and the upright are fleeced, however, our identifying with the rogue becomes more problematic: here, if we laugh, we do so at the expense of those who seem undeserving of exploitation. But, if not laughter, certainly a smile of complicity is permissible in the presence of even the most merciless of rogues; in fact, that display seems *required* whenever a spectator expresses sympathy with the unscrupulous (recall, again, Richard III), maybe because the smile is an automatic signal of appeasement that wards off the suspicion of criminal contagion. Usually, our response to rogues in comedy is ambiguously mixed, our laughter expressing sympathetic identification, our smiles unconscious expiatory reassurance, both of which confusedly converge in "mirth."

What is most significant about all three of these types—the fool, the wit, the rogue—is that they invite a response that confirms in the spectator a sense of his or her social eminency. In laughing *at* the fool, or *with* the wit, or (ambivalently) in complicity with the rogue's transgressions, we enjoy in comedy a release from the necessity of negotiating social compromise. Comedy may explicitly valorize that compromise, especially when it ends in promiscuous festivity, but *implicitly* the laughter of its audience serves the interests of the masterful individual alone. Such a conclusion accords with the empirical findings on the effects of laughter on the physiology and psychology of the organism: laughter, it's been learned over the last several years, can strengthen both the stress- and disease-fighting immune system (Berk et al., "Humor," "Laughter," "Mirth"; Dillon, Minchoff, and Baker; Martin et al.); it can alleviate pain and reduce psychological tension (Cogan et al.; Martin and Lefcourt; Nevo, Keinan, and Teshimovsky-Arditi; Zillmann et al.); it can increase creativity and flexibility of thought (Isen, Daubman, and Nowicki; Isen). All these reflect *phenotypic* advantages, and comedy may differ essentially from tragedy in licensing the drive toward self-serving fitness by the laughter of its spectators.[10] Whereas tragedy moves its hero toward isolation while implicitly valorizing the affiliative behaviors, comedy moves the hero toward union while implicitly valorizing the mastery of its beholders. Also, tragedy encourages empathic understanding of a kind that is foreign to "laughing" comedy: laughter is the sign of an incongruity mastered by a previously assimilated schema; as such, nothing is "new" to it, so to speak, and, unlike the pleasures of the tragic *katharsis*, the emotion that it engages is, however delightful, always one and the same. It is inimical, consequently, to the *work* of empathy, which not only deepens one's self-understanding but extends and enriches one's affiliative range.[11]

Apparently all of the types had their ancient origin in a figure whose behavior seems to confirm these conclusions, the so-called Trickster of oral narrative. Known by many names and under many forms, anthropomorphic as well as theriomorphic, the Trickster appears in both Eastern and Western cultures as a creature in which "seemingly contradictory roles are combined in a single personality" (Apte 214). Like the fool, he has little control over either his physical self or the world: the hands, for example, of a Winnebago Trickster get into a quarrel with themselves, the right slashing the left with a knife; "in another story he instructs his anus to keep watch over the roasted ducks while he sleeps, and when he finds out that they have been eaten by foxes, he tries to punish the offender by sitting on the fire but cannot endure the pain"; in still another, "he eats a bulb despite a warning that it will lead to defecation and almost drowns in the mountain of his own excrement" (Apte 215). But the Trickster is also a cunning rogue, and his insatiable appetite for food and sex hotly stimulates his invention. As Krishna (the hero of the *Mahabharata* and the narrator of the *Bhagavad-Gita*), he toys with the breasts of nubile young milkmaids on the pretext of recovering a stray ball, or he hides their clothes as they bathe in the river, agreeing to return them only if the owners emerge to claim them in the nude. The Zande Trickster, Ture (or "spider"), kills his father in his quest for a magic formula and seduces his mother-in-law. (But even armed with the formula he goes without food, and his penis confesses his incest.)

Like the type that I call the social wit, the Trickster is also a beneficial agent: Ture brings food and fire to the earth; Krishna slays demons in protection of his people, and the Oceanic Trickster, Maui-of-a-Thousand-Tricks, gives land and sun and vegetation to humanity. But apparently so inadvertent is so much of his benevolence that some anthropologists have demurred at the suggestion that the Trickster is a "cultural hero." "Tricksters," writes anthropologist Mahadev L. Apte, whose account I have followed above,

> are not culture heroes in the sense in which the term is commonly used. They are not noble, generous, caring, far-sighted, or altruistic. They certainly lack both a broad vision of the ultimate good of human societies and a motivation to act for it. As Boas . . . rightly noted, the fact that the tricksters' acts benefited humans is simply accidental, an unintentional by-product of the quest for self-gratification or trouble. (232)

Tricksters, in short, lack a sense of empathy, and they do so, I think, because they are conceived to excite laughter alone. When empathy inflects the social wit's behavior—when the Pedrolino of classical *commedia dell'arte* ceases to separate Isabella and Flavio, or to tease Franceschina, or to dupe the Dottore, regarding them no longer as objects of fun but as unfortunates deserving of fair-dealing— the laughter of the comedy evaporates. We are converging upon our previously implied point: that laughter and the movement toward affiliation in comedy are elements—to quote Nelson—"in conflict" (2).

It's not only the type, then, but also all humor in general that, for Nelson, opposes the closure of comedy: "In *As You Like It*, and in many other comedies, there is a tension between the forward movement of the plot, which is usually towards marriage, and the backward pull of the dialogue, which ridicules it" (46). Doubtless he is thinking of a scene like the following, in which the love-sick Orlando is teased by Rosalind, disguised as a boy but posing as herself, and incensed at her lover's tardiness:

> ROS. . . . I had as lief be woo'd of a snail.
> ORL. Of a snail!

ROS. Ay, of a snail; for though he comes slowly, he carries his house on his head—a better jointure, I think, than you make a woman; besides, he brings his destiny with him.

ORL. What's that?

ROS. Why, horns; which such as you are fain to be beholding to your wives for; but he comes armed in his fortune, and prevents the slander of his wife. (4.1.46–55)

Although Orlando protests that "my Rosalind is virtuous," every lover's nightmare has been rehearsed here in play. The teasing badinage of *As You Like It* presents marriage as a surreptitious contest of wills, a struggle, as it were, for phenotypic fitness, in which victory is measured in potential reproductive success. If the wife does not crown her husband with horns, she keeps him clapped in a (somewhat noisy) domestic zoo: "I will be more jealous of thee," quips Rosalind to Orlando, "than a Barbary cock-pigeon over his hen, more clamorous than a parrot against rain, more new-fangled than an ape, more giddy in my desires than a monkey" (4.1.133–35). This view of marriage, as a check to independence and a field of warring interests, threads clearly through comedy from Aristophanes to Shaw, whose John Tanner expresses it with trenchant vigor: "Marriage is to me apostasy, profanation of the sanctuary of my soul, violation of my manhood, sale of my birthright, shameful surrender, ignominious capitulation, acceptance of defeat" (Shaw 203). And marriage is, of course, not the only self-abrogation. "The comic attitude to children and childbirth has always," writes Nelson, "been ambivalent":

> Babies in comedy are left on mountainsides, in baskets, on doorsteps, or even in the left-luggage compartments of railway stations; but the assumption, in all but the darkest works, is that they will turn up again when they are old enough to be interesting. Aristophanes, in *The Frogs*, chides Euripides for dwelling too much on domestic things in his tragedies, but the rule against cooing over children applies just as strongly to comedy: children restrict freedom, and freedom is one of the defining characteristics of the comic hero and heroine. (72)

And yet the hero and heroine of romantic comedy stand as protests to that last remark. Their defining characteristic (as Tanner's case illustrates) is their willingness to give up their freedom—precisely that willingness that Nelson has argued is "in conflict" with the values of laughter. But the word "conflict," I think, is a misleading one, at least if the argument of comedy is grasped in full adaptationist terms. The "tension" of comedy that Nelson describes is an expression of the paradox of the sexual animal: intent on maximizing its inclusive fitness but inevitably compromising its "own" interests in the pursuit. Whereas laughter licenses the latter interests, the affiliative sentiments ensure that they widen to embrace an "inclusive" success. To be brief: romantic comedy serves ultimately the gene, not the phenotype that laughter preserves. As Shaw says (in diluting Schopenhauer with Bergson), it's the "Life Force" that finally "enchants."

It does so through the seductiveness of the smile, our response to the success and marriage of the hero, a response that legitimates our earlier having classed him with the rest of the comic types. Unless that hero is a hybridized creature, quasi-fool, -wit, or -rogue, he is not a character to excite our laughter; he is, rather, the figure of Frye's cool adjectives—"rather neutral and unformed." In the comic denouement, he acquires not so much definition as a kind of affective weight: he gains in substance as we smile in sympathy, especially at the spectacle of his union. The union need not be (although it usually is) marital: at the end of the *Menaechmi* it joins brother with brother; at the end of *The Winter's Tale*, husband with wife. What is essential is that the bitterest enemies exit as friends and that nobody kills anyone else. For in affiliations such as these, comedy offers the "understanding" of which it is most capable, even if inarticulately so. It doesn't deepen and refine the social emotions, as the *pathos* of tragedy tends to do; it rouses a pleasurably self-ratifying intuition: the sense, in Frye's words, that "this should be." Baudelaire called it "joy," and associated it with the smile; whereas the laugh was "satanic," a sign of "fallen humanity" (115, 122), the smile was "analogous to the wagging of a dog's tail, or to the purring of a cat" (120). His intuitions seem right, at least about the smile, for, like those "purely animal expressions of contentment" (120), it signals a willingness to bond and the pleasure of doing so—and, in sharing it with the hero of comedy, the spectator expresses both understanding and respect for the feeling that has ensured his union.

That the smile should be perceived as justifiably routing laughter is a measure of the hegemony of the gene. Nelson quotes a character in Goethe's *Elective Affinities* who is musing on the meretriciousness of the comic denouement:

> In a comedy we see a marriage as the final fulfillment of a desire which has been thwarted by the obstacles of several acts. The moment the desire is fulfilled the curtain falls, and this momentary satisfaction goes on echoing in our minds. . . . In the real world the play continues after the curtain has fallen, and when it is raised again there is not so much pleasure to be gained by seeing or hearing what is going on. (46)

Too cynical by half, of course. But, more important, irrelevant as a critique of romantic comedy. The very function of the latter is to confer that "momentary satisfaction"; its denouement may be likened to the *katharsis* of tragedy, which illuminates the destructiveness of the asocial will. Both genres, for all their formal dissimilarities, tend to encourage those behaviors that conscript the individual into the productive self-diminishments of cooperation and conjugation. Neither is completely unambivalent about the enterprise: Medea in her chariot may be facing, as she knows, a future of unrelieved remorse, but her revenge has nevertheless been exhilarating; and the Ubu Rois of comedy will never consent to self-control, much to the delight of those spectatorial rebels brandishing imaginary pschittaswords. But, in the main, Love is Best because it's an expedient ethic: it ensures the delivery of the selfish gene from one short-lived gamete-bearer to another. The attendants of that delivery may be splendidly various, as a consideration of these two literary modes suggest. In the long run, however, there is only one human story, and it is inscribed and reinscribed by the mortal coils for the sake of the mute—and quite inglorious—immortal ones.

Especially for the Western mind, the dissimilarities may seem paramount. Our usual tendency is to regard tragedy and comedy, not as performing similar adaptive functions, but as offering more or less veridical (and opposed) generic "visions" of human life. By "more or less veridical," I mean that one seems "more," and the other "less." Rarely is a literary critic able to resist the temptation to take sides in their ostensible debate. After describing or defining one of the genres in coarsely or subtly unflattering terms, the critic then holds up the other as the more incisive, more comprehensive, or simply more true. Here, for example, is Joseph W. Meeker, who begins, interestingly enough, with a position like my own, but who then goes on to depart radically from it, mainly by ignoring the spectator:

> As patterns of behavior, both tragedy and comedy are strategies for the res-
> olution of conflicts. From the tragic perspective, the world is a battleground
> where good and evil, man and nature, truth and falsehood make war, each
> with the goal of destroying its polar opposite. Warfare is the basic metaphor
> of tragedy, and its strategy is a battle plan designed to eliminate the enemy.
> That is why tragedy ends with a funeral or its equivalent. Comic strategy, on
> the other hand, sees life as a game. Its basic metaphors are sporting events
> and the courtship of lovers, and its conclusion is generally a wedding rather
> than a funeral. When faced with polar opposites, the problem of comedy is
> always how to resolve conflict without destroying the participants. Comedy
> is the art of accommodation and reconciliation. (37–38)

This is a crude example, but typical enough, because grounded in an as-sumption that is inseparable from critical practice, at least since the demise of structuralism: that literature is usually about human behavior, either as it is or as it ideally should be, and that one work of literature (or of philosophy or "theory") is preferable to another because it is persuasively faithful to that behavior. For Meeker, accommodation is ideally preferable to warfare, and, because comedy and not tragedy seems to enjoin accommodation, comedy is preferable to tragedy.

Even the most sophisticated of critics is drawn into this side-taking. Gellrich, for example, in deploring Aristotle's "distinct bias against a conflictual understanding of character and action," implies that, not only is tragedy always conflictual, but the human being itself is to be understood as a thing of rifts and aporias, the incarnate logomachy of postmodernist myth. The fundamental question is still, What is Man? and the conviction that still drives the study of literature is that somewhere in the multiplicities of the literary dynamics lies an answer to that question.

Now that generic distinctions have begun to collapse, it may seem likelier that the answers have become more subtle, and that Meeker's simple choice between the warrior and the sportsman is no longer a possible one. But, as I shall suggest in Chapter 7, the either/or that preeminently characterizes Western thought still constrains its conceptual powers. To think "philosophically" is to conceive the human being, not as the angelic and the diabolic, in Baudelaire's metaphor, that "move along parallel lines," but as fundamentally the one or the other: or—to shift the debate from the moral to the ontological—either as "essential" or "constructed," "unified" or "conflicted," "indeterminate" or (naively) "whole." Even the modern novelist (when that novelist is a "philosopher") is not immune to such reductionist thinking. But his or her fiction (when that fiction is persuasive) exacts a kind of mentation that throws it off. The thought of narrative apprehends the human being as what Wilson calls a "hodgepodge" of behaviors, and "fundamentally" reducible to none of them. If human life, as I've argued, serves the selfish gene, it does so in variegated (and often demonstrably unselfish) ways. To sample the variety— and yet descry the service—we need only open any mimetically compelling work of literature, but, to devise an illustration for the argument of this paragraph, we should conclude with a book by an artist and a philosopher. For us, the choice falls naturally on the ethicist who has already made an appearance in these pages: the Iris Murdoch of several volumes of philosophy and, among her many persuasive novels, of *A Fairly Honourable Defeat.*

7

Gilding the Mirror: Mimesis and Philosophy in A Fairly Honourable Defeat

Art cannot help changing what it professes to display into something different.
—Iris Murdoch, *Metaphysics as a Guide to Morals*

1

"What seems to me . . . true and important in Freudian theory," writes Iris Murdoch, iterating sentiments we have met with earlier in this book, "is as follows":

> Freud takes a thoroughly pessimistic view of human nature. He sees the psyche as an egocentric system of quasi-mechanical energy, largely determined by its own individual history, whose natural attachments are sexual, ambiguous, and hard for the subject to understand or control. Introspection reveals only the deep tissue of ambivalent motive, and fantasy is a stronger force than reason. Objectivity and unselfishness are not natural to human beings. (*Sovereignty* 51)

This is a theory of personality that owes as much to Murdoch's beloved Plato as to Freud. In the *Laws*, Plato's Athenian Stranger describes "each of us living beings" (in a metaphor that will not be lost on Murdoch's character Julius King) as "a puppet of the Gods," pulled toward vice by the "iron" cords of the "affections" and toward virtue by "the sacred and golden cord of reason." But reason, he adds, is also "called by us the common law of the state" (II.425), and it is clear that for at least the later Plato the virtuous man is formed less by the expression of inherent capacities than by an accession to the common will. In thus locating the source of moral authority outside the individual human being, he solves a problem that dogs Murdoch herself throughout all of her philosophical texts.

For if objectivity and unselfishness are indeed not "natural" to human beings—or, as Murdoch puts the case most recently in *Metaphysics as a Guide to Morals*, if "we cannot see the point of being moral beyond a certain level, we cannot *imagine* it except in terms of pure damaging disadvantage" (331)—then how is it that right action may be achieved merely by an exercise of "attention"? Such is Murdoch's repeated prescription for the attainment of moral integrity. Her often-cited example of the hypothetical mother M and of her daughter-in-law D offers a simple but highly problematic illustration. M feels hostility toward D, who, though "quite a good-hearted girl," seems "pert and familiar, insufficiently ceremonious, brusque, sometimes positively rude, always tiresomely juvenile." M's first thought is that her "poor son has married a silly vulgar girl." But because she is "an intelligent and well-intentioned person, capable of self-criticism, capable of giving careful and just *attention* to an object which confronts her," she resolves to "look again." And "gradually her vision of D alters": "D is discovered to be not vulgar but refreshingly simple, not undignified but spontaneous, not noisy but gay, not tiresomely juvenile but delightfully youthful, and so on" (*Sovereignty* 17–18). M has been morally transfigured, and the instrument for this change has been *vision*.

Genevieve Lloyd has identified the obvious weakness of this conclusion: "The struggle for just perception must, it seems, rest on a moral conviction that the real is indeed good; that there is goodness independent of ourselves, which we can come to see clearly by struggling out of the perceptual distortions of egoism. Yet we have been given no reason to believe that this is so" (64). M's change of perspective, in other words, certainly may invite our approval, but it by no means substantiates the assertion that by simply looking we may attain to greater accuracy of vision. "The world," Lloyd writes, "construed as 'there' independent of consciousness, we may say, surely does not contain value" (65). M's "discovery" of virtues in D has nothing to do with D herself; it merely records a greater willingness on M's part to tolerate and construe favorably what had before seemed tiresome and offensive. The appeal of Murdoch's argument is to the reader's sentimental weakness for good feeling—an appeal about which Murdoch-as-novelist seems to be intuitively (and inventively) shrewd. Hilda Foster counts precisely on the efficacy of this appeal when she argues with her husband, Rupert, in the opening scene of *A Fairly Honourable Defeat*:

" . . . Tallis is such a sort of *runt*."

"What a horrid word, Hilda. Surely that can't truthfully describe any-body."

"Why not, you high-minded old ass? Can 'sagacious, open-faced and virile' truthfully describe someone?"

"Who are you trying to describe?"

"You, of course!"

"Hilda, you should have been a philosopher." (25–26)

But the Murdoch of *The Sovereignty of Good* is not bent so shamelessly on rhetorical effect. She herself quickly acknowledges the weakness of her illustration ("Some people might say 'she [M] deludes herself'" [18]), but she persists by equating the "justice" of M's altered perspective with the generosity of vision made possible by "love." This equation, never entirely explicit, is crucial for the success of Murdoch's argument, both here and throughout the rest of her small philosophical oeuvre. Plato, somewhat prosaically, summarizes the position in "Above the Gods: A Dialogue about Religion," the second of Murdoch's *Acastos* dialogues, in response to a question from Timonax, "How do we find out what *is* good?"

> That's where love and desire come in. . . . Think of what learning something is like, something difficult like mathematics. You know how that feels when you're trying so hard to see something which *isn't yourself*, something *else*. You forget yourself. All your being and emotions are involved in trying to *understand*, and that's the sort of *desire* that actions come out of too, when you can't help responding because you really care. (103)

The desire to understand results, in effect, in a kind of epistemological receptivity, enabling one to take up a position of tolerance and respect (which Murdoch often tends to confuse with neutrality) toward the object, inanimate or human. And so it is that Lloyd can conclude that "objectivity" for Murdoch "is a matter of recognizing other centers of consciousness, other 'perspectives'; it is not a matter of representing a mind-independent reality from no perspective at all" (73).

But problems still persist. The psyche à la Freud (as Murdoch understands it) is no more willing to be generous than neutral: "The ego is indeed 'unbridled.' Continuous control is required" (*Metaphysics* 260). "Even its loving," she ruefully observes, "is more often than not an assertion of self" (*Sovereignty* 79). Having saddled herself with a model of "selfhood"—a concept, incidentally, that is never defined[1]—indebted heavily (if vaguely) to Freud's metaphysics, she is obliged to invent a faculty capable of recognizing and resisting "the fat relentless ego" (*Sovereignty* 52). That faculty, it turns out, is the "soul." "Without some . . . positive conception of the soul," she writes in the central essay of *The Sovereignty of Good*, "as a substantial and continually developing mechanism of attachments, the purification and reorientation of which must be the task of morals, 'freedom' is readily corrupted into self-assertion and 'right action' into some sort of *ad hoc* utilitarianism" (71). With this turn she is led ineluctably toward the kinds of theological constructs (as well as toward an explanation-by-homunculus) that are anathema to philosophical rigor. If the "self," which is presumably coextensive with the "soul," is "naturally" egocentric, then how explain (outside of social coercion, to which Plato resorts in the *Laws*) the emergence of an agency instinct with "rationality," generosity, and self-control? Like Freud's psychic "censors," the logical absurdity of which was exposed by Sartre, Murdoch's "soul" is a convenient ratchet introduced into the Freudian machinery to mitigate its logically predictable effects. In her latest book, she simply abandons all pretense of assimilating it to her model of the mind: "There is the selfish ego," she writes in *Metaphysics as a Guide to Morals*, "surrounded by dark menacing chaos, and the more enlightened soul perceiving the diversity of creation in the light of truth" (165).

Little wonder that she is inclined to dismiss psychoanalysis altogether as "a muddled embryonic science" (*Sovereignty* 26), even as, clearly lacking other models, she feels disposed to embrace its "truths."[2] When, in fact, she is unconstrained by its implications, she is apt to make generalizations about human nature that are as perceptive as they are inconsistent with her pronouncements about its "fundamental" selfishness: "We make, in many respects though not in all," she writes in "Existentialists and Mystics,"

> the same kinds of moral judgements as the Greeks did, and we recognize good or decent people in times and literatures remote from our own. Patroclus, Antigone, Cordelia, Mr Knightley, Alyosha. Patroclus' invariable kindness. Cordelia's truthfulness. Alyosha telling his father not to be afraid of hell. It is just as important that Patroclus should be kind to the captive women as that Emma should be kind to Miss Bates, and we feel this importance in an immediate and natural way in both cases in spite of the fact that nearly three thousand years divide the writers. And this, when one reflects on it, is a remarkable testimony to the existence of a single durable human nature. (177–78)

Elsewhere she takes seriously her own criticism of ethical philosophers misled by "a rationalistic desire for unity" and, setting aside all arguments about M's and D's and the operations of a "just" or "loving" vision, describes with great accuracy exactly how moral positions are embodied:

> When we apprehend and assess other people we do not consider only their solutions to specifiable practical problems, we consider something more elusive which may be called their total vision of life, as shown in their mode of speech or silence, their choice of words, their assessment of others, their conception of their own lives, what they think attractive or praiseworthy, what they think funny: in short, the configurations of their thought which show continually in their reactions and conversation. These things, which may be overtly and comprehensibly displayed or inwardly elaborated and

guessed at, constitute what, making different points in the two metaphors, one may call the texture of a man's being or the nature of his personal vision. ("Vision" 39)

Here Murdoch is thinking as an ethologist, for whom the human being is not "fundamentally" selfish or unselfish, "self" or "soul," but rather a complex amalgam of sometimes disparate behaviors that consort together in often instinctively functional ways. She puts this succinctly, though with disturbing qualifications, in *The Sovereignty of Good:* "What we really are seems . . . like an obscure system of energy out of which choices and acts of will emerge at intervals in ways which are often unclear and often dependent on the condition of the system in between the moments of choice" (54).

What is disturbing about this formulation is its implicit avowal that motivation (the human being's "obscure system of energy") is basically unintelligible. And in this Murdoch departs obviously from both the ethologist and Freud. Her authority is, of course, Ludwig Wittgenstein. "There may be no deep structure," she writes in "Metaphysics and Ethics": "This is the lesson of Wittgenstein" (120). It's a lesson that accords with her apparently strongly held conviction that life is (to use one of her favorite words) a "muddle." But it's also an idea that is incongruent with appeals to "attention." For the search for Good under such conditions becomes a fruitless exercise in the threading of an exitless maze. Her own words express it best: "If apprehension of good is apprehension of the individual and the real"— which is to say of particulars unassimilable to any "deep structure"—"then good partakes of the *infinite elusive* character of reality" (*Sovereignty* 42, my emphasis). M's task is "endless," in Murdoch's words (*Sovereignty* 23); in this light it's impossible as well.

If Murdoch has a penchant, as all this suggests, for painting herself into philosophical corners, she is unfortunately (or fortunately, depending upon how cozy one finds the corner) apt to take the novel as an object of speculation along with her. For her theories of fiction both rest on all these convictions and partake of their insoluble confusions. She has characterized her own novels as relatively "open" or "closed" and, in interviews and essays like "The Sublime and the Good" and "The Sublime and the Beautiful Revisited," has consistently championed the first over the second. A "closed" book is one in which "my own obsessional feeling about the novel is very strong and draws it closely together" (W. K. Rose 12), thereby giving it what she has described as "crystalline" autonomy: such a novel is "small, clean, resonant, and self-contained" ("Sublime and the Beautiful" 259). While seeming to express the uniqueness and separateness of the individual, it in reality eschews both history and "contingency"—the "messy, boundless, infinitely particular, and endlessly still to be explained" ("Sublime and the Beautiful" 260). Persons themselves—the "free," "separate," "independent" persons that we encounter in the characters of Tolstoy or Austen or George Eliot—withdraw, as it were, from its pages and are replaced by "the symbolic individual who *is* the literary work itself" ("Sublime and the Beautiful" 262, 266).

The "open" novel has, of course, the opposite character. In it a "Shakespearean" sensibility prevails, in that its characters are "not merely puppets in the exteriorization of some closely locked psychological conflict of [the writer's] own" ("Sublime and the Beautiful" 257). They are allowed their own autonomy by virtue of the novelist's "tolerance": "A great novelist is essentially tolerant, that is, displays a real apprehension of persons other than the author as having a right to exist and to have a separate mode of being which is important and interesting to themselves" ("Sublime and the Beautiful" 257). Murdoch's own novels are more "open" when "there are more accidental and separate and free characters" (W. K. Rose 12), and her goal (one that she may be said to be approaching, as, with *The Message to the Planet*, her narrative grows ever more tediously diffuse) is to write more of the open kind. "What I feel my work needs," she told W. K. Rose in 1968, "what makes it less good is that I'm not able to present characters with enough depth and ordinariness, and accidentalness" (11).

The notion that "accidentalness" is of the essence of the world, and should therefore be of the essence of art, crops up again and again in the essays. "Good art," Murdoch writes in *The Sovereignty of Good*, "reveals what we are usually too selfish and too timid to recognize, the minute and absolutely random detail of the world" (86). The implication is that, when human events, either on or off the page, do not smack of the "absolutely random," they are being configured by a "selfish" and "timid" mind. And, indeed, most of Murdoch's comments about aesthetic form make this point explicit: "Morality," she told Michael O. Bellamy, "has to do with not imposing form, except appropriately and cautiously and carefully and with attention to appropriate detail" (135). Presumably, an "instinctive" imposition of form would invite a deployment of egotistical impulses, but the qualifying phrase of that quotation begs by-now familiar questions. How is the naturally selfish ego to distinguish between the appropriate and the inappropriate? to proceed with caution and not heedlessness? to exercise precisely the right sort of attention? How, in short, is it to see beyond its own seductively kaleidoscopic fantasies at all? In at least one interview, Murdoch has declared that it often "turns out" that it doesn't:

> One starts off—at least I start off—hoping every time that . . . a lot of people who are not me are going to come into existence in some wonderful way. Yet often it turns out in the end that something about the structure of the work itself, the myth as it were of the work, has drawn all these people into a sort of spiral, or into a kind of form which ultimately is the form of one's own mind. (Kermode, "House" 63–64)

And so it is that art "charms reality, nature, into a formal semblance," with the lamentable result that "Hell itself" is turned "to favour and prettiness" (*Metaphysics* 122).

The writer is then left with an uncomfortable dilemma and the reader with an insuperable paradox. Form, Murdoch assumes, must be "imposed" upon mimetic art because without it the "minute and absolutely random" details of the world would add up simply to chaos, and yet the authorial ego that imposes that form is by nature "timid and selfish." And so the choice seems to be between formlessness and fantasy—unless the problem can be sidestepped by an appeal to Platonic transcendence. This is what Murdoch, ignoring Wittgenstein's antifoundationalist caveat, ultimately proceeds to do. Good art shares with nature, she concludes in *The Sovereignty of Good*, "a perfection of form which invites unpossessive contemplation and resists absorption into the selfish dream life of the consciousness" (85–86). That perfection and that unpossessiveness can only emanate, it seems to me, from a realm of perceptual and psychological ideality—a realm that forms a necessary, if subversive, supplement to Murdoch's avowedly materialist metaphysics.[3] In this view of things, the soul, unmoved, decodes the images of the eye, which, in its apprehension of napkin rings or of narrative lines, indeed sees perfection, though at a second or third remove. In short: (Murdoch's) Plato has taken flight from (Murdoch's) Freud.

But all of these contortions would be unnecessary if we simply scrapped the initial assumptions. Suppose we begin with the idea that human beings are *not* naturally selfish and that human life is *not* an absolutely random affair. The soul would then become a superfluous concept, and form something neither artifically "imposed" nor implicitly conferred by a Platonic deity. This, I suggest, is the lesson of Murdoch's novels, and none teaches it more lucidly than *A Fairly Honourable Defeat*.

2

The two Murdochs, the Platonic ethicist and the Freudian solipsist, are usefully schematized in this book, their views espoused by two separate characters: the civil servant and "Sunday metaphysician" (27), Rupert Foster, and the biochemist and former savant of germ warfare, Julius King. The fierce incompatibility of the two positions is brought out by the insolubility of their debates. For Julius, a natural lover of order, the world always takes the form of the mind, and that form invariably serves human selfishness. "It is not just that human nature absolutely precludes goodness," he tells Rupert, "it is that goodness . . . is not even a coherent concept, it is unimaginable for human beings, like certain things in physics" (224). Attachments are essential for human functioning, but for Julius—who is more consistent in this than his creator—they have nothing to do with the soul. "Human beings," he tells Morgan, his former lover,

> are roughly constructed entities full of indeterminacies and vaguenesses and empty spaces. Driven along by their own private needs they latch blindly onto each other, then pull away, then clutch again. Their little sadisms and their little masochisms are surface phenomena. Anyone will do to play the roles. They never really see each other at all. . . . Human beings are essentially finders of substitutes. (233)

What in Julius's opinion drives human life is vanity and lust for power: "Few questions are more important than: who is the boss?" (225).

Rupert, who is finishing a philosophical book (full, in Julius's words, of "cosy Platonic uplift" [222]), regards the search for "goodness" to be the end and justification of life: "We *experience*," he tells Julius, "the difference between good and evil, the dreariness of wickedness, the life-givingness of good" (222). Like Murdoch's Plato, for whom "the good is very, very far away" (Bigsby 220), Rupert experiences goodness as "something very much exterior to him[self]" but at the same time as something "very real" (359). It is manifested in "exercises in loving attention: loving people, loving art, loving work, loving paving stones and leaves on trees" (359). In fact love—"true love," which is "calm temperate rational and just" (255)—is, in Rupert's eyes, "the key" to all of life (138). "I am sure," he avers in the opening scene,

> that love tells in the end. . . . There are times when one's just got to go on loving somebody helplessly, with blank hope and blank faith. When love just *is* hope and faith in their most denuded form. Then love becomes almost impersonal and loses all its attractiveness and its ability to console. But it is just then that it may exert its greatest power. It is just then that it may really be able to redeem. (26)

This has struck some readers as flutily fatuous, readers who are eager to interpret Rupert's destruction in the machinery of Julius's mystifications as an inevitable consequence of his "silly optimism." But even Peter Conradi, from whom I have borrowed that judgment (163), concedes that Rupert's voice in the passage above is "very much the voice of *The Sovereignty of Good*" (172). Rupert's sentiments, to put it bluntly, are identical to Murdoch's own, a fact that has led to some rather desperate critical skirmishings from the admirers of the book. Rupert, it is concluded, is well intentioned but inept: he "represents a cosy and uninhabited version of Murdoch's own philosophy" (Conradi 163). Or he is merely superficial in his generosity: "Love, for him, implies interfering with other people's lives and bullying them" (Watrin 55). Or, according to one of the most sensitive readings, "his error lies in thinking that the golden cord [of Plato's reason] is the main one" (Dipple 189). What these judgments all have in common is Julius's conviction that vanity motivates Rupert's behavior. He is "easily gulled by pity, vanity, novelty, and fundamental humourlessness" (Conradi 175); "he projects his secret fears and passions, his own wishes on the world around him" (Watrin 55); like the other characters on which Julius "operates," he is basically "flawed by solipsism" (Dipple 182). None of this is the case, it seems to me; nor am I persuaded, as Murdoch's other critics are, that Julius's reading of human nature is in the main vindicated by the events of the narrative. To begin to understand the novel, we must resist the temptation to interpret it in the light of Murdoch's global conceptual terms, distributed between Julius and Rupert, and, first, look at the operations of "narrativity" here—which is to say, look at the behavior of the characters.

The opening scene, throughout which Murdoch's narrator remains unnervingly silent as Rupert and Hilda reveal themselves in dialogue, offers a fair sampling of that behavior, particularly as it evinces itself in thought. Rupert thinks with the precision and particularity of the trained academic mind; Hilda, who has had quite a bit to drink and who is suffering under the weather ("Oh don't *argue*, Rupert. It's too hot and I can't think" [12]), has been seduced into automatically instinctive responses. She is thinking in stereotypes: "I suppose queers are always a bit sly"; "those queer friendships are so unstable"; "all queers do like trouble" (15, 18). Rupert soon loses patience. "Any sentence," he protests, "beginning 'All queers . . .' is pretty sure to be false! It's like 'All married men . . .' 'All married men over forty deceive their wives.' " To which Hilda answers cheerfully, "Well, we know *that's* false" (18). The irony shouldn't be lost on the reader—Nabokov's ideal re-reader—who knows that Rupert will perish in the coils of a clandestine relationship with his sister-in-law; but neither should the point of this exchange be assumed to reside in its literary effect alone. Rupert is certainly right to object that Hilda's generalizations are literally false, but he is foolish to imply that they have no applicability to the world whatsoever. Later in this scene, Hilda will warn him that "you can't cheat nature, you can't cheat biology" (22). It is from the meaning-making cognitions of nature and biology that the stereotype in fact derives, cognitions—very largely "unconscious" in the perceiver—to which it owes its insidious power.

Rupert is, in his lucidity, like his colleague Axel, who likes "to argue about words" (34), who conducts his life according to well-reasoned principles, and whose "rationality"—his commitment to caution and circumspection—nearly costs him toward the end of the book his attachment with his lover Simon. Hilda, on the other hand, who's often characterized (here by Julius) as a "genuinely thinking being" (294), shares much with Simon himself, Rupert's volatile younger brother. In response to Axel's praise of what he sees as Julius's virtues ("Julius isn't a compromiser"; "Julius is a man with no nonsense about him" [34]), Simon thinks,

"Well I am [a compromiser]" and "I am a man with a lot of nonsense about me. . . . Nonsense is indeed the element in which I live" (34). Not confusion, but nonsense: Simon lives deeply steeped in his emotions, the intensities of which he cannot always control or understand. He remembers that, after Axel had once told him that neither must ever give into jealousy, he "had nodded his head, but he could no more control such feelings by acts of will than he could control the peristaltic movement of his gut" (30). So, too, Hilda, who, convinced at the novel's end of her husband's unfaithfulness, flees their home in Priory Grove, only to reflect later, "Why had she in an instant judged Rupert? Why had she had so little faith in her husband and her sister?" (417). Neither Simon nor Hilda, let me hasten to add, is (to recall Julius's image) the mere puppet of his or her passions. Although Simon cannot control his *feelings* of jealousy, he is quite capable of controlling his expressions of them—something that the sulking and door-slamming Axel seems often unable to do. And, although Hilda is proven wrong in assuming Rupert to be unfaithful, she does not, contrary to her own reproach, judge him "in an instant." It is not until she finds Morgan's unambiguous love letter, planted by Julius in Rupert's desk, that she allows the slowly accumulating evidence to overwhelm her. Throughout the novel, both she and Simon conduct themselves with intelligent intuition and restraint, and only Julius's capricious and unrelenting machinations (and, in Simon's case, Axel's "play[ing] for safety" [434]) can account for their entanglements in disaster.

Before taking up Rupert's case in detail, it's necessary to understand what "restraint" may mean, in both novels and life in general. Not only critics of this book but also Murdoch, as we have seen, assume that restraint is achieved by an exercise of "reason," which opposes the "lawlessness" of the passions. But it's useful to recall Mary Midgley's reminder that reason "is not the name of a character in a play": reason "is a name for organizing oneself" (*Beast* 258), and that means choosing between competing interests, both of which excite emotional claims. In other words, it is not a question of being passionate or passionless but of deciding *which* passion is to be given allegiance. Simon must choose, in *A Fairly Honourable Defeat*, for example, between obeying Julius's injunction against telling Axel of the trap set for Rupert and Morgan and, on the other hand, risking Julius's turning Axel against him by exposing the plot with the truth. His concern for his brother and sister-in-law is, for the greater part of the book, outweighed by his concern for himself, and, in choosing to keep silent, he may be said to be acting as reasonably as he can (especially given the accuracy of his intuitions about Axel's sensitivity and quick temper). His "rationality" has by no means silenced his passions, only, to use Midgley's word, "organized" them.

When Rupert enters into his determinedly therapeutic liaison with Morgan, he does so, we may then conclude, out of "passion," but it is a passion with at first only casual and inconsequential connections to either sex or vanity. Although "his very first feeling had been one of mad elation," since "human beings crave for novelty," this feeling, adds the narrator, "was only a momentary leap of the consciousness" (253). The passion that drives him most relentlessly is the same one that has produced his book: his conviction that "love really does solve problems" (255), that human beings are as capable of "unviolent unpossessive love" (254) as they are of greedy self-service. (That such an "intellectual" conviction can be an emotionally powerful incentive for action is suggested by Murdoch's own devotion to Rupert's task.) Axel is undoubtedly right about the long-awaited tome: it will be "a farrago of emotion" (35)—but not of the kind he envisages.

This tack, I should confess immediately, may seem naive to my psychologically sophisticated readers. Murdoch's is a narrator who is, after all, evasively indirect about her characters. Her usual practice is to adopt a reportorial stance just slightly outside their consciousnesses, so that her accounts of their reflections seem to hover ambiguously between transcription and interpretation. And so it is difficult to discern, in the passages I cite above, whether Rupert is being analyzed or simply "quoted." It's also hard to judge the tone: Are these reflections, whether of Rupert or of "Murdoch," set down with approval or derision? Rupert confesses, perhaps significantly, blithe ignorance of his own motivations:

> What he had said to Julius once had been true: he had come not so much to despise as simply to ignore the drama of his motives. He sought simply for truthful vision, which in turn imposed right action. The shadow play of motive was a bottomless ambiguity, insidiously interesting but not really very important. Could he do it here, latch himself onto the machinery of virtue and decent decision, and simply slide past the warm treacherous area of confusing attachment? (254)

An ominous question, certainly, but one that I think could be answered in the affirmative, were it not for Morgan's own treachery. For the *events* of the book support Rupert's intuitions: his motives may seem to him "bottomless," but the organization of his emotions is ultimately, albeit disastrously, in favor of his altruistic vision.

The crucial scene, what Morgan calls "the moment of maximum chaos" (357), occurs in chapter 13, part 2. Convinced by Julius's malicious manipulation of letters that each is in love with the other, Rupert and Morgan have been meeting to help the afflicted party "recover." Rupert has early suggested telling Hilda of the predicament, but Morgan has insisted on secrecy. Their meetings have now degenerated into bouts of mutual recrimination punctuated by brief interludes of tenderness beneath which lust has begun to stir:

> Rupert was thoroughly miserable. The loss of contact with Hilda made him feel reduced and mutilated. He hated telling lies and was in a state of abject fear in case his lies were discovered. At the same time, he craved for Morgan's

company, even quarreling with Morgan had become something necessary. They had endlessly discussed the situation and only succeeded in tangling it up to a mysterious degree. They had rationed their kisses. But he felt her passion and knew by now that she felt his. (358)

At this point, when a clear choice is inevitable—and before Peter, Rupert's son, barges into the room and brands both with irreversible incrimination—Rupert at first decides in favor of Hilda and himself:

"I think I've been a fool," said Rupert. "Maybe you'd better go away after all. I should have been tougher with you. Go away for six months. You know you can't lose me or my love. There's nothing to worry about. But I think we both need to calm down about this situation. While you're away I'll tell Hilda. I won't let it seem more important than it is." (360)

But Morgan is adamant:

"You took on this reponsibility, Rupert, and you've got to see it through. If I went away I'd go mad with worry. You don't know what you're saying. . . . I've got to *talk* to somebody, that's the only cure, Rupert, talk, talk, talk." (360)

And Rupert's response is to bow resignedly to the authority of his own conviction:

"I'm sorry," said Rupert. He stopped in front of her and resumed his glass. "I'm being selfish and unimaginative. Yes, we must go on." (360)

Readers of Murdoch's philosophy should ponder the irony that Rupert condemns himself precisely by an exercise of "tolerance." His is the "annihilation of self" in deference to "another center of consciousness," a move that promises the attainment of goodness in the Murdochian system of ethics. And he undertakes that annihilation with a strength of conviction that makes superfluous any operations of "soul." What we are seeing emerging here is a psychic dynamics that owe little to Plato or Freud. "Goodness" for Rupert is neither "very, very far away" nor opposed, with ghostly transcendental authority, to the passions of the "self." Rupert has, in Hilda's words, "instinctive . . . goodness of heart" (27). He can be called "egocentric" only by a Freudian deformation of that word: his overriding (though not only) "instinct" is to put Morgan's interests before his own. (The hard-core Freudians, I suppose, would say he has a "death instinct," but with the late Freud's naively tangled speculations we should have nothing to do here.) This reading renders problematic the juxtaposition of Rupert with Tallis Browne, who is often held up, in contrast to the former, as exemplary of the man of instinct. It also suggests the danger of abstracting a system of values from a reification of human response.

For Rupert is of course defeated by his goodness. And his defeat is ensured by Morgan's allegiance to the natural and the instinctual: "When one has such a deep instinctive need to do something," she tells herself, "then it cannot be wrong to do it" (184). Later she reflects upon the mess she has made of her life:

> Everything that I have done lately has been a disaster, thought Morgan, and yet each thing when it came along seemed absolutely *natural*. It was natural to fall in love with Julius, it was natural to feel sentimental pity for Rupert. How can one live properly when the beginnings of one's actions seem so inevitable and justified while the ends are so completely unpredictable and unexpected? (420)

The beginnings for Morgan seem so inevitable because she is undisposed to exercise moral choice—and they seem so justified because, once choice has been abdicated, the most primitively seductive of the emotions tend, as here, to take control. "It was a time of destiny," she concludes after her first meetings with Rupert, "not a time of decision. . . . She and Rupert had simply to hold hands. The gods would do the rest" (313). This attitude had carried her into her adulterous affair with Julius and had encouraged her, before the mix-up with Rupert, to expect a resumption of their relations: "We have not done with each other," she thinks, "and we are in the hands of the gods. Yes, that is it. With Julius one is in the hands of the gods, one has *fallen* into their hands" (184). Because those gods are, of course, Lawrencianly "dark," they manifest themselves in mythic terms: Julius had seemed to Morgan "almost all myth" (60), with him "everything was ritual" (92), and he and Morgan communicated with the "deep abysses" of their minds (92). What this seems to have meant in plainer terms is that he was, among other things, archetypal Hero and she archetypal Maid. "Seize me, be rough to me," she cries at their reunion: "Hold me and subdue me" (147).

Clearly she wants another mythic drama from Rupert—but of a somewhat different kind. Shortly after she pleads with him for more "talk, talk, talk," she explodes with reproach, frustrated by his horror at Peter's intrusion and by his fear of Hilda's losing faith in him:

> "Yes, you are a *coward*," said Morgan. "I think it would have been better and more honest if we'd just gone to bed, we both want to. Instead of having this endless nervewracking puling sort of *discussion*." (365)

A linguistic theorist who at bottom distrusts speech (and the psychic organization that it helps make possible), Morgan wants to live by the luxury of purely unreflective impulse. ("Morgan's living in Malory or something," Hilda had re-marked of her marriage to Tallis [249].) Such a self-surrender is made easy by the single-mindedness of her obsessions: "Morgan had a capacity," the narrator observes, "for dealing with one thing at a time, and not worrying about, almost not seeing, other features of the situation. Since she felt sure that she *ought* now to give Rupert her entire attention she found no difficulty in not reflecting too urgently about Hilda, about Peter, about Tallis" (313–14). Thus relieved of disturbingly competing emotional claims, Morgan, unlike Rupert, can feel confident that "there was really no conceivable alternative to the course which she was taking" (315). And so, while Rupert wrestles with his commitment to Hilda, his lust for her younger sister, and his allegiance to altruistic self-sacrifice, Morgan gives in to her crudest instincts, here not to submit to a godlike protector but to nurse a prostrate boy:

> It had become even plainer to her, and she felt this as a sign of her own continued rationality, that as a companion and as a person Rupert suited and matched her more than any man she had ever met. . . . Julius was far too erratic and domineering, and Tallis never really *held* me, she thought. Even a prostrate Rupert had over her a kind of authority to which her whole nature could calmly respond. It was, amidst all the hurly burly of Rupert's passions and her own aroused feelings, the calmness and steadiness of this response which most of all made her feel confident of the rightness of her decision to go on seeing him. . . . Perhaps indeed it was just from here that her warm sense of destiny arose. Rupert would help her to nurse Rupert through. (314–15)

That Morgan is, in Louis Martz's words, the "real villain" (54) of *A Fairly Honourable Defeat* is a fact oddly muted in the rest of the commentary on the novel. Perhaps from vaguely feminist motives, Dipple in fact chastizes Murdoch for having "diminished" Morgan's character (195). Over the criticism there hover the convictions, implied or completely unexpressed, that fictional characters cannot be convincing when "absolutely concentrated on [their] own being and suffering" (Dipple 195) and that women who are portrayed in an unfavorable light are an affront to womanhood in general. Both are romantic, if opposed, assumptions. The first is founded on the supposition that any person (or character) has the capacity to overcome all crippling limitations of temperament; the second is a covert expression of "essentialist" determinism, which assumes that universal traits are embodied in every individual and that fictional characters inevitably mirror those traits. (An only slightly more sophisticated version of the latter is the fashionable constructivist position: that the traits are culturally derived and imposed and that all female villains are social victims.)

But Morgan is, like human beings in general, a complex product of both nature and nurture, which alternately victimize and empower. Her inarticulate instincts are not all wrong, as we discover when Peter, in the scene at the abandoned railroad cutting, begs to make love to her: "She desired Peter, she wanted intensely to let him make love to her, here, now, in this magic place. But she felt with equal intensity, though entirely without clarity, the imposition of a veto. 'No'" (191). But such conventional taboos are rare in Morgan, mainly because of her love of daring. More powerful, even, than the tug of sexual submissiveness or of maternal tenderness (or dominance) is the appeal of recklessness—traceable, at least in part, to her sense of safety as Hilda's sister: "It was Hilda who was the deeply rooted tree. Morgan had indeed drawn a picture of the tree, the Hilda-tree, when she was six years old and had drawn a little bird in the branches which she announced to be herself" (151). Feeling thus secure in Hilda's love, she is much the more adventurous of the sisters. According to Hilda, Morgan "would have liked to be an adventurous boy hunting for other boys in Picadilly Circus Station" (16); when she witnesses scenes of anger and violence, like that in which Peter accuses Axel of hypocrisy and is in turn attacked as a parasite, her eyes grow "bright with interest," and she exclaims, "I adore violence!" (138). Hilda's deep-rootedness has paradoxically helped to license that adoration, and it also may have played a role in the impoverishment of Morgan's sympathies. "I love you. That's certain," Morgan tells her sister. "But I sometimes wonder if I'm capable of any other love whatever" (56).

Predictably, Morgan feels morally adrift. "How very peculiar one's mind is," she tells Rupert: "There's no foothold in it, no leverage, no way of changing oneself into a responsible just being. One's lost in one's own psyche. It stretches away and away to the ends of the world and it's soft and sticky and warm. There's nothing real, no hard parts, no centre" (96). What she habitually (and recklessly) seizes on as a "centre" is "that wicked and consoling force," destiny (153), which speaks from deep in the ancient animal brain of behaviors that should not be denied. Mythic lover, mythic mother, she is seduced into verbally unelaborated fantasies of life in "a heroic world" (58). Julius expresses it to her less exaltedly: "You are always wanting other people to act in some drama which you have invented. I think you are in a silly emotional frame of mind" (230).

If Morgan is too often emotionally "silly" (doubtless Julius is aware of the roots of that word), Rupert is, of course, too sophisticated. His error, in fact, lies precisely in his confidence that life is lived most intelligently—and morally—by conceptual, rather than by narrativic, strategies. We get a foretaste of that confidence fairly early in the novel when Tallis, disturbed by Peter's thefts, confronts Rupert with a question: "Why is stealing wrong?" As a man "who had not had a philosophical training for nothing" and who "was never startled by any question, however bizarre," Rupert answers with aplomb—and in abstract conceptual terms: "in a democratic society stealing is surely wrong not only for utilitarian reasons but because property is an important part of a structure generally agreed to be good and whose alteration in detail can be freely sought" (183). Tallis then takes his leave (after waiting "as if there might be something more to come" [183]), dissatisfied with a response that has failed to address the complex narrative of his relations with Peter, of Peter's relations with the larger world, and of his own ambivalence about the authority of that world born of his barely outmaneuvered despair.

Later, in the affair with Morgan, it's this faith in the conceptual with which Rupert allies fatally his "instinctive . . . goodness of heart." In trying to "slide past the warm treacherous area of confusing attachment," he stops his ears to the siren-calls of his narratively wise intuitions, and so renounces the one bond forged in inarticulate feeling that could have saved him from himself: his "sense of connection" with Hilda, that "loving communication which carried its own marks of truth" (343–44). His agony of course arises from the fact that he can't quite silence its call, even though both his upbringing and his training have left him ill-equipped to answer it. His love for Hilda has always been a "secret" (359), since he has felt himself deprived of "the direct language of love" (138–39). And so, impassioned by an innate "goodness" and yet awkward in discussions of intimacy, Rupert is the perfect gull for Julius's scheme—a scheme that can succeed only if all plain talk is avoided. (Morgan has been rendered scrupulous by Rupert's presumed "sensitivity," that of a man, according to Julius, suffering "some deep grief" [259].)

In an earlier literature, one less skeptical about the integrity of human motive, Rupert might have been a conflicted figure of high tragedy, but Murdoch's narrator, always removed, often mocking, seems incapable of elevating him above the ironic. That he ends up a grotesquely swollen carcass in a swimming pool, a victim of drunken befuddlement, apparently, rather than of a redeemingly more dignified suicide, suggests that we've been dealing, from Murdoch's perspective, not with tragic inevitability in this book but with "muddle" pure and simple, though muddle of a darkly comic kind. Rupert dies, but the narrative itself continues, its loose ends streaming out over a fitfully lit moral void: Tallis, martyred cuckold, toils away at his social work, wondering how to tell his irascible father that he, Leonard, is dying; Julius strolls the sunny boulevards of Paris, feeling "so much better now that he was not closely involved with human beings" (447); Axel and Simon, happy once more (though somewhat guiltily subdued in the affair of Rupert's death), stop for some wine in the south of France in a garden that seems almost a parody of Eden. Here still a pocket of muddle, obviously; there, for the moment, none.

3

But Murdoch's muddle is always very familiar because it is so faithfully and quintessentially human. Far from suggesting that there is no "deep structure," her novels reveal over and over that there is an extremely robust one. That structure arises from the biogram, from the ordinary dynamics of human relations, both the intelligibility and the predictability of which are essential for all art, especially the ironist's.

To begin with, hers is a world—to quote Murdoch in an interview—where "the ordinary human condition still seems to belong more to a man than to a woman" (Biles 119). Which is to say that men occupy the center of things, particularly of the political and socioeconomic spheres, where they conduct themselves with a self-confidence and self-importance that to women are often denied. (Morgan, who aspires to professional standing as a specialist in "glossematics," registers neither insult nor surprise when she is derided by Julius as possessing "the intellectual equipment of a sixth-form mistress or"—worse—"a literary critic" [259].) These men are bonded by their professional interests—at the anniversary party that opens the book, Axel immediately makes his way to Rupert, and the two men of government start talking shop—and are subtly graded by their rivalries: to Rupert it doesn't matter that Hilda never went to university, "yet it's important that Tallis got a second" ("You mention it," Hilda tells him, "about once a month" [25]). Like most high-ranking males everywhere, those here enjoy the perquisites and signs of status (Rupert's discretely diminutive swimming pool, Axel's powder-blue Hillman Minx) and, especially given the congestion of their tribal grounds, show strong territorial interests: Tallis, who is in most ways an embarrassment to his confreres, "lacks the concept of privacy," Rupert complains (23).

The women's status is, in turn, attached to the men's: Hilda doesn't mind Rupert's turning down a title, "though 'Lady Foster,'" she concedes, "would have sounded rather well" (27). Consequently, for them an attractive spouse is usually an older man, of some wealth, power, and prestige. Morgan was initially attracted by Tallis because he aroused her nurturing instincts: "My feeling about Tallis was like one's feeling about animals. I mean, that awful sort of naked pity and distress" (59). But life with him having proven "depressing," she now wants "a husband like Rupert," she tells Hilda: "A husband that *works*. Functions, I mean" (53). (Rupert, on the other hand, is, in typical male fashion, not insensible to her youth and beauty: of the two sisters, "Morgan was the handsome one now" [49].) Like the men, the women form same-sex ties of friendship and rivalry, but the tenor of both relations is altered by their sex. Friendship for the women— whom the men tend to sequester, though Tallis errs typically in this respect—is usually a family affair (neither Morgan nor Hilda seems to know a female non-affine), and the rivalry is covert to the point of invisibility: it is Morgan, we should remember, who insists to Rupert upon keeping Hilda in ignorance of their meetings.

Kin ties are here, as they are in life, the pivot around which human relations revolve. This is a tight little group of characters, and what holds them together as staunchly as sex is the consanguineal bond. That bond can be a source of conflict: both Rupert and Leonard are disappointed in their sons, and Leonard is provocatively free with his insults ("I don't know what I did," he bluntly tells Tallis, "to deserve such a stupid son" [438]). But Tallis's love remains undeflected, and Peter feels licensed throughout the book to persist in his adolescent rebellion: "Peter knew that it was a metaphysical impossibility that [Hilda's] love for him should diminish by one iota whatever he might or might not do, and this precisely enabled him to dismiss her altogether from his mind" (291). Most tellingly, it is to her sister that the villainous Morgan flees ("*We will not be divided*," she proclaims [389]) after destroying both Rupert and his marriage, and Hilda, apparently without demur, takes her prodigal sibling in. This sort of behavior strikes us as deplorable but humanly understandable; on the other hand, part of Julius's inhuman air results from his being totally without surviving family.

Predictably, relations outside family here are structured by the rites of reciprocity. Peter, still a callow adolescent, sneers self-righteously at those rites ("What you people call good manners is just hypocrisy and buttering each other up" [135]), but Axel, who has been compelled by his homosexuality to make an art of social diplomacy, sensibly defends them. Only those who suffer or choose marginalization—Peter, Leonard, Julius, and even Tallis to a certain extent—can afford to flout them with relative impunity. They're flouted, usually, in the name of "truth," but the effect in every case is self-absorbed and antisocial alienation. Peter retires into what Axel accurately calls his "dream world of drugs and layabouts and fuzzy fragments of Eastern philosophy" (136–37), Leonard into ethnocentric vituperation ("If I had my way all the bloody Jews would be deported to Palestine and all the bloody nig nogs would be sent back to wherever they came from. . . . And all Americans would be shot on sight" [107]). Julius manipulates lives for his amusement with a puppeteer's glacial detachment, and Tallis, while slaving for anonymous strangers, by his squalor keeps familiars at bay. Various degrees of "social deviancy" attach to all four of these characters. Age explains that of Peter and Leonard; grief for his murdered sister that of the insular, obsessed Tallis; the death camps, of course, that of Kahn-turned-(Caesar)/King.

Among the socially functional and comparatively unmutilated, life unfolds with its usual gregariousness, and its usual machinery of enabling deceit. Homosexuality is a fact here, as in all human cultures, but it is handled with typical Englishness by rarely acknowledging that it exists. (Murdoch should be commended, incidentally, for stripping it of its Freudian etiology in neurosis and depicting it as the Darwinian mystery that it is[4]—as, to quote Axel, a "completely ordinary way of being a human being" [37], for all its apparent and puzzling sacrifice of reproductive advantage.) What is also obvious is that there is a craving for a leader, for a "charismatic" who, by his strangeness and suave charm, can help focus diffuse social energies. Julius is the god ("He's not a saint. And yet—" [11]) upon whom most eyes are trained in *A Fairly Honourable Defeat*.

Finally, this is a familiar world of ceremony and art. The instinct to confer specialness upon life-events—a birthday, an anniversary, the production of a book—is apparent everywhere in this novel of aborted celebrations. As is the instinct to make and honor special things. When backed into an argumentative corner about the essential value of life, both Rupert and Morgan produce Shakespeare as its justification. Hilda's housekeeping is obviously artful occupation; for Simon, eager epicure, all experiences are "ceremonies" (39); and with Julius life itself is either art or filthy rubbish. Even Leonard, who is loftily scornful of the whole Beckettian pageant of futility, collects matchboxes of fine design.

For Murdoch, art means above all the imposition of form, and the example of Julius in this novel is meant to suggest how dangerous is the artist's power. Both Puck and Oberon, Julius works transformations upon his rude mechanicals that produce what Robert Hoskins has called a midsummer's nightmare. But Julius seems hardly a representative artist, especially of mimetic art. He in fact admits that if Morgan and Rupert "had been left to themselves there would have been no involvement, beyond [a] little bit of sentimentality" (402). In other words, his is a patently unnatural manipulation, a deformation of relationships to prove a specious point. If he succeeds in separating Rupert and Hilda, he does so, not because all human beings are simply motivated by vanity, but because, as I have suggested above, both the typical and individual dynamics of their characters, operating within certain (here largely artificial) constraints, tend to confer their own structure upon their destinies. Were this not the case, the novel would not convince us as successfully as it does that it is, in general as well as particular terms, an imitation of human life.

Apparently Murdoch thought that it should be more than that. And, either by a failure of nerve or by an unfortunate access of ambition, she felt it necessary to allegorize the action, to conceptualize it in Christian metaphor. "Of course, that book," she told Michael O. Bellamy, "is a theological myth":

> Julius King is, of course, Satan, and Tallis is a Christ figure, and Tallis' father (Leonard Browne) is God the Father, who finds that it's all gone wrong. . . . And then Morgan (Tallis' estranged wife and Julius' former mistress) is the human soul, for which the two protagonists are battling. When Julius recognizes who Tallis is, he can't help loving him. (135–36)

Apart from internal weaknesses in this scheme (if Leonard is an impotent God the Father, is Tallis an impotent Christ? and in what sense is Morgan soul-like?), it threatens to play havoc with the mimetic coherence of the narrative. Not only must Julius be bewitched by Tallis (and so befriend him, give him money, clean his house), but he must desire, in Elizabeth Dipple's words, "to be stopped and judged by good" (186). Thus some of the sentimental lapses of the book. During

a scene in which Simon has been teased by Julius and kept from emerging from
Rupert's swimming pool, he finally loses his temper and pushes his tormentor in;
and when Julius, who can't swim, is rescued, he murmurs something to Simon that
sounds like "Well done!" (375). Such a remark is clearly out of character, and, in
fact, the whole Tallis-as-Christ and Julius-as-Satan "battle" (which is, regrettably,
"very much there in the dialogue" [Bigsby 229]) seems an uncomfortably contrived
affair. It's a "credit" to Murdoch's "tact," as Dipple notes, that the allegory "is not
compulsively handled or absolutely central to a reading of the novel" (186).

The book itself actually resists its imposition by a respect for the ambivalences
of human sympathies. However "satanic" Julius King was meant to be, he exerts an
attraction upon both the other characters and the reader that cannot be ignored.
Not only does he exhale the exoticism of the outsider ("that weird fair Jewishness,"
as Hilda describes it [25]); he also has the affrontery to reject the etiquette of
ingratiation that usually knots the laces of social accord. "Exceptionally honest" is
Axel's description of him (34), and *nous autres* who are not—who are, like Simon,
flimsy compromisers in the face of what often seems social necessity—admire him
with a romantic ardor.

As for Julius' "foe," Tallis, he is for me the most ambiguously presented
character of the book. As late as 1982, Murdoch was describing Tallis in an
interview as the "only one real saint as it were, or symbolic good religious figure
in the books" (Bigsby 220), an assessment with which all critics of the novel
have concurred. Only Dipple emphasizes the difficulty of "perceiving the mythic
dimension" in Tallis (18) and concludes, with, I think, justice, that "it cannot
precisely fit in the framework of realism" (19). And it is the realism with which
Tallis is drawn that's most compelling. Suguna Ramanathan observes, for example,
that "the description of his filthy kitchen is one of the most unforgettable things
in Murdoch's work" (37). Memorable to me partly because it seems unjustified
in terms of the "myth." Admittedly, Tallis-as-Christ is a very busy man ("There's a
meeting of student volunteers, they're going to paint houses. Then there's someone
just out of jug I've got to see. Then there's a United Churchmen's Committee on
prostitution. Then I've got a class. Then there's a probation officer's study group
I promised to talk to. Then I've got to write a—" [210]), but even the busiest of
men can discard a jug of curdled milk. If in fact the kitchen is supposed to be a
metaphor (as it is for Richard Todd, of "contingent events" [89]), it completely
overwhelms its tenor with its vehicle.

In purely realistic terms, Tallis's perpetual state of squalor is best explained
by the impotence of his personal life. To the other characters of the book, Tallis
is very far from saintly: "hopelessly incompetent" (20), without "dignity" (21),
"feeble" (22), "completely spineless" (220)—these are the words that they use to
describe him when he is judged among themselves. And a good deal of his behavior
fits the judgments. After the ordinarily uncensorious Simon watches Tallis accept

a handshake from Julius, the man who had unceremoniously stolen his wife, he announces, "He ought not to have taken your hand" (85). And when Morgan hears of the incident, she seems stunned by Tallis's humiliating self-abasement, murmuring, "This is—somehow—the end" (103). A "saintly" Tallis is a man without aggression and even without much self-esteem, and we who need the one and crave the other find it difficult, however humblingly, to attend, as it were, to the fine points of his character. Especially when those points are themselves ambiguous. He generously befriends and takes in Peter, but, "with Tallis," as the narrator matter-of-factly records, "Peter had no role and lived in a state of vulnerability and nakedness which was not too far from despair" (112). He sets no boundaries on Morgan's life, but, though "at first all seemed very unworldly and spiritual and free," she ends up finding such freedom "frightening," growing terrified that she is losing her sense of identity (92).

In short, without the *crudities* of instinct, especially of male instinct, Tallis seems a curiously unsympathetic creature. Rupert and Hilda both try to convince him that "authority" is what is needed with Morgan: Tallis listens in silence and, to Hilda's exasperation, rescues a stray fly from his glass (180). Authority *is*, in fact, what Morgan is after, but Tallis is not the man to supply it; when, later, he attempts to restrain her with force, he merely causes a ludicrous scene. As Todd has observed, Tallis works most effectively with people who are "not closely bound to him" (104). In a scene at a restaurant, he impulsively slaps a tough whose gang is roughing up a Nigerian, while Axel, Simon, and Julius stand by. And yet, for all of what Dipple calls his "spontaneous knowledge" (21)—he also acts decisively when Julius reveals his deceptions—he remains a character about whom the reader feels a perhaps abject sense of ambivalence. Murdoch's narrator seems to feel the same way. Her first description of him is quite unfairly unflattering: "He had a shiny bumpy forehead and very wide apart very light brown eyes and a short shiny nose and a small and slightly prissy mouth" (83). "Prissy" is an obviously loaded adjective; one is tempted to protest, like Rupert to Hilda, that surely such a word can't truthfully describe anybody. But sophisticated readers don't expect truth from their narrators, just cues on how to think and feel.

It may be objected that I am simply thinking like a man, like an aggressive and competitive sexist, in singling out these traits in Tallis. But I take comfort in the fact that, in doing so, I'm probably picking up most of the right cues: "I think perhaps," Murdoch told Jack I. Biles, "I identify with men more than with women" (119). Not that those cues have been deliberatively planted; obviously Murdoch's view of Tallis—her reflective, analytical view in the interviews—is different from my own. But the Murdoch who entertains that perspective is not the mimetic novelist. "Art," she writes in *The Fire and the Sun*, "cheats the religious vocation at the last moment and is inimical to philosophical categories" (87). This is the art of *A Fairly Honourable Defeat*, one that rejects the reductionism of parable and philosophy (in which category I would include both Plato and Freud)[5] in favor of an account of human relations that is at once more complex and more coherent. Tallis is certainly not the simple "runt" to which Hilda's early description reduces him; but neither is he the "one real saint" who inspires in either the other characters or the reader an unambiguous sympathy. "Art accepts and enjoys the ambiguity of the whole man," writes Murdoch (*Fire* 82), and, indeed, we tend to judge Tallis with the whole of our intuitive selves—with our admiration for the sincerely committed altruist and our contempt, perhaps secret, for the ineffectual male.

It may be impossible, given our penchant for categorization, to resolve the two Tallises into a single image. Thus our feeling that this novel, like genuinely mimetic art as a whole, retains a teasing and fascinating suspensiveness; that it is, as it were, a message to the planet that never quite achieves full legibility. Thus, too, our respect for it, a respect that for many real students of literature may not be too far from veneration. For it leaves us with the inarticulate conviction that the simplifications of a Freud or a Plato (or the Murdoch of *The Sovereignty of Good*) have, in our imaginative experiencing of the book, been temporarily overcome, and that we have become more whole and clear to ourselves even while we've become less communicable in analytical terms. We have been reintroduced to our own specialness as a species and, at least during the time we have shared these characters' skins, have been neither brute nor Platonic demigod, neither the fat relentless ego nor a sovereign of Good, but—exhilaratingly and chasteningly—the human animal.

Plainspoken Postscript

Someone in the audience [at the MLA Convention] was asking Angelica if she would agree that the novel, as a distinct genre, was born when Epic, as it were, fucked the romance. She gave the suggestion careful consideration.
—David Lodge, *Small World*

According to Peter Brooks, moderator of the 1991 Tenth Anniversary Symposium at the Whitney Humanities Center of Yale University, there is "a restless sense in contemporary scholarship that the humanities experience both the privilege and the burden of having no fixed place from which to speak" ("Introduction" 83). His words accurately capture the feeling of martyrdom that emanates from many of the self-crucified on the rood of poststructuralist indeterminacy, but they hardly express the contemporary reality of the humanities, especially as they flourish in institutions like Yale: there are, in fact, a *number* of "fixed" places from which they speak, all of which are very familiar to anyone even casually conversant with academic fashion. Those places constitute the new orthodoxies of the humanities, and, although the positions they represent have long since overshot the point of self-parody, they continue to dominate the journals, the symposia, the graduate seminars like the impenetrable crystal spheres of medieval astronomy. Like those spheres, they serve mainly a political purpose: they preserve the clouds of emancipatory glory that trailed after the student revolutionaries of the 1960s, now all full (or at least tenured) professors in charge of curricular academic affairs. On the page of the *Yale Journal of Criticism* that faces Brooks's address, we find a characteristically lyrico-pretentious statement of that purpose: "Can there be an atopicality of the community that nonetheless gathers, a community going nowhere, but ecstatic, a community of shattered egos, where the control towers come tumbling down, and where the other is genuinely anticipated?" (Ronell 80).

The contemporary humanities are a church preserving a faith, a house, like Our Father's, having many rooms, in which the devout are invited to gather for ritual confessions of solidarity. "Since the death," as Howard Felperin writes, "of the godlike author,"

> any number of idols have been erected in His place under the names of our diverse theoretical schools as the ultimate reference of literature and resting-point for its study. Each of these schools promises its own version of salvation through correct interpretation in a grounded, and by that token valid, reading

of texts. . . . Just as God was once the ground of being, from Whom all things come and to Whom they return, the transcendental Signified toward which all textuality—the "books" of nature and of revelation—points and on which it was based, so our theoretical schools, while generally denying the divine or metaphysical basis of the textuality they study[,] have displaced but by no means dispensed with the notion of a transcendental signified, a kind of bottom-line for reading, that justifies and guides their operations. (204)

The symposium at the Whitney Center offers a fairly typical illustration. Its participants having been chosen "because their work was exemplary, setting standards and raising issues of interest far beyond the boundaries of a single discipline," they were convened for an anniversary to address once again all the "large issues of perennial concern to the humanities" (Brooks, "Introduction" 84, 85): the nature of the self, the boundaries of knowledge, the epistemology of narrative, the foundations of judgment, and the "authority, tradition, and future of the disciplines." A tall order, obviously, but the participants seem to have gone at their "rubrics" with both confidence and zeal, and, if we may judge by the "Introduction," there was a sense of scholarly excitement and adventure about it all, the feeling that knowledge was being advanced, in Brooks's carefully innocuous phrase, "in new and productive ways" ("Introduction" 90).

And how was it being advanced? The speakers on "the self" showed no concern with the last half-century of research by developmental psychologists into the ways the self-concept is acquired; they showed no familiarity with the recent and ground-breaking work in the neurosciences investigating the links between selfhood and consciousness; they in fact showed no interest in defining what the "self" is or possibly could be. The "places" from which they spoke defined it for them, and those places are deserts of drearily arid familiarity: psychoanalysis and deconstruction. Juliet Mitchell, for example, offered ("through two literary channels, *King Lear* and 'Anna O'") some "speculative theses on hysteria and the traditionless self." As one might expect, the "theses" amount to the usual psychoanalytic mystifications, in which fantasizing babies seek incest with the mother, then, denied, turn to the father, finally using him *as* "a mother," whatever such twaddle may mean: "never agreeing to symbolize the difference between the sexes (the law of castration), she or he demands 'all' from this seductive mother-father" (98). The absurdities of Freud and of his French expositors can't be done any sort of justice here;[1] suffice it to say that psychoanalysis is a "discipline" now regarded by most scientists as, at best, an intellectual backwater and that its "speculative theses" represent epistemological advancement only for the credulous (I speak from experience) and professionally upward-bound. And for those seeking "ecstatic" community, of course: Mitchell's "hysteric" turns out to be one who can neither forget nor "repress" the "polymorphous delights of infantile sexuality" (93).

Psychoanalysis is such an appealing place from which today's "humanists" can speak because it ministers to both of their sentimental obsessions: on the one hand, it confirms through its iron "laws" (the "law of castration," for example) their total victimization by forces (the "control towers") that render them piteously helpless; on the other, it obscurely promises, in its Lacanian strains, an endlessly self-liberating "mobility of desire." Psychoanalytic gospel can be conscripted, therefore, to any purpose or vision, a fact especially true of the hieratic *Ecrits*, which offers as many readings as it has readers. Nothing so bourgeois as evidence should come between those readers and their Scripture (or, in the words of "theorist," Pierre Macherey, "A rigorous knowledge must beware of all forms of empiricism, for the objects of any rational investigation have no prior existence but are thought into being" [5]), because that may endanger the ideological confirmations that are synonymous with the decoding of the text. Thus the humanist's fondness not only for "theory" but also for philosophy of the "speculative tradition." With its indifference to matters of empirical verification, even to formulation that would permit such procedures, European philosophy offers itself to the student as an easily mastered Genius Theory of Knowledge: to "do philosophy" one simply attaches oneself to a "thinker"—Kant, Heidegger, Derrida—and then reads the world (or its works) through his or her "system." Like psychoanalysis, the system is safely closed: its accountability to fact is essentially irrelevant.

I can illustrate what I mean with another paper from the symposium, this one by Martha Nussbaum entitled "Emotions as Judgments of Value." The paper, to my mind, has an admirable aim: to restore the emotions to their rightful place as important ways of knowing. But the way Nussbaum goes about doing this would seem incomprehensible to the practicing psychologist of emotion. Two sets of objections in "the philosophical tradition" that have been lodged against the emotions are summarized—the first that they "are blind forces, deriving from some animal part of our nature that does not partake in judgment" (205); and the second that, though "not innate, but socially taught, not blind bodily impulses, but complex cognitive operations," they nevertheless proffer judgments that are "false" (206)—and then Nussbaum proceeds to ally herself with the second position while rejecting its evaluation of the emotions as "false." She does this, apparently, on wholly intuitive grounds: because that position "is based on a deep conception of what emotions are, and one that I believe to be more or less correct" (208). There is no consultation of the immense and increasingly more sophisticated psychological literature on the emotions; no hesitation over the naive distinction between the "innate" and the "taught," over the hopelessly anachronistic phrase "animal part of our nature," or over the unintelligibility of the metaphor of the emotions as "blind" forces or bodily impulses; no indication that anything other than "the philosophical tradition" need be consulted on an issue bearing directly on psychological fact. If one wants to find out anything about the emotions, read the Stoics and then one's heart.

This is not irresponsible scholarship because it's really not scholarship at all. It's consulting Holy Writ and then preaching to the converted. Not one of the smallest ironies produced by the current "human sciences" is that, following upon their zeal in "deconstructing" authority, they've created a highly visible cadre of authorities whose appeal lies mainly in the receptivity—or adaptability—of their work to ideological pieties. And so, if serious science is to be represented at the symposium, it must be represented by the anthropologist Clifford Geertz, one of the proselytizers, like Nussbaum, for the postmodern hegemony of the "culturally constructed" and the "local." Even his session is a tribute to his faith: it's entitled, not "How 'Local' Is Human Knowledge?" but rather "'Local Knowledge' and Its Limits." Since the issue has, obviously, already been decided, it remains for Geertz only to denigrate the opposition: "most (conceivably all) universals are so general as to be without intellectual force or interest, are large banalities lacking either circumstantiality or surprise, precision or revelation, and thus are of precious little use" (130). In defense of which dismissiveness he does what John Mellencamp would call his best James Dean:

> The renunciation of the authority that comes from "views from nowhere" ("I've seen reality and it's real") is not a loss, it's a gain, and the stance of "well, I, a middle-class, mid-twentieth-century American, more or less standard, went out to this place, talked to some people I could get to talk to me, and think things are sort of rather this way with them there" is not a retreat, it's an advance. (132)

How to argue against such wise-but-inarticulate *faux-naïf* charm?

Significantly, Geertz' co-participant of the session, unlike all the other speakers, thinks it necessary to join the ranks of the respondents: Jack Goody presents not a piece of independent argument but a response to Clifford Geertz. To take an original line before such universally respected orthodoxy is obviously a wasted effort, although Goody tries gingerly to do so: "The problems of humanity are of course far from identical, but any elucidation of them involves a bifocal vision, both on the particular and on the general, or rather on the more particular and on the more general" (145). But lest the heresy of such notions breed suspicion about the wisdom of inviting Goody into the inner sanctum, Brooks assures his readers in the "Introduction" that he quickly returned to his senses: "neither [Geertz nor Goody], as the ensuing discussion made clear, believes that the dream of a critical 'metalanguage,' still prevalent in many sectors of the social sciences, can be anything but an illusion" (86).

It must be illusory because such a language would make "a spurious claim to authority" (Brooks, "Introduction" 89), and authority, as almost all of these authorities would certainly tell us, is what has been deconstructed. Thus the spectacle of the symposium: of humanists assuming "the privilege and the burden" to speak on any subject whatsoever. Not that such a transgression of disciplines is necessarily to be deplored (as this book itself bears witness): what is to be deplored is the ideological selectivity that now dictates which disciplines—and which positions within those disciplines—are invested with the mantle of truth. French Freud speaks for the self; European philosophy for "values"; Clifford Geertz's nearsighted relativism for the anthropological study of the species; Gould and Lewontin's behavioral Lysenkoism for whatever scant attention is to be paid to human biology. And it's easy to name the other "places" from which "we" speak: Do we wish to know anything about power? Read Foucault. Gender? Read Nancy Chodorow. Shakespeare (or, as some New Historicists would write, "Shakespeare")? Read Stephen Greenblatt and his ilk.

Such, in general, has been the priestly legacy of poststructuralism. Joseph Carroll has recently summarized the reasons that legacy has for so long prevailed. As I pointed out at the beginning of this postscript, the principal reason is a political one: "The political norm that typically governs poststructuralist thinking is that of anarchistic utopianism" (467). Affiliating itself "with every form of radical opposition to prevailing or traditional norms" (467), poststructuralism offers the ambitious academic a fairly comfortable and lucrative career even as it sanctifies his or her ideals and agonistic fantasies. And it also "privileges" that career in professional terms. "It is hardly surprising," as Carroll observes, "that rhetoricians, aggrieved at the continually increasing authority and efficacy of science, would insist that the laws of discourse take precedence over the laws of science" (31). Finally, these motivating factors "form an uneasy alliance with a quasi-religious desire to preserve an area of human subjectivity or spirituality that is somehow, mystically, distinct from the objective world that can be known by science":

> The desire to identify literature with a realm of the spirit, and to segregate this realm from the objectively knowable world, has animated a broad spectrum of critical theory. It is the guiding spirit of Sidney's Christian Platonism; it dominates Kant's *Critique of Judgment*; and it is a central motive behind Romantic theory, Husserlian phenomenology, Russian formalism, and the more doctrinaire version of the New Criticism represented by John Crowe Ransom. The various traditions of transcendental aesthetic theory provide a large context for the poststructuralist hostility to positive scientific understanding, and these traditions join with that range of utopian social theory that wishes to invest human social ideals with an autonomous creative power that transcends the constraints of an evolved human nature. (31)

But that "positive scientific understanding," as Carroll insists, will come to dominate even the humanities, and it will do so, "in spite of all prejudice and all entrenched interests," because "of the irresistible force of its explanatory power" (468). Carroll is alluding to a specific kind of understanding—to the Darwinian paradigm that informs this book—and his argument is precisely my own: that "the evolutionary explanation of human experience is . . . a more complete and adequate theory of the development and nature of life, including human life, than any other theory currently available to it," and that it "thus necessarily provides the basis for any adequate account of culture and of literature" (467). Where its eventual triumph will leave poststructuralism and its disciples is, intellectually and professionally, nowhere, for the poststructuralist paradigm "operates on principles that are radically incompatible with those of evolutionary theory" (468). Carroll concludes with a blunt assessment of the historical and institutional implications of this incompatibility:

> If my polemical contentions are basically right, a very large proportion of the work in critical theory that has been done in the past twenty years will prove to be not merely obsolete but essentially void. It cannot be regarded as an earlier phase of a developing discipline, with all the honor due to antecedents and ancestors. It is essentially a wrong turn, a dead end, a misconceived enterprise, a repository of delusions and wasted efforts. (468)

Already as early as 1983, the anthropologist Robin Fox, in his *Red Lamp of Incest,* had issued a warning to the humanities: "For what it is worth let me appeal to the philosophers who seem to be in an impasse over the theory of mind: If you do not quickly educate yourselves in neuropsychology and brain evolution, then the issue may pass from your hands" (xiv). The words were prescient, and in fact the issue is now clearly the province of those philosophers—Dennett, Flanagan, Paul and Patricia Churchland—who most assiduously undertook the education. There is little likelihood, of course, that the study of literature will pass out of English departments into other hands, but there is every likelihood that, if it continues on its present course, its reputation as a laughingstock among the scientific disciplines will come to be all but irreversible. Given the current state of scientific knowledge, it is still possible for literary theory to recover both seriousness and integrity and to be restored to legitimacy in the world at large. It can do both, I think, only if it abandons the hermetic anthropocentrism of poststructuralism for the more inclusive view that evolution affords. "Had we known no other animate life-form than our own," Mary Midgley observes, "we should have been utterly mysterious to ourselves as a species" (*Beast* 18). Her verbs suggest that there was a point of divide at which the mysteriousness began to dissipate, and that point was of course the date of publication of *The Origin of Species.* Its author clearly understood the implications of his work for the future of philosophical thought: "Origin of man," he confided to his "M" notebook, "now proved. . . . He who understands baboon would do more towards metaphysics than Locke" (539, no. 84e). Primatologists have already entered upon the immensely exciting project of revising those metaphysics.[2] And not only primatologists: anthropologists, psychologists, behavioral biologists, neuroscientists, philosophers of mind—researchers in dozens of disciplines, now working within the evolutionary paradigm, are beginning to define human nature in a persuasively definitive way. Meanwhile, the humanities paddle about in intellectual sandboxes. So long as they stay there, with Foucault and Lyotard and Kristeva and Lacan, they'll have nothing to show for their work but blank slates.

Close your Deleuze; open your Darwin.

Notes

Preface

1. As Livingston points out, contemporary literary theory does not concern itself (as theory in the sciences always does) with the issues of "veracity, falsehood, or testability" (*Literary Knowledge* 14). And he continues:

> Again and again a substantive literary theory makes claims concerning its own autonomy and supremacy which crumble in the face of any serious confrontation with research on related topics in other fields. It usually turns out as well that the substantive literary theory derived a good part of its material by means of a series of selective appropriations of some "theory" (generalities) circulating in other disciplines. Structuralism is a good example, for its proposed unification of the human sciences ultimately rests on a series of analogies based on some general ideas taken from a particular vein of linguistics—a vein of linguistics, moreover, that is highly problematic. (17)

For an exhaustive critique of the intellectual irresponsibility of current literary theory, see Levin; for two insiders' views of how scientific theories in particular have been abused by the humanities and social sciences, see Gross and Levitt.

2. In addition to Livingston and Levin, see Argyros; Brodribb; Cole; Dillon; Easterlin and Riebling; Eddins; Edmundson; Ellis; Felperin; Fischer; Frank; Freadman and Miller; Jackson; Pavel, *Feud;* Roustang; Simpson; and, especially, Carroll.

3. For a full discussion of Frye's transcendental archetypalism, see Carroll 382–90.

4. For a provocative history of representation in science, politics, and art from pre- to postmodern times, see Redner.

Chapter 1

1. I refer the reader who suspects me of overstating the case (if an animal of such improbability still exists) to a fairly recent "Point of View" article in the *Chronicle of Higher Education.* There, Betty Jean Craige, author of *Laying the Ladder Down:*

The Emergence of Cultural Holism, begins by observing that Darwin "revolutionized the study of living forms by replacing the assumption of rigid species types with a new concept of populations." Darwin's population-thinking, she rightly points out, exploded the "essentialist" view of species. But she then concludes, in a series of assertions that would have bewildered Darwin himself, that various traits or behaviors observed within or between species have therefore "no natural foundation": "If there is no natural 'chain of being,' the perception of rank-order among individuals, species, races, or any other category is culturally derived." The pecking-order among chickens is, in other words, a cultural construction of the perceiver. The authority for such conclusions resides in the incoherent assumptions of the "cultural studies" movement and of the somewhat muddled constructivist arguments of a book like Donna Haraway's *Primate Visions,* characteristically over-valued by readers in the humanities. For the fullest argument in defense of the notion of Darwin as a proto-deconstructionist—a lamentably misguided project, to my mind—see Beer.

2. For an intriguing account of the mounting support for this position from the neurosciences, see A. R. Damasio's *Descartes' Error.*

3. De Sousa argues that emotions may be regarded as "instincts" but that they represent a special class of "H" or human instincts as opposed to what he calls "T" or "Tinbergen" instincts, after the eminent ethologist Nikko Tinbergen. The latter identified (for example, in animals such as gulls) predictable sequences of stereotyped responses to precise "releasing stimuli" that led to fitness-promoting behaviors of a relatively fixed type. "Emotions, by contrast," writes de Sousa, "determine motivation. And motivation, even where it concerns simple biological needs such as attachment or the 'four F's,' does not determine fixed patterns of behavior" (84).

4. As developmental psychologist Jerome Kagan points out in his recent *Galen's Prophecy,* new evidence suggests that an emotion like "fear" may be subdivided into at least three different "states," those "produced by innate releasers, conditioning, and unfamiliarity," and that "it is likely that different brain circuits are associated with each of the fear states" (95, 96).

5. This frequently recurring word in the psychological literature may prove a misleading metaphor, since the neuropsychological evidence now suggests that "the neural bases for specific emotions are different" (Kagan, *Galen's Prophecy* 45).

6. As Michael Gazzaniga points out, however, Merzenich's findings may be interpreted in two radically different ways: "The issue . . . is whether the seemingly new cortical maps [that emerge from Merzenich's experiments with monkeys] reflect a change in the underlying neural structure through growth and reorganization, or whether the changes reflect a selection process where a preexisting inactive circuit is activated by a change in the environmental stimulus." In other words, does the brain fabricate new structures or merely draw upon

hitherto "inactive" ones? "At this writing," Gazzaniga concludes, "it is not known which of these possibilities is true" (51).

7. See the recent article by Ekman ("Strong Evidence for Universals"), as well as that by Izard ("Innate and Universal Facial Expressions"), for vigorous defenses of their position against cultural-constructivist critiques.

8. Doubtless the human penchant for dichotomizing phenomena originates in this system's binary dynamics—which itself is born of the fundamental opposition/interplay of organism and world. For the necessity of preserving a distinction between the two, see my remarks toward the end of this chapter.

9. Searle argues that we do not have to resort to anatomical comparisons of brain structures to infer such analogous behaviors in other animals (in dogs, let us say) and we needn't do so "because I can see that the causal basis of the behavior in the dog's physiology is relevantly like my own. . . . I can see, for example, that these are the dog's ears; this is his skin; these are his eyes; that if you pinch his skin, you get behavior appropriate to pinching skin; if you shout in his ear, you get behavior appropriate to shouting in ears" (73).

10. For the most recent elaborations of and arguments in defense of the position expressed by Midgley's italicized remark, see the essays in Byrne and Whiten and the excellent overview in Quiatt and Reynolds (139–211); for a report on recent research that suggests that "feeding complexity" also plays a crucial role in "bootstrapping" cognitive intelligence, specifically among the primates, see Fischman.

11. This fact is noted, not by Wrangham, but by Michael P. Ghiglieri (346, 347), whose references suggest he is characterizing the behavior of female human primates in terms of their behavior among nomadic hunter-gatherers.

12. Paleoanthropologist Robert A. Foley suggests that hominid bonds became strengthened "into long-term stable relationships" with the evolution of the larger-brained infants of early *Homo,* possibly *Homo erectus* (152).

13. The correlation is only a rough one, however, and some anthropologists discount dimorphism as necessarily related to mating patterns (Fisher 335 n. 31). The correlation still seems robust to a physiologist like Jared Diamond (see below).

14. "The other primates": a coinage of Earl W. Count to distinguish nonhuman primates from human ones without laborious circumlocution ("all primates except *Homo sapiens sapiens,*" etc.) or pejorative condescension ("the lower primates").

15. As the evolutionary psychologists John Tooby and Leda Cosmides point out, however, many eminently legitimate explanations in the sciences could be classified (and so dismissed) as just-so stories: "even physics and geology run the 'risk' of addressing such Kiplingesque post hoc questions as why Mercury has an orbit that deviates from the predictions of Newtonian mechanics, why Asia has the Himalayas, or why the universe has its present set of four interactions, temporal asymmetry, background radiation, and particle distribution. In science,

this is usually called 'explanation'" (77). Moreover, "Gould himself," writes Daniel C. Dennett, "has endorsed some of the most daring and delicious of adaptationist Just So stories, such as the argument by Lloyd and Dybas (1966) explaining why cicadas (such as 'seventeen-year locusts') have reproductive cycles that are prime-numbered years long—thirteen years, or seventeen, but never fifteen or sixteen, for instance" (*Darwin's Dangerous Idea* 246). The fact of the matter is that Gould enthusiastically embraces those "just-so stories" about human adaptation that accord with his Marxist politics (see, for example, *Ever Since Darwin* 260–67), while dismissing all the others as sociobiological *ignes fatui.*

16. Maccoby and Jacklin answered their critics—notably Todd Tieger, who, in 1980, challenged their findings on aggression—in their "Sex Differences in Aggression: A Rejoinder and Reprise," a rebuttal generally held in high esteem by psychologists of sexual behavior (see Block 1337). Fausto-Sterling, who relies heavily upon Tieger's critique in the defense of her own arguments, does not mention Maccoby and Jacklin's article.

17. In her first chapter, Fausto-Sterling announces that *Myths of Gender* is "a scientific statement *and* a political statement" since it is written from "a feminist standpoint" (12, 11). Although she herself insists that "in the study of gender (like sexuality and race) it is inherently impossible for any individual to do unbiased research" (10), she claims with equal confidence that her own perspective is superior to that of the "many others" who have gone before her: "Because of my different angle of vision, I see things about the research methods and interpretations that many others have missed" (11). Exactly what that "angle of vision" is becomes clear by the end of the book. Confessing there that she has left certain areas of gender research unexplored, she explains why further disputation would be unnecessary: *"because I fully believe* that the same combination of inadequate research and inappropriate model building would turn up . . . , the general lesson emerges clearly without having to dwell on every available example" (220, my emphasis). If one is fully convinced of the inadequacies of a study before one even reads it, it's fairly easy to mount sophistical arguments to dismiss all the evidence in its favor. Fausto-Sterling's "science" is seductively akin to Stalinist genetics, constructed on the politically correct conviction that Mendel could not possibly have been right.

18. It's the failure to recognize this fact that permits most opponents of biologically based theories of human nature to dismiss the claims of the latter. But as primatologist Sarah Blaffer Hrdy points out in a recent review of Nancy Scheper-Hughes's *Death without Weeping: The Violence of Everyday Life in Brazil,* such dismissals rest upon fundamental misconceptions about the role of genetic programming in behavior:

Ms. Scheper-Hughes, like the French writer Elisabeth Badinter and others, believes that by documenting lapses in mother love she disproves the existence of a biological basis for maternal emotions. In doing so, these writers mistakenly equate a biological basis with some genetically determined, instinctive or automatic response that causes mothers to nurture any infant they bear, regardless of circumstances. The problem lies with definitions of maternal behavior that presuppose nurturing and fail to reflect the full range of situation-dependent maternal responses actually found in nature.

That there is a "range" of responses does not in turn imply, of course, unconstrained behavioral plasticity. It implies, on the other hand, that an organism is programmed to respond to its environment in terms of what E. O. Wilson calls "behavioral scaling":

> Behavioral scaling is variation in the magnitude or in the qualitative state of a behavior which is correlated with stages of the life cycle, population density, or certain parameters of the environment. It is a useful working hypothesis to suppose that in each case the scaling is adaptive, meaning that it is genetically programmed to provide the individual with the particular response more or less precisely appropriate to its situation at any moment in time. In other words, the entire scale, not isolated points on it, is the genetically based trait that has been fixed by natural selection. (*Sociobiology* 20)

In the human organism, the emotional system sets the limits of that scale.

19. Recent meta-analyses of gender differences in behavior conclude, like Maccoby and Jacklin, that "males show more aggression than females for both physical aggression and verbal aggression" (Hyde 61) and that males are "more assertive" than females, having "slightly higher self-esteem" (Feingold 429). For a rare social-psychological study assimilating these findings (and others) to the evolutionary perspective presented here, see Kenrick and Trost.

20. "A comparison of the contexts of aggression in nonhuman primates and humans reveals striking similarities. . . . In both groups, aggression usually occurs in the contexts of competition for resources, sexual partners and status, personal defense, protection of conspecifics, play, policing, intergroup encounters, etc. These similarities point to the [human's] primate legacy" (Chapais 210).

21. Anthropologist Helen Fisher sees in such behavioral differences the source for differences in styles of intimacy expressed by men and women. She quotes the sociologist Harry Brod: "Numerous studies have established that men are more likely to define emotional closeness as working or playing side by side, while women often view it as talking face to face" (204).

22. For one of the most recent human studies, see Baucom, Besch, and Callahan; for a survey and critique, see Rubin, Reinisch, and Haskett. (Although

the latter study precedes the former by several years, it still has important relevance for the findings of Baucom et al.)

23. In the course of an extremely blurry survey of these studies, at least those conducted before 1985, Fausto-Sterling lodges three principal criticisms against them: first, there were no direct "blind" observations of the behaviors, the researchers relying upon interviews and pencil-and-paper tests; second, the effect of genital surgery upon the patients was not taken into account; and, third, the effects of the cortisone therapy were not considered. To take the last objection first: some patients in these studies—specifically the children of progestogen-treated mothers—received no cortisone treatments at all, and, for those that did, it is not immediately clear why cortisone, which "can cause mood elevation and even hyperactivity" (Fausto-Sterling 136), should have affected anything other than activity level in the recipients. As for the surgery, Fausto-Sterling argues that it could have had the effects that have been attributed, circumstantially, to circumcision ("male/female differences in activity, wakefulness, and irritability" [136]). But, again, not all of the patients were "feminized" surgically—certainly, none of the CAH boys were—and the effects attributable to surgical correction can account for only one aspect of the reported behaviors.

The fact that the behaviors were reported and not observed leads Fausto-Sterling, predictably, to suspect observer bias, since all the informants who were interviewed "knew that at birth there had been questions concerning the children's gender" and "such knowledge could lead to nonconscious but nevertheless inaccurate assessments of . . . behavior" (137). This does not seem to have been the case. One of the researchers, Anke A. Ehrhardt, "found that the parents [of CAH girls] were either not specifically concerned about their behavior, or if concerned, usually about tomboyism, they tended to encourage femininity. That is, they tended to oppose rather than to encourage those temperamental characteristics of their daughters that appeared to be sequelae of their specific prenatal hormone condition" (Ehrhardt and Meyer-Bahlburg 1314). Of course, if one is convinced that "nonconscious" assessments have flawed the studies, such assurances are to little avail. Fortunately, we now have two new studies in which the actual behavior of CAH children, observed at play with their sibling controls, is reported and analyzed. In the first (Berenbaum and Hines), CAH girls, unlike their unaffected counterparts, were seen to show a marked preference for masculine toys, playing with cars, for example, for the same amount of time as did the so-called normal boys. In the second (Hines and Kaufman), CAH girls were found to be "more likely than unaffected girls to identify boys as playmates" (1052). No difference was found in the "rough-and-tumble" play of CAH and unaffected girls, but athletic and similar activity was not assessed by either study. And Hines and Kaufman conclude: "in light of clear evidence that rough-and-tumble play is influenced by prenatal androgen exposure in experimental animals, including nonhuman primates . . . , it would seem unlikely that this aspect of sex-typical behavior would be selectively exempt from hormonal influence in human beings" (1049). Only further research—not feminist faith—will confirm or disprove this conclusion.

24. For one of the most recent and accessible discussions of the "sexual brain," see LeVay; for MRI and PET-scan studies confirming that "differences [between the sexes] in cognitive and emotional processing have biological substrates" (Gur et al. 528), see Shaywitz et al., and Gur et al.

25. As Tooby and Cosmides put it, "'biology' is not some substance that is segregated or localized inside the initial state of the organism at birth, circumscribing the domain to which evolutionary analyses apply."

> It is also in the organization of the developmentally relevant world itself, when viewed from the perspective imposed by the evolved developmentally relevant mechanisms of the organism. Thus, nothing the organism interacts with in the world is nonbiological to it, and so for humans cultural forces are biological, social forces are biological, physical forces are biological, and so on. (86)

As for the tendency to explain all behaviors as "learned," they point out that "'learning'—like 'culture,' 'rationality,' and 'intelligence'—is not an explanation for anything, but is rather a phenomenon that itself requires explanation. . . . Under closer inspection, 'learning' is turning out to be a diverse set of processes caused by a series of incredibly intricate, functionally organized cognitive adaptations, implemented in neurobiological machinery" (122, 123).

26. For recent (and sympathetic) reviews of feminist "interventions" in behavioral biology, especially as it concerns gender, see the "Bibliographies and Guides" in Rosser 181–85 and Lewontin's "Women"; for a rare but important critique of constructivist thinking by a feminist literary critic—one that "throws into question the stability and impermeability of the essentialist/constructionist binarism" (2)—see Fuss.

27. But I hasten to add that I share none of the pervasive romanticizing of the feminine in which the maternalists indulge. As Sarah Blaffer Hrdy observes:

> Widespread stereotypes devaluing the capacities and importance of women have not improved either their lot or that of human societies. But there is little to be gained from countermyths that emphasize woman's natural innocence from lust for power, her cooperativeness and solidarity with other women. Such a female never evolved among the other primates. Even under those conditions most favorable to high status for females—monogamy and closely bonded "sisterhoods"—competition among females remains a fact of primate existence. (*Woman* 190)

28. For the argument that "a slide into relativism" was "not even remotely Kuhn's intention" (276), see Churchland 271–77; for Kuhn's own account of his frustration with admirers and critics, see Horgan, "Profile."

29. In *The Fragmentation of Reason*, Stephen P. Stich attacks the thesis that "natural selection prefers reliable inferential systems—those that do a good job at producing truths and avoiding falsehoods—to unreliable ones" (60). Drawing attention to gene-selection processes that can in fact be deleterious to organismic fitness (random drift, pleiotropy, heterozygote superiority, meiotic drive), he first demonstrates the noncontestable point that "it is simply not the case that evolution inevitably produces close approximations to optimally well-designed systems" (67). But it's a big step, of course, from a system that functions in a suboptimal way (any engineer, my biologist friends tell me, can design a better body than the human being's) to one with "unreliable" equipment, and so, as Stich himself realizes, he must now argue the possibility that "variations in inferential strategies across persons or societies are largely *independent* of genetic factors" (69, my emphasis).

To do so, he unfortunately repairs to a poor analogy, asserting that "it is entirely possible that the cognitive mechanisms subserving inference are similar in important ways to the cognitive mechanisms underlying language comprehension" (69). He assumes that the "nativist" arguments about language acquisition have been exploded (although most linguists are beginning to come to John L. Locke's conclusion: that "the classic opposition—genes versus the environment [in the matter of language acquisition]—now appears to be rather shopworn and empty" [423]) and so concludes that so-called humanly possible languages "need not share any common core or any other common features" (71). But this fact (if it is a fact) says nothing about the nature of the inferential system, since the structure of a language can be wildly arbitrary so long as its speakers agree upon observing the rules that the structure consistently generates. Human inference, on the other hand, must deal with various constancies and intractabilities in both the physical and the social worlds—and a human being with no sense of, say, cause and effect would not last very long in either. The general problem with Stich's argument is that he never defines what he means by "inferential system" or the kinds of "truths" that he maintains that that system may do without. For a recent defense of the position (my own) that "adaptations are biological knowledge, and knowledge as we commonly understand the word is a special case of biological knowledge" (xv), see Plotkin; for a study that distinguishes carefully between the "rationality" necessary for the survival of the human mind and the "rationality" only incidental to that survival, see Anderson; for the argument that mathematics in particular "is strongly associated with our own genetic make-up" (176), see Barrow.

30. The field work of early primatological study provides an illuminating example. Most primatologists now agree that the principal factor behind both the

cohesiveness and longevity of at least half of all primate groups is the social bond between female members. But when the science was still young, one of the first of its practitioners, Irven DeVore, found his attention focused almost exclusively on the behavior of the males among the olive baboons under his scrutiny. "That's the thing that hits you when you first see baboons," he has recently told a *Science* reporter: "the big, rowdy males. When they move, things happen. They also had shifting coalitions, and this was so new that everyone seized on it as being of the utmost importance. What I didn't see during my time in the field was a single male transfer [a rather common olive baboon phenomenon]" (M[orell] 428).

My own attention throughout this book is biased in favor of (which is to say, largely focused upon) male behavior. Most of this bias is deliberate, however, as the phenomenon I am dealing with—the literature of our species—has for more than two thousand years been predominantly a male enterprise, one that reflects (especially when it comes to comedy) the epistemological practices of the male of that species more accurately and consistently than the female's. Feminist criticism, particularly of women's literature, is now attempting to correct the bias, but I'm skeptical of much, if not most, of its value. Outside of appeals to pseudosciences like psychoanalysis or the sociology inspired by it, that criticism makes no attempt to ground its analyses in empirically responsible evidence or argument, usually resorting to a "constructivist" ideology (it's a mistake to call it a paradigm) derived from the pantheon of fashionable "thinkers." At any rate, it may be fruitless at this point to generalize about women's literature, at least about the ways it differs from men's, both because the sample we must work with is hazardously small and because many women writers, as the critics put it, have been constructed by the phallocentric discourse.

31. A fascinating and dramatic illustration of this fact is provided by the recent discovery that a tiny shrimplike Antarctic amphipod (*Hyperiella dilatata*) typically enslaves the even tinier *Clione limacina*, a pteropod or "sea butterfly." To avoid being eaten by the local species of fish, which find the sea butterfly distasteful, the amphipod grasps the latter by its serrated feet, and the sluglike captive lives out its life gripped tightly to the back of its enslaver (McClintock and Janssen).

32. The reader interested in Goldberg's thesis—if only for the fact that *The Inevitability of Patriarchy* was once listed in the *Guinness Book of World Records* as having received the highest number of rejections for an eventually published book—should consult the more recent edition (entitled, unfortunately, rather more ambiguously *Why Men Rule*), in which he addresses past criticism of his work.

33. It is the failure to recognize that cultural "superstructures" are founded upon *emotional* tendencies that leads Daniel C. Dennett (among other theorists) into the error of concluding that cultures are *"able to overpower or escape* biological constraints in most regards" (*Darwin's Dangerous Idea* 491). My argument is that a culture is *not*, as Dennett declares it to be, "a *largely* autonomous system of symbols

and values" (ibid.); rather, a culture's symbols and values arise directly out of the human emotional system—the system that, in de Sousa's words, "we see the world 'in terms of' " (196). Because an ambitious book like William H. Durham's *Coevolution: Genes, Culture, and Human Diversity* takes no account of that system, its discussion of gene-culture coevolution seems to me seriously weakened.

34. Alexander Argyros would call them, properly, *chaotically* constrained ambivalences. I regret that I do not have the space to enlist chaos theory in the elaboration of the general argument of this book. The curious reader will find much that is suggestive (and supplemental to that argument) in Argyros's *Blessed Rage*.

35. John Horgan defines "heritability": "A trait that stems entirely from genes, such as eye color, is defined as 100 percent heritable. Height is 90 percent heritable; that is, 90 percent of the variation in height is accounted for by genetic variation, and the other 10 percent is accounted for by diet and other environmental factors" ("Eugenics" 124). Horgan, who is senior writer for *Scientific American*, not himself a geneticist, is among those skeptical of the heritability research, but in "Eugenics" he offers little in the way of criticism of it except for untested suppositions and conjectural allegations from scientists unsympathetic to behavioral genetics. As the psychologist Matt McGue and his sixteen international co-signers point out in a subsequent letter to the editor, Horgan's "baseless accusations" (such as his suggestion that, because Hitler was an "enthusiastic eugenicist," he, "presumably, had much in common with the modern behavioral genetics researcher") "are merely an attempt to win with scare tactics that which has not been won in the research laboratory."

What Horgan's article succeeds in showing is not what is announced by the cover behind which it appears—"The Dubious Link between Genes and Behavior"—but rather the difficulty that geneticists are having in linking specific behaviors to specific sets of genes. But this, as biologist Evan Balaban suggests, is a difficulty endemic to all genetic research: "It is very rare," Horgan quotes Balaban as saying, "to find genes that have a specific effect. . . . For evolutionary reasons, this just doesn't happen very often" ("Eugenics" 127).

For one of the most recent mainstream contributions to the genes-behavior debate, see the special edition of *Science* (June 17, 1994) devoted to "Genes and Behavior," especially the article by Bouchard, "Genes, Environment, and Personality," and that by Plomin, Owen, and McGuffin, "The Genetic Basis of Complex Human Behaviors." For a fascinating account of the first scientific study proving genetic linkage to a complex human behavior (in this case, male homosexuality), see Hamer and Copeland.

36. The aptness of "evolutionary psychology" is not, however, the major reason for its inscription on the revolutionaries' flag; nor is it, as Robert Wright explains, the only phrase under which they march:

The various revolutionaries stubbornly refuse to call themselves by a single, simple name, the sort of thing that would fit easily onto a fluttering banner. They once had such a name—"sociobiology," Wilson's apt and useful term. But Wilson's book drew so much fire, provoked so many charges of malign political intent, so much caricature of sociobiology's substance, that the word became tainted. Most practitioners of the field he defined now prefer to avoid his label. . . . People sometimes ask: What ever happened to sociobiology? The answer is that it went underground, where it has been eating away at the foundations of academic orthodoxy. (6–7, footnote omitted)

I resurrect Wilson's "apt and useful term" in the next chapter, and flourish it without apology. For those readers seeking a less abbreviated account of the "substance" of sociobiology, I recommend Wright's lucid and lively book. For one of the most enlightened defenses of it from the biologist's point of view, see Goldsmith; for an exhaustive critique by a philosopher of science—one that concludes that "human sociobiology is being tried [by its detractors] in a court where the law is outdated and ill designed for cases of emerging fields that aim to extend past work in various situation-dependent ways" (413)—see Holcomb.

37. From the long perspective (as Hahlweg and Hooker argue), evolutionary epistemology is itself "essentially nonfoundational" (29). They quote Konrad Lorenz:

The realization that all laws of "pure reason" are based on highly physical or mechanical structures of the human central nervous system which have developed through many eons like any other organ, on the one hand shakes our confidence in the laws of pure reason and on the other hand substantially raises our confidence in them. Kant's statement that the laws of pure reason have absolute validity, nay that every imaginable rational being, even if it were an angel, must obey the same laws of thought, appears as an anthropocentric presumption. Surely the "keyboard" provided by the forms of intuition and categories—Kant himself calls it that—is something definitely located on the physico-structural side of the psychophysical unity of the human organism. . . . But surely these clumsy categorical boxes into which we have to pack our external world "in order to be able to spell them as experiences" (Kant) can claim no autonomous and absolute validity whatsoever. This is certain for us the moment we conceive them as evolutionary adaptations. . . . At the same time, however, *the nature of their adaptation shows that the categorical forms of intuition and categories have proved themselves as working hypotheses* in the coping of our species with the absolute reality of the environment (in spite of their validity being only approximate and relative).

Thus is clarified the paradoxical fact that the laws of "pure reason" which break down at every step in modern theoretical science, nevertheless have stood (and still stand) the test in the practical biological matters of the struggle for the preservation of the species.

Chapter 2

1. A phrase like "the individual gene" is a form of technical shorthand and will be used as such throughout this chapter. Apparently, as sociobiologists are well aware, most genes function in the aggregate. Or, in Sober and Lewontin's more careful formulation, "selection acts on multilocus genotypic configurations and not on the genotype at a single locus, let alone on the separate genes at that locus" (221).

2. For an extended explanation of the reproductively functional character of female sexual attractiveness, see Symons.

3. More recently, Helen Fisher has proposed that human "females evolved two *alternative* strategies to acquire resources: some women elected to be relatively faithful to a single man in order to reap a lot of benefits from him; others engaged in clandestine sex with many men to acquire resources from each. This scenario roughly coincides with the common beliefs: man, the natural playboy; woman, the madonna or the whore" (94).

4. It shouldn't be inferred from these remarks that women are less sexually active than men, either inside or outside marriage. As Robert L. Smith's cross-cultural statistics make clear (604, 606), the frequency of pre- and extramarital sex is roughly about the same for men and women. (For more dramatic documentation, see Fisher 89–94, 260–72.) The important difference, as Buss has argued recently, seems to be between men's and women's attitudes toward "casual sex." Whereas "women's desires in a short-term sex partner strongly resemble their desires in a husband," the preferences of men, "in marked contrast, shift abruptly with the mating context" (*Evolution* 88). Women value stability and generosity in such a partner; men, indifferent to the economic advantages that accrue to such traits (as well as to the kindness and understanding they seek from a spouse), pursue strategies that would have reaped immediate reproductive benefits for an ancestral male. Men's sexual fantasies say it all: "The most striking feature of [male fantasy]," as Bruce Ellis and Donald Symons observe, "is that sex is sheer lust and physical gratification, devoid of encumbering relationships, emotional elaboration, complicated plot lines, flirtation, courtship, and extended foreplay" (qtd. in Buss, *Evolution* 82). And the more partners, the better: "A key male sexual fantasy is to have sexual access to dozens of fresh, beautiful women who respond eagerly" (Buss, *Evolution*

82). Interestingly, Buss notes that, when men and women are both freed of the "dictates and demands" of the opposite sex—that is, when homosexuality relieves them of the same—their "permanent mating preferences" are, on average, identical to their "casual mating proclivities" and that those proclivities (at least before AIDS) "reveal fundamental differences between men and women in the centrality of casual sex" (*Evolution* 84–85):

> Whereas male homosexuals often cruise the bars, parks, and public rest rooms for brief encounters, lesbians rarely do. Whereas male homosexuals frequently search for new and varied sex partners, lesbians are far more likely to settle into intimate, lasting, committed relationships. . . . This evidence suggests that when men are unconstrained by the courtship and commitment requirements typically imposed by women, they freely satisfy their desires for casual sex with a variety of partners. (*Evolution* 84)

5. For an extended argument to the effect that "the nuclear family—with all its drawbacks, difficulties and dangers—is a biologically derived way of living which comes naturally to us and which generates an emotional force of enduring and unquenchable power" (64), see Mount.

6. Qtd. in Barash 157; "bosses" is my addition.

7. For a full account of the terms and conditions under which reciprocal altruism is thought to have evolved, see Axelrod; Axelrod and Dion; Cosmides and Tooby; R. Boyd; Sigmund 155–206; and Casti.

8. As Damasio and his wife, Hanna, explain in their book *Lesion Analysis in Neuropsychology,* their work takes into account the lesions that are produced "by neurological disease or by a surgical procedure" (7). This means that the behavioral deficits that he describes can be attributed to genetic as well as environmental factors. Indeed, studies of monozygotic and dizygotic twins have turned up high heritability coefficients for altruism: see the summary in Krebs 111.

9. Marvin Harris offers a more detailed and subtle development of the argument (which owes its earliest formulations to Jack Goody), but the persuasiveness of his reasoning is weakened by the poverty of his assumption that men differ from women only "in stature, weight, and musculature, and in reproductive physiology, especially with respect to pregnancy and lactation" (57). That there should be differences in aggressiveness, neurological structure, and genetic dispositions is a possibility that he dismisses as "vague, subjective, facile, and hypothetical" (57).

10. It suggests "invariant," as well. But, as Robert Foley points out, "the path of social evolution within the genus *Homo* is likely to be diverse and complex" (152). From the early *Australopithecus afarensis,* with its probable paucity of "close and exclusive relationships between individual males and females" (151), through *Homo erectus,* with its probable pattern of long-term, stable, perhaps polygynous

unions, there appear to have been "marked behavioral differences between archaic and modern hominids" (153).

11. The !Kung have lost their mobility and have thereby acceded to hierarchical governance because of a recently developed tendency to hoard nontransportable "wealth": see Yellen. The Russian gravesite of a Cro-Magnon people, dating from 28,000 years ago, has turned up elaborate ornamental beadwork on two children's skeletons, suggesting to anthropologist Randall White that perhaps "the children had inherited a high social rank. If so, hierarchical societies arose—contrary to what some have assumed—well before economic systems based on agricultural production" (64).

12. Joan B. Silk expresses the consensus view: "Male dominance over females is characteristic of . . . vervets, macaques, squirrel monkeys, talapoins, Hanuman langurs, mantled howler monkeys, *gorillas, orang-utans, chimpanzees,* and baboons" (215, my emphasis). (The female-dominated bonobos are the odd-hominoids-out.) Some anthropologists have minimized the continuity between the great apes and human beings, arguing, as Susan Carol Rogers does, that male dominance in human societies is nothing more than a powerful "myth." But Martin King Whyte's measured formulation of the issue suggests that, although gender relations in humans are more subtle and more varied than those among their great-ape kin, they adhere to the general primate pattern: "there is substantial variation from societies with very general male dominance to other societies in which broad equality and even some specific types of female dominance over men exist. Women seem never to fully dominate men in all of social life, but the degree of male dominance ranges from total to minimal" (167–68). Most significant for my subsequent discussion is the fact that "politics is the realm of social life that is most dominated by males" (Whyte 58). Of the preindustrial societies for which relevant data exist, 88 percent (65 cultures) include only males in intermediate or local leadership positions, and, in the two cultures in which women's political status is highest, men are more numerous in such positions while women are equally powerful, or men are more powerful while women are equally numerous (Whyte 57). The statistics show little departure from this pattern for leadership posts in kinship and/or extended family units.

13. The "most striking finding" of psychologist Alice H. Eagly's recent meta-analysis of gender and the effectiveness of leaders was that "leadership roles defined in relatively masculine terms favored male leaders and that roles defined in relatively feminine terms favored female leaders" (Eagly, Karau, and Makhijani 137). What those "terms" were are clearly specified in the article: "women were more effective than men in leadership roles that were feminine in the sense that our respondents judged they required considerable interpersonal ability, defined as the ability to cooperate and get along with other people. Men were more effective than women in roles that were masculine in the sense that our respondents judged they required

considerable task ability, defined as the ability to direct and control people" (137). For a study of Irish working-women's groups that supports the same conclusions, see Veeder; for an extended account of three feminist organizations that were able "to maintain non-hierarchical organization while at the same time achieving, to a reasonable extent, organization goals" (117), see Iannello.

14. I have slightly revised the original sentence (it reads " . . . only the more dominant get a chance to breed") to accord with the most recent research. It is still clear, as Chapais points out, that "the scope of dominance-based power amounts to securing priority of access to physical resources (space, food, water, sleeping sites) and mates" (197). But "priority of access" does not neatly translate into success of acquisition, especially where mates are concerned. Female primates (including, of course, human primates) are rarely merely passive (or browbeaten) recipients of the sexual favors of the males, and reproductively successful males, like the human adolescents I described in Chapter 1, are those that can add other skills to their proven ability to muscle their way up the hierarchy. "Males," write anthropologists James Silverberg and J. Patrick Gray, in reference specifically to male baboons, "do not increase mating success directly through their dominance interactions with other males, but through their abilities to form nonagonistic relationships ('friendships') with females and their offspring" (20).

15. In one of the most recent reviews and reformulations of the subject, Penelope J. Oakes, S. Alexander Haslam, and John C. Turner conclude that there is no "*necessary* basis on which stereotypes distort reality. Of course, stereotyping (as other forms of person perception) can be a route to overgeneralization and other distortions, but . . . it is not *by definition* distorted simply because it represents people as other than unique individuals" (125). The "individual," as they point out, is itself, like the stereotype, a categorical phenomenon: "*Both person and group perception are categorization.*"

> The issue of validity, therefore, is not a matter of opposing unreal, categorized groups to real, uncategorized individuals, of seeing either groups or individuals, of one or the other level of perception always being more real or valid than the other, but of doing both or either when appropriate. We suggest that this is precisely what people do. They define people as individuals in one context and as groups in another. (189)

The alert reader will have realized that the biogram, as I am developing it, is a group-categorization phenomenon.

16. For one of the most recent studies of the continuing wage gap between men and women, see England.

17. Sociologist Beth Anne Shelton, in a recent and regionally unrestricted study, also concludes that, between 1975 and 1987, "women's and men's paid labor

time became more similar than did their housework time. In addition, a significant part of the convergence in women's and men's housework time was a function of a decrease in women's housework time rather than an increase in men's housework time" (145).

Chapter 3

1. For one of the most accessible discussions of the phenomenon, see Calvin 117–22, 172–74.

2. For a particularly fascinating example of how the brain "half-creates" its perceptions, see Dennett on the "color phi phenomenon" (*Consciousness* 120–26).

3. Tooby and Cosmides have summarized the research on young children's principles of categorization:

Recent research suggests that young children . . . distinguish the animate from the inanimate worlds, and make very different inferences about the two. . . . Natural kinds are viewed as having invisible "essences" that bear a causal relation to their perceptual attributes, whereas artifacts are defined by how their perceptual attributes subserve their (intended) function. In general, being a member of a natural kind carries more inferential weight than being perceptually similar. In addition, children give more weight to natural kind membership when reasoning about traits that actually *are* more likely to vary as a function of membership in a natural kind, such as breathing, than when reasoning about traits that are more likely to vary as a function of perceptual similarity, such as weight or visibility at night. (71–72)

4. For a decisive critique of the idea that "words determine thoughts" (56), see Pinker 55–67; for an anthology of the most recent empirical research into "thought without language," see Weiskrantz.

5. The identification, in the pages that follow, of one hemisphere or the other as "verbal" or "analytic" or "holistic" is a form of shorthand for which I beg the reader's indulgence. As Joseph B. Hellige points out in the most recent synthesis of hemispheric research, "it is rarely the case in the intact brain that one hemisphere can perform a task normally whereas the other is completely unable to perform the task at all. Instead, even when hemispheric asymmetry for a task exists, it is typically the case that both hemispheres have the ability to perform the task, even though one may do a better job than the other" (29). Moreover, most tasks are distributed in subtle ways *between* the two hemispheres: for example, "the left hemisphere seems dominant for the production of overt speech, for the

perception of phonetic information, for using syntactic information, and for certain aspects of semantic analysis. However, the right hemisphere seems dominant for certain other aspects of language, including the use of pragmatic aspects of language (e.g., narrative-level linguistic information) and the use of intonation and prosody to communicate emotional tone" (61–62). Finally, nowhere do I intend to imply that a "fundamental dichotomy" exists that may be identified by my shorthand notations. "It is . . . possible," writes Hellige, "that no single information-processing dimension will ever be able to account for all hemispheric asymmetries," adding that the empirical evidence indeed favors that possibility (58).

6. Dennett concedes as much when, at the end of his *Consciousness Explained*, he writes:

> I haven't replaced a metaphorical theory, the Cartesian Theater, with a *non*metaphorical ("literal, scientific") theory. All I have done, really, is to replace one family of metaphors and images with another. . . . It's just a war of metaphors, you say—but metaphors are not "just" metaphors; metaphors are the tools of thought. (455)

7. As I pointed out in Chapter 1, the so-called prototypical emotions develop in the infant shortly after birth, and it's apparently by virtue of their development that this "reading" of other agents is made possible. Paul L. Harris argues, for example, that, "quite early in the first year of life, babies adjust their social behaviour to the emotion expressed by their caretaker [specifically, by their caretaker's face]. By the end of the first year of life, they extend this selectivity to objects in the environment; they seem to recognize that adults do not simply express emotion, rather they express emotion in a targeted fashion toward particular objects" (23). Later, as young children, they "grasp that people's emotional reactions differ depending on the beliefs and desires they have about a situation" (2), and they find that, "if they examine a situation in the light of the beliefs or desires that another person brings to it, they can proceed to simulate the intentions or emotions of that person" (3). For a detailed discussion of these developments, see both Harris and Perner.

8. Cf. the remark by the cognitive neuroscientist and philosopher of mind Paul M. Churchland: "the cognitive priority of the preverbal over the verbal shows itself, upon examination, to be a feature of almost all of our cognitive categories" (144).

9. Linguist Lois Bloom has in fact pointed out that the "most important" class of meanings expressed by young children learning language occurs "in sentences with the constituents subject-verb-object, utterances like 'Mommy pigtail,' 'read book,' and 'Baby do it,'" and that the "majority" of children's sentences express "action relations between animate nouns as actor or agent subjects and inanimate objects affected by the action" (16). Such sentences are, of course, narratives in small.

10. I quote this remark trusting that the reader will assume that the "unity and meaning" of which Johnson speaks arise from the pleasures (and demands) of the social life. But, to be acccurate with respect to Johnson, I should point out that he, following such philosophers as Paul Ricoeur and Alasdair MacIntyre, is actually arguing that the unity and meaning for which we "strive" offer the kind of existential closure sought by Sartre's Roquentin, one that knits up the "gaps, disjunctions, reversals, fractures, and fragmentations that constitute what Ricoeur calls the 'discordance' of human existence" (170). Although widely accepted by narrative theorists, this seems to me a somewhat myopically (and romantically) modern notion of the function of narrative. It may arise, in part, from Johnson's essentially constructivist view of human nature ("We inhabit this world . . . as beings who are *constituted by* sedimented cultural practices, institutions, and meanings" [161]), a view shared by many other critics (Mark Turner, for example) who have been influenced by cognitive science. As Derek Bickerton notes, in disapproval, "Cognitive scientists are not, for the most part, interested in evolution" (113).

11. Marcia Barinaga, in a recent number of *Science*, observes that "neural-network models . . . show that alternation of states that resemble S[low]W[ave] and REM sleep helps adjust the strength of neural connections in a way that would allow memories to be stored and retrieved" ("To Sleep" 604). Two studies that support those conclusions (Wilson and McNaughton; Karni et al.) appear in the same issue.

12. Carrithers was anticipated by Robert Scholes in identifying narrativity as a property of perceivers rather than of texts: "I should like to employ the word 'narrativity,'" writes Scholes in *Semiotics and Interpretation*, "to refer to the process by which a perceiver actively constructs a story from the fictional data provided by any narrative medium" (60). But, as Philip J. M. Sturgess implies in his recent *Narrativity: Theory and Practice*, among narratologists Scholes's is an anomalous position. Many influential theorists, from Propp through Greimas and Jameson, regard narrativity as a property immanent in a (verbal) text—the dubiety of which conviction is lucidly exposed by Sturgess. But even he insists that "one is obliged . . . to apply the concept of narrativity, as its very name seems to demand, to the operations of narrative rather than of the reader," conceding to Scholes only that "readers will possess a certain *awareness* of narrativity, based on their previous reading experience" (14, 15). And in failing to embed narrativity in the preverbal social matrix of the developing perceiver's world, Sturgess, like the other narratologists whom he criticizes, seems to end up attributing anthropomorphic agency to narrative qualities themselves. "Narrativity," he writes,

> is a quality that operates along the syntagmatic axis of a narrative, indeed one may say that in effect it produces this axis. It does so not by way of some sub- or pre-textual stratum, whether distinct from the linguistic level

or not, but by way of its own ability to produce properly "sequential" units which ultimately in their combination together will form the narrative itself. As can and will be seen, this is an understanding of the term narrativity to which I am most sympathetic. (21–22)

But ghostly, disembodied "qualities" are completely without generative "ability," either to operate along axes or to produce sequential units. Only human minds, as Sturgess later makes explicit ("The agent in this process [of elaborating narrative] is of course the author" [63]), may be attributed with such powers—and, consequently, with the power to invest a text with, or to engage a text by virtue of, what both Scholes and Carrithers call narrativity. Henceforth I'll use the word as they do.

13. Locke continues: "This [genetic] possibility is suggested by studies identifying a pattern of autosomal recessive inheritance in multiple-incidence families . . . , a higher frequency of maternal illness and other prenatal risk factors in single-incidence families . . . , and a higher concordance for autism in monozygotic than dizygotic twins" (317; references omitted).

14. It may be of some significance that she is equally deficient in what most would call aesthetic sensitivity. At one point during their talk, Sacks "found some horsetails (one of my favorite plants) in a muddy patch . . . and became excited about them. Temple glanced at them, said 'Esquisetum,' but did not seem stirred by them, as I was" ("Neurologist's Notebook" 112). Later she confesses that she is indifferent to music and that she is puzzled by words like "sublime": she "had spent much time with a dictionary, trying to understand them. She had looked up 'sublime,' 'mysterious,' 'awe,' and 'numinous,' but they all seemed to be defined in terms of one another" (124). "You get such joy out of the sunset," she tells Sacks. "I wish I did, too. I know it's beautiful, but I don't 'get' it" (124).

15. For a recent survey of that error, see D. Kuhn.

16. Although some theorists have maintained that both the perception and the production of emotional responses are equally divided between the two hemispheres—the right hemisphere dominant for "negative" emotions and the more "verbal" left dominant for "positive" ones—Hellige points out that the bulk of the evidence "is more consistent with the hypothesis that the right hemisphere is dominant for producing and perceiving emotion, regardless of valence, rather than with the alternative" (50). Consequently, the shift to logico-verbal processing may entail a reduction in affective sensitivity.

17. Churchland is even more critical of Dennett's account of consciousness as a linguistically "emergent" phenomenon, arguing that "the social institution of language has nothing to do with the genesis of consciousness" and that, "on the best evidence and theory available, the higher animals are just as conscious as we are" (269, 271).

18. For a fascinating theory of how such selection may work, see Calvin 261–72; for a full discussion of temperament and its role in the construction of the self, see Ornstein, *Roots* 35–99, and especially Kagan, *Galen's Prophecy.*

19. For a critique (undertaken, unfortunately, from a psychoanalytic point of view) of the romantic tendency of contemporary theorists like Deleuze and Baudrillard to glorify the schizophrenic "loss of self," see Glass.

20. Hanna Damasio and her colleagues have recently argued that it is to the frontal lobes that we should also (collaterally?) attribute "the planning and execution of personally and socially suitable behavior, . . . the aspect of reasoning known as rationality" (1102).

21. As I indicate below, Consciousness-2, according to Bickerton, emerged only after the advent of language; narrativity, however, preceded language, being a probable possession of the alloprimates as well as of other "lower" animals. Such is also the opinion of Baron-Cohen, who uses the word "mindreading" for my "narrativity": "The limitation of a language faculty without an accompanying mindreading system suggests that mindreading may have preceded language in evolution" (132). It is certainly the case, though, as he suggests, that "mindreading is enabled by the language faculty" (131).

22. Bickerton uses the word "language" for Jackendoff's "conceptual structures" throughout his book, but, "by language," he insists,

> I do not mean sound waves coming out of mouths, or conventionalized marks on pages, or French, Latin, Swahili, or any of the other local manifestations of language. I am talking about the infrastructure of language: the properties and consequences of the system of neuron ensembles and connecting nerve fibers that made possible, first, the first and only symbolic system for transmitting objective information that emerged on this planet, and second, the refinement of that symbolic system whose use we enjoy today. (160, footnote omitted)

He adds that "all that one needs to make [Jackendoff's] account compatible with mine is to introduce the on-line/off-line distinction and rename conceptual structure 'Language-with-a-big-L'" (118).

23. For a recent answer to Dennett—which argues that "there *is* a theater" and that "the action on its stage is being scrutinized by an observer" (144)—see Harth.

Chapter 4

1. "What is it to imagine? We have examined a number of dimensions along which imaginings can vary; shouldn't we now spell out what they have in common?

Yes, if we can. But I can't. Fortunately, an intuitive understanding of what it is to imagine . . . is sufficient for us to proceed with our investigation" (Walton 19, paragraphing simplified).

2. To give Walton his due, I shouldn't omit mention of his speculations to the effect that "a Darwinian explanation may be available" for our understanding of "psychological participation in games of make-believe": "Probably it has survival value. So evolutionary pressures may be responsible for our being organisms of a kind susceptible to quasi emotions in situations in which they might enrich our psychological participation in games of make-believe" (245 n). But it is not at all clear how this explanation—correct, in my opinion—squares with Walton's idea that "there is no such thing as the way the world is in itself."

3. On the play-ritual-art connection, see especially Dissanayake, *Homo* 42–49.

4. Throughout, I quote the Fagles translation; numbers in parentheses are line numbers.

5. The importance of the first two items of this series should be self-evident; on the role that probability plays in the reception of narrative, see below.

6. Pfeiffer argues that each figure in the caves "is part of a series, a procession of some sort, and it may have been intended to be viewed sequentially" (236).

7. Unless otherwise indicated, all parenthetical references in this paragraph as well as in the three paragraphs that follow are to Pitcher and Prelinger.

8. Walton seems to me right in arguing that the so-called painful emotions are not necessarily disagreeable in themselves. Of sorrow, for example, Walton writes: "What is clearly disagreeable, what we regret, are the things we are sorrowful *about*—the loss of an opportunity, the death of a friend—not the feeling or experience of sorrow itself. . . . One may *want* to experience sorrow, and may find a certain enjoyment or satisfaction in the fact that one does experience it" (257). In this position, he is anticipated (among others) by Oscar Mandel: "Art gives us the adventure and withholds the pain; exercises our emotions but allays their discomfort; arouses fear without danger, pity without injury, love without responsibility, defeat without humiliation, luxury without work, power without effort" (81). These positions are useful, of course, in tackling the issue of audience response in Western tragedy.

9. In this their stories resemble all folktales of the world: "The hero folktales of various cultures exhibit four types of content. . . . In the first type, one power overwhelms another, and the minor power makes no attempt at response. In the second, one power overwhelms another, and the minor power attempts a response but fails. In the third type, one power overwhelms another, who then nullifies the threat. And in the fourth, one power overwhelms another, who nullifies the threat, and the original circumstances are substantially transformed" (Winner 323).

10. Nell's findings seem to contrast with those of Appleyard, who emphasizes that "dark themes" are "prominent" in adolescent literature (109). But one suspects

that Appleyard is somewhat distorting the evidence in favor of his general thesis—that developing readers move through the four literary "modes" into which Frye organizes all imaginative literature: the preadolescent through romance, the adolescent through tragedy, the college reader through irony, and the adult through comedy. It is true that many of the books that are "popular with teenagers" often conclude with sentimental disaster (*Love Story*), but the sentimentality, much more often than not, supports what most readers would call a "positive" theme (true love is stronger than selfishness).

11. "Since, as [Barbara Herrnstein] Smith points out, 'there is no formal principle which in itself can prevent a poem from continuing indefinitely' (30), all modes of discourse, including narrative discourse, must justify their conclusions by what Smith calls thematic principles: the coming of evening or winter, the death or marriage of the hero, the end of the world" (Leitch 42). What this suggests is that readers or spectators perceive closure, and therefore structure, in events or actions of human life: the achievement of a purpose, or the failure to achieve it; the passage from one life-stage into another—adolescence into adulthood, bachelorhood into marriage, and so forth.

12. Argyros is best at distinguishing between literary and analytical/critical thinking:

> Criticism, or the kind of analytic or philosophical discourse of which it is a subset, almost exclusively engages the neocortical regions of the brain, its primary sphere of influence being the dominant hemisphere of the cerebrum. Literature, on the other hand, can trigger a much wider range of neural and hormonal events. Especially in its performance, great literature tunes in to all the levels of the remarkable evolutionary palimpsest of our species' nervous system. As most theoreticians of literature from Aristotle on have known well, literature is as effective in speeding up breathing (a brain stem function) and in producing emotional response (probably a limbic system function) as in provoking temporal and spatial conceptualization (a function of the two hemispheres of the neocortex, and, probably, of their interaction across the corpus callosum). In other words, although literature's choices are partly accessible to the conscious, self-reflective level of the human brain, they also affect an enormous range of brain states, most of which are not directly available to conscious examination. . . . Criticism reduces the complex psychic arsenal of a literary text (itself already a reduction of pure cultural possibility) to those categories of analytic or synthetic thought within the purview of the higher cortical functions. (205)

13. For the argument that drama in particular, "in all its varied forms, represents an important cultural mechanism for introducing people to novel ways of feeling,

supplementing their education as natural psychologists, and thus in the long run promoting mutual understanding between members of the social group" (110), see Humphrey 93–117.

Chapter 5

1. For an extended account of what *all* human cultures have in common, thereby resulting in a portrait of the "Universal People," see Brown 130–41.

2. In a section of their *Homicide* entitled "On the Cross-Cultural Ubiquity of Blood Revenge," Daly and Wilson point out that *"lethal retribution is an ancient and cross-culturally universal recourse of those subjected to abuse"* (226, emphasis in original).

3. Like Oscar Mandel, I think that illustrations of tragedy can be "drawn from any form: the drama, the novel, the poem, the short story," since tragedy is more "an idea about human existence" than it is a strictly dramatic genre (9). I'm reluctant to adopt Frye's word *mythos* in discussing tragic works, as it seems to confer on those works an air of (arbitrary) fictionality; instead I'll use "genre" (for tragedy and, later, for comedy) in its general sense of "kind." As most of my illustrations are from the dramatic literature, I have referred frequently and naturally to the "spectators" of tragedy, although "audience" should sometimes be understood.

4. The familiar feeling of "all passion spent" at the end of many tragedies arises, I would argue, from the tendency of postclassical tragedians to conclude on a "comic" upswing—with an affiliative or a laughable gesture. Thus Samson's father (in Milton's *Samson Agonistes*, where the famous phrase appears) communicates to the Chorus in the final scene his intention to "send for all my kindred, all my friends / To fetch [the dead Samson] hence and solemnly attend / With silent obsequy and funeral train / Home to his Father's house" (lines 1730–33). Many other examples should flock to the reader's mind: in the epilogue to *Crime and Punishment*, Raskolnikov is redeemed by Sonia's love; Theseus adopts the once-persecuted Aricia at the end of Racine's *Phèdre*; and Edgar notoriously is joined to Cordelia at the conclusion of Tate's *King Lear.* Mirthful endings, in which either the characters laugh or the audience is encouraged to do so, may be found in the epilogues of pieces as various as Chaucer's *Troilus and Criseyde*, Shaw's *Saint Joan*, and the Stravinsky/Auden/Kallman *Rake's Progress.* Classical tragedies (as opposed to what we would now call tragicomedies) rarely end on such a note; in Seneca's corpus, for example, only the unusual *Hercules on Oeta*, recalling in its conclusion the fate of Oedipus in the *Oedipus at Colonus*, transcends the somberness of its catastrophe.

5. I use "hero" throughout this chapter as a gender-neutral term.

6. For this distinction I am indebted to de Sousa (85).

7. Throughout, I quote the Fagles translation; parenthetical numbers refer to lines.

8. The antagonism that Fox describes had been played out in Greece in the previous century, when Cleisthenes disarmed the powerful "tribes" of Attic kin by inventing what the classicist H. D. F. Kitto calls "a preposterous paper constitution":

> He created ten brand-new "tribes"—all provided with ancestors—each composed of a roughly equal number of "demes" (or "parishes"), but not contiguous. . . . Then since each tribe would contain farmers and hill-men, artisans and traders from Athens and the Piraeus, and men who lived in boats, local and family loyalties could do little in the election of archons ["mayors"]: they could find expression only in the open Assembly, where they could be recognized for what they were. (106)

9. "We can go some way to finding a parallel in modern life, for we probably know of families not really very affectionate where a wrong done to one member is immediately resented by all. And if we asked a brother we knew disliked his sister why he entered a quarrel over her in which he hadn't a hope of winning, he might even to-day fall back on an answer like Antigone's, 'Why, she's my sister, isn't she?'" (Mason 56).

10. She is also thinking with a woman's. For not only has she been deprived of the traditional woman's role as guardian of the funeral rites, but, at least according to the Sentry of the play, she has been overcome by instinctive nurturant feelings at the sight of her brother's exposed corpse. When she finds that his body has been denuded of her ritually sprinkled dust, she cries "a sharp, piercing cry, / like a bird come back to an empty nest, / peering into its bed, and all the babies gone" (471–73).

11. My list differs slightly from Steiner's own. His includes: man versus woman, age versus youth, society versus the individual, the living versus the dead, and men versus the gods. Like Fox, I don't interpret Antigone's claim as an "individual" grievance; she is acting on behalf of her kin. As for Steiner's living/dead antagonism, it doesn't seem to be dramatized within the play: the conflict is between the living *over* the dead. If the "gods" can be interpreted as I have explained them, the last pairing may be phrased as emotion versus deliberation—and perhaps Steiner himself would concur. I have also toned down some of Steiner's hyperbole: *Antigone*, he writes, expresses "*all* the principal constants of conflict" (my emphasis), but intergroup conflict, which I discuss below, arises only as background to the play.

12. Throughout, I quote the Campbell translation; numbers in parentheses are page numbers.

13. Janko reproduces the passage in an appendix:

Since music happens to belong among pleasant things, and virtue is concerned with feeling delight correctly and loving and hating [correctly], clearly one should learn, and become habituated to, nothing so much as judging correctly, i.e. feeling delight in decent characters and fine actions. Rhythms and songs contain especially close likenesses of the true natures of anger and mildness, bravery, temperance and all their opposites, and of the other [traits of] character: this is clear from the facts—we are moved in our soul when we listen to such things. Habituation to feeling pain and delight in things that are like [the truth] is close to being in the same state regarding the truth [itself]. (Aristotle 58)

Although Janko writes that the theory of *katharsis* that he has elaborated from this passage "is, and seems likely to remain, highly controversial" (xx), it is the same theory offered by Humphry House in his (posthumously published) *Aristotle's Poetics* of 1956:

A tragedy rouses the emotions from potentiality to activity by worthy and adequate stimuli; it controls them by directing them to the right objects in the right way; and exercises them, within the limits of the play, as the emotions of the good man would be exercised. When they subside to potentiality again after the play is over, it is a more "trained" potentiality than before. This is what Aristotle calls *katharsis*. Our responses are brought nearer to those of the good and wise man. (109–10)

Recently Elizabeth S. Belfiore has argued that, although formulations such as these have "the advantages of precision and clarity, and of being based on an interpretation of specific ancient texts" (278), they are not faithful to Aristotle's thought. That thought, she proposes, is—at least as regards *katharsis*—"allopathic," grounded in the belief that opposites are self-correcting. And so, in tragedy, "an opposing extreme of tragic emotion is applied, like a drug, to a preexisting, opposite emotional extreme of shamelessness. Tragedy accomplishes a katharsis of these opposite, shameless emotions, carrying them away with it as it departs from the soul" (341). Belfiore's evidence is very persuasive, but my argument remains unaffected: Aristotle's conception of *katharsis* is not crucial to my own.

14. See Chapter 4, note 8.

15. "Because of bounded rationality, the docile individual will often be unable to distinguish socially prescribed behavior that contributes to fitness from altruistic behavior [that does not]. In fact, docility will reduce the inclination to evaluate independently the contributions of behavior to fitness. Moreover, guilt and shame will tend to enforce even behavior that is perceived as altruistic. Hence the docile individual will necessarily also incur the cost . . . of altruism" (Simon 1667).

16. For a discussion of computer models that bear out the hypothesis that "cooperation is most likely in small [social] groups with lengthy interactions" (78), see Glance and Huberman.

17. "The ideal number of citizens was ten thousand, which would imply a total population of about 100,000. . . . At the outbreak of the Peloponnesian War [431–404 B.C.] the population of Attica was probably about 350,000, half Athenian (men, women and children), about a tenth resident aliens, and the rest slaves" (Kitto 66, paragraphing simplified).

Chapter 6

1. Steiner weakens this observation by adding, "of agonistic misunderstanding, in language itself." Misunderstanding is only one source of conflict, and the conflicts that arise from language represent a "late . . . phase" of human contest.

2. I should add that Morreall's formula is self-evidently applicable only to what Paul Ekman calls the "enjoyment" laugh; for a critique of Morreall's argument that "a pleasant psychological shift is a causally necessary condition for [all] laughter," see Pfeifer 157–72.

3. Among empirical humor theorists, Lawrence La Fave, Jay Haddad, and William A. Maesen are the harshest in their assessment: Freud's *Jokes* offers "a pseudo-sophisticated, non-nullifiable 'theory' of humour which appears profound to the fuzzy-minded"—a judgment that leads them to conclude that "it would be exceedingly difficult to find a person of at least average intelligence who knows less about humour than did Freud" (81).

4. To give Sutton his due, I should note that he concedes, in passing (and in a parenthesis), that ridiculousness "perhaps" involves "some form of perceived incongruity" (42); but his casualness and indifference to precision—humor, as I shall argue, involves a *masterable* incongruity—do not strengthen his position.

5. Sometimes the incongruity may arise simply through the operation of telling a joke: the framing of discourse as a joke to be "got" conveys to the audience that mastery should follow. And so, although a pun (for example) may be grasped through the mental superimposition of two equally congruent schemata (and not through the "resolution" of an incongruity by a congruence), its comprehension depends upon the listener's sensitivity to the "discrepancy" of which it marks a linguistic departure. In other words, the pun must be understood as an incongruent disruption of "ordinary" communicative language.

6. Doubtless it was the affective unreality of the misshapen and the ugly that once licensed public laughter at their expense (see O'Connor). The sense of incongruity was the *cause* of that laughter, but the latter could be given open

expression because its targets were not being regarded as human; that is, there was no attempt at empathic identification with the objects of the laughter. Such barbarity is, of course, still with us. The videotape of the assault on Reginald Denny, the trucker who was pulled from his cab and beaten after the recent Los Angeles riot, shows one of the thugs laughing, his arms raised in triumph, after smashing Denny's head with a brick. The attacker is clearly oblivious to Denny's pain (or, in the words of Antonio Damasio, encountered earlier in this book, he doesn't feel that pain "in the flesh"); Denny is simply a target, and, when the brick meets the target after a chancy throw, the reaction of the attacker is exultation, mainly over his own ballistic mastery.

7. In keeping with my view of romantic comedy as (generally) male wish-fulfillment, the word "hero" when it is used in this chapter will mean a male hero. If, in fact, all the comic types originated in the Trickster figure (see below), my restriction of the hero's sex seems additionally justified, since Tricksters "are basically considered to be males" (Apte 214).

8. Toward the end of the novel, Lypiatt is revealed to be possessed of a sensibility that belies the judgment that he is merely stupid, but this is an instance of what I called earlier a character's "moving . . . out of 'type.'"

9. For a full discussion of such types, see Ritter.

10. By "self" (in "self-serving") I mean the "atomic" self, not the extended self that, say, Antigone serves. Tragedy often focuses upon a hero who feels keenly an obligation to kin or group; the laughter of comedy, I am suggesting, ministers to the "selfish" phenotype.

11. As humor theorists have pointed out, "laughter can reveal group allegiances, communicate attitudes, and help in establishing and reaffirming dominance in a status hierarchy. . . . Additionally, . . . some of humor's major functions have to do with aiding members of small groups to engage in smooth interactions" (Chapman 135). But these regulatory functions should not be confused with those that invite or affectively deepen affiliation—the province, as I shall emphasize below, not of the laugh but of the smile.

Chapter 7

1. Murdoch circles around the term in *Metaphysics as a Guide to Morals* without ever settling upon a definition: "Philosophically, should 'self' be taken as an initial problem, or simply assumed or postulated as a carrier of experience or consciousness, or should we take something else, society or language or genes, as fundamental? Is the self part of the world, or should it be seen as constructing the world?" (148).

2. Her continuing ambivalence over psychoanalysis emerges in a particularly ambiguous passage in *Metaphysics as a Guide to Morals:* "The 'unconscious mind' is a deep abode of ambiguous images. Freud's treatment of these may be narrowed by his lack of consideration of the deeply moral nature of soul activity. This omission may be deemed essential to a scientific account. But if we regret the omission we may be led to doubt the scientific claim" (307).

3. "Perhaps (I believe) Christianity can continue without a personal God or a risen Christ, without beliefs in supernatural places and happenings, such as heaven and life after death, but retaining the mystical figure of Christ occupying a place analogous to that of Buddha: a Christ who can console and save, but who is to be found as a living force within each human soul and not in some supernatural elsewhere" (*Metaphysics* 419).

4. For provocative meditations on that mystery that are congruent with evolutionary theory, see Hamer and Copeland; for recent encapsulations of the nature/nurture debate about homosexuality, see Levay and Hamer; Byne.

5. Murdoch herself calls Freud "a self-styled modern disciple of Plato" (*Metaphysics* 20).

Postscript

1. On the scientific status of Freudian psychoanalysis, see especially Edelson and Grünbaum; for an evolutionary critique of classical psychoanalytic theory, see Gazzaniga 159–77; on Lacan, see Roustang. Slavin and Kriegman have attempted an ambitious revision of psychoanalysis along evolutionary lines; for a summary of the synthetic work done prior to the appearance of their book, see Nesse and Lloyd.

2. For one of the most valuable of recent contributions, see de Waal's *Good Natured.*

Works Cited

Omitted are titles of Shakespeare's plays, quotations from which are identified parenthetically in the text by act, scene, and line.

Abernethy, Virginia. "Female Hierarchy: An Evolutionary Perspective." Tiger and Fowler 123–34.

Aeschylus. *The Oresteia.* Tr. Robert Fagles. Harmondsworth, Eng.: Penguin, 1979.

Alexander, Richard D. *Darwinism and Human Affairs.* Seattle: U of Washington P, 1979.

———. "The Search for a General Theory of Behavior." *Behavioral Science* 20 (1975): 77–100.

Alexander, Richard D., and Katharine M. Noonan. "Concealment of Ovulation, Parental Care, and Human Social Evolution." Chagnon and Irons 436–53.

Altieri, Charles. *Act and Quality: A Theory of Literary Meaning and Humanistic Understanding.* Amherst: U of Massachusetts P, 1981.

Ames, Louise Bates. "Children's Stories." *Genetic Psychology Monographs* 73 (1966): 337–96.

Anderson, John R. *The Adaptive Character of Thought.* Hillsdale, NJ: Erlbaum, 1990.

Appleyard, J. A. *Becoming a Reader: The Experience of Fiction from Childhood to Adulthood.* Cambridge: Cambridge UP, 1990.

Apte, Mahadev L. *Humor and Laughter: An Anthropological Approach.* Ithaca: Cornell UP, 1985.

Argyros, Alexander J. *A Blessed Rage for Order: Deconstruction, Evolution, and Chaos.* Ann Arbor: U of Michigan P, 1991.

Ariès, Philippe. *Centuries of Childhood: A Social History of Family Life.* Tr. Robert Baldick. New York: Knopf, 1962.

Aristotle. Poetics I *with the* Tractatus Coislinianus/A Hypothetical Reconstruction of Poetics II/The Fragments of the On Poets. Tr. Richard Janko. Indianapolis: Hackett, 1987.

Artaud, Antonin. *The Theater and Its Double.* Tr. Mary Caroline Richards. New York: Grove, 1958.

Auerbach, Erich. *Mimesis: The Representation of Reality in Western Literature.* Tr. Willard Trask. Garden City, NY: Doubleday, 1957.

Axelrod, Robert. *The Evolution of Cooperation.* New York: Basic Books, 1984.

Axelrod, Robert, and D. Dion. "The Further Evolution of Cooperation." *Science* 242 (1989): 1385–90.

Barash, David. *The Whisperings Within*. New York: Harper and Row, 1979.

Barinaga, Marcia. "The Brain Remaps Its Own Contours." *Science* 258 (1992): 216–18.

——. "How Scary Things Get That Way." *Science* 258 (1992): 887–88.

——. "To Sleep, Perchance to . . . Learn? New Studies Say Yes." *Science* 265 (1994): 603–04.

Barkow, Jerome H. "Sociobiology: Is This the New Theory of Human Nature?" Montagu 171–97.

Barkow, Jerome H., Leda Cosmides, and John Tooby, eds. *The Adapted Mind: Evolutionary Psychology and the Generation of Culture*. New York: Oxford UP, 1992.

Baron-Cohen, Simon. *Mindblindness: An Essay on Autism and Theory of Mind*. Cambridge: MIT P, 1995.

Barrow, John D. *Pi in the Sky: Counting, Thinking, and Being*. Oxford: Clarendon, 1992.

Barthes, Roland. *A Barthes Reader*. Ed. Susan Sontag. London: Cape, 1982.

Baucom, Donald H., Paige K. Besch, and Steven Callahan. "Relation Between Testosterone Concentration, Sex Role Identity, and Personality Among Females." *Journal of Personality and Social Psychology* 48 (1985): 1218–26.

Baudelaire, Charles. "The Essence of Laughter and More Especially of the Comic in Plastic Arts." Tr. Gerard Hopkins. *The Essence of Laughter and Other Essays, Journals, and Letters*. Ed. Peter Quennell. New York: Meridian Books, 1956. 109–30.

Beer, Gillian. *Darwin's Plots: Evolutionary Narrative in Darwin, George Eliot, and Nineteenth-Century Fiction*. London: Routledge, 1983.

Belfiore, Elizabeth S. *Tragic Pleasures: Aristotle on Plot and Emotion*. Princeton: Princeton UP, 1992.

Bellamy, Michael O. "An Interview with Iris Murdoch." *Contemporary Literature* 18 (1977): 129–40.

Belsey, Catherine. *Critical Practice*. London: Routledge, 1980.

Berenbaum, Sheri A., and Melissa Hines. "Early Androgens Are Related to Childhood Sex-typed Toy Preferences." *Psychological Science* 3 (1992): 203–06.

Berg, Elizabeth L. "Impossible Representation: A Reading of *Phèdre*." *Romanic Review* 73 (1982): 421–37.

Bergson, Henri. "Laughter." *Comedy: An Essay on Comedy [by] George Meredith/Laughter [by] Henri Bergson*. Ed. Wylie Sypher. New York: Doubleday Anchor, 1956. 61–190.

Berk, Lee S., et al. "Humor Associated Laughter Decreases Cortisol and Increases Spontaneous Lymphocyte Blastogenesis." *Clinical Research* 36 (1988): 435A.

——. "Laughter Decreases Cortisol, Epinephrine and 3,4 Dihydroxyphenyl Acetic Acid (Dopac)." *The Federation of American Societies for Experimental Biology (FASEB) Journal* 2 (1988): A1570.

——. "Mirth Modulates Adrenocorticomedullary Activity: Suppression of Cortisol and Epinephrine." *Clinical Research* 36 (1988): 121.

Berke, Bradley. *Tragic Thought and the Grammar of Tragic Myth*. Bloomington: Indiana UP, 1982.

Berlyne, D. E. *Aesthetics and Psychobiology*. New York: Appleton-Century-Crofts, 1971.

Betzig, Laura L. *Despotism and Differential Reproduction: A Darwinian View of History*. New York: Aldine, 1986.

Bickerton, Derek. *Language and Human Behavior*. Seattle: U of Washington P, 1995.

Bigsby, Christopher. "Interview with Iris Murdoch, London, 5 December 1979." *The Radical Imagination and the Liberal Tradition: Interviews with English and American Novelists*. Ed. Heide Ziegler and Christopher Bigsby. London: Junction Books, 1982. 211–30.

Biles, Jack I. "An Interview with Iris Murdoch." *Studies in the Literary Imagination* 11 (1978): 115–25.

Bleier, Ruth, ed. *Feminist Approaches to Science*. New York: Pergamon, 1986.

Block, Jeanne H. "Differential Premises Arising from Differential Socialization of the Sexes: Some Conjectures." *Child Development* 54 (1983): 1335–54.

Bloom, Harold. *The Breaking of the Vessels*. Chicago: U of Chicago P, 1982.

Bloom, Lois, et al. *Language Development from Two to Three*. Cambridge: Cambridge UP, 1991.

Bohannan, Laura. "Shakespeare in the Bush." Spradley and McCurdy 21–31.

Bohannan, Laura, and Paul Bohannan. *The Tiv of Central Nigeria*. London: International African Institute, 1969.

Bouchard, Thomas J., Jr. "Genes, Environment, and Personality." *Science* 264 (1994): 1700–1701.

Bouchard, Thomas J., Jr., et al. "Sources of Human Psychological Differences: The Minnesota Study of Twins Reared Apart." *Science* 250 (1990): 223–28.

Bowlby, John. *Attachment*. New York: Basic Books, 1969. Vol. I of *Attachment and Loss*. 3 vols. 1969–80.

Boyd, John D. *The Function of Mimesis and Its Decline*. 2d ed. New York: Fordham UP, 1980.

Boyd, Robert. "The Evolution of Reciprocity when Conditions Vary." Harcourt and de Waal 473–89.

Brereton, Geoffrey. *Principles of Tragedy: A Rational Examination of the Tragic Concept in Life and Literature*. Coral Gables: U of Miami P, 1968.

Breuer, Georg. *Sociobiology and the Human Dimension*. Cambridge: Cambridge UP, 1982.

Brodribb, Somer. *Nothing Mat(t)ers: A Feminist Critique of Postmodernism*. North Melbourne: Spinifex, 1992.

Brooks, Peter. "Introduction: Constructing Traditions—Renovation and Continuity in the Humanities." *Yale Journal of Criticism* 5 (1992): 83–90.

———. *Reading for the Plot: Design and Intention in Narrative*. New York: Knopf, 1984.

Brown, Donald E. *Human Universals*. Philadelphia: Temple UP, 1991.

Bruner, Jerome. *Acts of Meaning*. Cambridge: Harvard UP, 1990.

————. *Actual Minds, Possible Worlds*. Cambridge: Harvard UP, 1986.

Buss, David M. *The Evolution of Desire: Strategies of Human Mating*. New York: Basic Books, 1994.

————. "Sex Differences in Human Mate Preferences: Evolutionary Hypotheses Tested in 37 Cultures." *Behavioral and Brain Sciences* 12 (1989): 1–49.

Byne, William. "The Biological Evidence [for Male Homosexuality] Challenged." *Scientific American* May 1994: 50–55.

Byrne, Richard, and Andrew Whiten, eds. *Machiavellian Intelligence: Social Expertise and the Evolution of Intellect in Monkeys, Apes, and Humans*. Oxford: Clarendon, 1988.

Cairns, Robert B. "An Evolutionary and Developmental Perspective on Aggressive Patterns." Zahn-Waxler, Cummings, and Iannotti 58–87.

Calvin, William H. *The Cerebral Symphony: Seashore Reflections on the Structure of Consciousness*. New York: Bantam, 1990.

Campbell, Donald T. "Stereotypes and the Perception of Group Differences." *American Psychologist* 22 (1967): 817–29.

Carrithers, Michael. "Narrativity: Mindreading and Making Societies." *Natural Theories of Mind: Evolution, Development and Simulation of Everyday Mindreading*. Ed. Andrew Whiten. Oxford: Blackwell, 1991. 305–17.

Carroll, Joseph. *Evolution and Literary Theory*. Columbia: U of Missouri P, 1995.

Casti, John L. "Cooperation: The Ghost in the Machinery of Evolution." *Cooperation and Conflict in General Evolutionary Processes*. Ed. John L. Casti and Anders Karlqvist. New York: Wiley and Sons, 1994. 63–68.

Caws, Peter. *Structuralism: The Art of the Intelligible*. Atlantic Highlands, NJ: Humanities P International, 1988.

Cervantes, Miguel de. *The Siege of Numantia*. Tr. Roy Campbell. *The Classic Theatre*. Ed. Eric Bentley. Vol. 3. Garden City, NY: Doubleday, 1959. 97–160.

Chagnon, Napoleon A. "Is Reproductive Success Equal in Egalitarian Societies?" Chagnon and Irons 374–401.

Chagnon, Napoleon A., and William Irons, eds. *Evolutionary Biology and Human Social Behavior*. North Scituate, MA: Duxbury, 1979.

Chapais, Bernard. "Primates and the Origins of Aggression, Power, and Politics among Humans." Loy and Peters 190–228.

Chapman, Antony J. "Humor and Laughter in Social Interaction and Some Implications for Humor Research." McGhee and Goldstein 135–57.

Chapman, Antony J., and Hugh C. Foot, eds. *Humour and Laughter: Theory, Research and Applications*. London: Wiley, 1976.

√ Charney, Maurice, ed. *Comedy: New Perspectives*. New York: New York Literary Forum, 1978.

Cheney, Dorothy L., and Robert M. Seyfarth. "Truth and Deception in Animal Communication." Ristau 127–51.

Churchland, Paul M. *The Engine of Reason, The Seat of the Soul: A Philosophical Journey into the Brain.* Cambridge: MIT P, 1995.

Cogan, Rosemary, et al. "Effects of Laughter and Relaxation on Discomfort Thresholds." *Journal of Behavioral Medicine* 10 (1987): 139–44.

Coghill, Nevill. "The Basis of Shakespearian Comedy." *Essays and Studies, 1950: Being Volume Three of the New Series . . . Collected for The English Association by G. Rostrevor Hamilton.* London: Murray, 1950. 1–28.

Cole, Steven E. "The Scrutable Subject: Davidson, Literary Theory, and the Claims of Knowledge." *Literary Theory after Davidson.* Ed. Reed Way Dasenbrock. University Park: The Pennsylvania State UP, 1993. 59–91.

Condry, John C., and David F. Ross. "Sex and Aggression: The Influence of Gender Label on the Perception of Aggression in Children." *Child Development* 56 (1985): 225–33.

Conradi, Peter J. *Iris Murdoch: The Saint and the Artist.* New York: St. Martin's, 1986.

Corballis, Michael C. *The Lopsided Ape: Evolution of the Generative Mind.* New York: Oxford UP, 1991.

Corneille, [Pierre]. "Discours de la tragédie et des moyens de la traiter selon le vraisemblable ou le nécessaire." *Théâtre.* Ed. Pierre Lièvre and Roger Caillois. Vol. 1. Paris: Gallimard (Bibliothèque de la Pléiade), 1950. 86–118.

Cornford, Francis MacDonald. *The Origin of Attic Comedy.* 1914. New York: Anchor Books, 1961.

Cosmides, Leda, and John Tooby. "Cognitive Adaptations for Social Exchange." Barkow, Cosmides, and Tooby 163–228.

Cothey, A. L. *The Nature of Art.* London: Routledge, 1990.

Count, Earl W. "The Biological Basis of Human Sociality." *American Anthropologist* 60 (1958): 1049–85.

Courtney, Richard. *Drama and Intelligence: A Cognitive Theory.* Montreal: McGill-Queen's UP, 1990.

Craige, Betty Jean. "Point of View." *Chronicle of Higher Education* 6 Jan. 1993: A56.

Crawford, Charles, Martin Smith, and Dennis Krebs, eds. *Sociobiology and Psychology: Ideas, Issues and Applications.* Hillsdale, NJ: Erlbaum, 1987.

Crews, Frederick. "The Grand Academy of Theory." *New York Review of Books,* May 1986; rpt. Frederick Crews, *Skeptical Engagements.* New York: Oxford UP, 1986. 159–78.

Crews, Frederick. Foreword. Easterlin and Riebling vii–x.

Crook, John Hurrell. "Consciousness and the Ecology of Meaning: New Findings and Old Philosophies." *Man and Beast Revisited.* Ed. Michael H. Robinson and Lionel Tiger. Washington, DC: Smithsonian Institution P, 1991. 203–23.

———. *The Evolution of Human Consciousness.* Oxford: Clarendon, 1980.

Crowley, Daniel J. "An African Aesthetic." *Journal of Aesthetics and Art Criticism* 24 (1966): 519–24; rpt. *Art and Aesthetics in Primitive Societies: A Critical Anthology*, ed. Carol F. Jopling. New York: Dutton, 1971. 315–27.

Csikszentmihalyi, Mihaly. *Beyond Boredom and Anxiety.* San Francisco: Jossey-Bass, 1975.

Culler, Jonathan. *Flaubert: The Uses of Uncertainty.* Ithaca: Cornell UP, 1974.

———. *Structuralist Poetics: Structuralism, Linguistics and the Study of Literature.* Ithaca: Cornell UP, 1975.

Cummings, E. Mark, et al. "Early Organization of Altruism and Aggression: Developmental Patterns and Individual Differences." Zahn-Waxler, Cummings, and Iannotti 165–88.

Daly, Martin, and Margo Wilson. *Homicide.* New York: Aldine de Gruyter, 1988.

Daly, Martin, Margo Wilson, and Suzanne J. Weghorst. "Male Sexual Jealousy." *Ethology and Sociobiology* 3 (1982): 11–27.

Damasio, Antonio R. *Descartes' Error: Emotion, Reason, and the Human Brain.* New York: Putnam, 1994.

Damasio, Hanna, et al. "The Return of Phineas Gage: Clues about the Brain from the Skull of a Famous Patient." *Science* 264 (1994): 1102–05.

Damasio, Hanna, and Antonio R. Damasio. *Lesion Analysis in Neuropsychology.* New York: Oxford UP, 1989.

Darwin, Charles. *Charles Darwin's Notebooks, 1836–1844: Geology, Transmutation of Species, Metaphysical Enquiries.* Ed. Paul H. Barrett et al. Ithaca: Cornell UP, 1987.

———. *The Descent of Man and Selection in Relation to Sex.* 2 vols. New York: Appleton, 1872.

———. *The Expression of the Emotions in Man and Animals.* 1872. New York: Appleton, 1896.

———. *The Origin of Species by Means of Natural Selection.* 6th ed. London: John Murray, 1872.

Dawkins, Richard. *The Extended Phenotype: The Gene as the Unit of Selection.* Oxford: Freeman, 1982.

———. "In Defence of Selfish Genes." *Philosophy* 56 (1981): 556–73.

———. *The Selfish Gene.* New ed. Oxford: Oxford UP, 1989.

Dennett, Daniel C. *Consciousness Explained.* Boston: Little, Brown, 1991.

———. *Darwin's Dangerous Idea: Evolution and the Meanings of Life.* New York: Simon and Schuster, 1995.

Derrida, Jacques. *Of Grammatology.* Tr. Gayatri Chakravorty Spivak. Baltimore: Johns Hopkins UP, 1976.

de Sousa, Ronald. *The Rationality of Emotion.* Cambridge: MIT P, 1987.

de Waal, Frans B. M. "Chimpanzee's Adaptive Potential: A Comparison of Social Life under Captive and Wild Conditions." *Chimpanzee Cultures.* Ed. Richard W. Wrangham et al. Cambridge: Harvard UP, 1994. 243–60.

————. *Good Natured: The Origins of Right and Wrong in Humans and Other Animals.* Cambridge: Harvard UP, 1996.

Diamond, Jared. *The Third Chimpanzee: The Evolution and Future of the Human Animal.* New York: HarperCollins, 1992.

Dillon, Kathleen M., B. Minchoff, and K. H. Baker. "Positive Emotional States and Enhancement of the Immune System." *International Journal of Psychiatry in Medicine* 15 (1985–86): 13–17.

Dillon, M. C. *Semiological Reductionism: A Critique of the Deconstructionist Movement in Postmodern Thought.* Albany: State U of New York P, 1995.

Dipple, Elizabeth. *Iris Murdoch: Work for the Spirit.* London: Methuen, 1982.

Dissanayake, Ellen. *Homo Aestheticus: Where Art Comes From and Why.* New York: Free P, 1992.

————. *What Is Art For?* Seattle: U of Washington P, 1988.

Donald, Merlin. *Origins of the Modern Mind: Three Stages in the Evolution of Culture and Cognition.* Cambridge: Harvard UP, 1991.

Dunbar, R. I. M. "The Evolutionary Implications of Social Behavior." *The Role of Behavior in Evolution.* Ed. H. C. Plotkin. Cambridge: MIT P, 1988. 165–88.

Dyson-Hudson, Rada, and Eric Alden Smith. "Human Territoriality: An Ecological Reassessment." *American Anthropologist* 80 (1978): 21–41; rpt. Hunt 367–93.

Eagly, Alice H., Steven J. Karau, and Mona G. Makhijani. "Gender and the Effectiveness of Leaders: A Meta-Analysis." *Psychological Bulletin* 117 (1995): 125–45.

Easterlin, Nancy, and Barbara Riebling, eds. *After Poststructuralism: Interdisciplinarity and Literary Theory.* Evanston: Northwestern UP, 1993.

Eddins, Dwight, ed. *The Emperor Redressed: Critiquing Critical Theory.* Tuscaloosa: U of Alabama P, 1995.

Edelman, Gerald M. *Bright Air, Brilliant Fire: On the Matter of the Mind.* New York: Basic Books, 1992.

————. *The Remembered Present: A Biological Theory of Consciousness.* New York: Basic Books, 1989.

Edelson, Marshall. *Hypothesis and Evidence in Psychoanalysis.* Chicago: U of Chicago P, 1984.

Edmundson, Mark. *Literature against Philosophy, Plato to Derrida: A Defence of Poetry.* Cambridge: Cambridge UP, 1995.

Ehrhardt, Anke A., and Heino F. L. Meyer-Bahlburg. "Effects of Prenatal Sex Hormones on Gender-Related Behavior." *Science* 211 (1981): 1312–18.

Eibl-Eibesfeldt, Irenäus. *Human Ethology.* New York: Aldine de Gruyter, 1989.

————. *Love and Hate: The Natural History of Behavior Patterns.* Tr. Geoffrey Strachan. New York: Schocken, 1974.

Eisenberg, Nancy, and Paul A. Miller. "The Relation of Empathy to Prosocial and Related Behaviors." *Psychological Bulletin* 101 (1987): 91–119.

Ekman, Paul. "Strong Evidence for Universals in Facial Expressions: A Reply to Russell's Mistaken Critique." *Psychological Bulletin* 115 (1994): 268–87.

Ekman, Paul, and Wallace V. Friesen. "Constants across Cultures in the Face and Emotion." *Journal of Personality and Social Psychology* 17 (1971): 124–29.

———. "A New Pan-Cultural Facial Expression of Emotion." *Motivation and Emotion* 10 (1986): 159–68.

Ekman, Paul, Robert W. Levenson, and Wallace V. Friesen. "Autonomic Nervous System Activity Distinguishes among Emotions." *Science* 221 (1983): 1208–10.

Elia, Irene. *The Female Animal.* Oxford: Oxford UP, 1985.

Ellis, John M. *Against Deconstruction.* Princeton: Princeton UP, 1989.

England, Paula. *Comparable Worth: Theories and Evidence.* New York: Aldine de Gruyter, 1992.

Fausto-Sterling, Anne. *Myths of Gender: Biological Theories about Women and Men.* New York: Basic Books, 1985.

Feingold, Alan. "Gender Differences in Personality: A Meta-Analysis." *Psychological Bulletin* 116 (1994): 429–56.

Felperin, Howard. *Beyond Deconstruction: The Uses and Abuses of Literary Theory.* Oxford: Clarendon, 1985.

Feshbach, Seymour, and Norma Deitch Feshbach. "Aggression and Altruism: A Personality Perspective." Zahn-Waxler, Cummings, and Iannotti 189–217.

Fischer, Michael. *Does Deconstruction Make Any Difference? Poststructuralism and the Defense of Poetry in Modern Criticism.* Bloomington: Indiana UP, 1985.

Fischman, Joshua. "New Clues Surface about the Making of the Mind." *Science* 262 (1993): 1517.

Fisher, Helen E. *Anatomy of Love: The Natural History of Monogamy, Adultery, and Divorce.* New York: Norton, 1992.

Flanagan, Owen. *Consciousness Reconsidered.* Cambridge: MIT P, 1992.

Flohr, Heiner. "Biological Bases of Social Prejudices." Reynolds, Falger, and Vine 190–207.

Foley, John Miles. *Oral Tradition in Literature: Interpretation in Context.* Columbia: U of Missouri P, 1986.

Foley, Robert A. "Evolutionary Ecology of Fossil Hominids." *Evolutionary Ecology and Human Behavior.* Ed. Eric Alden Smith and Bruce Winterhalder. New York: Aldine de Gruyter, 1992. 131–64.

Foley, R. A., and P. C. Lee. "Finite Social Space, Evolutionary Pathways, and Reconstructing Hominid Behavior." *Science* 243 (1989): 901–06.

Foner, Nancy. *Ages in Conflict: A Cross-Cultural Perspective on Inequality between Old and Young.* New York: Columbia UP, 1984.

Forabosco, Giovannantonio. "Cognitive Aspects of the Humor Process: The Concept of Incongruity." *Humor* 5 (1992): 45–68.

Foster, George. "The Anatomy of Envy: A Study in Symbolic Behavior." *Current Anthropology* 13 (1972): 165–202.

Foucault, Michel. *The Birth of the Clinic: An Archaeology of Medical Perception.* Tr. A. M. Sheridan Smith. New York: Pantheon, 1973.

———. *The Order of Things [Les Mots et les choses]: An Archaeology of the Human Sciences.* New York: Vintage, 1973.

Fox, Robin. "Prejudice and the Unfinished Mind: A New Look at an Old Failing." *Psychological Inquiry* 3 (1992): 137–52.

———. *The Red Lamp of Incest: An Enquiry into the Origins of Mind and Society.* Notre Dame: U of Notre Dame P, 1983.

———. "The Virgin and the Godfather: Kinship versus the State in Greek Tragedy and After." *Journal of the Steward Anthropological Society* 17 (1987–88): 141–92.

Frank, Manfred. *What Is Neostructuralism?* Tr. Sabine Wilke and Richard Gray. Minneapolis: U of Minnesota P, 1989.

Freadman, Richard, and Seamus Miller. *Re-Thinking Theory: A Critique of Contemporary Literary Theory and an Alternative Account.* Cambridge: Cambridge UP, 1992.

Freedman, Daniel G. *Human Sociobiology: A Holistic Approach.* New York: Free P, 1979.

Freud, Sigmund. *Jokes and Their Relation to the Unconscious.* Tr. and ed. James Strachey. New York: Norton, 1963.

Fry, William F., Jr. "The Appeasement Function of Mirthful Laughter." *It's a Funny Thing, Humour.* Ed. Antony J. Chapman and Hugh C. Foot. Oxford: Pergamon, 1977. 23–26.

Frye, Northrop. *Anatomy of Criticism: Four Essays.* Princeton: Princeton UP, 1957.

Fuchs, Victor R. "Sex Differences in Economic Well-Being." *Science* 232 (1986): 459–64.

Fuss, Diana. *Essentially Speaking: Feminism, Nature & Difference.* New York: Routledge, 1989.

Galin, David. "Implications for Psychiatry of Left and Right Cerebral Specialization." *Archives of General Psychiatry* 31 (1974): 572–83.

Gardner, John. *On Moral Fiction.* New York: Basic Books, 1978.

Gazzaniga, Michael S. *Nature's Mind: The Biological Roots of Thinking, Emotions, Sexuality, Language, and Intelligence.* New York: Basic Books, 1992.

Gazzaniga, Michael S., and Joseph E. LeDoux. *The Integrated Mind.* New York: Plenum, 1978.

Geertz, Clifford. "'Local Knowledge' and Its Limits: Some *Obiter Dicta.*" *Yale Journal of Criticism* 5 (1992): 129–35.

Gellrich, Michelle. *Tragedy and Theory: The Problem of Conflict since Aristotle.* Princeton: Princeton UP, 1988.

Gerrig, Richard J. *Experiencing Narrative Worlds: On the Psychological Activities of Reading.* New Haven: Yale UP, 1993.

Ghiglieri, Michael P. "Sociobiology of the Great Apes and the Hominid Ancestor." *Journal of Human Evolution* 16 (1987): 319–57.

Glance, Natalie S., and Bernardo A. Huberman. "The Dynamics of Social Dilemmas." *Scientific American* March 1994: 76–81.

Glass, James M. *Shattered Selves: Multiple Personality in a Postmodern World.* Ithaca: Cornell UP, 1993.

Goffman, Erving. "Gender Display." *Studies in the Anthropology of Visual Communication* 3 (1976): 69–77; rpt. Tiger and Fowler 60–86.

Goldberg, Steven. *The Inevitability of Patriarchy.* New York: Morrow, 1973.

———. *Why Men Rule: A Theory of Male Dominance.* Chicago: Open Court, 1993.

Goldsmith, Timothy H. *The Biological Roots of Human Nature: Forging Links between Evolution and Behavior.* New York: Oxford UP, 1991.

Goody, Jack. "Local Knowledge and Knowledge of Locality: The Desirability of Frames." *Yale Journal of Criticism* 5 (1992): 137–47.

Gordon, Robert J. *The Bushman Myth: The Making of a Namibian Underclass.* Boulder, CO: Westview, 1992.

Gould, Stephen Jay. *Ever Since Darwin: Reflections in Natural History.* New York: Norton, 1977.

———. "Sociobiology: The Art of Storytelling." *New Scientist* 80 (1978): 530–33.

Gross, Paul R., and Norman Levitt. *Higher Superstition: The Academic Left and Its Quarrels with Science.* Baltimore: Johns Hopkins UP, 1994.

Grünbaum, Adolf. *The Foundations of Psychoanalysis: A Philosophical Critique.* Berkeley and Los Angeles: U of California P, 1984.

———. *Validation in the Clinical Theory of Psychoanalysis: A Study in the Philosophy of Psychoanalysis.* Madison, CT: International Universities P, 1993.

Gur, Ruben C., et al. "Sex Differences in Regional Cerebral Glucose Metabolism during a Resting State." *Science* 267 (1995): 528–31.

Gutwirth, Marcel. *Laughing Matter: An Essay on the Comic.* Ithaca: Cornell UP, 1993.

Hahlweg, Kai, and C. A. Hooker. "Evolutionary Epistemology and Philosophy of Science." *Issues in Evolutionary Epistemology.* Ed. Kai Hahlweg and C. A. Hooker. Albany: State U of New York P, 1989. 21–150.

Hamer, Dean, and Peter Copeland. *The Science of Desire: The Search for the Gay Gene and the Biology of Behavior.* New York: Simon and Schuster, 1994.

Hamilton, W. D. "The Genetical Evolution of Social Behaviour, I." *Journal of Theoretical Biology* 7 (1963): 1–25; rpt. Hunt 7–21.

Hampson, Elizabeth, and Doreen Kimura. "Sex Differences and Hormonal Influences on Cognitive Function in Humans." *Behavioral Endocrinology.* Ed. Jill B. Becker, S. Marc Breedlove, and David Crews. Cambridge: MIT P, 1992. 357–98.

Haraway, Donna. *Primate Visions: Gender, Race, and Nature in the World of Modern Science.* New York: Routledge, 1989.

————. *Simians, Cyborgs, and Women: The Reinvention of Nature*. New York: Routledge, 1991.

Harcourt, Alexander H., and Frans B. M. de Waal. *Coalitions and Alliances in Humans and Other Animals*. Oxford: Oxford UP, 1992.

Hardy, Barbara Nathan. *Tellers and Listeners: The Narrative Imagination*. London: Athlone, 1975.

Harris, Marvin. "The Evolution of Human Gender Hierarchies: A Trial Formulation." Miller 57–79.

Harris, Paul L. *Children and Emotion: The Development of Psychological Understanding*. Oxford: Blackwell, 1989.

Harth, Erich. *The Creative Loop: How the Brain Makes a Mind*. Reading, MA: Addison-Wesley, 1993.

Hawkesworth, Mary E. "Knowers, Knowing, Known: Feminist Theory and Claims of Truth." *Signs* 14 (1989): 533–57.

Heilman, Robert Bechtold. *Tragedy and Melodrama: Versions of Experience*. Seattle: U of Washington P, 1968.

Hellige, Joseph B. *Hemispheric Asymmetry: What's Right and What's Left*. Cambridge, MA: Harvard UP, 1993.

Hernadi, Paul. "On the How, What, and Why of Narrative." W. J. T. Mitchell 197–99.

Hinde, Robert A. *Individuals, Relationships, and Culture: Links Between Ethology and the Social Sciences*. Cambridge: Cambridge UP, 1987.

Hines, Melissa, and Francine R. Kaufman. "Androgen and the Development of Human Sex-typical Behavior: Rough-and-Tumble Play and Sex of Preferred Playmates in Children with Congenital Adrenal Hyperplasia (CAH)." *Child Development* 65 (1994): 1042–53.

Hobbes, Thomas. "Human Nature: or The Fundamental Elements of Policy." *The English Works of Thomas Hobbes of Malmesbury*. Ed. William Molesworth. Vol. 4. London: Bohn, 1840. 1–76.

Hobson, J. Allan. *The Dreaming Brain*. New York: Basic Books, 1988.

Hochschild, Arlie, with Anne Machung. *The Second Shift: Working Parents and the Revolution at Home*. New York: Viking, 1989.

Hoffman, Martin. "Is Altruism Part of Human Nature?" *Journal of Personality and Social Psychology* 40 (1981): 121–37.

Holcomb, Harmon R., III. *Sociobiology, Sex, and Science*. Albany: State U of New York P, 1993.

Holden, Constance. "The Genetics of Personality." *Science* 237 (1987): 598–601.

Holland, Norman. *The Brain of Robert Frost: A Cognitive Approach to Literature*. New York: Routledge, 1988.

Horgan, John. "Eugenics Revisited." *Scientific American* June 1993: 120–31.

————. "Profile: Reluctant Revolutionary." *Scientific American* May 1991: 40–49.

Horner, John, and James Gorman. *Digging Dinosaurs*. New York: Workman, 1988.

Hoskins, Robert. "Iris Murdoch's Midsummer Nightmare." *Twentieth Century Literature* 18 (1972): 191–98.

House, Humphry. *Aristotle's Poetics*. Rev., with a preface by Colin Hardie. London: Hart-Davis, 1956.

Hrdy, Sarah Blaffer. "The Myth of Mother Love." Rev. of *Death without Weeping: The Violence of Everyday Life in Brazil*, by Nancy Scheper-Hughes. *New York Times Book Review* August 30, 1992: 11.

———. *The Woman That Never Evolved*. Cambridge: Harvard UP, 1981.

Humphrey, Nicholas. *Consciousness Regained: Chapters in the Development of Mind*. Oxford: Oxford UP, 1984.

Hunt, James H., ed. *Selected Readings in Sociobiology*. New York: McGraw-Hill, 1980.

Huxley, Aldous. *Antic Hay*. 1923. New York: Perennial Library, 1965.

Hyde, Janet Shibley. "Gender Differences in Aggression." *The Psychology of Gender: Advances through Meta-analysis*. Ed. Janet Shibley Hyde and Marcia C. Linn. Baltimore: Johns Hopkins UP, 1986. 51–66.

Iannello, Kathleen P. *Decisions without Hierarchy: Feminist Interventions in Organization Theory and Practice*. New York: Routledge, 1992.

Ike, Ben W. "Man's Limited Sympathy as a Consequence of His Evolution in Small Kin Groups." Reynolds, Falger, and Vine 216–34.

Inglis, James, and J. S. Lawson. "Sex Differences in the Effects of Unilateral Brain Damage on Intelligence." *Science* 212 (1981): 693–95.

Isaacson, Robert L. *The Limbic System*. 2d ed. New York: Plenum, 1982.

Isen, Alice M. "Positive Affect, Cognitive Processes, and Social Behavior." *Advances in Experimental Social Psychology* 20 (1987): 203–53.

Isen, Alice M., K. A. Daubman, and G. P. Nowicki. "Positive Affect Facilitates Creative Problem Solving." *Journal of Personality and Social Psychology* 52 (1987): 1122–31.

Izard, Carroll E. *The Face of Emotion*. New York: Appleton-Century-Crofts, 1971.

———. "Innate and Universal Facial Expressions: Evidence from Developmental and Cross-Cultural Research." *Psychological Bulletin* 115 (1994): 288–99.

Jackendoff, Ray. *Consciousness and the Computational Mind*. Cambridge: MIT P, 1987.

Jackson, Leonard. *The Poverty of Structuralism: Structuralist Theory and Literature*. London: Longman, 1991.

Jameson, Fredric. *The Political Unconscious: Narrative as a Socially Symbolic Act*. Ithaca: Cornell UP, 1981.

———. *Postmodernism, or the Cultural Logic of Late Capitalism*. Durham: Duke UP, 1991.

Johnson, Allen W., and Timothy Earle. *The Evolution of Human Societies: From Foraging Group to Agrarian State*. Stanford: Stanford UP, 1987.

Johnson, Mark. *The Body in the Mind: The Bodily Basis of Meaning, Imagination, and Reason*. Chicago: U of Chicago P, 1987.

————. *Moral Imagination: Implications of Cognitive Science for Ethics.* Chicago: U of Chicago P, 1993.

Jolly, Alison. "Conscious Chimpanzees? A Review of Recent Literature." Ristau 231–52.

Jung, Carl. *Collected Works.* Ed. Herbert Read, Michael Fordham, and Gerhard Adler. 2d ed. 20 vols. Princeton: Princeton UP, 1970–.

Kagan, Jerome. *Galen's Prophecy: Temperament in Human Nature.* New York: Basic Books, 1994.

————. *Unstable Ideas: Temperament, Cognition, and Self.* Cambridge: Harvard UP, 1989.

Karni, Avi, et al. "Dependence on REM Sleep of Overnight Improvement of a Perceptual Skill." *Science* 265 (1994): 679–81.

Keller, Evelyn Fox. *A Feeling for the Organism: The Life and Work of Barbara McClintock.* San Francisco: Freeman, 1983.

Kenrick, Douglas T., and Melanie R. Trost. "The Evolutionary Perspective." *The Psychology of Gender.* Ed. Anne E. Beall and Robert J. Sternberg. New York: Guilford, 1993. 148–72.

Kermode, Frank. "The House of Fiction: Interviews with English Novelists." *Partisan Review* 30 (1963): 62–65.

————. "Secrets and Narrative Sequence." W. J. T. Mitchell 79–97.

————. *The Sense of an Ending.* New York: Oxford UP, 1967.

Kimura, D. "Sex Differences in the Brain." *Scientific American* September 1992: 119–25.

Kitto, H. D. F. *The Greeks.* Harmondsworth, Eng.: Penguin, 1957.

Knox, Bernard. Introduction [to *Antigone*]. Sophocles 35–53.

Koch, Walter A. *The Biology of Literature.* Bochum, Ger.: Brockmeyer, 1993.

Konner, Melvin. *The Tangled Wing: Biological Constraints on the Human Spirit.* New York: Harper and Row, 1982.

Krebs, Dennis. "The Challenge of Altruism in Biology and Psychology." Crawford, Smith, and Krebs 81–118.

Kreitler, Hans, and Shulamith Kreitler. *Psychology of the Arts.* Durham: Duke UP, 1972.

Kristeva, Julia. *Semiotikè: Recherches pour une sémanalyse.* Paris: Seuil, 1969.

Kuhn, Deanna. *The Skills of Argument.* Cambridge: Cambridge UP, 1991.

Kuhn, Thomas S. *The Structure of Scientific Revolutions.* 2d ed. Chicago: U of Chicago P, 1970.

La Fave, Lawrence, Jay Haddad, and William A. Maesen. "Superiority, Enhanced Self-Esteem, and Perceived Incongruity." Chapman and Foot 63–91.

Lakoff, George. *Women, Fire, and Dangerous Things: What Our Categories Reveal about the Mind.* Chicago: U of Chicago P, 1987.

Lakoff, George, and Mark Johnson. *Metaphors We Live By.* Chicago: U of Chicago P, 1980.

Langer, Susanne K. *Mind: An Essay on Human Feeling*. Vol. 1. Baltimore: Johns Hopkins UP, 1967.

Laski, Marghanita. *Ecstasy: A Study of Some Secular and Religious Experiences*. New York: Greenwood, 1968.

Laughlin, Charles D., Jr., and Eugene G. d'Aquili. *Biogenetic Structuralism*. New York: Columbia UP, 1974.

Laughlin, Charles D., Jr., John McManus, and Eugene G. d'Aquili. *Brain, Symbol, and Experience: Toward a Neurophenomenology of Human Consciousness*. Boston: Shambhala, 1990.

Le Guin, Ursula K. "It Was A Dark and Stormy Night; or, Why Are We Huddling about the Campfire?" W. J. T. Mitchell 187–95.

Leech, Clifford. *Tragedy*. London: Methuen, 1969.

Leitch, Thomas M. *What Stories Are: Narrative Theory and Interpretation*. University Park: Pennsylvania State UP, 1986.

Lerner, Gerda. *The Creation of Patriarchy*. Oxford: Oxford UP, 1986.

LeVay, Simon. *The Sexual Brain*. Cambridge: MIT P, 1993.

Levay, Simon, and Dean H. Hamer. "Evidence for a Biological Influence in Male Homosexuality." *Scientific American* May 1994: 44–49.

Levin, Richard. "The New Interdisciplinarity in Literary Criticism." Easterlin and Riebling 13–43.

Levowitz, Herbert J. "Smiles and Laughter: Some Neurologic, Developmental, and Psychodynamic Considerations." Charney 109–16.

Levy, Robert I. "Emotion, Knowing, and Culture." *Culture Theory: Essays on Mind, Self, and Emotion*. Ed. Richard A. Shweder and Robert A. LeVine. Cambridge: Cambridge UP, 1984. 214–37.

Lewis, Paul. *Comic Effects: Interdisciplinary Approaches to Humor in Literature*. Albany: State U of New York P, 1989.

Lewontin, R. C. "Women versus the Biologists." *New York Review of Books* 7 Apr. 1994: 31–35.

Lewontin, R. C., Steven Rose, and Leon J. Kamin. *Not in Our Genes: Biology, Ideology, and Human Nature*. New York: Pantheon, 1984.

Lex, Barbara W. "The Neurobiology of Ritual Trance." *The Spectrum of Ritual: A Biogenetic Structural Analysis*. By Eugene G. d'Aquili, Charles D. Laughlin, Jr., John McManus, et al. New York: Columbia UP, 1979. 117–51.

Linden, Eugene. "Megacities." *Time* 11 Jan. 1993: 30–35.

Livingston, Paisley. *Literary Knowledge: Humanistic Inquiry and the Philosophy of Science*. Ithaca: Cornell UP, 1988.

———. *Literature and Rationality: Ideas of Agency in Theory and Fiction*. Cambridge: Cambridge UP, 1991.

———. *Models of Desire: René Girard and the Psychology of Mimesis*. Baltimore: Johns Hopkins UP, 1992.

Lloyd, Dan. *Simple Minds.* Cambridge: MIT P, 1989.

Lloyd, Genevieve. "Iris Murdoch on the Ethical Significance of Truth." *Philosophy and Literature* 6 (1982): 62–75.

Locke, John L. *The Child's Path to Spoken Language.* Cambridge: Harvard UP, 1993.

Lopreato, Joseph. *Human Nature and Biocultural Evolution.* Boston: Allen and Unwin, 1984.

Lorenz, Konrad. *On Aggression.* Tr. Marjorie Kerr Wilson. New York: Harcourt, Brace, and World, 1966.

Loy, James D., and Calvin B. Peters, eds. *Understanding Behavior: What Primate Studies Tell Us about Human Behavior.* New York: Oxford UP, 1991.

Luria, A. R. *The Man with a Shattered World: The History of a Brain Wound.* Tr. Lynn Solotaroff. New York: Basic Books, 1972.

Maccoby, Eleanor Emmons, and Carol Nagy Jacklin. *The Psychology of Sex Differences.* Stanford: Stanford UP, 1974.

———. "Sex Differences in Aggression: A Rejoinder and Reprise." *Child Development* 51 (1980): 964–80.

Macherey, Pierre. *A Theory of Literary Production.* 1966. Tr. Geoffrey Wall. London: Routledge, 1978.

Mahler, Margaret S. *On Human Symbiosis and the Vicissitudes of Individuation.* New York: International Universities P, 1968.

Mandel, Oscar. *A Definition of Tragedy.* New York: New York UP, 1961.

Mandler, George. *Mind and Body: Psychology of Emotion and Stress.* New York: Norton, 1984.

Marks, Lawrence E. *The Unity of the Senses: Interrelations among the Modalities.* New York: Academic P, 1978.

Marshall, Lorna. "Sharing, Talking and Giving: Relief of Social Tensions among the !Kung." *Kalahari Hunter-Gatherers: Studies of the !Kung San and Their Neighbors.* Ed. Richard B. Lee and Irven DeVore. Cambridge: Harvard UP, 1976. 350–69.

Martin, Rod A., and Herbert M. Lefcourt. "Sense of Humor as a Moderator of the Relation between Stressors and Moods." *Journal of Personality and Social Psychology* 45 (1983): 1313–24.

Martin, Rod A., et al. "Humor, Coping with Stress, Self-Concept, and Psychological Well-Being." *Humor* 6 (1993): 89–104.

Martz, Louis L. "Iris Murdoch: The London Novels." *Twentieth-Century Literature in Retrospect.* Cambridge: Harvard UP, 1971; rpt. as "The London Novels," *Iris Murdoch: Modern Critical Views,* ed. Harold Bloom. London: Chelsea House, 1986. 39–57.

Maryanski, Alexandra, and Jonathan H. Turner. *The Social Cage: Human Nature and the Evolution of Society.* Stanford: Stanford UP, 1992.

Mason, Bobbie Ann. *The Girl Sleuth: A Feminist Guide.* New York: Feminist P, 1975.

Mason, H. A. *The Tragic Plane.* Oxford: Clarendon, 1985.

Maynard-Smith, J., and G. T. Price. "The Logic of Animal Conflict." *Nature* 246 (1973): 15–18.

McClintock, James B., and John Janssen. "Pteropod Abduction as a Chemical Defence in a Pelagic Antarctic Amphipod." *Nature* 346 (1990): 462–64.

McCollom, William G. *The Divine Average: A View of Comedy.* Cleveland: P of Case Western Reserve U, 1971.

McFadden, George. *Discovering the Comic.* Princeton: Princeton UP, 1982.

McGhee, Paul E. "The Role of Arousal and Hemispheric Lateralization in Humor." McGhee and Goldstein 13–37.

McGhee, Paul E., and Jeffrey H. Goldstein, eds. *Handbook of Humor Research.* Vol.1, *Basic Issues.* New York: Springer-Verlag, 1983.

McGue, Matt, et al. "Letters to the Editors: Genes and Behavior." *Scientific American* November 1993: 8.

Meeker, Joseph W. *The Comedy of Survival: Studies in Literary Ecology.* New York: Scribner's, 1974.

Merchant, Carolyn. *The Death of Nature: Women, Ecology, and the Scientific Revolution.* San Francisco: Harper and Row, 1980.

Midgley, Mary. *Beast and Man: The Roots of Human Nature.* Ithaca: Cornell UP, 1978.

———. "Rival Fatalisms." Montagu 108–34.

Miller, Barbara Diane, ed. *Sex and Gender Hierarchies.* Cambridge: Cambridge UP, 1993.

Mitchell, Juliet. "From *King Lear* to *Anna O* and Beyond: Some Speculative Theses on Hysteria and the Traditionless Self." *Yale Journal of Criticism* 5 (1992): 91–107.

Mitchell, Robert W. "The Evolution of Primate Cognition: Simulation, Self-Knowledge, and Knowledge of Other Minds." *Hominid Culture in Primate Perspective.* Ed. Duane Quiatt and Junichiro Itani. Boulder: UP of Colorado, 1994. 177–232.

Mitchell, W. J. T., ed. *On Narrative.* Chicago: U of Chicago P, 1981.

Mohanty, S. P. "Us and Them: On the Philosophical Bases of Political Criticism." *Yale Journal of Criticism* 2 (1989): 1–31.

Molfese, Dennis L., and Jacqueline C. Betz. "Electrophysiological Indices of the Early Development of Lateralization for Language and Cognition, and Their Implications for Predicting Later Development." *Brain Lateralization in Children: Developmental Implications.* Ed. Dennis L. Molfese and Sidney J. Segalowitz. New York: Guilford, 1988. 171–90.

Molière, Jean Baptiste Poquelin de. *The Misanthrope and Tartuffe.* Tr. Richard Wilbur. San Diego: Harvest/HBJ, 1965.

Montagu, Ashley, ed. *Sociobiology Examined.* Oxford: Oxford UP, 1980.

M[orell], V[irginia]. "Seeing Nature through the Lens of Gender." *Science* 260 (1993): 428–29.

Morreall, John. *Taking Laughter Seriously.* Albany: State U of New York P, 1982.

Mount, Ferdinand. *The Subversive Family: An Alternative History of Love and Marriage.* London: Unwin, 1983.

Mowrer, O. Hobart. *Learning Theory and Behavior.* New York: Wiley, 1960.

Moyer, Kenneth Evan. "Kinds of Aggression and Their Physiological Basis." *Communications in Behavioral Biology* 2, part A (1968): 65–87.

Murdoch, Iris. *Acastos: Two Platonic Dialogues.* New York: Viking, 1987.

———. "Existentialists and Mystics: A Note on the Novel in the New Utilitarian Age." *Essays and Poems Presented to Lord David Cecil.* Ed. W. Robson. London: Constable, 1970. 169–83.

———. *A Fairly Honourable Defeat.* Harmondsworth, Eng.: Penguin, 1972.

———. *The Fire and the Sun: Why Plato Banished the Artists.* Oxford: Clarendon, 1977.

———. "Metaphysics and Ethics." *The Nature of Metaphysics.* Ed. D. F. Pears. London: Macmillan, 1957. 99–123.

———. *Metaphysics as a Guide to Morals.* New York: Viking Penguin, 1993.

———. *The Sovereignty of Good over Other Concepts.* London: Routledge and Kegan Paul, 1970.

———. "The Sublime and the Beautiful Revisited." *Yale Review* 49 (1960): 247–71.

———. "The Sublime and the Good." *Chicago Review* 13 (1959): 42–55.

———. "Vision and Choice in Morality." *Dreams and Self-Knowledge.* Aristotelian Society, Supplementary Volume 30 (1956): 32–58.

Murray, Gilbert. *The Classical Tradition in Poetry.* Cambridge: Harvard UP, 1927.

Nagel, Thomas. *Mortal Questions.* Cambridge: Cambridge UP, 1979.

Nell, Victor. *Lost in a Book: The Psychology of Reading for Pleasure.* New Haven: Yale UP, 1988.

Nelson, T. G. A. *Comedy: An Introduction to Comedy in Literature, Drama, and Cinema.* Oxford: Oxford UP, 1990.

Nesse, Randolph M., and Alan T. Lloyd. "The Evolution of Psychodynamic Mechanisms." Barkow, Cosmides, and Tooby 601–24.

Nevo, Ofra, Giora Keinan, and Mina Teshimovsky-Arditi. "Humor and Pain Tolerance." *Humor* 6 (1993): 71–88.

Norell, Mark A., et al. "A Theropod Dinosaur Embryo and the Affinities of the Flaming Cliffs Dinosaur Eggs." *Science* 266 (1994): 779–82.

Novitz, David. *Knowledge, Fiction & Imagination.* Philadelphia: Temple UP, 1987.

Nussbaum, Martha. "Emotions as Judgments of Value." *Yale Journal of Criticism* 5 (1992): 201–12.

Oakes, Penelope J., S. Alexander Haslam, and John C. Turner. *Stereotyping and Social Reality.* Oxford: Blackwell, 1994.

O'Connor, John J. "Physical Deformity and Chivalric Laughter in Renaissance England." Charney 50–62.

Ornstein, Robert E. *The Evolution of Consciousness: Of Darwin, Freud, and Cranial Fire—The Origins of the Way We Think.* New York: Prentice Hall, 1991.

———. *The Roots of the Self: Unraveling the Mystery of Who We Are.* New York: HarperCollins, 1993.

Ortony, Andrew, Gerald L. Clore, and Allan Collins. *The Cognitive Structure of Emotions.* Cambridge: Cambridge UP, 1988.

Palca, Joseph. "Insights from Broken Brains." *Science* 248 (1990): 812–14.

Paley, Vivian Gussin. *Boys and Girls: Superheroes in the Doll Corner.* Chicago: U of Chicago P, 1984.

Palmer, Richard H. *Tragedy and Tragic Theory: An Analytical Guide.* Westport, CT: Greenwood, 1992.

Panksepp, Jaak. "The Psychobiology of Prosocial Behaviors: Separation Distress, Play, and Altruism." Zahn-Waxler, Cummings, and Iannotti 19–57.

Pavel, Thomas G. *The Feud of Language: A History of Structuralist Thought [Le Mirage linguistique].* Tr. Linda Jordan and Thomas G. Pavel. London: Blackwell, 1989.

———. *Fictional Worlds.* Cambridge: Harvard UP, 1986.

Penfield, Wilder. *The Mystery of the Mind: A Critical Study of Consciousness and the Human Brain.* Princeton: Princeton UP, 1975.

Perner, Josef. *Understanding the Representational Mind.* Cambridge: MIT P, 1991.

Pfeifer, Karl. "Laughter and Pleasure." *Humor* 7 (1994): 157–72.

Pfeiffer, John E. *The Creative Explosion: An Inquiry into the Origins of Art and Religion.* New York: Harper and Row, 1982.

Pinker, Steven. *The Language Instinct.* New York: William Morrow, 1994.

Pitcher, Evelyn Goodenough, and Ernst Prelinger. *Children Tell Stories: An Analysis of Fantasy.* New York: International Universities P, 1963.

Plato. "Laws." *The Dialogues of Plato.* Tr. B. Jowett. Vol. 2. New York: Random House, 1937.

Plomin, Robert, Michael J. Owen, and Peter McGuffin. "The Genetic Basis of Complex Human Behaviors." *Science* 264 (1994): 1733–39.

Plotkin, Henry. *Darwin Machines and the Nature of Knowledge.* Cambridge: Harvard UP, 1994.

Plutchik, Robert. *Emotion: A Psychoevolutionary Synthesis.* New York: Harper and Row, 1980.

Pollio, Howard R. "Notes Toward a Field Theory of Humor." McGhee and Goldstein 213–30.

Power, Margaret. *The Egalitarians—Human and Chimpanzee: An Anthropological View of Social Organization.* Cambridge: Cambridge UP, 1991.

Purdie, Susan. *Comedy: The Mastery of Discourse.* New York: Harvester Wheatsheaf, 1993.

Quiatt, Duane, and Vernon Reynolds. *Primate Behaviour: Information, Social Knowledge, and the Evolution of Culture.* Cambridge: Cambridge UP, 1993.

Racine, Jean. *Phèdre.* Tr. Margaret Rawlings. New York: Dutton, 1962.

Radway, Janice A. *Reading the Romance: Women, Patriarchy, and Popular Literature.* Chapel Hill: U of North Carolina P, 1984.

Ramanathan, Suguna. *Iris Murdoch: Figures of Good.* New York: St. Martin's, 1990.

Rappaport, Roy A. "The Sacred in Human Evolution." *Annual Review of Ecology and Systematics* 2 (1971): 23–44.

Redner, Harry. *A New Science of Representation: Towards an Integrated Theory of Representation in Science, Politics and Art.* Boulder, CO: Westview, 1994.

Reiner, Anton. "An Explanation of Behavior." Rev. of *The Triune Brain in Evolution: Role in Paleocerebral Functions,* by Paul D. MacLean. *Science* 250 (1990): 303–05.

Reynolds, Vernon, Vincent Falger, and Ian Vine, eds. *The Sociobiology of Ethnocentrism: Evolutionary Dimensions of Xenophobia, Discrimination, Racism and Nationalism.* London: Croom Helm, 1987.

Riggs, Larry W. "Molière's 'Poststructuralism': Demolition of Transcendentalist Discourse in *Le Tartuffe.*" *Symposium* 44 (1990): 37–57.

Ristau, Carolyn A., ed. *Cognitive Ethology: The Minds of Other Animals. Essays in Honor of Donald R. Griffin.* Hillsdale, NJ: Erlbaum, 1990.

Ritter, Naomi. *Art as Spectacle: Images of the Entertainer since Romanticism.* Columbia: U of Missouri P, 1989.

Rogers, Susan Carol. "Female Forms of Power and the Myth of Male Dominance: A Model of Female/Male Interaction in Peasant Society." *American Ethnologist* 2 (1975): 727–56.

Ronell, Avital. "Support Our Tropes II: Or, Why in Cyburbia There Are a Lot of Cowboys." *Yale Journal of Criticism* 5 (1992): 73–80.

Rosch, Eleanor. "Principles of Categorization." *Cognition and Categorization.* Ed. Eleanor Rosch and Barbara B. Lloyd. Hillsdale, NJ: Erlbaum, 1978. 27–48.

Rose, Hilary. "Beyond Masculinist Realities: A Feminist Epistemology for the Sciences." Bleier 57–76.

Rose, W. K. "An Interview with Iris Murdoch." *Shenandoah* 19 (winter 1968): 3–22.

Rosenfield, Israel. *The Strange, Familiar, and Forgotten: An Anatomy of Consciousness.* New York: Knopf, 1992.

Rosser, Sue V. *Biology and Feminism: A Dynamic Interaction.* New York: Twayne, 1992.

Rothbart, Mary K. "Incongruity, Problem-Solving and Laughter." Chapman and Foot 37–54.

Rousseau, Jean-Jacques. "Discourse on the Origin and Foundations of Inequality among Men." *Basic Political Writings.* Tr. and ed. Donald A. Cress. Indianapolis: Hackett, 1987.

Roustang, François. *The Lacanian Delusion.* Tr. Greg Sims. New York: Oxford UP, 1990.

Rubin, Robert T., June M. Reinisch, and Roger F. Haskett. "Postnatal Gonadal Steroid Effects on Human Behavior." *Science* 211 (1981): 1318–24.

Rue, Loyal. *By the Grace of Guile: The Role of Deception in Natural History and Human Affairs.* New York: Oxford UP, 1994.

Ruse, Michael. *Taking Darwin Seriously: A Naturalistic Approach to Philosophy.* Oxford: Blackwell, 1986.

Rushton, J. Philippe, and Ian R. Nicholson. "Genetic Similarity Theory, Intelligence, and Human Mate Choice." *Ethology and Sociobiology* 9 (1988): 45–57.

Sacks, Oliver. *The Man Who Mistook His Wife for a Hat and Other Clinical Tales.* New York: Harper, 1970.

———. "A Neurologist's Notebook: An Anthropologist on Mars." *New Yorker* 27 December 1993–3 January 1994: 106–25.

Sagan, Carl. *The Dragons of Eden: Speculations on the Evolution of Human Intelligence.* New York: Ballantine Books, 1977.

Sahlins, Marshall. *The Use and Abuse of Biology: An Anthropological Critique of Sociobiology.* Ann Arbor: U of Michigan P, 1976.

Sams, Eric. "Taboo, or Not Taboo? The Text, Dating and Authorship of *Hamlet*, 1589–1623." *Hamlet Studies* 10 (1988): 12–46.

Savin-Williams, Ritch C. *Adolescence: An Ethological Perspective.* New York: Springer-Verlag, 1987.

Schank, Roger C. *Tell Me a Story: A New Look at Real and Artificial Memory.* New York: Scribner's, 1990.

Scholes, Robert. "Language, Narrative, and Anti-Narrative." W. J. T. Mitchell 200–208.

———. *Semiotics and Interpretation.* New Haven: Yale UP, 1982.

Searle, John R. *The Rediscovery of the Mind.* Cambridge: MIT P, 1992.

Serres, Michel. "Thanatocratie." *Critique* 298 (1972): 199–227.

Shatz, Carla J. "The Developing Brain." *Scientific American* September 1992: 61–67.

Shaw, Bernard. *Man and Superman: A Comedy and a Philosophy.* London: Penguin, 1957.

Shaywitz, Bennett A., et al. "Sex Differences in the Functional Organization of the Brain for Language." *Nature* 373 (1995): 607–09.

Shelton, Beth Anne. *Women, Men and Time: Gender Differences in Paid Work, Housework and Leisure.* New York: Greenwood, 1992.

Shepard, Roger N. "Evolution of a Mesh between Principles of the Mind and Regularities of the World." *The Latest on the Best: Essays on Evolution and Optimality.* Ed. John Dupré. Cambridge: MIT P, 1987. 251–75.

Shepard, Roger N. "The Perceptual Organization of Colors: An Adaptation to Regularities of the Terrestrial World?" Barkow, Cosmides, and Tooby 495–532.

Shettel-Neuber, J., J. B. Bryson, and L. E. Young. "Physical Attractiveness of the 'Other Person' and Jealousy." *Personality and Social Psychology Bulletin* 4 (1978): 612–15.

Shklovsky, Viktor. *Theory of Prose.* 1925. Tr. Benjamin Sher. Elmwood Park, IL: Dalkey Archive P, 1990.

Shultz, Thomas R. "A Cognitive-Developmental Analysis of Humour." Chapman and Foot, 11–36.

Sigmund, Karl. *Games of Life: Explorations in Ecology, Evolution, and Behaviour.* New York: Oxford UP, 1993.

Silk, Joan B. "Primatological Perspectives on Gender Hierarchies." Miller 212–35.

Silverberg, James, and J. Patrick Gray. "Violence and Peacefulness as Behavioral Potentialities of Primates." *Aggression and Peacefulness in Humans and Other Primates.* Ed. James Silverberg and J. Patrick Gray. New York: Oxford UP, 1992. 1–36.

Silverman, Irwin. "Race, Race Differences, and Race Relations: Perspectives from Psychology and Sociobiology." Crawford, Smith, and Krebs 205–21.

Simon, Herbert A. "A Mechanism for Social Selection and Successful Altruism." *Science* 250 (1990): 1665–68.

Simpson, David. *The Academic Postmodern and the Rule of Literature: A Report on Half-Knowledge.* Chicago: U of Chicago P, 1995.

Slavin, Malcolm Owen, and Daniel Kriegman. *The Adaptive Design of the Human Psyche: Psychoanalysis, Evolutionary Biology, and the Therapeutic Process.* New York: Guilford, 1992.

Smith, Barbara Herrnstein. *Poetic Closure.* Chicago: U of Chicago P, 1968.

Smith, Robert L. "Human Sperm Competition." *Sperm Competition and the Evolution of Animal Mating Systems.* Ed. Robert L. Smith. New York: Academic P, 1984. 601–59.

Sober, Elliott, and Richard C. Lewontin. "Artifact, Cause, and Genic Selection." *Conceptual Issues in Evolutionary Biology: An Anthology.* Ed. Elliott Sober. Cambridge: MIT P, 1984. 210–31.

Sophocles. *The Three Theban Plays: Antigone, Oedipus the King, Oedipus at Colonus.* Tr. Robert Fagles. Harmondsworth, Eng.: Penguin, 1984.

Spradley, James P., and David W. McCurdy, eds. *Conformity and Conflict: Readings in Cultural Anthropology.* 4th ed. Boston: Little, Brown, 1980.

Springer, Sally P., and Georg Deutsch. *Left Brain, Right Brain.* 3d ed. New York: Freeman, 1989.

Steiner, George. *Antigones.* Oxford: Clarendon, 1984.

Stern, Daniel N. *The Interpersonal World of the Infant: A View from Psychoanalysis and Developmental Psychology.* New York: Basic Books, 1985.

Stevens, Anthony. *Archetype: A Natural History of the Self.* London: Routledge and Kegan Paul, 1982.

Stich, Stephen P. *The Fragmentation of Reason: Preface to a Pragmatic Theory of Cognitive Evaluation.* Cambridge: MIT P, 1990.

Sturgess, Philip J. M. *Narrativity: Theory and Practice.* Oxford: Clarendon P, 1992.

Sulloway, Frank J. *Freud, Biologist of the Mind: Beyond the Psychoanalytic Legend.* New York: Basic Books, 1979.

Sutton, Dana F. *The Catharsis of Comedy.* Lanham, MD: Rowman and Littlefield, 1994.

Symons, Donald. "Beauty Is in the Adaptations of the Beholder: The Evolutionary Psychology of Human Female Sexual Attractiveness." *Sexual Nature, Sexual Culture.* Ed. Paul R. Abramson and Steven D. Pinkerton. Chicago: U of Chicago P, 1995. 80–118.

Tannen, Deborah. *You Just Don't Understand: Women and Men in Conversation.* New York: Morrow, 1990.

Taub, David, and Patrick Mehlman. "Primate Paternalistic Investment: A Cross-Species View." Loy and Peters 51–89.

Taylor, Shelley E., and Jonathon Brown. "Illusion and Well-Being: A Social Psychological Perspective on Mental Health." *Psychological Bulletin* 103 (1988): 193–210.

Teisman, M. W., and D. L. Mosher. "Jealous Conflict in Dating Couples." *Psychological Reports* 42 (1978): 1211–16.

Tieger, Todd. "On the Biological Basis of Sex Differences in Aggression." *Child Development* 51 (1980): 943–63.

Tiger, Lionel. *Men in Groups.* 2d ed. London: Boyars, 1984.

Tiger, Lionel, and Heather T. Fowler, eds. *Female Hierarchies.* Chicago: Beresford Book Service, 1978.

Tiger, Lionel, and Robin Fox. *The Imperial Animal.* 1971. New York: Holt, 1989.

Todd, Richard. *Iris Murdoch: The Shakespearian Interest.* New York: Barnes and Noble, 1979.

Tomkins, Silvan S. "Affect as Amplification: Some Modifications in Theory." *Emotions: Theory, Research, and Experience.* Ed. Robert Plutchik and Henry Kellerman. Vol. 1. New York: Academic P, 1980. 141–64.

Tooby, John, and Leda Cosmides. "The Psychological Foundations of Culture." Barkow, Cosmides, and Tooby 19–136.

Trivers, Robert. "The Evolution of Reciprocal Altruism." *Quarterly Review of Biology* 46 (1971): 35–57; rpt. Hunt 38–68.

———. "Parent-Offspring Conflict." *American Zoologist* 14 (1974): 249–64; rpt. Hunt 111–30.

———. "Sociobiology and Politics." Elliott White 1–43.

Turner, Fredrick. *The Culture of Hope.* New York: Free P, 1995.

———. *Natural Classicism: Essays on Literature and Science.* New York: Paragon, 1985.

Turner, J. "Social Categorization and Social Discrimination in the Minimal Group Paradigm." *Differentiation between Social Groups: Studies in the Social Psychology of Intergroup Relations.* Ed. Henri Tajfel. London: Academic P, 1978. 101–40.

Turner, Mark. *Reading Minds: The Study of English in the Age of Cognitive Science.* Princeton: Princeton UP, 1991.

Turner, Victor. "Social Dramas and Stories about Them." W. J. T. Mitchell 137–64.

van Hooff, J. A. R. A. M. "A Comparative Approach to the Phylogeny of Laughter and Smiling." *Non-Verbal Communication.* Ed. R. A. Hinde. Cambridge: Cambridge UP, 1972. 209–41.

van den Berghe, Pierre. *Human Family Systems: An Evolutionary View.* New York: Elsevier North Holland, 1979.

Veeder, Nancy W. *Women's Decision-Making.* Westport, CT: Praeger, 1992.

Walton, Kendall L. *Mimesis as Make-Believe: On the Foundations of the Representational Arts.* Cambridge: Harvard UP, 1990.

Watrin, Jany. "Iris Murdoch's *A Fairly Honourable Defeat.*" *Revue des Langues Vivantes* 38 (1972): 46–64.

Weeks, Jeffrey. "Questions of Identity." *The Cultural Construction of Sexuality.* Ed. Pat Caplan. London: Tavistock, 1987. 31–51.

Weisfeld, Glenn E. "Social Dominance and Human Motivation." *Dominance Relations: An Ethological View of Human Conflict and Social Interaction.* Ed. Donald R. Omark, F. F. Strayer, and Daniel G. Freedman. New York: Garland STPM P, 1980. 273–86.

Weiskrantz, L., ed. *Thought without Language.* Oxford: Clarendon, 1988.

Wenke, Robert J. *Patterns in Prehistory: Humankind's First Three Million Years.* 3d ed. New York: Oxford UP, 1990.

White, Elliott, ed. *Sociobiology and Human Politics.* Lexington, MA: Lexington Books, 1981.

White, Hayden. "The Value of Narrativity in the Representation of Reality." W. J. T. Mitchell 1–23.

White, Randall. "The Dawn of Adornment." *Natural History* May 1993: 61–66.

Whyte, Martin King. *The Status of Women in Preindustrial Societies.* Princeton: Princeton UP, 1978.

Wilbur, Richard. Introduction [to *Tartuffe*]. Molière 159–63.

Wilde, Oscar. *The Importance of Being Earnest.* Ed. Henry Popkin. 1895. New York: Avon Books, 1965.

Willhoite, Fred H., Jr. "Rank and Reciprocity: Speculations on Human Emotions and Political Life." Elliott White 239–58.

Wilson, Edward O. *On Human Nature.* Cambridge: Harvard UP, 1978.

———. *Sociobiology: The New Synthesis.* Cambridge: Harvard UP, 1975.

Wilson, Edward O., and Charles Lumsden. *Genes, Mind, and Culture: The Coevolutionary Process.* Cambridge: Harvard UP, 1981.

Wilson, James Q. *The Moral Sense.* New York: Free P, 1993.

Wilson, Margo, and Martin Daly. "The Man Who Mistook His Wife for a Chattel." Barkow, Cosmides, and Tooby 289–322.

Wilson, Matthew A., and Bruce L. McNaughton. "Reactivation of Hippocampal Ensemble Memories during Sleep." *Science* 265 (1994): 676–79.

✓ Wilson, Timothy D., and Jonathan W. Schooler. "Thinking Too Much: Introspection Can Reduce the Quality of Preferences and Decisions." *Journal of Personality and Social Psychology* 60 (1991): 181–92.

Winner, Ellen. *Invented Worlds: The Psychology of the Arts.* Cambridge: Harvard UP, 1982.

Winson, Jonathan. *Brain and Psyche: The Biology of the Unconscious.* Garden City, NY: Anchor, 1985.

Witelson, Sandra. "Les Différences sexuelles dans la neurologie de la cognition: Implications psychologiques, sociales, éducatives et cliniques." *Le Fait féminin.* Ed. Evelyne Sullerot. Paris: Fayard, 1978. 287–303.

Wittgenstein, Ludwig. *Philosophische Untersuchungen/Philosophical Investigations.* Tr. G. E. M. Anscombe. New York: Macmillan, 1953.

Wrangham, Richard W. "The Significance of African Apes for Reconstructing Human Social Evolution." *The Evolution of Human Behavior: Primate Models.* Ed. Warren G. Kinzey. Albany: State U of New York P, 1987. 51–71.

✓ Wright, Robert. *The Moral Animal: The New Science of Evolutionary Psychology.* New York: Pantheon Books, 1994.

Yellen, John E. "The Transformation of the Kalahari !Kung." *Scientific American* April 1990: 96–105.

Young, Dudley. *Origins of the Sacred: The Ecstasies of Love and War.* New York: Harper Perennial, 1992.

Zahn-Waxler, Carolyn, E. Mark Cummings, and Ronald Iannotti, eds. *Altruism and Aggression: Biological and Social Origins.* Cambridge: Cambridge UP, 1986.

Zillmann, Dolf, et al. "Does Humor Facilitate Coping with Physical Discomfort?" *Motivation and Emotion* 17 (1993): 1–21.

Index

Abernethy, Virginia, 53
Acastos (Murdoch), 181
Aeschylus, 109, 110, 141, 169
Agamemnon, 109, 110
Agamemnon (Aeschylus), 141
age-ranking, universality of, 52
aggression: and warfare, 57; biological basis of, 22, 24, 27–28; different neural controls for, 25; evolutionary origins of, 21, 25–26, 213 n. 20; functions of, 24, 25–26; gender differences in, 21–26, 213 n. 19; in nonhuman primates, 24, 213 n. 20; in preschool child, 25; kinds of, 25, 213 n. 20
Alcestis (Euripides), 136
Alexander, Richard D., 15, 21, 39, 45, 60, 61, 80, 171
alliance behavior: in nonhuman primates, 26; male propensity to learn, 26; origins and functions of, 26–27
"alpha" female (human), characteristics of, 27. *See also* hierarchies
"alpha" male (human), characteristics of, 25, 27. *See also* hierarchies
Altieri, Charles, 120
altruism. *See* reciprocal altruism
Ames, Louise Bates, 115
Amis, Kingsley, 165
analytical psychology, 77
Anderson, John R., 216 n. 29
Anna Karenina (Tolstoy), 128
Antic Hay (Huxley), 169
Antigone, 141, 182, 232 nn. 9, 11, 235 n. 10. See also *Antigone*
Antigone (Sophocles), 232 n. 11; analysis of, 142–46
Appleyard, J. A., 117, 118, 119, 120, 121, 122, 123, 129, 229–30 n. 10
Apte, Mahadev L., 172, 173, 235 n. 7
archetypes: ambivalence inherent in, 79; kinds of, 78–79; origins and functions of, 77–79

Argyros, Alexander J., xiv, xv, 111, 209 n. 2, 218 n. 34, 230 n. 12
Ariel, 170
Ariès, Philippe, 46
Aristophanes, 174
Aristotle, 64, 124, 128, 135, 136, 137, 139, 140, 145, 148, 153, 163, 167, 177, 230 n. 12, 233 n. 13
Arnold, Tom, 171
art: adaptive value of, 106, 107; and arousal, 67; and defamiliarization, 106–7; and play, 106, 229 n. 3; and ritual, 106, 229 n. 3; and "set," 107; apprehended as meaningful because of evolved mind, 111; as exercise of narrativity, 107; as "making special," 106, 107; enculturating role of, 12; in nonliterate societies, 107. *See also* comedy, imagination, mimesis, narrative, narrativity, reader, tragedy
Artaud, Antonin, 130, 150
Asad, Talal, 4, 5
assortative mating, 48
As You Like It (Shakespeare), 166, 173–74
Auden, W. H., 231 n. 4
Auerbach, Erich, 123
Au rebours (Huysmans), 130
Austen, Jane, 184
Austin, J. L., xiii
autism, 86, 227 n. 13; and aesthetic sense, 227 n. 14; and narrativity, 86–97
Axelrod, Robert, 221 n. 7

Bacon, Sir Francis, 31
Badinter, Elisabeth, 212 n. 18
Baker, K. H., 172
Bakhtin, Mikhail, 92
Balaban, Evan, 218 n. 35
Barash, David, 221 n. 6
Barinaga, Marcia, 11, 12, 226 n. 11
Barkow, Jerome H., 15
Baron-Cohen, Simon, 86, 228 n. 21